Feminist English Literature

Second and Revised Edition

Edited by
Manmohan K. Bhatnagar

ATLANTIC
PUBLISHERS & DISTRIBUTORS (P) LTD

Published by

ATLANTIC

PUBLISHERS & DISTRIBUTORS (P) LTD

7/22, Ansari Road, Darya Ganj, New Delhi-110002
Phones : +91-11-40775252, 40775214, 23273880, 23275880
Fax: +91-11-23285873
Web: www.atlanticbooks.com
E-mail: orders@atlanticbooks.com

First Edition 2003

Printed & bound in India by Atlantic Print Services

Preface

Feminism is a rapidly developing critical ideology of great promise. It has evolved into a philosophy encompassing diverse fields of human activity in society. The feminist theory with its varied articulations and ramifications in a literary context constitutes a significant segment for critical endeavour.

The present anthology provides a broad spectrum on Feminist English Literature with in-depth analysis of the works of Kamala Das, Kamala Markandaya, Anita Desai, Rama Mehta, Shashi Deshpande, Uma Vasudevan, Githa Hariharan, Nina Sibal, Arundhati Roy, Jane Austen, Virginia Woolf, Margaret Atwood, Jean Rhys, Ellen Glasgow, F. Scott Fitzgerald, Toni Morrison, and others.

The volume also contains articles on feminist theory, the emerging self of women in Indian English Fiction, and general appraisal of women novelists with regard to their portrayal of the Woman's question.

I express my deep gratitude to all contributors who have worked hard to write their papers.

Manmohan K. Bhatnagar

Contents

List of Contributors

M.K. Bhatnagar. Head, Department of English, M.D. University, Rohtak, Haryana.

Sharad Rajimwale. Professor, Department of English, Jai Narain Vyas University, Jodhpur, Rajasthan.

M. Rajeshwar. Professor, Department of English, Kakatiya University, Warangal, Telangana.

S.P. Swain. Head, Department of English, Rourkela Municipal College, Rourkela, Odisha and **A. Naik**.

A.G. Khan. Reader, S.S. in English, Vikram University, Ujjain, Madhya Pradesh.

Mallikarjun Patil. Professor, Department of English, Karnatak University, Dharwad, Karnataka.

Bimaljit Saini. Assistant Professor, Department of English, G.B. Pant University of Agriculture and Technology, Pantnagar, Uttarakhand.

Rama Kundu. Professor, Post-Graduate Department of English, Burdwan University, Burdwan, West Bengal.

Najma Mahmood. Reader, Department of English, A.M.U. (Women's College), Aligarh, Uttar Pradesh.

Padma Srinivasan. Reader, Department of English and Comparative Literature, Madurai Kamaraj University, Madurai, Tamil Nadu.

F.A. Inamdar. Reader, Department of English, Veer Narmad South Gujarat University, Surat, Gujarat.

Surekha Dangwal. Vice-Chancellor, Doon University, Dehradun, Uttarakhand.

Attia Abid. Women's College, Aligarh Muslim University, Aligarh, Uttar Pradesh.

Shruti Das. Lecturer, Department of English, K.B. College, Barang, Cuttack, Odisha.

Sanjay Kumar. Lecturer, Languages Group BITS, Pilani, Rajasthan.

Vibha Jain. Project Assistant, SSL Jain PG College, Vidisha, Madhya Pradesh.

1

Feminist English Literature—An Introduction

M.K. BHATNAGAR

Feminist Literature in English is certainly not a recent innovation. It has been there ever since perspectives on life were recorded in the medium of literature, though it certainly has come to its own of late of recent origin again is the feminist perception of literature. Feminist criticism in its broadest implication has three distinct subdivisions, each with its own adherents. The first two are well defined and frequently practised without raising any ideological outrage. These are: The examination and analysis of the portrayal of women characters by themselves or in relationship with their male counterparts, and the appreciation of female authors. What is noteworthy is the fact that in the last few years these commonly accepted critical practices have been overhauled to accommodate the possibility of exclusively feminist perceptions of human relationships. Uma Vasudevan's *Shreya of Sonagarh* makes the reader aware of this new found angle of perception. The third direction is that of the so-called 'prescriptive criticism' that attempts to set standards for literature that is 'good' from the feminist perspective.

Feminism in the Indian context is a by-product of the Western liberalism in general and feminist thought in particular. The indigenous contributing factors have been the legacy of equality of sexes inherited from the freedom struggle, constitutional rights of women, spread of education and the consequent new awareness among women. The Indian woman caught in the flux of tradition and modernity saddled with the burden of the past but both to cast off her aspirations constitutes the crux of aspirations constitutes the crux of feminism in Indian literature. In literary terms, it precipitates in a search for identity and a quest for the definition of the self. In critical practice, it boils down to scrutinizing empathetically the plight of women characters at the receiving end of human interaction.

Feminist English Literature is a spectrum of many colours and shades—soft, prominent, and strident. The voices emanating therefrom vary from the traditional-but-conscious-of-their-selves to exclusively self-seeking with a seeming vengeance. When clearly articulated, well-argued and precisely defined feminist sentiments rather than mere faint echoes thereof can be traced even in early works like Mary Shelley's *Frankenstein* and Jane Austen's *Pride and Prejudice*, one feels chary of dubbing feminism as merely a late twentieth century phenomenon. The feminist perspective on literature—creative or critical—whether in a Third World country or elsewhere, has had to confront issues of similar persuasion: male chauvinism, sexist bias, psychological and even physical exploitation, hegemonistic inclinations in not merely the male but also the female sections of society, the utter disregard for the female's psychological, cultural, familial, and spiritual quests. Predictably enough, the ways out suggested subtly or propagated more avowedly have ranged from mild protest, seeking accommodation through moderation, love and persuasion to carving out of a self-sufficient exclusivist self.

The articles included in the present anthology form an insightful sample of the incisive critical endeavour being undertaken in our universities and higher institutions of learning. They are in-depth analyses of works of feminist persuasion. The authors and texts covered are unmistakably milestones in literature in English across the world. The studies incorporated here include scholarly articles on Kamala Markandaya's *A Silence of Desire*, Rama Mehta's *Inside the Haveli*, Shashi Deshpande's *Roots and Shadows* and *That Long Silence*, Uma Vasudeva's *Shreya of Sonagarh* and *The Song of Anasuya*, Nina Sibal's *Yatra*, Shobha De's *Socialite Evenings*, Anita Desai's entire corpus from *Cry, The Peacock* to *Baumgartner's Bombay*, Kamala Das's creative outpourings, Margaret Atwood's essay in giving her inner perceptions 'a local habitation and name', her rendering of feminine sensibility in *The Edible Woman*, the quest-motif in the works of Jean Rhys, Anita Desai, Geetha Hariharan and Margaret Atwood, *A Doll's House, Frankenstein, Pride and Prejudice*, Virginia Woolf's *Between the Acts*, Ellen Glasgow's *The Miller of Old Church*, Toni Morrison's *Whole Range of Novels*, and F. Scott Fitzgerald's *Portrayal of Women.* Besides these erudite studies of single texts, individual authors or a group of authors, the anthology also includes lucid exposition of the varied nuances of feminism, interspersed in different articles, preceding detailed consideration of texts under study. Not merely that. Also included is a wide ranging study of the treatment of the neurotic phenomenon in Indian English fiction with special reference to the portrayal of the emerging self of women characters. A quick glance at the range of these studies indicates the wide horizon opening up for exploration from this perspective. A perusal of the studies is bound to open up new vistas of appreciation and understanding.

2

Kamala Das—Need for Re-Assessment

SHARAD RAJIMWALE

Ms. Kamala Das has mostly been assessed as a writer in the genre of confessional poetry. She has been ranked with such poetesses of dissatisfaction and discontent as Sylvia Plath and Ann Sexton, though the comparison is seen by many as undeserving.

There are essentially two sides to Ms. Das's poetry; one is that which is extraordinarily centred around her own self, probing the malaise and morbidity that seem to clamp on her poetic vision. Over the years, it is this side that has been turned to our view, and she has been dismissed and rated accordingly.

Why not leave
Me alone, critics, friends, visiting cousins,
Every one of you? Why not let me speak in
Any language I like?

Things that came from her pen was something new, as no woman writer had ever before written with such power and honesty. The other side emerges from this, or seen from another angle, is a dimension of it. Her poetry constitutes not just a compelling expression of personal experiences and a forceful subjective voice, but more importantly, a phenomenon unlike any other in Indian English poetry. She is the first woman poet to crack the mould, and establish an attitude and viewpoint the Indian readers were quite unfamiliar with.

I wore a shirt and my Brother's trousers,
cut my hair short and ignored My womanliness.

Readers whose tastes and expectations were formed by compositions like "Morning Serenade", "Our Casuarina Tree", "The Queen's Rival", "Caprice", "The Lady of the Night" and such like, were shocked and staggered, by what Kamala Das wrote. It was so unconventional, so hurtfully new, so outrageously anti-traditional. What the general readers reacted to immediately was the bold and frank confessional tone she wrote in and broad imagery seeking to convey the hurts and humiliations she received in her personal life. It is true that personal voice is very strong in her, and from one point of view it provides a very limited scope. However, this voice is so strong that it extends beyond the personal world of anguished feelings and assumes wider significance.

I am sinner,
I am saint. I am the beloved and the
Betrayed. I have no joys which are not yours,
No aches which are not yours,
I too call myself I

There is a strange power in the way she conveys meaning through concrete imagery which have pictorial vividness, tactile immediacy, and auditory impact. The areas of experience these images reveal have long lain submerged; it required unusual courage to bring them to light. A profoundly restless spirit fired by the "passional force", to use D.H. Lawrence's expression, that originates in a mind that sees and hears and is aware of a disharmonious life, of the hurt inflicted by coercive subjugation and complete obliteration of the self, needed a new idiom, a new repertoire of images and symbols and a new poetic approach, the conventional being woefully inadequate. One easily discerns ruggedness in her metre, savagery in her images, a complete denial of all that the Toru Dutt—Sarojini Naidu—Nilima Devi tradition stood for.

"Sleek crows flying/ like poison on wing", "a meagre rain that smelt of dust in/ Attics and the urine of lizards and mice", "The city morgues are full of unclaimed cadavers", "You heard the sparrows in gutters", "I am moved by fancies that are curled/ Around these images, and cling".

Such expressions, and they come so naturally, so forcefully, cannot be dismissed as expressions of a fevered mind or a warped personality verging on nymphomaniac tendencies, as has usually been done. They are different tones and pitches of a voice articulating her deep mistrust of the conventional.

The conventional modes in Indian English poetry have been unable to convey reality, rather they have only glossed it over. Kamala Das confronts reality in its brutal and ugliest forms. Her poetic techniques and language coalesce with her mood and with her experience content.

> I who have lost my way and beg now at stranger's doors
> to Receive love, at least in small change?

Her most notable strength lies in confronting the reality of her experiences which in poem after poem becomes symptomatic of the general suffering of countless women. As Ms. Margaret Dickie observes in a different context,

> ...if the voices of women are not mute, neither are they the voice of the dominant culture. They are rather new voices at the fringes of society, where language changes and develops. Woman's poetry has always been a channel for such voices.

What Sylvia Plath, Adrienne Rich, Judith Wright, Margaret Atwood, Anne Sexton, Phyllis Webb, Margaret Avison, Rosemary Sullivan, and Susan Griffins are doing in British, American, Canadian, and Australian poetry was begun by Kamala Das in Indian English poetry. These woman poet's gesture of defiance and self-assertion snowballed into a movement first and later on a genre. It took a Kamala Das here to say without mincing words,

> I am not yours for asking
> Not because of morality
> but because
> I don't feel the need.

She was joined after a few hesitations by Mamta Kalia, Eunice de Souza, Margaret Chatterjee, Sunita Namjoshi, Gauri Deshpande and a whole generation of younger poetesses to establish an image of woman totally unencumbered by the conventional falsifying colours. This was not a personal matter but a whole generation's pangs of birth, not an individualistic attitudinizing but a painful transformation coming over feminine consciousness.

> To fight for the dignity and true emancipation of women is the most difficult task especially because it involves values and attitudes that are deep-rooted not only in the minds of men but also in the consciousness of women.... The period of transition manifests contradictory patterns, the subjugation and the emergence of new forms of bondage and subjugation in the new era of dominance of money and market.... The concept of freedom of women in practice is grossly vulgarized throwing up extremely grotesque and distorted forms of 'freedom' in a "transitional society combining the worst of both worlds".

Kamala Das's poetry embodies agonies of women emerging from that state of subjugation and bondage, and seeking to establish their identity and the self. Obviously, this is not an easy and uncomplicated process, as this involves discarding a lot, adopting a defiant attitude and probing the bruised self that expresses itself in so many different moods ranging from despair and dejection to anger and bewildered sense of rootlessness. This is best expressed through felt emotions in an intensely personalised idiom. It is easy enough to see in such a stance a dislocated mind suffering the nightmares of a shut-in life devastated and laid bare by a hyper-sexed, self-willed and schizophrenic woman. This is precisely what prevailing critical attitude to her poems highlights, which is not only lamentably lop-sided, but indicative of an alarmingly impoverished angle of critical outlook in Indian English Criticism. In a vein which issues from this dominant critical approach, her poems are seen as the expression of the pitiable plight of a defenceless woman who needs love, consideration and sympathy and desires a loving husband, warmth and home.

Such an interpretation comes from a reluctance to give up the traditional mental attitude, for what is more heartwarming than the return of the defiant woman to the conventional age-old mould of the 'categorizers'? It misses the basic point about her poetry; it is essentially a poetry of protest, of defiance and of emphatic assertion, all other moods ranging from weak feminine sense of helplessness and submission, to a restless search for happiness and shelter are different expressions of this basic Promethean spirit which is eager to break the rusted shackles and have its voice heard.

> As the convict studies
> His prison's geography
> I study the trappings
> of your body, dear love,
> For I must someday find
> An escape from its snare

Whether she explores her sexual experiences and encounters or the seamy side of public life, cities, dwellings, and streets—there can always be noted the defiant, ironical tone in her poetry. No other Indian English poet employed irony to such devastating effect before Kamala Das—it is caustic, it is Virgilian, it is profoundly demolishing. It evokes both pity and anger, sympathy and ire.

Kamala Das's poetry presents Indian woman in a way that has outraged the usual male sense of decency and decorum. Kamala Das inaugurates a new age for woman poets by doing so, an age seeking to forge new idiom, a new medium and newer modes of address, constituting a total rejection of the conventional modes of poetic expression of the dominant culture. The shock generated by this is something resembling the shock created by the experimental poets of the 1920s (Hulme, Pound, and Eliot) who decided that the time had come to liberate English poetry from the Georgian decadence and rejuvenate it. Though no such high claims can be made for Kamala Das, her importance as an inaugurator of a new poetic awareness for Indian woman poets is an established fact. As a critic has observed, "She deals with the conflict between passivity and rebellion against the male-oriented universe. Her poetry is the acknowledgement and celebration of the beauty and courage of being a woman".

Her medium is a passionate inflamed assertion of that being which has remained mute, suppressed, and battered through nameless centuries.

"The central problem in poetry is always the problem of reality, less on the social and more on the psycho-spiritual plain. The existential conditions impinge intensely on the female psyche. The acceptance or rejection, denial or disapproval at the emotional level, whether in love or death creates in her inner storm, a mutiny within", says Elizabeth Smart.

When Kamala Das writes,

> Of what does the burning mouth
> Of sun, burning in today's
> Sky remind me ... Oh, yes, his
> Mouth and...his limbs like pale and
> carnivorous plants reaching
> Out for me...

She is not celebrating unbridled sensuality, but projecting the stereotype of a wronged woman and at once asserting the need to establish her voice and identity. As someone observed, we see in her "the calm centre of the storm, the triumphant surge of affirmative projection that comes with a clear perception of despair by an energetically creative spirit".

Those who naively condemn her for her unpretentious frankness and bold portrayal of the living fabric of the passional man-woman relationship defaced and distorted by aberrations coming from socially—culturally determined attitudes, fail to see the basic force and drift of her poetry. Alicia Ostriker, a contemporary critic, says:

> The belief that true poetry is genderless—which is a disguised form of believing that true poetry is masculine—means that we have not learned to see women poets generically, to recognise the tradition they belong to....

With Kamala Das it is essentially a matter of attuning our critical vision to "the hidden vistas" of her inner world which has so much to offer to our perturbed, questioning minds. For her poetry is not "a continual self-sacrifice, a continual extinction of personality". As she says in *My Story*: "A poet's raw material is not clay or stone; it is her personality. I could not escape from personality". And again,

> One's real world is not what is outside him. It is the immeasurable world inside him that is real. Only the one who has decided to travel inwards, will realize that his route has no end.

Only, Kamala Das's inner world has not remained her personal demesne, it has acquired profound symbolic significance for all bruised and battered womankind.

WORKS CONSULTED

1. "The Alien in Contemporary American Women's Poetry", Margaret Dickie, *Contemporary Literature*, Wisconsin University, XXVIII, 3, 1987.
2. *Women in Indian Society*, ed., Rehana Ghadially, Sage Pub., 1988.
3. *Kamala Das* by Devendra Kohli, New Delhi: Arnold-Heinemann, 1974.
4. Quoted by Manorama B. Trikha in "Contemporary Canadian Poetry by women: A Cosmos of Miscellany", *Meerut Journal of Comparative Literature and Language*, special no. Canadian studies, Vol. V, No. 1, 1992.
5. *Kamala Das*, Devendra Kohli, N.D.: Arnold-Heinemann, 1974.
6. "Skating the Language: The Emergence of Women's Poetry in America", *Contemporary Literature,* Wisconsin University, 29.2, Summer 1988.
7. *Selected Essays*, T.S. Eliot, Penguin, London.
8. *My Story*, by Kamala Das.

3

The Unconscious Desire and its Fulfilment in Kamala Markandaya's *A Silence of Desire*

M. RAJESHWAR

Kamala Markandaya's *A Silence of Desire* depicts the unconscious desire of a housewife, Sarojini, to fight the decay of her self within the marital relationship. She protests unconsciously, but in a manner approved by the society, against her husband, and by extension against the whole society, for giving her a listless and mechanical life which her psyche perceives quite clearly as being responsible for her fast deteriorating self. Her husband, Dandekar, to whom her strange behaviour and defiance come as a big shock, neurotically reacts and goes through a phase of suffering and soul-searching. Since it all happens unconsciously neither of them has a clear understanding of the real motives for their behaviour. In the light of the knowledge of depth psychology I would like to integrate into the discussion here such aspects of the novel as Dandekar's jealousy, his rationality and its loss on being subjected to traumatic experiences, the strategies of his psyche to win Sarojini back, Sarojini's preference for a faith-healer over modern medicine and her deep attachment with the Swamy and argue that the whole effort of Sarojini's psyche has been to voice her desire to protest against the imminent loss of her self and that of Dandekar to get back his peace and domestic harmony and then conclude that both the protagonists emerge wiser than before—she having made her point and he having recognized his 'integral' but non-sexual 'wholeness' with her.

Dandekar bases his life upon some certainties: "Three children, no debts, a steady job, a fair pile of savings that his wife methodically converted into gold-bangles, a necklace, ear-rings and brooches less for ornamentation than the security it represented."[1] As a wife Sarojini is "good with the children, and excellent cook, an efficient manager of his household, a woman who still gave him pleasure after fifteen years of marriage... she did most things placidly...and from this calm proceeded the routine and regularity that met the neat and orderly needs or his nature" (p. 7). He does not want a change in this routine even in the wildest of his dreams. Even a trivial change like his daughters' buying tiffin provokes him to roundly remonstrate with his wife. This secure world comes off at the seams once its main pivote, his wife, frequently absents herself from the house and lies about it. Dandekar's first feeling is a suspicion of her fidelity. Her lies and his discovery of a stranger's photograph in her trunk strengthen his suspicion. Still, it is strange that after fifteen years of shared living Dandekar should suspect her fidelity the first thing instead of considering other possibilities. There appears to be an element of abnormally intense jealousy in him which is often the case with people prone to neurotic reaction. His leniency towards his colleagues Joseph and Mahadevan who believe in free love and inherent unfaithfulness of women respectively shows him to be secretly entertaining similar thoughts. But they have undergone a thorough repression. He therefore readily projects his own feelings onto his wife. As Freud puts it, projected jealousy is

> derived in both men and women either from their own actual unfaithfulness in real life or from impulses towards it which have succumbed repression.[2]

The common experience is that marital fidelity is maintained only in the face of great temptations. Persons consciously denying to themselves these temptations, like Dandekar, will find it inevitable to use the unconscious mechanism of projecting their own impulses to unfaithfulness onto the other person to get relief from the pressure exerted by these temptations. Freud continues:

> This strong motive can then make use of the perceptual material which betrays unconscious impulses of the same kind in the partner, and the subject can justify himself with the reflection that the other is probably not much better than he is himself.[3]

The situation has not varied from the days of Othello and Desdemona. Dandekar's repressed unfaithfulness informs his moral errantry during his neurotic grapple with the difficulties imposed upon him by adverse circumstances.

Dandekar feels so intensely jealous that he makes two attempts to trail Sarojini risking in the process his reputation and interests at the office. The desire to find out with whom she is carrying on an affair consumes him "like a fire" (p. 68). He succeeds the second time. To his dismay he finds Sarojini amidst a group of people and in the company of a Swamy to whom she confesses to be going to get cured of a painful growth in her womb by faith and prayer.

It is very interesting to examine Sarojini's reasons for going to the faith-healer and not to a medical doctor. She had a rigid religious tutelage and consequently she has not kept up with the changing times. Upon developing the growth she expects to meet the same fate as her mother and grandmother who suffered from the same disease, underwent an operation but did not survive. She refuses to recognize the tremendous advance made by the medical science. These are the verbalised reasons. However, the important reasons lie in her unconscious. Fifteen years of married life has made it clear to her that the rest of her life is going to be as dull and drab as it has always been. Her life becomes so mechanical and routine that we find her attending to her household chores with a predictable regularity which Dandekar has grown to like so much. She does not betray her emotions at all. Her repressed anger, accumulated over the years, against the person responsible for the meaninglessness of her life assumes a negative identity symbolically put in the novel as the tumour. She knows all too well Dandekar's Western frame of mind and scientific attitude. By going to the Swamy, which she knows will be disapproved of by him, she unconsciously protests against him just as Tara protested against her pedantic husband Brihaspati by physically running away with Soma in the Rigvedic myth. Sarojini does it differently, in a manner that is sanctioned by tradition and achieves the desired effect. In her unconscious the Swamy plays the lover and the father at the same time as we shall see next.

Once she starts meeting the Swamy regularly complications develop. It soon becomes impossible to wrench herself free from the magnetic pull of the Swamy. This point calls for a little theoretical enquiry. In offering to heal, all these mystics follow a familiar but complex method discussed at length by Sudhir Kakar in his book *Shamans, Mystics and Doctors*. They know that only lonely, neglected and distraught people seek their help. Therefore, the first thing they see to is that an enhancement of the 'individual,' as against the all-embracing community and the isolation of the individualistic society, is assured. Then they annex this newly developed self to themselves which results in a relatively greater childlikeness in the followers. The event becomes a symbolic enactment of a similar experience in childhood. Sudhir Kakar, strongly echoing Freud, puts it succinctly:

> The whole transformation process has its roots in, and is a replication of, psychic events in that early period of childhood when the child, in the face of the many narcissistic hurts and disappointments that the ending of infancy brought in its wake, sought to recapture his early feelings of "greatness" through a new route, where he projected his greatness into the idealized image of a parent and then partook of it himself by setting up a configuration in the psyche: "you are great but I am a part of you."[4]

The unconscious substitution of the guru in place of the father requires afresh the mechanisms of idealization and identification. The follower achieves a "psychological symbiosis" with the Master through these processes. Idealization of the analyst and identification with him do happen at certain stages of psychoanalysis too. The difference is that they are tactical and temporary in psychoanalysis whereas in mystical cults they are strategic and are meant to be permanent. The idealization and internalization of the guru is usually sought to be cemented by such strategic methods as meditating upon the guru's face which indeed Sarojini does. The result of all this is that the ailing follower replaces his feelings of dependence, insignificance, inertness, limitation and circumscription with the guru's dependability, omnipotence, energy and all-pervasive presence in the unconscious.[5] It sets in motion the follower's healing transformation similar to what is obtained in psychoanalysis.

The Swamy of *A Silence of Desire* follows a similar method and Sarojini is completely taken in. Markandaya does not go into the healing rituals at the Swamy's place. But enough evidence is offered to strengthen our theoretical perspective:

> She was sitting, cross-legged, on the man's [the Swamy's] right. His hand was on her bowed head, and he was murmuring to her, his voice sometimes falling to a whisper, a soft stream of indistinguishable words. In a rough circle about them sat a small group of men and women, listening—so engrossed that no one turned as he [Dandekar] burst in. No one had even stirred; they were simply unaware of his presence. (pp. 79-80)

It is therefore not surprising that Sarojini should feel better every time she goes there. She is aware that the pain is there but it does not touch her in the Swamy's presence. What the Swamy actually ministers to is not the alleviation of the pain her body experiences but the pain her psyche experiences—the pain born of a sense of neglect and worthlessness. Her neurotic need for love and self-importance are amply attended to by him. It produces a temporary euphoria which neutralizes the physical pain for the time being. Before Sarojini knows it, the Swamy's image is internalized and going to him becomes something of an addiction. She lacks the necessary intellectual resources to discriminate between the needs of her body and psyche. She therefore falls into the false belief that "without faith I shall not be healed" (p. 87). As is evident, the Swamy's method works only in the treatment of imaginary illnesses. Rajam, the garrulous cousin of Sarojini, has in fact been cured by the Swamy of her terrible pains which the doctors have diagnosed as imaginary.

While thus Sarojini is happy in her pain, Dandekar goes through a period of acute mental torture. The certainties of his life appear to be crumbling down. He finds "the pattern of his life being twisted out of shape" (p. 77). The cumulative effect of it is that he growe "withdrawn, questioning, introspective" (p. 98).

His exposure to Western thinking has rendered him particularly unsuitable to uncritically participate in the world of Sarojini. We find him at that point of turning away from religion which Freud thinks "is bound to occur with fatal inevitability of a process of growth."[6] Dandekar is, for example, careful to point out that the tulasi plant which his wife worships with great devotion is merely "a plant; one did not worship plants" (p. 5). His disregard for rituals is symbolic of the reenactment of the overcoming of childhood neurosis which of necessity everybody suffers in the process of taming the unruly instinctual demands. Religion is by extension "the universal obsessional neurosis of humanity; like the obsessional neurosis of children."[7] This much desirable psychic progression of Dandekar is suddenly disrupted by the onslaught of great anxiety caused by his wife the relationship with whom becomes strained and hence the chief source of pain for him. Attempting to work out solutions at the infantile level to problems requiring adult rationality is quite in keeping with the logic of neurosis. He unconsciously believes that hie wife, whose love and acquiescence he has taken so much for granted, has deserted him for good and he experiences acute anxiety and pain just like an infant who equates the loss of perception of its mother with the loss of the mother herself and becomes anxious about it.[8] With the passage of a few months Dandekar realises that his wife can be with him and yet not give him the assurance which she formerly used to give. This, as in the case of an infant, becomes for him "a new and much more enduring danger and determinant of anxiety."[9] His anxiety makes him do things which earlier he would not think of doing even in dreams. Knowing well that he is financially strained he becomes exaggeratedly generous, purposelessly talks aloud, risks his social reputation by visiting houses of ill-fame and commits such blunders in his work that they almost earn him the sack. His rationality deserts him and he sees nothing wrong in worshipping the tulasi himself!

He feels so drained of thought that it requires his kindly colleague Sastri to advise him to initiate some steps to set things right. His genuine efforts to talk some sense into Sarojini's head and his pitiable pleadings with the Swamy to dissuade her from seeing him end up in a fiasco as they are bound to, for reasons we have already considered. In addition, in the Swamy's presence, he feels so detached from himself and attracted to the Swamy that he is moved to donate money to the Swamy's fund. The Swamy seems to touch an atavistic chord in him as he surely does in others including the fierce Deputy District Magistrate, Ghose. Nothing seems to matter in the Swamy's presence.

The realities of life are, however, different. One cannot afford to lose sight of them for long. Dandekar finds it now impossible to reconcile these two worlds. He feels as though he is fighting "something invisible" (p. 170). Questions siege his mind allowing it no respite to find answers.

> 'Questions, questions, questions,' Dandekar's knuckles dug into his forehead. They crowd into my brain and it's like you [Sastri] said, I don't know the answers. I suppose it's because I've never had to think much about anything until now, but I don't seem able to think straight, do anything. All I know is I can't go on like this. (p. 171)

He is indeed unable to go any further. Nature itself takes care of it. He comes down with severe shingles and is bedridden for fourteen days. The illness serves several purposes simultaneously although Dandekar appears to regard it as mere inconvenience. Firstly, as the doctor rightly diagnoses, it provides a relatively safer outlet for the anxiety that has been brewing in his unconscious for the past few months. Secondly, it becomes a device employed by his unconscious to hold Sarojini down to him. After all no woman, however irresponsible, will leave her husband to suffer and go away for a selfish reason. But here the strategy fails. While not neglecting her duties as a wife, Sarojini nevertheless continues to visit the Swamy. Thirdly, it allows him some breathing space to make some key discoveries about himself and his relation with Sarojini. The "heat and pain and those stabbing, lucid moments" of the two weeks of his illness sensitise him to the suffering of Sarojini and sober him. Her body does not arouse him sexually any more. He now looks at her "from another aspect of love" (p. 191) and sees "the flesh flower pale and beautiful under the thin blue cotton she wore without desire" (p. 191). He wants her back now "not merely because he desired her," but because of "a spiritual ingrowing which made it impossible for him to be whole so long as any part of her was missing" (p. 191). Markandaya subtly conveys the changed perspective of Dandekar through the image of a night storm which is followed by a gentle drizzle in the morning.

Dandekar pins all his hopes on his boss, Chari. Although Chari does not assure him of anything he nevertheless assigns the task of enquiring into the Swamy's activities to his deputy, Ghose, and when that yields only limited results he takes up the matter himself. He does not order the Swamy to quit the place but his efforts do not really go waste. The Swamy is clever enough to see that his position as a spiritual guide and faith-healer has become controversial. He therefore thinks it wise to quietly leave the place. For Sarojini this proves to be traumatic. She feels so distraught and dazed at the Swamy's disappearance that for a split second Dandekar feels that if it is within his power to bring him back he would do it. Inconsolate as she is with the loss she at the same time realises, unconsciously again, that she still matters a great deal to her husband. Otherwise why would he suffer so much on account of her? She is therefore restored, body and soul, to Dandekar—to the world of hard facts, her 'honeymoon' with irrationality being over and her 'desire' being fulfilled. Her desire to voice her protest had something revolutionary about it. It was her last ditch effort to save herself from falling into self-preservatory negativism issuing directly from psychological repression unleashed by the social institution of family. She undergoes the required operation and is eventually cured of the ailment.

Dandekar too regains a semblance of happiness by shedding the physical nature of his desire and with the distinct realization that his wife is an essential and indispensable part of his world, that it will not be in his interest to take her for granted and finally that henceforth his relation with her should be on the basis of love and equality.

NOTES

1. Kamala Markandaya, *A Silence of Desire* (London: Putnam, 1960), p. 6. Further references to this edition are parenthesized within the text of the article.
2. Sigmund Freud, "Some Neurotic Mechanisms in Jealousy, Paranoia and Homosexuality," *On Psychopathology*, tr. James Strachey (Harmondsworth: Penguin, 1979, rpt. 1983), p. 198.
3. *Ibid.*
4. Sudhir Kakar, "The Path of the Saints," in his *Shamans, Mystics and Doctors: A Psychological Inquiry into India and its Healing Traditions* (New Delhi: Oxford University Press, 1982), p. 145.
5. *Ibid.*, pp. 146-47.
6. Sigmund Freud, *The Future of an Illusion*, tr. James Strachey (Harmondsworth: Penguin, 1964), p. 227.
7. *Ibid.*, p. 226.
8. Sigmund Freud, "Anxiety, Pain and Mourning," *On Psychopathology*, p. 330.
9. *Ibid.*, p. 331.

❑❑❑

4

Images of Alienation—A Study of Anita Desai's Novels

S.P. SWAIN

In Anita Desai's novels, imagery lends a poetic, lyrical colouring to the problems of the estranged self and project reality through "artistic parallels more powerful and eloquent than common collocation of words" (Prasad 1984: 54). Besides enriching the artistic and aesthetic value of the novels, images in Desai, enlarge the critical and interpretative horizon of her art. They suggest the protagonist's totality of experience and build up the overall tonality of the novels. Images in Desai are not confined to the world of art only. There are scientific images too. Both these images produce esthetic effects and impart a tangible shape to stirred up emotional states of the alienated self. To Anita Desai, "it is the image that matters, the symbol, the myth" (Srivastava 1984: 04). There is in her a persistent search for the most appropriate symbols and images in the expression of the subterranean and the subconscious.

Image may be an epithet, a metaphor, a symbol or a simile in the form of a mental picture. It derives its origins from 'imago'. It is an 'artificial imitation' of the external form of any object, while 'symbol' deriving its origin from symbolism, is something which stands for, represents or denotes something else (not by exact resemblance, but by vague suggestion, or by some accidental or conventional relation).

Anita Desai's mastery over words is manifested in her felicitous and deft use of images. Her imagery is always in character which suits the lone plight of her characters. In Desai's novels, the struggle of the alienated self takes place through a dialectic of images, through an intricate pattern of imagery. Her novels are based on the texture of a rich and splendid medley of images which is functional rather than decorative. The core images of alienation are found enmeshed with other images arising out of it. Each image holds within it the seeds of the self's own destruction and Desai's dialectical method is a constant building up and splitting down of the images that come out of the character's alienational experience. The images do not conflict with or contradict each other but are in perfect harmony and accord with the nature of the character's alienation. Sometimes these images become congested and dense. Desai does not make use of scientific and Biblical imagery in her novels. Most of the Desai novels deal with images suggesting the identification of human beings with the forces of isolation. Through imagery, Desai achieves the polarisation of the opposites. In her novels there are a number of symbols which have a contextual signification. In Anita Desai's novel characters are found to be 'thinking in images', i.e. images which strike the mind as the projection of other minds in immediate contact with social realities. Thus Maya's character is projected through Monisha, Monisha's through Sita's and so on.

Anita Desai uses symbolic and functional imagery as the sole ingredient of her art. Her images are literal, metaphorical and frequently symbolical. Imagery in Anita Desai may be considered to constitute the poles of an axis on which her fictional world revolves. The symbolic world of her fiction, the themes of despair, death, desolation and socio-psychic fragmentation have been picturesquely presented through telling and tantalising images. Imagery in her novels, besides articulating the estranged sensibility and the changing moods of her introverted characters, reflect their mental isolation. Botanical, zoological, meteorological and colour images add to the aesthetic beauty and textural density of her novels. Besides these primary images, she employs certain stray images which move along the periphery of her works but are nonetheless important to the theme of alienation. Of all the contemporary Indian English novelists, Anita Desai is avowedly the most powerful imagist novelist in whom images give a poetic and lyrical colouring to the problem of the alienated self.

Cry, The Peacock, Desai's maiden novel, teems with numerous striking images illuminating the dark and shadowy realms of Maya's consciousness and her deteriorating psychic states. The botanical image of the "sapless and sere neem tree" which figures in Part-II, Ch. 2, of the novel and the image of "the silk-cotton trees" whose "huge, scarlet blooms" were "squashed into soft yellowish miasma" (34), symbolically project the inner void and isolation of a childless housewife. The images of petunias and lemon blossoms suggest the temperamental isolation between Gautama and Maya, unlike Gautama, is able to distinguish the smell of the petunias from that of lemon blossoms. To Maya, Gautama's hand appears as cool and dry as the bark of an old and shady tree. "The blossoms of the lemon tree were different, quite different: of much stronger, crisper character, they seemed cut out of hard moon shells, but a sharp knife of mother-of-pearls, into curving scimitar petals that guarded the heart of fragrance..." (19).

But who guarded the heart of Maya? For her, Gautama is a repelling, not a refreshing presence. The limes reveal the flagging love-life of Maya and Gautama, an ill-assorted couple languishing in silence and incommunication.

In *Fire on the Mountain*, Nanda Kaul wants to withdraw from the milieu and merge with the pine trees. Free from all "unwelcome intrusion and distraction" (3), she longs for the privacy, seclusion, tranquility and solidity of trees: "She stepped, backwards into the garden and the wind suddenly billowed up and threw the pine branches about as though to curtain her" (3). The news of Raka's visit to Carignano shatters Nanda's hope for privacy and isolation. Raka's arrival would pose a threat to her "privacy achieved only at the very end of her life" (36). The image of the "yellow rose-creeper" that "had blossomed so youthfully last month but was now reduced to an exhausted mass of grey creaks and groans again" (17), symbolises the wilting and withering of her hope for a cloistered life.

In *Baumgartner's Bombay*, Hugo's isolation during his infancy is portrayed through the image of the 'fir-tree': "...he did not belong to the picture-book world of the fir-tree..." (36).

Botanical and zoological images occur in clusters to denote the isolation of Nanda. Residing in the mute, and desolate milieu of Carignano, she seeks an identity, different from all bewildering passions, the identity of "a charred tree trunk in the forest, a broken pillar of marble in the desert, a lizard on a stone wall. A tree trunk could not harbour irritation nor a pillar annoyance. She would imitate death, like a lizard. No one would dare rouse her. Who would dare?" (*Fire on the Mountain*, 1977: 23).

No one dare rouse her, since she would attract no one's concern for her tense and trying moments. She should prefer total isolation: "She asked to be left to the pines and cicadas alone..." (3).

Alienated from her great-grandmother, Raka begins to listen "to the wind in the pines and the cicadas all shrilling incessantly in the sun with her unfortunately large and protruding ears, and thought she had never before heard the voice of silence" (10). The sighing of the pines and the cicadas inspires in her the urge for isolation silence and serenity.

Raka's isolation is instinctive and unimposed. It is spontaneous and natural. It is the isolation of a roe, playful and fanciful. She could often be found: "...scrambling up a stony hillside...or wandering down a lane in a slow straying manner, stopping to strip a thorny bush of its few berries or to examine an insect under a leaf..." (46). Wishing to be left to the pines and cicadas, Nanda withdraws herself totally from the world of "bags and letters, messages and demands, requests, promises and queries" (3). Raka and Nanda, components of "the bareness and stillness of the Carignano garden", of "the starkness of rocks, pines and mountains" (4), want no one and nothing else. Seeking an absolute isolation here, she fancies she could merge with the pine trees and be mistaken for one. "To be a tree, no more and no less" (4) is all she desires. She wants to be alone and to have Carignano to herself in this period of her life, "when stillness and calm were all that she wished to entertain" (17). The imagery used highlights Nanda Kaul's longing for a secluded and still life. Nanda despises almost everyone who comes her way: her haughty, complacent daughter, Asha, her pale and fragile granddaughter Tata, her elusive, volatile and cadaverous great-granddaughter Raka and her old, decrepit and emaciated companion Ila Das.

In *Voices in the City*, Anita Desai uses the image of the 'weed' to portray the dehumanisation of Nirode. He is "a dripping gargoyle, grotesque, offensive, comic" (54). Nirode is wearied by his own incertitude in which "he swept back and forth like a long weed undulating under water, a weed that could live only in aqueous gloom, would never rise and sprout into clear day light..." (63-64).

Look at Amla's reaction to Monisha's withdrawal and confinement: "This sister had wandered away into some unholy garden of her own, stood there now like one of those lifeless statues on the brink of the stone fountain, and seemed not to realise that the fountain was dry and what confronted her was no ripple and tickle of cool water but only dry, hard flag stones" (149).

There is also Aunt Lila's garden which with its oppressive spirit of melancholy preys upon Amla and her thoughts. Aunt Lila has allowed it to "run wild" with its "dark unbreathing atmosphere", its "unmown grass" and "its infertile trees, contrasting sharply with the garden in Kalimpong" (148). The garden is a veritable picture of abandonment and neglect with none to domesticate it with mown grass.

Dharma also has a garden. He finds himself "inexorably drawn away from his island, back to the mainland again" (223-24). One is reminded of the garden of Carignano in *Fire on the Mountain* which, too, presents a dreary, desolate, forlorn picture suggesting Nanda Kaul's isolation.

Of the different kinds of images, zoological imagery insistently impinges on the reader's consciousness in *Cry, The Peacock*, *Where Shall We Go this Summer?*, and *Fire on the Mountain.* The image of dead Toto, besides introducing the death motif in *Cry, The Peacock,* serves as the symbol of an abandoned self doomed to loneliness:

> All day the body lay rotting in the sun. It could not be moved onto the verandah for, in that April heat, the reek of dead flesh was overpowering and would soon have penetrated the rooms.... Crows sat in a circle around the corpse, and crows will eat anything, entrails, eyes, anything. Flies began to hum amidst the limes, driving away the gentle bees and the unthinking butterflies. (5)

Gautama, the fly, is driving away gentle bees like Maya and the dead Toto, to utter desolation and isolation. The image of dead Toto is projected in different forms to describe Maya's psychic derangement and her ineluctable obsession with death. Several disturbing and horrifying images of slimy, creeping, crawling creatures such as rats, snakes, lizards and iguanas figure in close succession in a crescendo till Maya pushes Gautama over the parapet.

The image of rats suckling their young symbolises Maya's harrowing obsession with her childlessness: "Rats will suckle their young most tenderly. I know this, as now I lived quite near one, with seven young ones nestling between her legs..." (145-46).

The image of the domestic cat is metamorphosed into the horrifying iguanas. On seeing it, she wails out:

> Iguanas! My blood ran cold, and I heard the slither of its dragging tail even now, in white day light. Get off—I tell you, get off Go. (147)

Maya stands for the domestic cat who under pressure goes wild and neurotic like the iguanas. The iguanas suggest her neurosis and melancholy. The animal images in Maya's mind indicate her submerged instinctive drives.

Maya is exasperated to hear the cooing of the doves. She must drive them away? yet dares not disturb their amour. The doves in a mood for mating, cooed to one another. But, could Maya coo to Gautama? Oh, no their mating was to Maya, an omen of ill-fortune, of alienation, for their coo was a tedious repetition of the fatal words, 'Go Away' (35). The alienation of the copulating doves is an ephemeral one, whereas hers is far more enduring. Theirs is natural and instinctive, hers, though natural, is self-imposed and compulsive. With the mounting tensions in her aberrant mind, Maya thinks of rats and lizards, projections of her abandoned self and her fast disintegrating sensibility.

The image of the caged monkeys on the railway platform stirs and excites her agony. She too is caged within her nostalgic remembrances. It signifies her loss of privacy, her isolated life, a life of domestic imprisonment. It is her self-image. The monkeys boisterously struggling inside the cage for liberation and release remind Maya of her own alienation and estrangement. She is sensitively prone to self-reflection which dismantles her emotional stability and self-identity. Her thought-current transforms itself into a swift flux of fragmentary images frothing to the surface under the impact of certain external stimulus.

The image of the peacock and its anguished shriek for mating call "Piya, Piya" reaches out to Maya. She responds woefully to it, but not Gautama:

> 'Can you hear them, Gautama?
> Do you....?'
> 'Hear what?' (175)

Gautama remains listless to the cry. He is isolated from the milieu. He has no sexual urge. Maya the 'pea-hen' fails to get a response from Gautama, the 'peacock'.

In *Voices in the City*, the prey-predator image forms an integral part of the zoological imagery. Amla's longing to flee is expressed through the image of the horses bursting forth to release themselves from the massed impatience and the lust of the mob. The horses symbolise the possibility of isolation and escape from the pressures of conformity. The prey-and-predator image occurs in the race-course scene in which a horse, while running fast, falls on the ground hurt, and then a flock of hungry birds swoops down. We remember the abandoned corpse of Toto, encircled by crows and rotting in the sun. The characters in the city live corpse-like, isolated from the general current of life, going their own way. Calcutta itself is imaged as an ugly, ghastly monster in whose lethal grip the three desperate preys—Nirode, Monisha and Amla—gape and gasp for breath. Monisha calls Calcutta "this devil city" (117), "unrelenting city" (236). Images of putrefaction, like filth, squalidness and adversity create in Monisha a distaste and dislike for the city. Amla keenly feels the demonic, ogre-like presence of the city, its throbbing pulse attracts as well as repels:

> ...this monster city that lived no normal, healthy and red-blooded life but one that was subterranean, underlit, stealthy and odorous of mortality, had captured and enchanted—or disenchanted—both her sister and brother.... (150)

The city with its callousness presents a subtly tilting picture of aloofness to Amla:

> At every turn, on every road, the city thrusts its ugly apathy at her like a beggar thrusting his mutilated hand through the window and laughing because he knows she must pay him her conscience money.... (193)

Amla calls Calcutta a 'harsh' and 'insidious' city. It is a city with a brooding, dull, weary and vacant face. "...this city, this city of yours, it conspires against all who wish to enjoy it, doesn't it?" (153). Vacant and brooding and at the same time rapacious, the city has a Janus-like existence. This ogre and monster city gobbles Monisha, while it leaves the remaining two—Nirode and Amla—awfully battered and shattered. Calcutta is an 'overpopulated burrow'. Its sewers and gutters are choked with 'grime, darkness, poverty and disease'.

Washed in the monsoon, Calcutta presents a moving picture of desolation and dissolution, decay and disintegration:

> ...watching the sodden walls of unlit houses peel away in the wet, film posters dissolve and fade, seeing motor-cars and trams stranded hub-high in water, noticing how the crowds had melted away, vanished and only a solitary rickshaw—heroically mobile amidst all the waterlogged vehicles—churned and splashed nobly through.... (54)

The solitary rickshaw, 'heroically mobile amidst all the waterlogged vehicle is an apt image symbolising the 'singlehanded struggle' of Nirode in the suffocating and stifling environ of the city.

In *Where Shall We Go This Summer?*, the tumult and chaos in Sita's mind has also been symbolically projected through the image of the monsoon winds:

> I wanted the book to follow the pattern of the monsoon to gather darkly and threateningly, to pour down wildly and passionately, then withdraw quietly and calmly. (Ram, "Desai Interviewed", *WLWE* 97-98)

Again in *Fire on the Mountain*, we have an image of the whirlpool pointing to Nanda Kaul's incarceration and staticity: "...life would swirl on again, in an eddy, a whirlpool of which she was the still, fixed eye in the centre" (24).

The imagery of urban squalor, soulless pursuit of the characters for material prosperity and mundane pleasures create a cumulative impression of alienation. Spiritually alienated, they are doomed to rave and roam for ever in the desert of desolation, disturbed infrequently by vague forebodings and apprehensions.

In *Bye-Bye, Blackbird*, the image of the city occurs in a different perspective. It points to the void of existence, which is mutely repulsive and incomprehensively cold. The silence and emptiness of the houses and streets of London make Dev uneasy. The hollowness of the city bewilders him: "...the houses and blocks of flats, streets and squares and crescents—the English habit of keeping all doors and windows tightly shut—of guarding their privacy—It remains incomprehensible to him. It never fails to make Dev uneasy to walk down a street he knows to be heavily populated and yet finds it utterly silent, deserted—a cold wasteland of brick and tile" (70). Acutely tormented by the agony of silence and solitude in the city, he develops a disgust for London. He becomes a rebel like Nirode, the artist-rebel in *Voices in the City*. The Waterloo station serves as an image to reveal the emotional estrangement of the black-birds. The lone and solitary image of the station—all smoggy and hazy—objectively projects the isolation of the blackbirds in England. In that hazy atmosphere, none could see the other. Each remain alienated from the other behind the thick screen of smog. None could even hear the other. Alienation—physical and emotional—persists throughout. The melancholic haze of departure and the anguish of separation seem to have seized every word and feeling of the couple:

> As in an old film, the dialogue was blurred, almost inaudible, merely an accompaniment to the scene—words snatched away and sank into the haze of departure, the fog of preconceived absence. (257)

Monisha sees Nirode as a "broken bird" in the aviary, alienated in his own way and subdued and silenced by the fever and fret of life: "Lying on a mat in his tin-shed room, so solitary on a roof-top splattered with pigeon-droppings and a million cigarette stubs that speak of nights of insomnia and despair... (125-26).

In *Where Shall We Go This Summer?*, Anita Desai emblematically delineates the conflict in Sita's life through the image of a crowd of crows attacking an eagle, "wounded or else too young to fly" (38). This trivial incident serves as an apt objective correlative to Sita's alienation from her husband.

The image of the jelly fish has been used to highlight Sita's entanglement and her consequent alienation:

> Perhaps I am only like the jelly fish washed up by the waves, stranded there on the sand bar. I was just stranded here by the sea, that is all. I had not much to do with it at all, she sadly admitted.... (149)

Sita's identification with the jelly fish only suggests her castaway and shipwrecked self, an image which is repeated in *Baumgartner's Bombay*, in the depiction of the alien plight of Hugo Baumgartner.

In *Fire on the Mountain*, Raka is "a mosquito flown up from the plains to tease and worry" (40). Raka (literally means the moon) is ironically likened to one of "those dark crickets that leap in fright but do not sing" (39). She is "lizard-like" (42), "a pet insect" (54), "higher than the eagles" (61), or "a mosquito, minute and fine" (39). Raka moves about in Kasauli like a 'soundless moth', solitary and isolated.

Nanda Kaul views Raka as "an uninvited mouse or cricket" (85), stealthily entering the barren and rugged world of Carignano. Pining for a secluded life, she would lie down motionless like "a lizard on a stone wall" (23).

Through zoological images, Anita Desai juxtaposes the animal world with the human to suggest the cannibalistic and predatory nature of man. Preet Singh's sexual assault on Ila Das, for instance. Ila's cold-blooded rape and murder is gruesome and horrifying. Carnal images indicate our low instincts and desires, our base and ignoble motives. Reference to animals serves as an interface imagery.

In *Cry, The Peacock*, the isolation between Maya and Gautama is brought out by the image of the horse, a symbol of animal blindness and apathy to the splendour of nature. The denizens of Calcutta in *Voices in the City* are compared to "gutter rats" and "apparitions seen in delirium" (97).

In *Clear Light of Day*, the despair and isolation of Bim is projected through the image of the mosquito:

> They had come like mosquitoes—Tara and Bakul, and behind them the Misras, and somewhere in the distance Raja and Benazir—only to torment her and mosquito-like sip her blood. All of them fed on her blood—Now when they were full, they rose in swarms, humming away, turning their backs upon her. (153)

The zoological image of a snail, slowly, resignedly making its way from under the flower up a clod of earth only to tumble off the top onto its side—"an eternal, miniature Sisyphus" (2), symbolically illuminates the character of Bim in *Clear Light of Day*, who withdraws herself from the El Dorado of life to shoulder all alone the responsibility of looking after her mentally retarded, dumb brother, Baba, and her widowed Aunt Mira. She is a "lone crusader" in the arena of life's "conflicts and confrontations".

In *Baumgartner's Bombay*, we see the loneliness and destitution of Hugo shivering on a hot summer night "as abjectly as a dog who senses he is about to be turned out into the street..." (133). Baumgartner's rootlessness, his sense of not belonging, his terrifying loneliness have been articulated through the image of the dog. Feline and canine images, a part of the zoological imagery, play a crucial role in crystallising the predicament of the self living in closed and sequestered worlds. Desai stresses Hugo's homelessness through the image of cats. As time rolls, the cats flock round him, the cats that haunt the alleys of Colaba, homeless and nomadic like himself: "Baumgartner could contemplate homelessness for himself but not for his cats.... His room filled and overflowed with them, with their scrawny progeny..." (204).

Throughout, Hugo remains an outsider, a flotsam panting for self-identification and self-projection:

> An isolated youth in an increasingly unsafe and threatening land and then, a solitary foreigner in India—like a mournful turtle—Baumgartner carried everything with him; perhaps it was the only way he knew to remain himself. (109)

'Captivity' and 'internment', an extension of the image of entrapment and encagement "had provided Baumgartner with an escape from the fate of those in Germany, and safety from the anarchy of the world outside" (131). Hugo's isolation is a kind of protection. But to Elaine Y.L. Ho, it is desperation and destruction:

> His squalid room is cut off from, but also hemmed in by, the poverty and degradation of the streets. It is a marginal refuge from the real world and from a past that lingers and that he cannot retrieve meaningfully; nor will the past allow him to survive in his marginality. (*WLWE* 104)

Nur in *In Custody* is a veritable prisoner of his own self. He "had not escaped from his cage for all that—he was trapped as Deven was, even if his cage was more prominent.... Still it was a cage in a row of cages. Cage, cage, Trap, trap" (131). This image of the trapped animal and menagerie brings to our mind the lone selves of Maya, Nirode and Dev. The stress on the words, 'Cage' and 'Trap' bears out the quagmired self of Deven both in his public and private life. Without any control over these forces, Deven remains alienated and ruffled. "An agonised dog" (126), he is left out in the cold, reeling under the throes of the agony of life.

The vehicles of steel, though devised to save time, are in reality "self-destructive". The self is imprisoned in its desire to save time: "A vehicle of steel is only a steel trap. Man is not set free by the aeroplane, he is trapped in it" (153). Getting trapped is also getting isolated from the self as well as the society.

Auditory image in Desai is a part of the synaesthetic imagery. The sounds produce anticipatory sensations. In *Fire on the Mountain*, Raka hears the call of the cuckoos, but instead of dutiful domestic birds, they emerge as symbols of demented birds that rave and beckon Raka on to faery lands forlorn where there is "no sound, only silence, no light, only shade" (90). The sound that carries with it the sensation of solitude is symbolically an echo of Raka's own voice crying for isolation.

The house is a recurring image that resonates in the novels of Anita Desai. In Attia Hossain's *Sunlight on a Broken Column*, the house stands for country, home and families divided against each other and in Arun Joshi's *The Last Labyrinth*, it is the symbol of dirt and squalor. It is a whore: "...money was dirt, a whore. So were houses..." (11). But in Desai, the house stands for the individual self divided from within. It is the symbol of despair and desolation. House imagery in Desai evokes a sense of desertion and incarceration. It throws light on the musings of the lacerated self's immured existence. In her novels, the house occurs as an inorganic imagery serving as the focus of her thematic vision. It is metaphorically pictured through the symbols of walls, boundaries and barriers.

In *Voices in the City*, there are allusions to large Victorian houses "screened by royal palms" (125) and "old Georgian houses lined still" (142) which indicate gloomy and dejected minds, languishing in self-isolation and solitary confinement. "The houses here have aged with grace, and faintly lit by low gas lamps glowing a pale blue in the foliage...grown very old and deserted long ago to the vicissitudes of soot-black rain and plaster peeling sun" (125). Nirode fears his isolation from his own past, his childhood home. The image of the house is projected through the symbol of a "shell". Nirode is encaged in his "small shrunken shell" (110). But he steps out of it for self-expression. In Desai, there is a curious merging where the body becomes the house often referred to as a 'shell' or a 'cage'.

The house to Monisha is a prison. In the first few pages of the novel, the concept of her husband's house as a prison, cage comes across very strongly. She does not belong to it, does not relate to it. Her husband, on the other continues securely in his own cage. To him, the house is a symbol of safety and shelter. The house to Monisha is also an object of intimidation. The four-tiered balances with metal railings were so intricately criss-crossed that one could not so much thrust one's head through them. "Enclosing shadows like stagnant well water" (109), it was enough to depress her. She longs to thrust her head out of the window but the bars are too closely set. After all what was there to see. Other houses, other walls and other bars. In the privacy of her room, she is oppressed by a terrifying sound that repeats like the motif of a nightmare, from which there seemed no escape. The atmosphere in and around the house seemed to stifle her self-expression. She is encaged in the house. Like Nirode, she cannot step out of it. It is impossible to avoid in any corner of this house, "the damp pressure of critical attention" (159).

Nirode, "stared across the road at the white, cell-like suburban houses with their barred windows" (72). To him these houses where "there are no ethics" (117) serve as the symbol of a lacerating and disintegrating sense of anguish and agony. He says to David, "And have you taken a room at that robbing house again" (67). To him they are "slaughter houses" (42) that ruin our sensibility but to Dharma his house was "as quiet as his face" (46). Desai uses the image of the house to portray men and women leading scattered and disunited lives in this city of commerce: "Lives spent in waiting...always behind bars, those terrifying black bars that shut us in, in the old houses, in the old city" (120).

In *Where Shall We Go This Summer?*, Desai makes an artistic and symbolic use of the house imagery. The house here is linked with the pale and melancholic psychic life of Sita. In Bombay, she lived in a flat on a height, but now isolating herself from the hubbub and commotion around, she retreats to the house built by her father in Manori Island. She has the desire to set the house right but she discovers, to her amazement, the house abandoned in a sorry and awful state:

> ...a waste of ashes she saw, the cold remains of the bonfire her father had lit here to a blaze. Ashes, white and waste. Dust lay as casually as sound on a beach, spider webs spanned the corners of the unfurnished room like skeletal palm leaves. The odour was bats and mildew, and silence boomed like the silence of undersea caves. It had no air of providing shelter from the sea or the beach...it was as much a natural part of them as an abandoned shell or lump of twisted driftwood. (28)

The house, besides exposing the battered and fractured self of Sita, projects her wish to withdraw into an isolated and illusory world of impregnable silence and muted movements. But later, realising the futility of her living in an imaginative world of illusions, she compromises with the harsh realities of existence and returns to Bombay.

The use in *Fire on the Mountain* is a static and iterative image appearing in clusters with the image of the garden and other botanical and inorganic images as portrayed in the picture of the Carignano: the house that consoles Nanda and satisfies her:

> She turned around and gazed at her house instead, simple and white and shining on the bleached ridge. On the north side, the wall was washed by the blue shadows of the low, dense apricot trees. On the east wall the sun glared, scoured and sharp. It seemed so exactly right as a house for her, it satisfied her heart completely. (5)

Nanda Kaul's house becomes her refuge. Desai sharply contrasts this with "that house—his house, never hers" (18), the perfect house she dutifully ran for her husband and family but to which she never really belonged.

Carignano, the desolate and haunted house in Kasauli inscapes the life of Nanda. But unlike Sita, she does not live in Carignano by choice. She lives there under compulsion deserted by her sons and daughters after the death of her husband. Yet she is content with its stark, secluded and sunny splendour. Symbolically, the seclusion and serenity of Carignano defines the stillness and freedom, Nanda has been able to achieve in her old age. Carignano is Nanda and Nanda Carignano. The humming and hectic part of Carignano is made out of Nanda's own past—the past that goes back to her days as a housewife. It is juxtaposed with her awfully busy life in the past—ordering "too many servants" (29) entertaining "too many guests" (29) and tending "so many children" (29) and grandchildren. But Carignano, like Nanda, is burried in the silent spaces of inner vastness.

The image of the burnt house "at the top of the hill" (90) used in Chapter 18, Part-II, of the novel, mirrors the wild and unbridled nature of Raka with her irrepressible desire to set the forest on fire and her irresistible attraction towards "the ravaged, destroyed and barren spaces in Kasauli" (91):

> At the top of the hill was the burnt house she had come to visit. It was only the charred shell of a small stone cottage. The verandah roof was already torn off and flung onto the hillside, the paving stones on the floor were cracked and gaping. The doors swung rotten, the window-frames hung askew, shattered glass lay amongst the cinders. The stairs were a tumable of rocks and weeds.... (90)

The house imagery used in this novel is chiefly functional in nature. The house in this novel has its own history, that relentlessly links Nanda to other tormented and exiled women. Even this tranquil mountain resort, Carignano, that resonates in Nanda's experience, explodes and culminates in the rape and murder of her childhood friend, and alter ego, Ila Das.

In *Clear Light of Day*, the house throws light on the variegated moods of Tara and the behavioural eccentricities of Bim. The image of empty rooms suggest abandoned husbands. The old unchanged decrepit house in Old Delhi to which Tara returns evokes the feeling of stagnation and the resultant sense of boredom and nausea. Raja and Bim feel alienated in their own shabby house. In contrast to the house of Hyder Ali where there is company, colour and charm, his (Raja's) own house is "dismal, dusty, grimy and uncharming" (49).

In Part-II of the novel, we have the subtle image of a house abandoned by Hyder Ali. Bim too, is abandoned by Raja and Aunt Mira. Look at the neighbours derelict houses in Chapter 1: "On the either side of their garden were more gardens, neighbours' houses, as still and faded and shabby as theirs, the gardens as overgrown and neglected and teeming with wild uncontrolled life..." (23-24).

Throughout, the house image figures as an ominous and threatening presence characterised by a detonating and a palpitating silence. This static image of the house symbolically projects Bim's stifled anger and acerbity, her longing for silence and staticity. The house lingers long in the reader's mind. It becomes a symbol of the past to which both Tara and Bim try to feel indifferent since they abhor returning to their childhood, "all that dullness, boredom, waiting" (122) where life seemed to have bypassed them. Bim's "dark and smouldering" (140) house horrifies her. Looking at the past she gets terrified and grows despondent to such an extent that she "seemed to stampede through the house like a dishevelled storm..." (148). Tara eventually becomes reconciled to her life in the house which at the outset only seemed to appease her expectations from life. She frees herself "of this shabby old house that looked like a tomb in the moonlight" (159).

In *Village by the Sea*, Hari's house in the village, Thul, serves as a symbol of neglect and abandonment:

> The hut should have been rethatched years ago...the old palm leaves were dry and tattered and slipping off the beams. The earthen walls were crumbling. The

> windows gaped, without any shutters. There was no smoke to be seen curling up from under a cooking-pot on a fire as in other huts.... (9)

The house image brings out the forlorn self of Hari as well as the rural folk of Thul who crushed under poverty and despair, live split lives on the verge of decay and death.

The derelict house in *In Custody*, reflects on Deven's failure to form congenial and harmonious conjugal ties. It also reveals the couple's marital isolation and conjugal chaos leading to insanity.

Siddiqui's dilapidated, derelict and blackened house, which has neither lights nor curtains to colour the gloom, symbolises his incarcerated and immured self-seeking an escape into the open and lucid atmosphere of Delhi. The kitchen in the house which is "unspeakably filthy" (134) serves as an image of waste and putrefaction projecting the isolation and neglect into which the house has fallen. Deven is vaguely pleased, rather nauseated to look at this house "blackened by neglect" (134) which symbolises the "state in which everyone else lived in Mirpore" (134).

In *Baumgartner's Bombay*, the house serves as a contrast between the protagonist's past and the present. Hugo Baumgartner's "old, crowded, slum-like house off Free School Street, in the lane too narrow for traffic but wide enough for people, pigs, stray dogs, even a few intrepid rickshaws" (171) serves as a contrast to the European quarter he had known before the war—its great houses with deep verandahs and green shutters, high walls and tall palms... (171). But the house hardly provides any refuge to the disconsolate and expatriate self of Hugo from the conundrum of city-life:

> Not that the house provided any kind of shelter from the city. Down at the bottom of the lane there was a gap in the wall where the gate had once been and one entered through that into the walled compound that was really only partially walled since the wall had crumbled and in many places disappeared, allowing beggars, cattle, stray dogs and vendors of the whole

> locality to wander in and set up wherever they found space. (174)

Even then Hugo "entered the house, mounted the stairs, careful not to step on the beggars and lepers and prostitutes who inhabited every landing, and at last achieved the small cell that was his room. He had no sense of being walled away from the outer world as he had had in the camp" (175).

The house is concerned with the quest for self-identification. Be it Nanda, Sita or Deven, the house serves as a symbol of consummation. Having relinguished her present self, Nanda Kaul totally merges with the house. The organic alien identifies with the inorganic alien—the derelict house. This identification of Nanda with the house is an assertion of self. For most of the protagonists in Desai the house is the symbol of their decaying and moribund self. Disgruntled with their self-existence, the characters have a frantic desire to assert their identity with the forlorn and forsaken house. Besides portraying the sickening self of the alienated protagonists, the house image brings to the surface their straying into the world of death and desolation, of illusions and longings, in quest of meaning and value. It lays bare the inner rumblings of their psychic life. The house brings about a spatio-temporal continuity to the alienated self in its quest for identity in a world as menacing and lonely as the house in which the lone self strives and thrives. The house in Desai novels is not only a symbol of shelter and protection but also of incarceration and laceration. It is the house that fails to house the abandoned self.

In *Clear Light of Day*, Bim's emotional estrangement is projected through the image of a flock of mynahs and the dog who serve as a foil to her isolation:

> Bim said nothing. In the small silence, a flock of mynahs suddenly burst out of the green domes of the trees and, in a loud commotion of yellow beaks and brown wings disappeared into the sun. While their shrieks and cackles still rang in the air, they heard another sound, one that made Bim stop and stare and the dog lift his head, prick up his ears and then charge madly across to

> the eucalyptus trees that grew in a cluster by the wall... bellowed in that magnificent voice. (6)

In *Baumgartner's Bombay*, Anita Desai has portrayed the alienation of Hugo through the image of the curtain:

> He felt his life blur, turn grey, like a curtain wrapping him in its dusty felt. If he became aware from time to time, that the world beyond the curtain was growing steadily more crowded, more clamorous, and the lives of others more hectic, more chaotic, then he felt only relief that his had never been a part of the mainstream. (Desai, 1989: 211)

A depleted self, Hugo is enshrouded in his own isolation. Desai delineates the estrangement of Hugo through auditory images, especially the German songs, mostly nursery rhymes which occur only at critical moments when the narrative documents the isolation of Baumgartner from his parents or from his peers. They point directly to Hugo's socio-cultural roots and his psychic displacement that begins in early childhood as he flounders to acculturise and identify himself with the German milieu. The song of the rider imagistically portrays his childhood disappointment and his estrangement from his apathetic father:

> Hoppe, hoppe, Reiter,
> wenn er fallt, dann schreit et.
> Falt er in die Hecken,
> fressen ihn die Schnecken,
> fallt er in den Klee,
> Schreit er gleich: O weh.... (35)

The verse "comments on young Hugo's inability to assume and act out a role of his own choice and refers this disablement to archetypal situations (encoded in the song itself) of frustration, impotence, and loss of self-identity" [Ho, *WLWE* (32), 98].

Hugo is disowned, rather rejected by his father and is tagged to his mother in a bond of subjection. With both, his is the pitiable plight of a prisoner: "He looked at her with the hatred of one prisoner for another" (Desai, *Baumgartner's Bombay*, 35). In this context, the observation of Elaine, Y.L. Ho is worth noting:

> The child's alienation is entered into German culture, while the narrative re-enacts the culture as the incidental experience of one of its subjects. [*WLWE* (32), 98]

The song also expresses young Hugo's failure at establishing a cultural rapport with the milieu. It is these childhood experiences of frustration and failure that disallows him a secure social place and a concrete self-identity. Hence his alienation from the milieu. The nightmarishly pungent and redemptive world of contrasts in the following rhyme enciphers the polarities of integration and alienation. It also pictures the non-conformist child Hugo, who declines to sleep—an outsider and a prey to katabolic forces:

> Schlaf, Kindlein, Schlaf!
> Da draussen gehn zwei Schaf!
> Ein schwarzes und e in weisses,
> und wenn das Kind nicht schlafen will,
> dann kommt das Schwarz und beist es,
> Schlaf, Kindlein, Schlaf! (37)

A Jew in the German social milieu, the young Hugo lives like a 'prisoner' marginalised from society. Even the episode narrated through the German nursery rhymes point to young Hugo's sensation of being an alien in his own schoolroom. Ironically, he is stigmatized in Jewish School and it is here that he becomes gradually conscious of the alienation that will soon become his identity. Hence, his alienation is not an outcome of his ageing but it is the offshoot of the idyllic little happenings and affairs of his searing infancy.

Stellar imagery in Desai's fiction is a part of the synaesthetic imagery. Stellar images which follow one after the other focus on the obsessions and longings of the lonely self. In *Cry, The Peacock*, it illuminates the agonizing "solitude" of Maya, the psychic "distance" between her and her elderly husband. It lays emphasis on Maya's deep obsession with death and desolation, separation and loneliness: Death lurked in those spaces, the darkness spoke of distance, separation and loneliness—loneliness of such preparation that it broke the bounds of that single word and all its associations, and went spilling and spreading out and about, lapping the starts, each one isolated from the other by so much (24). The stars isolated from each other symbolically suggest the gulf between Maya and Gautama, though it is mainly psycho-temperamental.

The lunar image, which is another part of the colour imagery, only emphasises the "morbid" and "etiolated" self of Maya chasing shadows and silences, but never meeting them. Always aloof, she grows into pale and melancholic feminine image of a housewife. The "pale, hushed glow of the rising moon...her rim climbing swiftly above the trees, its vast pure surface...waxen white, virginal, chaste and absolute white, casting a light that was holy in its purity, a soft, suffusing glow of its chastity..." (240) is but a reflection of Maya's gloomy, pale, and virgin life. The "stark gaze of the moon" (97) in the waiting silence of the night conveys her hopeless predicament. The image of the moon assumes deeper significance with the death of Gautama at the hands of Maya towards the end of the novel.

In *Voices in the City*, colour imagery (especially images of light and dark) is functional. The image of darkness in Part-II of the novel projects the forlornness of Monisha's broken heart in the face of the dark and dangerous forces of life:

> I will have only the darkness. Only the dark spaces between the stars, for they are the only things on earth that can comfort me, rub and balm into my wounds, into my throbbing head, and bring me this coolness, this stillness, this interval of peace. Even sleep has not this sweet, swaying stillness as these immensities of night sky to which I top my face, allowing them to fall into my eyes, and fall. Sleep has nightmares. This, this empty darkness, has not so much as a dream. It is one unlit waste, a desert to which my heart truly belongs. (140)

Light and dark imagery, an extension of colour imagery explores the dim and dark corridors of the souls of Nirode and Monisha. It suggests their emotional estrangement and their abortive desire for a life of detachment in the deafening cacophony of Calcutta. It also reflects the caged isolation, psycho-physical torture, phantasmagoric and paralytic life, bogged and defeatist attitudes and dim apprehensions of failures, of darkness and stillness of Nirode, the bohemian artist. Like Adit, Nirode is haunted by "the black sensation of not belonging" (205). He longs for "shadows, silence, stillness—and well, he told himself, that was exactly what he would always be left with. He remained in the half-dark—and each light on that street served to show up an expanse of wall, a doorway, a balcony that was darkly shadowed—and bled with longing to go" (8).

The image of the moon in *Bye-Bye, Blackbird* points to Dev's existentialist predicament and his feeling of silence and stillness, of estrangement and incertitude in England. The lunar image occurs with the botanical imagery forming a cluster image: "In the night, Dev lay on his back, smoking a cigarette and watching the moon fill the pool of the ceiling with its thin polar light in which the long weeds and fronds of garden shadows languorously swayed and danced. The rush of the stream, grown louder now in the stillness of night, added to the illusion of being afloat in a water world as a shadow island—light, unanchored, disembodied as the mere shadow of a round wet leaf" (169).

Shut in by the "barbed wire fence", Hugo Baumgartner wants to shut out both the human and natural incursions of all sorts. His longing for shadows, silence and darkness is an attempt on his part to shut out both the human and natural incursions: "Baumgartner lay with his arms across his eyes, shutting out the probing needles of sun and heat, wishing, there were some way of shutting out the voices as well..." (118).

The landscape image occurs in *In Custody* to project Deven's dry and drab existence, his immured life: "...the impassable desert that lay between him and the capital with its lost treasures of friendships, entertainments, attractions and opportunities. It turned into that strip of no man's land that lies around a prison, threatening in its desolation" (24).

The desolation and waste Deven sees outside is a projection of the dismay and void within him. "Deven stared out at the white dust and yellow weeds, the leafless thorn trees, the broken fences, isolated tin and brick sacks and the scattered carcasses of cattle that littered the landscape and yet rendered it more bleak and bare under the empty sky" (28). The landscape image stresses the psychic states of the protagonists and points to the bitterness and harshness on the milieu from which the self craves to withdraw. It mirrors their psychoscape.

Maya's impending doom and estrangement is communicated through the various dance images. These images of dance are the symbols of death and desolation, which obliquely connote isolation and separation. The dance image figures as an iterative image which emphasises an escalating sense of fatality and despair. The Kathakali dance that "rose out of realms of silence into one thunderous drumming" (28), suggests Maya's psychic journey from stillness and silence to chaos and confusion. The bear dance is related to Maya's past, her childhood experiences which drive her to near-madness and hysterical derision. Of all the dance images, the image of the dancing Shiva and the Peacocks is thematically linked to the centrality of Maya's alienated self. The dance of Shiva gains a new mythological meaning. It stands for "divine isolation", a way out of the existential predicament in which Maya is entrapped and encaged. It is the symbol of "escape" and "liberation" from death and despair. The dance of the peacocks, portrayed in Chapter 3 and later on referred to in Chapter 6, Part-II, is the most poignant of all the images used in the novel. The bacchanalian and frenzied dance of the peacocks at the advent of monsoon is pregnant with meaning. In Maya, despair becomes hysterical and neurotic: "Pia, pia", they cry. "Lover, lover, Mio, mio—I die, die...like Shiva's, their dance of joy is the dance of death, and they dance knowing that they and their lovers are all to die.... Before they mate, they fight. They will rip each other's breasts to strips and fall, bleeding, with their beaks open and panting" (95).

Like the peacocks frantically longing for sexual communion, Maya craves for the company of Gautama, his touch and tickle. The cry of the peacocks becomes the symbol of the pathetic cry of Maya's bruised soul. Her suicide at the end of the novel becomes an enactment of her long-cherished desire for isolation in death.

There are a number of stray images in Desai's novels. The image of the barbed-wire, an extension of the image of a caged bird, occurs in *Baumgartner's Bombay*, symbolising the desperate, deserted and isolated life of Hugo, whose life seems cobwebbed and unsightly, like the "strands of—barbed wire wrapped around the wooden posts and travelling in circles and double circles around the camp" (111).

The image of a rushing and whistling train "leaving the small signalman waving a pointless flag, lonely and sad at the door of his whitewashed hut in the middle of the desert" (56) in *Cry, The Peacock*, evokes the world of loneliness. So it does in *Voices in the City*. So it does in, *In Custody*, where the train whistle reminds Deven of "Prisoners in their bars, mocked... in their cells" (132), condemned and subjected to death-like isolation.

The image of the island as an interface imagery in Anita Desai. Like the image of "incarceration" and "entanglement", it forms a common link between the different images of isolation. Each character in Desai's novels is an island unto itself. The image of the island mirrors the individual's alienated plight, its abandonment. The island of Manori in *Where Shall We Go This Summer?* is the symbol of Sita's marooned life. She returns to the island but its inhabitants go on, completely oblivious of her presence. She remains isolated from the island till the very end, an "island on the island" (Ram, "Island on the Island", *WLWE* 98).

Solar imagery along with the images of light and darkness forms a base to show the to and fro movement of the self from light to darkness and from sadness to happiness. It again becomes a part of the synaesthetic imagery.

In *Clear Light of Day*, the image of the morning sun is unlike the one painted in *Bye-Bye, Blackbird*. The former attracts and enlivens, but the latter repels and isolates. Tara bows her head to "the morning sun that came slicing down, like a blade of steel on to the beck of her neck" (1). The morning sun here is not homely but alien that acquires a brutal and harsh nature through the use of the words 'slicing down' and 'blade of steel'. It is not a playful and cheerful sun, it is formidable and intimidating. It triggers off the feel of alienation in Tara, who drops the screen and remains isolated from its ghastly sight: She actually got up and went to the door and lifted the bamboo screen that hung there, but the blank white glare of afternoon slanted in and slashed at her with its flashing knives so that she quickly dropped the screen (21).

In *Cry, The Peacock*, Maya's psychic estrangement is described in terms of the light pouring in from her window: The light from the open window was too bright: it hurt my eyes like a giant red thumb pressed into the sockets of my eyes, end bit up Gautama's face luridly (144).

In *Clear Light of Day*, Desai evokes, through Tara's reactions to the light of the full moon, a sense of the eerie: "Like snow, its touch was cold, marmoreal and made Tara shiver.... She could not free herself of them, of this shabby old house" (158-59).

The most striking and powerful image projecting isolation and estrangement is the image of the cow drowned in the well in *Clear Light of Day*. The cow was drowned but was never taken out. It becomes the symbol of nausea, Nausea generating isolation: "That looked like a tomb in the moonlight, a white-washed tomb rising in the midst of the inky shadows of trees and hedges, so silent—everyone asleep, or stunned by moonlight" (159). Again, in *Clear Light of Day*, the children, unlike their mother, who continually broke apart into violent eruptions of emotion, seemed rigid, encased in separate silences like larvae in stiff-spun cocoons.

In Desai's novels, one comes across a symbolic link between different images, which form an interface, a common bond. Imagery is primarily used to capture and crystallise a wide range of experiences. It lends clarity and vividness to the situation she describes, events she documents and characters she delineates. Most of the images are so sharply condensed and chiselled that they resemble a piece of painting.

The characters in Anita Desai's fictional world are victims of alienation. They experience a fragmentation and disintegration which is conveyed through images. Words like 'tunnel', 'net', 'cobweb', 'snare', 'hedge', 'cage', 'tomb', evoke a sense of incarceration and isolation in which the characters live. The images of isolation, at times, overlap adding to the lyrical and rhythmic splendour of her novels. They are simple but histrionically powerful. Highly functional, they form an integral part of the fiction. Seldom decorative or ornamental, they reveal a world inside, a world of the inner weather. Never otiose, they help maintain the dominant mood of the novel throughout the succession of parts, and set up a fundamental identity between the form and the content; the space and the time. They appeal to the poetry of life. These images, observes Amina Amin, "look contrived and far-fetched, a striving after effect for its own sake, without relevance to the emotions felt or the situations described" (*Littcrit*, 36). And she is wrong. Desai's images are neither unnatural nor unrelated. In the words of Madhusudan Prasad, "Desai's imagery which is chiefly anticipatory, pre-figurative or demonstrative in nature is always considerably functional.... Lusciously lyrical, her image patterns are singularised by interrelatedness and continuity" (*Perspectives on Anita Desai*, 76).

Unlike Narayan's fictional society, the isolation of Desai's protagonists leaves them bereft of control and protection other than what they can generate for themselves. Desai's writing functions through its orchestration of sensory images, while Narayan's operates through ironically counterpointed situations, characters and conversations. Nanda Kaul in *Fire on the Mountain* longs to be "a tree, no more and no less", and this sort of isolation leads the protagonist into a state of silent alienation. The images of destruction and violence portray the plight of the protagonist inexorably driven towards self-effacement and self-annihilation. Thus, images of isolation in Desai's novels lay bare the dark passions and bruised emotions of the individual soul languishing in self-alienation and struggling for self-identification.

The simple but dramatically powerful images in Desai trace the growth of the self from a state of seething discontent and despair to a state of psychic submission and spiritual consolation. Images of anguish in the external world of sights and sounds mature to images of spiritual identification of the inner world of the psyche. Rhythmically condensed, subtly chiselled colour images are knitly woven into the characters to point out the emotional chiaroscuro through successive stages of alienation leading to self-identification.

WORKS CITED

Amin, Amina. "Imagery as a Mode of Apprehension in Anita Desai's Novels", *Littcrit*, 18, Vol. 10, No. 1, 1984.

Desai, Anita, 1980. *Cry, The Peacock*, New Delhi: Orient Paperbacks.

—— 1982. *Voices in the City*, New Delhi: Orient Paperbacks.

—— 1982. *Where Shall We Go This Summer?*, New Delhi: Orient Paperbacks.

—— 1985. *Bye-Bye, Blackbird*, New Delhi: Orient Paperbacks.

—— 1977. *Fire on the Mountain*, New Delhi: Allied Publishers.

—— 1980. *Clear Light of Day*, New Delhi: Allied Publishers.

—— 1983. *The Village by the Sea*, New Delhi: Allied Publishers.

—— 1984. *In Custody*, London: Heinemann.

—— 1988. *Baumgartner's Bombay*, Harmondsworth: Penguin.

(Citations from the text kept within parentheses in the paper are from these editions of Desai's novels.)

Ho, Elaine Y.L. "The Languages of Identity in Anita Desai's *Baumgartner's Bombay*", *World Literature Written in English* (*WLWE*), Arlington, Vol. 32, No. 1 (1992).

Joshi, Arun, 1981. *The Last Labyrinth*, New Delhi: Orient Paperbacks.

Prasad, Madhusudan. "The Novels of Anita Desai: A Study in Imagery", in Ramesh K. Srivastava (ed.). *Perspectives on Anita Desai*, Ghaziabad: Vimal Prakashan, 1984.

Ram, Atma. "Interview with Anita Desai", *World Literature Written in English*, Arlington, 16, April 1, 1977.

—— "Island on the Island: Anita Desai's *Where Shall We Go This Summer?*", *WLWE*, Arlington, Vol. IV, No. 2, November 1975.

Srivastava, R.K. 1984. *Perspectives on Anita Desai*, Ghaziabad: Vimal Prakashan.

5

Inside the Haveli—The Silent Transformation

A.G. KHAN

I

Late Rama Mehta could convincingly accomplish, what the Bombay-based loud mouthed 'Socialite' and gossip/scandal machines could not. Her "sensitive piece of realistic fiction written with naturalness and poise"[1] performs a delicate job with ease, grace and sincerity. She had enormous opportunities to find excuse for voyeurism in a haveli shrouded in dark or could have reduced it into a suspense thriller; but handled with a sense of mission and conviction, Rama Mehta refrained from sex and violence as Iyengar appreciates, "there is romance but no cheap sex, tension but no violence."[2]

Sarla Barnabas finds it a fictionalised version of an academic study conducted in the international year of women sponsored by Nehru Memorial Museum and Library culminating in "*Indian Women: From Purdah to Modernity*." She regards it more of a documentary, the narrative style in the earlier pages as a clear proof. She feels that it has neither plot, nor character study and had no epic pretensions. Yet, she appreciates that it "encompasses a microcosm of traditional values".[3]

That traditions are not mere chains of slavery passed on by the past; they also have "strength and security", though it means "isolation and stagnation".[4] It is for this reason Mehta deserves commendation that she did not allow her protagonist to succumb to stagnation or helplessness. On the other hand, she could reconcile herself to the idea that the "anachronism" had a meaning too. "How could she allow little discomfort to blind her to the great tradition of the family" (pp. 34-35).

In this process of silent revolution without blowing trumpets or without offending any, she induces her mother-in-law with a feeling of warmth towards modernity. She deviated from "dissatisfaction to acceptance, from tolerance to generosity, and finally to magnanimity"[5] (p. 259). That family is not a battle ground for skirmishes and the desired results can be achieved through patience and perseverance has been ably demonstrated. And in this process of 'give and take' the heroine also gets transformed. What appeared to be a prison acquired the status of home, sweet home, to the extent that she said, "I don't want to leave Udaipur now" (p. 137).

Sarla emphasises the fact that tradition was not a ruthless demonstration of male chauvinism alone. The various restrictions imposed by the system were not solely for the women—men also had their own mores of conduct. Turbans and Churidars in the street was an established norm of etiquette. Be it Udaipur, Hyderabad or Bhopal; the "sanctity" of purdah was as much respected by males as by females. When women had to move out of houses drumbeaters used to proclaim and the males used to turn their backs towards the street. "It was system not a mere arrogance of chauvinism."[6]

The "doll kept in a glass for a marionette show" (p. 89), the "unwilling prisoner" from a "constricted, suffocating atmosphere of the haveli" was able to open a few windows to allow some breeze of freedom is a matter of triumph—women's awakening. She does not shout from the house top cliche like "women lib" but yet manages significant contribution in her own humble way.

The two important approvals that she could thus obtain were: right of the girl for education irrespective of their class distinction, and, right of the mother to have a say in deciding marriage of her daughter. What responsibility the grandparents used to discharge was slowly but surely granted to parents. She does not call it a "victory". In all her humility, issues like the marriage of Vijay, her own daughter or education of Sita even after her marriage are convincingly tackled by her. An Amazon like attitude would have thrown the peace of the haveli to shambles; but a subservient role brought her "Bhagwant Singhji's esteem and affection." Similarly, child marriage was also delayed considerably—a marvel in Rajasthan even today.

Class distinction did matter in issues related to girls. Birth of a daughter was no "cause of rejoice" as Gangaram, the servant, sighs. But when a daughter is born to the owners of the haveli, it assumes a different significance. It becomes an occasion for celebration. As Pariji declares "So what if it is a girl? After all it is the first time in sixty years that there are four generations under the roof of the haveli" (p. 7). This has a relevance today when girl child is terminated in the foetus itself; in spite of so-called modernity. In fact, modernity provides the weapons to determine sex of the child and then to terminate it. The twenty-first century is in no way brighter than the dark medieval ages when people used to bury their daughters in sand lest they should be humiliated by others.

When Geeta came to Haveli, she was merely tolerated. Her delinquency (of having studied in college) was forgiven with the hope:

"even an educated girl can be moulded. That I was not wrong in selecting you..." (p. 26). Thus began the dis-orientation process to refashion an educated girl "into a model daughter-in-law".[7] The final result was fortunately, contrary to expectations and the educated girl did succeed in ensuring approval of her plans. Not only this, she could create an awareness among the elderly ladies that gone were their days and they should put no obstructions against the forces of change. What the son fervently hoped:

My mother's generation will die and with it the traditional way of life (p. 112) was foreseen by Kanwarani Sa and she insisted her daughter-in-law not to "think of us all the time" (p. 140). It is because of such recognition that she encouraged Geeta to go ahead with her plans of educating girls and maid-servants "Binniji, don't let yourself be disturbed by Nandu bai Sa" (p. 140).

The "mod" have their sessions of Meddona and Beauty contests and on special occasions they stage a march with placards not to shout "women lib" but to exhibit their expensive Saris and precious jewellery. Here is the vision—Don't just leave your children to the care of ayahs and Khansamas. Discharge your duty as mother and give the maid servants also an opportunity to learn and grow. This will require abstaining from Kitty parties and boozing sessions. Would Namita Gokhale or Shobha De stoop to conquer this way?

II

Z.N. Patil examined the whole work as a sociological case study examining the various symptoms of ailment in the society. He enlists a number of taboos that governed the haveli and made its inhabitants to conform to these norms. He begins by pointing out the North-South difference in attitude towards daughter-in-law. While brides in south have no such restrictions; in north they cannot talk with members of family directly. Daughters or maid servants are required to communicate the wishes of the two groups. The "authority taboo" enjoins on the married couple not to demonstrate concern or affection. Even parents should not make a show of their filial love by kissing a child or caressing them. This affects consequent kinship in which verbal as well as non-verbal behaviour are restricted. This also affects even "textile behaviour" even among women, daughters-in-law are expected to keep their heads covered.[8] Barnabas records that women belonging to 65-80 age group admitted that they had not seen the faces of their daughters-in-law, though they had been in the family for two to three decades. Geeta was always in a perplexed state wondering how on earth she would be distinguishing one guest from the other. At the time of touching the feet—the feet were the focus of attention, faces irrelevant. It is this anonymity "befitting" a housewife that Kanwarani Sa was not given a name—throughout the novel she was Bhagwat Singhji's wife. Women are not expected to peep into male quarters or to stare at the paintings of the ancestors (that too without an escort)! Patil enlists the "purdah taboo", and "reticence taboo" in which women do not speak until they are asked to. Similarly, the "child bed and menstrual taboo" serves a much needed relief. The women, at least for a few days, avail themselves of rest from the hard work they are enjoined to perform. The "death taboo" prohibits close relatives to mourn the death by weeping loudly—decorum should be maintained. So also is the "burial or cremation taboo" compelling purification before entering the house.[9]

And yet, the customs have a brighter side too. A daughter-in-law is expected to show courtesy to the maid servants of the family also. Much do we lambast about old generation, or the feudal system. But the norms they had set are not despicable. Today, when parents are disobeyed, to respect the servants is something unusual. Not only this, even "greatly disliked relatives are received with utmost courtesy and show of joy".[10]

The language is plain and simple without any intention to perform gymnastics in linguistics. The novel divided into three sections, each covering five years traces the evolution of silent transformation. Recipient of Sahitya Akademi Award (1979); the novel, is the Swan Song that the distinguished lady gifted us.

REFERENCES

1. K.R.S. Iyengar, *Indian Writing in English* (New Delhi: Sterling Publishers, 1987), Sixth ed., 752.
2. *Ibid.*, 753.
3. Sarala Barnabas, Rama Mehta's *Inside the Haveli*: The winds of change in *Recent Commonwealth Literature* (Vol. I), ed. by Dhawan *et al.* (New Delhi: Prestige Books, 1989), p. 245.
4. *Ibid.*, 246.
5. *Ibid.*, 257.
6. *Ibid.*, 259.
7. *Ibid.*, 249.
8. Z.N. Patil, Indian Kinship Organization and Taboo Customs as Reflected in Rama Mehta's *Inside the Haveli*, in *Recent Commonwealth Literature* (Vol. II) (New Delhi: Prestige Books, 1989), p. 29.
9. Barnabas, p. 218: Dipankar Ray exploits the opportunity of the "purdah" to describe a highly erotic situation. The haveli provides promiscuous privacy too! (*Hell-Bent, Gold Nib Books, Bombay,* 1989).
10. *Ibid.*, p. 245.

❑❑❑

6

Roots and Shadows— A Feminist Study

S.P. SWAIN

I

The term feminism was first used by the French dramatist Alexander Dumas, the younger, in 1872 in a pamphlet 'L' 'Homme-femme' to designate the then emerging movement for women's rights. An anti-masculinist movement of the women for the assertion of their individual rights, feminism is also called Aphraism after Aphra Behn, a seventeenth-century feminist and political activist.

Feminism recognises the inadequacy of male-created ideologies and struggles for the spiritual, economic, social and racial equality of women sexually colonised and biologically subjugated. An expression of the mute and stifled female voice denied an equal freedom of self-expression, feminism is a concept emerging as a protest against male domination and the marginalisation of women. Sarah Grimke observes:

> Man has subjugated woman to his will, used her as a means to promote his selfish gratification, to minister to his sensual pleasure, to be instrumental in promoting his comfort; but never has he desired to elevate her to that rank she was created to fill. He has done all he could do to debase and enslave her mind.... (*Letters on the Equality of the Sexes*, 10ff)

Feminism strives to undo this tilted and distorted image of woman whose cries for freedom and equality have gone and still go unheard in a patriarchal world, a malist culture. Thus denied the freedom to act and choose on their own, women remained solely inside the field of vision, mere illusion to be dreamt and cherished. A woman is a woman, and a woman she must remain but not a 'man's shadow-self', 'an appendage', 'an auxiliary' and the 'unwanted and neglected other'. A woman is held to represent the 'otherness' of man, his negative. The development of Feminist thought at the outset of this century has brought about a perceptive change in our outlook towards women. Now, women are one with man and not their 'otherness'.

Men have taken up the cudgels for women. No longer are they callous to their sexual and gender exploitation. Gandhiji gave a new direction and dimension to the Feminist movement in India and freed women from passivity and servility. Raja Rammohan Roy and Pd. Ishwar Chandra Vidyasagar did no less. The ideal of Ardhangini enshrined in Indian culture renders man as the complement of woman, her other half. Together, they make a whole. Prakriti and Purusha are one. Man and woman are one in the concept of Ardhanariswara. Traditionally, India is a male-dominated culture. Indian woman 'covered with many thick, slack layers of prejudice, convention and ignorance' has hardly any autonomous existence. "Our country belongs to its men" (143), observes Aunt Lila in Anita Desai's *Voices in the City.* The woman's voice is an insurgent, subaltern voice. The Indian woman today is no longer a Damayanti. She is a Damini or a Nora or a Joan of Arc. Social reformers championing the cause of woman like Raja Rammohan Roy, Pd. Ishwar Chandra Vidyasagar and Mahatma Gandhi gave a new direction to the Women's Lib in India. Thus, feminism has now emerged as a new way of life, free of the "dependence syndrome" [Nahal in Singh (ed.) *Feminism*, 1991: 17]. A new perspective has dawned on the Indian social horizon with the feminine psyche trying to redefine woman's role in the society and re-assert her self-identity. This paper intends to study the incarceration of the self of Indu and her assays to get out of this 'encagement and entrapment' by asserting her feminity through self-realization and self-discovery.

II

Elaine Showalter posits three phases in the growth of feminist tradition: "limitation, protest and self-discovery" (*Literature*, 13). Shashi Deshpande's novels are directly related to all these phases. They encapsulate her artistic vision of feminity as alienation. In her novels, she explores and exposes the long-smothered wail of the incarcerated psyche, imprisoned within the four walls of domesticity. Here we have the heroine protagonist sandwitched between tradition and modernity, between illusion and reality and between the mask and the face. Thus positioned, the Deshpande woman disowns a ritualistic and tradition-bound life in order to explore her true self. Concerned with a woman's external quest for an authentic selfhood and an understanding of the existential problems of life, the Deshpande heroine is all agog to retain her individuality in the teeth of disintegrating and divisive forces that threaten her identity as a woman. Shashi Deshpande has dealt graphically with the problems that confront a middle-class educated woman in the patriarchal Hindu society. Deshpande's is not "the strident and militant kind of feminism which sees the male as the cause of all troubles" (Deshpande interviewed, *Literature Alive*, 1987: 08). Rather her novels deal with the psychic turmoil of woman within the limiting and restricting confines of domesticity. The Deshpande heroine is not like the women of Anita Desai, neurotic and hysterical. She is not a Maya or a Monisha ever ready to face the "ferocious assaults of existence" (Desai interviewed, *Times of India*, 1979). Deshpande does not make her woman characters stronger than they actually are in their real life. She declares that her "characters take their own ways" and that her "writing has to do with woman as they are" (Deshpande interviewed, *op. cit.*). Woman as presented in her novels is an incomplete self, a partial being. She is in need of someone to shelter her, be it her father, brother or husband. Indu, the protagonist in *Roots and Shadows* says, "This is my real sorrow, that I can never be complete in myself" (34). Bogged down by existential insecurity and uncertainty, women in the novels of Shashi Deshpande are in quest of refuge which in *Roots and Shadows* is portrayed through the image of the house.

III

Roots and Shadows explores the inner self of Indu, who symbolises the New Women who are educated and who live in close association with society brushing aside all narrow social conventions. They have the freedom to talk about anything they like and are also free to think of their own caged selves besides politics, corruption and what not. Married to Jayant Indu freely moves with Naren and uses such words like “kiss”, “rape”, “deflowered”, “orgasm” (78), etc. in her conversation with him. Indu says:

> We’re gay and whimsical about our own people, our own country. We are rational, unprejudiced, broadminded. We discuss intelligently, even solemnly, the problems of unemployment, poverty, corruption, family planning. We scorn the corrupt, we despise the ignorant, we hate the wicked.... And our hearts bleed, Naren, for Vietnam, for the blacks, for the Harijans.... But frankly, we care a damn. Not one goddam about anything but our own precious selves, our own precious walled-in lives. (25)

Through the character of Indu, Deshpande is portraying the inner struggle of an artist to express herself, to discover her real self through her inner and instinctive potentiality, i.e. creative writing. Indu wants to bid adieu to her monotonous service-life but her husband, Jayant, is not one with her. He is a barrier to her feminine urge for self-expression since he believes that one person like Indu can do nothing against the whole system by wielding her pen:

> What can one person do against the whole system. No point making a spectacle of yourself with futile gestures. We need the money, don’t we? Don’t forget, we have a long way to go. (17)

Look at the diametrically opposite temperaments of the husband and the wife. One is sympathetic to the ills of the society, the 'system' as Deshpande puts it, whereas the other is nonchalant. One is a writer in quest of an artistic selfhood while the other is a philistine, in pursuit of materialistic happiness. Despite these temperamental differences, Indu is quite submissive. Hence, she had not asked him, "To go where?". Instead she had silently gone back to her work, hating it and hating herself. Her self-alienation increases as she becomes aware of the contradiction between her desire to conform to a cultural ideal of feminine passivity and her ambition to be a creative writer. Thus, Indu perceives herself as a shadow of the female self, a negative, an object. Miller observes that "when one is an object, not a subject, all of one's own psychical and sexual impulses and interests are presumed not to exist independently" (*Towards a New Psychology of Women*, 63). But why doesn't Indu ask Jayant? It is because, she is hedged in, she is incarcerated, unable to "go on" (18) through the ordeal of life and "feeling trapped" (*ibid.*), seeing herself "endlessly chained" (*ibid.*) to the long dusty road that lay ahead of her. But with Akka's summons she heaves a sigh of relief:

> It had been a welcome reprieve. A chance to get away. To avoid thinking about what was happening to me... to Jayant and me...and our life together. (18)

A woman's role is not only confined to the centripetal needs of the family in which she lives but also to its centrifugal needs. It is here that a woman has to be more than her domestic role as a submissive housewife. She has to become a 'society lady' as Shobha De would put it. But there also, she is a meek and yielding creature. Centuries of tradition have made her so and she takes pride in such suffering. But we do not find Indu expressing such pride in her suffering. She cannot bear with the suffering she had to face in the family and hence she breaks away from it and marries Jayant. In the family, she was an incomplete being, without a sense of the wholeness of personality. But with Jayant she feels a sense of completion and wholeness:

> I had felt incomplete, not as a woman, but as a person, and in Jayant I had thought I had found the other part of my whole self. (51)

But did she attain wholeness and the integration of personality? No. She is often haunted by a "usual feeling of total dis-orientation" (33). An outsider, she remains untouched by the milieu:

> For some reason I was an outsider. The waves of sorrow, sympathy and comradeship rippled all around me, but left me untouched. (30)

Her feeling of isolation from the milieu is almost Camuesque. One is reminded of Camus' *The Outsider.* Meursault says:

> Mother died today. Or may be yesterday. I don't know. I had a telegram from the home: 'Mother passed away. Funeral tomorrow. Yours Sincerely'. That doesn't mean anything. (*The Outsider*, 09)

Such a state also reminds us of Sartre's Roquentin, who, unable to share the collective joy of the Bouvillois, stands alone: "But, after all, it was their Sunday, not mine" (*Nausea*, 81). Not only that, Roquentin also feels "so far away from them" (*ibid.*, 224).

This is an instance of total disorientation and isolation from which Indu too suffers. Often, we find in the novel references to her 'loneliness', suggested through the image of 'dust and barrenness' (10) and 'dark room' (21):

> Then we are out. It is dusty, a totally barren place. The glare and the heat are both fierce. I am alone now and move along people I don't know. ...I had rejected the family, tried to draw a magic circle around Jayant and myself. I had pulled in my boundaries.... 'I am alone'. (10)

And again her disorientation finds expression when she says: "Our own people? Who are they? Where do I draw the boundary?" (11).

Indu reckons her roots in breaking away from the family but she ultimately discovers that these family-bonds are the root of one's being and keep on dogging one like shadows. In fact, these roots are the shadows. Shadows that one can't flee from:

> We flatter ourselves that we've escaped the compulsions of the past; but we're still pinioned to it by little things. (34)

Even the trifles and trivia which dog her like shadows, uproot her from her social moorings.

As a woman, Indu is hardly left with any choice. Her life is so acutely circumscribed that she cannot make quick decisions and hence fails to arrive at concrete determinations:

> Inner strength...I thought of the words as I looked down on Mini's bowed head. A woman's life, they had told me, contained no choices. And all my life, specially in this house, I had seen the truth of this. The women had no choice but to submit, to accept. And I had often wondered...have they been born without wills, or have their wills atrophied through a lifetime of disuse? (06)

Indu recognises her displacement and marginalisation as a woman, a process of ego dissolution begins. She finds herself merging into others, experiencing a loss of boundaries. The authoritative and dominating male has not only suppressed the female voice for articulation but also brought silence, dullness and repulsion to the houses these women live in:

> The house was silent, as if tired of its pretence of liveliness. A few women who had been left behind, and who had been carrying on an interminable argument in the kitchen, their voices, rising and falling monotonously, were now hustled out by an authoritative male voice. (06)

Women like Indu can neither express themselves nor choose for themselves. They can neither love nor hate but be content with "the gift of silence" (33) that marriage had taught them. In silence, Indu pines for love, almost frantically:

> Jayant and I...I wish I could say.... But I cannot...I want to be loved, I want to be happy. The cries are now stilled. Not because I am satisfied, or yet hopeless, but because such demands now seem to me to be an exercise in futility. Neither love nor happiness come to us for the asking. (13)

Marriage is a fate traditionally sanctioned to women by society. But marriage is not the same thing to a man as to a woman. The two sexes are different from each other, though one has the necessity of the other. De Beauvoir observes:

> ...this necessity has never brought about a condition of reciprocity between them; women have never constituted a caste making exchanges and contracts with the male caste upon a footing of equality. (*The Second Sex*, 446)

A woman like Indu is allowed no direct influence upon her husband. Neither upon the future nor upon the world. She has to reach out beyond herself towards the social milieu only through her husband. But does the husband allow? He is impervious and indifferent to her emotional urges. Instead, it is Indu who has to cater to the needs of his inner urges and drives:

> But my marriage had taught me this too. I had found in myself an immense capacity for deception. I had learnt to reveal to Jayant nothing but what he wanted to hear. I hid my responses and emotions as if they were bits of garbage. (38)

In such a situation, Indu feels alienated from Jayant. To Ann Foreman, women experience themselves as the fulfilment of other people's needs:

> Men seek relief from their alienation through their relations with women; for women there is no relief. For these intimate relations are the very ones that are the essential structures of her oppression. (*Femininity as Alienation*, 102)

Indu is interested in creative writing—a means to articulate her feminine voice, to forge moments in art that are arresting and original. To this Jayant says 'No' because they need money and they have a long way to go but "To go where?" (19), Indu could not ask for she had no right to ask. It is the authoritative husband who has the say and not a meekly submissive wife like her. O.P. Bhatnagar rightly remarks:

> ...the novel deals with a woman's attempt to assert her individuality and realize her freedom. It depicts how it brings her into confrontation with family, with male-dominated society. ("Indian Womanhood: Fight for

> Freedom" in Shashi Despande's *Roots and Shadows*, unpublished paper)

Jayant betrays her hopes for harmony and integration, for peace and happiness. He fails to be her 'alter ego'. Neither is he 'a sheltering tree', to protect her in weal and woe. Instead she finds that she has relinquished her identity by surrendering before Jayant's masculinity, by becoming his wife. Willingly, she yields to the demands of marriage and moulds herself up to the dictates of her husband. But she never blames him for it is men who 'tear' and women who 'bear'. Indu exists and yet does not exist. There are women in our society who hate the rearing of a child. They are simply sex objects who produce children and leave them to their hapless lot. Indu is one such woman who does not believe in mothering. She is a woman who 'bears' and not the one who 'rears'. In an act of unreflecting defiance against patriarchy, she believes that a woman should deprive herself of the satisfaction that comes from not only bearing a child but also playing a major role in his/her personal development. In this sense, she is an anti-radical feminist. She says:

> Having children...it isn't something you should think and plan about. You should just have them. And yes... end up like Sunandatya. Pure, female animal. (115)

Probably, she believes that a female's job is only to reproduce and breed and to take care of the offspring's growth and development is the look-out of the male. This seems to be a blot on her feminity. A fluid character as she is, Indu, willingly bears all and acts up to the expectations of her husband:

> Always what he wants, what he would like, what would please him. And I can't blame him. It is not he who has pressurized me into this. It is the way I want it to be.... Have I become fluid with no shape, no form of my own. (54)

Marriage subjugates and enslaves woman. It leads her to "aimless days indefinitely repeated, life that slips away gently toward death without questioning its purpose" (de Beauvoir, 1974: 500). Women pay for their happiness at the cost of their freedom. De Beauvoir emphasized that such a sacrifice on the part of a woman is too high for anyone since the kind of self-contentment and security that marriage offers woman drains her soul of its capacity for greatness:

> She shuts behind her the doors of her new home. When she was a girl, the whole countryside was her homeland; the forests were hers. Now she is confined to a restricted space.... (de Beauvoir, 1974: 502)

Indu, true to her feminine virtues, plays the role of an ideal housewife but the role of a wife restricts, rather circumscribes her self-development—firstly by taking away her freedom of thought and expression and secondly by denying her the scope of giving free play to her artistic (creative) potentiality. Regarding a woman's role-playing, Rosemarie Tong observes:

> Sometimes women play their roles not so much because they want to, as because they have to in order to survive economically and/or psychologically. Virtually all women engage in the feminine role playing. (Tong, 1993: 208)

Jaya is discontented with this pre-ordained role of a woman. She has so many choices but for a married woman like her, she is left with a few or practically no choice save what her husband wills and desires. She cannot unburden herself. Her feminine instinct is curbed and suppressed. Despite all these, she is reluctant to admit failure and drags on with her marital life which encloses and imprisons her true self. She confesses to Naren:

> As a woman I felt hedged in by my sex. I resented my womanhood because it closed so many doors to me. (87)

Even in her professional life too, she has to curtail her freedom and submit to the dictates of the editor. She cannot give up her job which fails to be self-satisfactory. Jayant wants her to compromise with the profession of a writer. But could she compromise? The uncompromising Indu surrenders at times before Jayant just for show only. She is the very embodiment of the feminist principle which is an uncompromising pledge, and an antidote to exploitation and oppression of women. This uncompromising stance that Indu assumes is ventilated through her dialogic imagination. Woman like Indu are alienated from the product upon which they work: their body. Tong further observes:

> A woman may say that she diets, exercises, and dresses for herself, but in reality she is probably shaping and adorning her flesh for men. A woman has little or no say about when, where, how or by whom her body will be used. (*Feminist Thought* 187)

Whatever Indu does, it is only to please Jayant, and to please him is her way of life:

> Now, I dress the way I want. As I please!... As I please? No, that's not true. When I look in the mirror, I think of Jayant. When I dress, I think of Jayant. When I undress, I think of him. Always what he wants. What he would like. What would please him. And I can't blame him.... It's the way I want it to be. (49)

A woman's responding and relating to other's needs may detract her from her own sense of identity, of her becoming so fluid as to assume any shape. Indu feels as if she had become so fluid that she has no tangible shape, no form of her own. Without wants of her own, what is her identity in the family? Indu minus the "I" of course renders her an ideal woman—"a woman who sheds her 'I', who loses her identity in her husband's" (49), a woman who bears everything without a drop of tear. Marriage has reduced Indu to a state of "total surrender" (52). Through Indu, Deshpande voices her views of marriage:

> It's a trap...that's what marriage is. A trap? Or a cage? ...a cage with two trapped animals glaring hatred at each other...isn't so wrong after all. And it's not a joke, but a tragedy. But what animal would cage itself? (59)

Women's experience is primarily defined through interpersonal, usually domestic and filial relationships: serving the needs of others. Her identity exists "largely as being—for—others (needing to please; narcissist vanity and deriving security from her intimacy with others) rather than being—for—itself" (Waugh 1989: 43). Indu experiences herself as a woman given to physical narcissism in her self-reflexive concern with the body often "looking in the mirror" (49), thus trimming herself up to please Jayant, to please her narcissist self. She loves being "looked at" (54). In this context, it is quite relevant to note what Berger says:

> A woman must continually watch herself. She is almost continually accompanied by her own image of herself.... She has to survey everything she is and everything she does.... Her own sense of being in herself is supplanted by a sense of being appreciated as herself by another.... Men act and women appear. Men look at women. Women watch themselves being looked at.... The surveyor of woman in herself is male: the surveyed female. Thus, she turns herself into an object—and most particularly an object of vision: a sight. (*Ways of Seeing* 1972: 46-47)

Indu loathes womanhood for it is thrust upon a girl and for its association with the idea of "uncleanliness" (79). In order to assert her right to an independent existence, she longs to escape from the burden and responsibilities of womanhood. She fears her becoming a mother and hence scorns her "introduction to the beautiful world of being a woman" (79):

> "Tell me Indu, why do you fight against your womanhood so much?"
>
> "Do I?"
>
> My womanhood...I had never thought of it until the knowledge had been brutally, gracelessly thrust on me the day I had grown up.
>
> "You're a woman now," Kaki had told me. "You can have babies yourself".
>
> I, a woman? My mind had flung off the thought with an amazing swiftness...felt an immense hatred for it.
>
> "And don't forget", she had ended, "for four days now you are unclean. You can't touch anyone or anything." (79)

Indu fails to establish emotional rapport with Jayant for "it shocks him to find passion in a woman. It puts him off" (83). She confesses to Naren:

> When I am like that, he turns away from me. I've learnt my lesson now. And so I pretend, I'm passive. And unresponsive. I'm still and dead. And now, when you tried to kiss me, I thought...this is Jayant. So that's all I am, Naren. Not a pure woman. Not a too faithful wife. But an anachronism. A woman who loves her husband too much. Too passionately. And is ashamed of it. (83)

Such is the paradoxical situation in which Indian women are enmeshed. Like Indu they lead ambivalent lives. The cherish within their hearts deep and profound love but when the occasion comes for expressing it they retrace. Willing to wound, they hesitate to strike. They are loyal and obedient women who have been nourished and reared by a traditionally bogged society. Indu says:

> As a child they had told me I must be obedient and unquestioning. As a girl, they had told me I must be meek and submissive. Why? I had asked. Because you are a female. You must accept everything, even defeat, with grace because you are a girl, they had said. It is the only way, they said, for a female to live and survive. (158)

But as said earlier, Indu is a woman of free thinking, her thoughts are with the coming generation of women steeped in a scientific rational way of life. She has her own say to what people say:

> And I...I had watched them and found it to be true. There had to be, if not the substance, at least the shadow of submission. But still, I had laughed at them, and sworn I would never pretend to be what I was not. (158)

Should woman as passive characters put on a hypocritical stance towards themselves as well as the society? Should they out of fear for the male put on the mask of unreasonable submission? These are the questions that the society puts before the dominating male. Woman as a subordinate sex is characterized by obedience and submission, and under male dominance women have "developed a tendency to prevail by passive means" (Klein 1971: 167). Women surrender before men whom they really love. But does Indu submit before Jayant's masculinity because she loves him? No. Indu is scornful of love. To her "love is a big fraud, a hoax, that's what it is.... It's false" (173). She surrenders since she did "not want conflict" (159). She had clung tenaciously to Jayant, to her marriage "not for love, alone" (159) but because she was "afraid of failure" (*ibid.*). She wanted to show to the family and the world that her marriage was a success and so she had put on the mask of an obedient and subservient wife:

> And so I went on lying, even to myself, compromising, shedding bits of myself along the way. Which meant that I, who had despised Devdas for being a coward, was the same thing myself. I had killed myself as surely as he had done. (159)

Indu's problematic of "becoming" expresses Deshpande's feminist polemics against sexual and gender roles imposed upon women in a patriarchal malist culture. Such 'relative identity', or rather the 'received role models' distort and problematize her self-perception. Such a world reduces women like Indu to a mere thing or a mind-less body. With her peremptory and subjugating voice, her feminine instinct for articulation is suppressed. Ever ready to please Jayant, Indu acquiesces to his wills and desires and does everything to reflect his image. Indu gradually realises that she doesn't exist for her but for Jayant, that archetypal male, imperialistic and subjugating. She feels in her a sense of existential angst and insecurity. Look at a fear-stricken and lacerated woman railing at her family and the malist world where a girl is "never claimed" but is "set apart from the others" (81):

> This is my family. These are my people. And yet...I hate them. I despise them. They're mean and petty and trivial and despicable. I had always told myself...I won't be like them. I won't live like them. And I thought...I've got away. But to what, Naren?... Are we doomed to living meaningless futile lives? Is there no escape? I'm afraid, Naren...I'm afraid.... (160)

Indu ultimately realises that she has been chasing shadows, leaving her roots far behind in the family and in Jayant. Naren with whom she develops an adulterous relationship is a mere shadow to her. Naren has no permanent place in her memory. Hence, she decides to go back to Jayant who she feels is totally innocent. It is she who is to blame for the marital discord in their lives. She has created a hell out of a heaven. She, the narcissist who "had locked herself in a cage and thrown away the keys" (85), forgotten the roots, feeding on only dreams and shadows. She has failed in love not Jayant. She has escaped from the familial responsibilities of the home, chasing after oneirodynic and uncrystallising shadows. She realises that marriage had stunted and hampered her individuality for she saw it as a 'trap' and not a bond and that the home where the family is housed, she saw it as a 'cage'. Now she realises that all those were mere illusions and not reality and all the struggles of her life was an act of futility:

> But what of my love for Jayant, that had been a restricting bond, tormenting me, which I had so futilely struggled against? Restricting bond? Was it not I who made it so? Torment? Had I not created my own torment? Perhaps it was true.... There was only one thing I wanted now...and that was to go home...the one I lived with Jayant. That was my only home.... I would put all this behind me and go back to Jayant.... I knew I would not tell Jayant about Naren and me.... That had nothing to do with the two of us and our life together. But there were other things I had to tell him. That I was resigning from my job. That I would do the kind of writing I had always dreamt of doing. (187)

Thus, Indu's uncompromising and paradoxical feminine self that frantically longed for self-expression for the articulation of her feminine voice, finally finds its roots in the home and with her husband. Shadows disappear from her vision and she sees the clear light of day with the realization and discovery of her authentic female self. Thus "in the end, comes the realization that freedom lies in having the courage to do what one believes is the right thing to do and the determination and the tenacity to adhere to it. That alone can bring harmony in life" (Bhatnagar, *op. cit.*).

The meek, docile and humble Indu finally emerges as a bold, challenging, conscious and rebellious woman. She resigns her job, thus defying the male authority, hierarchy and the irony of a woman's masked existence. Her self-discovery is the frightening vision of the feminine self's struggle for harmony and sanity. She comes out of her emotional upheaval, to lead a meaningful life with her husband Jayant. Her 'home-coming' is ironical since the home she had discarded becomes the place of refuge, of solace and consolation. It is Akka's house which makes her realize many things and offers ample opportunities to know herself, her inner life. It is here that she is able to discover her roots—an independent woman and a writer and what the shadows are—a daughter, a mother and a commercial writer. She begins to see life in a new light. Have a fresh look at Akka's house:

> Yes, the house had been a trap too, binding me to a past I had to move away from. Now, I felt clear, as if I had cut away all the unnecessary uneven edges of me. (204)

Indu now, feels a sense of hope for life, for existence. She negates the ideas of non-existence. She says:

> No, there is no such thing. To accept it will be to deny the miracle of life itself. If not this stump, there is another. If not this tree, there will be others. Other trees will grow, other flowers will bloom, other fragrances will pervade. Other airs...I felt as if I was watching life itself...endless, limitless, formless and full of grace. (202)

Marriage to Indu is a "cold-blooded bargaining to meet, mate and reproduce" (03). That's all. The tragedy of her marriage is that it fails to assure her the promised happiness. It mutilates her; it dooms her to repetition and routine, the monotony of "meet, mate and reproduce" (03). Almost always it annihilates her. But a woman is not to blame for it. "It is the masculine code, it is the society developed by the males and in their interest, that has established the woman's situation in a form that is at present a source of torment for both the sexes" (de Beauvoir 1988: 500).

Indu's liberation is a biological-revolution. She detests the idea of woman as a 'rearing machine', a caretaker of the child. In playing such a role she yields herself, though reluctantly, before patriarchy—"the systematic subordination of women" (Firestone 1970: 01). She seems to question herself as to why should women take care of the offspring? Why not men? Perhaps she wants to eliminate this division of labour based upon sex—the sexual caste system. But in thinking so, she puts on the garb of an abnormal girl ('masculine girl') who does not want to be a mother and hence lose her self-worth, her feminity. Since "women are socially and culturally conditioned to be mothers" (Oakley 1974: 187), she should have gladly accepted the role of rearing a child like that of an ideal mother. But she does not, thereby alienating herself from her feminity.

All mothers need children not to abandon her (the child) to her fate but to nurse her. Unless a woman's 'maternal instinct' is satisfied, she will become increasingly frustrated and forlorn. Indu should accept the role of an ideal mother, if she at all has a 'maternal instinct' and should not renounce, in the name of 'liberation', all that female biology has to offer. Perhaps, Indu wants to assert herself and hence believes that since motherhood is a patriarchal institution, each woman has to deny herself, even temporarily, the experience of mothering, so that the patriarchal institution is destroyed once and for all. Such is Indu's feminist vision which "has recoiled from female biology" (Rich 1979: 31). But as women struggle to elude patriarchal oppression in order to assert their feminity, they gradually become alienated from the socio-familial milieu for "feminity is itself alienating" (Foreman 1977: 151).

The greatest crime for Indu is that she is born a girl. She feels that womanhood is a curse: "I had committed a great crime by being born a girl" (126). Being a female Indu "could neither assert, nor demand or proclaim" (132). She "doesn't fit into the world" (102). Then where does she belong? She doesn't know: "Where do I belong?" (*ibid.*). It is this search for roots that moves her to affirm her identity through the assertion of her feminine self:

> ...assert yourself. Don't suppress it. Let it grow and flourish, never mind how many things it destroys in the bargain. (132)

The novel ends with a note of affirmation. Indu asserts her individuality as a woman and also as a partaker in the endless cycle of life. She lives to see life with the possibilities of growth. Thus, she has discovered the meaning of life in her journey to individuation. Through the character of Indu, Deshpande has registered her awareness of the arrest to feminine development brought about by an economic system given to sheer materialistic happiness and inhabited by philistines like Jayant, and a patriarchal family-structure which produce in women dependency, insecurity, lack of autonomy, and an incomplete sense of their identity.

WORKS CITED

Beauvoir, Simone de. *The Second Sex* (trans.) H.M. Parshley, Harmondsworth, 1974.

—— London: Pan Books, 1988.

Berger, John. *Ways of Seeing*, Harmondsworth, 1972.

Camus, Albert. *The Outsider* (tr. Joseph Laredo), Penguin Books Ltd., 1983.

Desai, Anita. *Voices in the City,* Delhi: Orient Paperbacks, 1982.

—— "An Interview with Yasodhara Dalmia", *The Times of India*, April 29, 1979.

Deshpande, Shashi. Interview by Vanamala Viswanatha, "A Woman's World...", *Literature Alive,* 1, December 3, 1987.

—— *Roots and Shadows,* New Delhi: Orient Longman, 1983. (Issued as a Disha Book, 1992.)

(All citations from this text in the paper are from the Disha edn. of the novel and are followed by page numbers within parentheses.)

Firestone, Shulamith. *The Dialectic of Sex*, New York: Bantam Bks., 1970.

Foreman, Ann. *Feminity as Alienation: Women and the Family in Marxism and Psychoanalysis*, London, 1977.

Grimke, Sarah. *Letters on the Equality of the Sexes and the Condition of Woman,* New York: Burt Franklin, 1970.

Klein, Viola. *The Feminine Character,* London: Routledge, 1989.

Miller, Jean Baker. *Towards a New Psychology of Women,* Harmondsworth, 1983.

Nahal, Chaman. "Feminism in English Fiction: Forms and Variations" in Sushila Singh (ed.), *Feminism and Recent Fiction in English,* New Delhi: Prestige, 1991.

Oakley, Ann. *Woman's Work: The Housewife, Past and Present*, New York: Pantheon Books, 1974.

Rich, Adrienne. *Of Woman Born,* New York: W.W. Norton, 1979.

Sartre, Jean Paul. *Nausea*, Penguin Books Ltd., 1965.

Tong, Rosemarie. *Feminist Thought*, London: Routledge, 1993.

Waugh, Patricia. *Feminine Fictions*, London: Routledge, 1989.

7

Articulation of the Feminine Voice: Jaya in Shashi Deshpande's *That Long Silence*

S.P. SWAIN

> A free and autonomous being like all creatures—(a woman) finds herself living in a world where men compel her to assume the status of the Other.
>
> —*Simone de Beauvoir*

In *That Long Silence*, Shashi Deshpande delineates the delicate swings of mood, the see-saw moments of joy and despair, the fragments of feelings perceived and suppressed, the life of senses as well as the heart-wringing anguish of the narrator protagonist Jaya, a housewife and a failed writer. The novel depicts the life of Jaya at the level of the silent and the unconscious. A sensitive and realistic dramatisation of the married life of Jaya and her husband Mohan, it portrays an inquisitive critical appraisal to which the institution of marriage has been subjected to in recent years. It centres round the inner perception of the protagonist, a woman who is subtly drawn from inside, a woman who "finds her normal routine so disrupted that for the first time she can look at her life and attempt to decide who she really is" (King, Debonair: 97). But could she?

The question, "who am I?" (24) haunts her so obsessively that she fails to find herself. She is "an utter stranger, a person so alien that even the faintest understanding of the motives of her actions seemed impossible" (69). Hence, her agonised cries—"I can't hope, I can't manage. I can't go on" (70). In such a stifling and suffocating domestic ambience and patriarchal set-up, she finds her female identity effaced. Her feminine dilemma is expressed in her vacillating state of mind: "I could and couldn't do, all the things that were womanly and unwomanly... (83). Jaya is Suhasini and also "Seeta", the pseudonym she assumes to write columns about the plight of the middle-class housewife. Both "Suhasini" and "Seeta" are as Jaya says, "the many selves waiting to be discovered...each self-attached like a Siamese twin to a self of another person, neither able to exist without the other" (69). Hence, if life is "to be made possible" (193), she is to live neither as "Suhasini" or "Jaya", nor as "Seeta" or "anti-Kusum". She is to live but not in fragments.

Seething discontent within and without make her bounce upon the spring-board of life. She loses all hold on it and keeps on oscillating in opinions and choices, yet to decide "who she really is" (King: *ibid.*). Deshpande reveals the consciousness of Jaya through an exposition of her mind in the process of thinking, feeling and reacting to the stimuli of the moment and situation. In doing so, she goes on to assert the feminine psyche of the protagonist, all ago, to break away from the stranglehold of a quagmired social fabric rooted in patriarchy which repels as it attracts. In her tiny old flat in Dadar, Bombay, Jaya lives like an introvert, often given to brooding and reminiscing with a lot of self-reflection in order to discover her true self:

> And I was Jaya. But I had been Suhasini as well. I can see her now, the Suhasini who was distinct from Jaya, a soft smiling, placid, motherly woman. A woman who lovingly nurtured her family. A woman who coped. (16)

Memories plunge in often linked by the ambivalent association of ideas. Each incident, a mini-story, a fiction in itself, imparts an unexplored vision to the narrative. The dejections and disappointments of unrequited selfhood, the illusions and pinings of love and the yearnings for companionship make up the stream of Jaya's consciousness. Recalling the ions of her split self-entangled in her memory, she creates a world of harmony, a world of fantasy, understanding, authentic selfhood and a composite self: "Ours has been a delicately balanced relationship, so much so that we have even snipped off bits of ourselves to keep the scales on an even keel" (07). Jaya is not totally a silent and mute sufferer. She is an actor participant as well as an observer in the novel. She steps out of the narrative-action as a witness as it were, a critic to perceive the tenor of the story filtered through a female consciousness:

> Sensual memories are the coldest. They stir up nothing in you.... These emotions and responses seemed to belong to two other people, not to the two of us lying here together...whatever my feeling had been then, I had never spoken of them to him. In fact, we had never spoken of sex at all. (95)

Like Shourie Daniel's Mira Cheriyan, the witnessing critic in Jaya is perpetually probing and protecting her autonomy. She revolts but in silence. Silence was her natural condition. When her husband, Mohan, talks about women being treated very cruelly by their husbands which he calls strength, she passionately bursts into rumination:

> He saw strength in the woman sitting silently in front of the fire, but I saw despair. I saw a despair so great that it would not voice itself. I saw a struggle so bitter that silence was the only weapon. Silence and surrender. (36)

Like Dorothy M. Richardson, Shashi Deshpande endeavours "to render current existence as reflected in the consciousness of her heroine" (Allen, 1967: 03). Veena Sheshadri says in her interview:

> Why the author has chosen a heroine who only succeeds in evoking waves of irritation in the reader? Perhaps it is because a competent writer like her is never satisfied unless she is tackling new challenges. Also, she believes in presenting life as it is and not as it should be; and there must be thousands of self-centred women like Jaya, perennially gripping about their fate, but unwilling to do anything that could result in their being tossed out of their comfortable ruts and into the big, bad world of reality, to fend for themselves. (*Literature Alive*, 1988: 94)

Jaya is a modern predicament and the flood of consciousness that ensues out of it is a silent stream of thoughts and feelings. She knows pretty well that in order to get by in a relationship one has to learn a lot of tricks and "Silence is one of them.... You never find a woman criticising her husband, even playfully, in case it might damage the relationship" (Cunningham, *The Indian Post*: 6). Jaya succumbs and surrenders to Mohan without revolting. Silently, she wills to his will. She never says 'Yes' when her husband asks her whether he has hurt her. She endures everything, tolerates all kinds of masculine oppression silently: "...in the emotion that governed my behaviour to him, there was still the habit of being a wife, of sustaining and supporting him" (48). Hence, it is Jaya who makes "the first conciliatory move..." (82). A dominating husband and a suffering wife—that is her tie with Mohan. She does not immediately react to the situation but the reader is insinuated through the flashback technique used by the author especially at critical junctures in the psychic life of Jaya. Lying solitary in her room, her mind shuttles between the past and the present and thus covers the whole span of her life. At times Deshpande executes the stream-of-consciousness technique to project the psychic reverberations of her characters in order to make the story more real and authentic. Her heroines like Jaya are rebels but only passive ones whose incarcerated lamentations are but cries in the wilderness, "mute and desperate calls to restructure the groove of society" (Menon, *Commonwealth Quarterly*: 32). Rebellion and suffering in Jaya has a proclivity for being transmuted into an artistic expression. In her there is an inner need for creativity and fulfilment but this creative expression in her is inhibited due to lack of privacy, of sheer physical space to reflect and work in. Virginia Woolf attributed woman's lack of creativity to her not having a room of her own. Nayantara Sahgal recalls that until she wrote *Rich Like Us* in the United States on a Woodrow Wilson Fellowship, she never had a room of her own where she could write undisturbed and "where there are no interruptions" (Sahgal, *The Hindustan Times*, Sunday Magazine, Jan. 11, 1987). In case of Jaya, strong social and family pressure stifles her creativity and holds all creative activities in subservience to her role as a home-maker. Feminists like Helene Cixons and Luce Irrigarary identify the feminine at levels of silent and unconscious. Jaya says, "Like a disease, a disability I had to hide from everyone" (97). Her urges are silent and mute pinings passively manifested in moments of crisis and in "chaotic sequence of events and non-events" (167) that made up her life. She is silent because, "It was so much simpler to say nothing. So much less complicated" (99). The metaphor of silence for her is a retreat, a defence mechanism which helps her to express herself more comprehensively and artistically.

The first person narrative serves as an apt means to channelise the flow of her agonised reminiscences, her ruthless and crushing need to use words, to become a writer. She says:

> Why am I thinking of these things now? Is it because I find myself struggling for words? Strange—I've always found writing easy. Words came to me with a facility that pleased me; sometimes shamed me too—it seemed too easy. But now, for some reason, I am reminded of the process of childbirth. The only memory of it that remains with me is that of fear—a fear that I was losing control over my own body. And so I resisted. (01)

Jaya being renamed as Suhasini after her marriage is not a case of the loss of identity since Jaya and Suhasini are the two facets of the same coin and these two collateral names of the Deshpande protagonist are symbolical in their socio-familial import. Jaya, her premarital name means 'victory' and Suhasini, the postmarital name given to her by her husband means "a soft smiling, placid motherly woman. A woman who lovingly nurtured her family. A woman who coped" (15). Jaya is a woman who adjusts and accommodates unlike the modern women who find themselves "forced into the background by the claims of culture" and hence they adopt "an inimical attitude towards it" (Freud, 1939: 73). She is not the structurally patterned woman of the traditional Indian Society where woman was chiefly confined to the hearth and man to the world, where woman was the follower and man the leader, where woman was the sufferer and man the ordainer. She does not want to be a "Sita following her husband into exile" or a "Savitri dogging Death to reclaim her husband" or a "Draupadi stoically sharing her husband's travails..." (11). She believes that there is pain in hostility, and rebellion is anguish and agony. Hence, she adopts a subaltern and subservient attitude:

> No, what I have to do with these mythical women? I can't fool myself. The truth is simpler. Two bullocks yoked together...it is more comfortable for them to move in the same direction. To go in different directions would be painful; and what animal would voluntarily choose pain? (11-12)

In this way, Jaya attempts to demythify/demystify her actions through the animal imagery of "two bullocks yoked together" (11). But she is never safe when yoked. So she flounders to break out of the yoke:

> Stay at home, look after your babies, keep out the rest of the world, you are safe. That poor idiotic woman Suhasini believed in this. I know better, now I know that safety is always unattainable. You are never safe. (17)

Past disappointments 'flashback' across her mind 'fading out' the consciousness of her present plight in the milieu. The memories of the past enlighten the present and the recurring images, the Sparrow story and the myths (like the Ramayana) lend a universal touch to her tragic predicament. The nursery rhymes and the trivial scenes though unrelated to the sequence of the narrative, yet have a thematic import. They portray the abandoned and the lonely Jaya's drift of thought and her evanescent mood captured through the broken and fragmentary stream of consciousness:

> "A husband is like a sheltering tree,"... "Take your pain between your teeth, bite on it, don't let it escape...". (32)

Jaya's self-questioning attitude comes as a split in the narrative. She broods over the metaphor of the "Sheltering tree":

> A sheltering tree. Without the tree, you are dangerously unprotected...equally logically and vulnerable. This followed logically. And so you have to keep the tree

> alive and flourishing, even if you have to water it with deceit and lies. This too followed, equally logically. (32)

Struggling with the threats to her freedom and her integrity, Jaya desperately needs to protect herself from dissipating and sinking in the crumbling world around her. Her hysterical laugh at the absurdity of marriage echoes the insane woman's laughter. It symbolises her cousin Kusum's insanity through which she tries to define herself negatively. Hence, the self-questionings "Who am I?" (24). She thinks, "Am I going crazy like Kusum" (125). Such digression in the narrative sequence as this piece of reminiscence plays a unique part since the novelist's aim is to document the flow of human consciousness in different directions unmindful of its taxing effects on the readers whose sensibilities have been nurtured on the scientific and modern ideal of reality. An individual's real self exposes itself more in his irrational, irrelevant and fragmented currents of thoughts and emotions rather than in his well thought out responses to life. Deshpande thus presents the subterranean and subliminal impressions of human life through digressions in the narrative.

In their stream of thoughts, both Jaya and Mohan look at their marital relationship where there is nothing but suppressed silence. Disgruntled with Mohan and at the consigning social milieu, Jaya wants to flee from the cribbed confines of an incarcerated domestic life in order to find a new identity for herself, a new mooring for her fugitive self. Communication at the domestic and personal level is a failure: "Nothing. Nothing between us...nothing between me and Mohan. We live together but there had been only emptiness between us" (185). Jaya had never confessed her "frenetic feelings" to Mohan as it had seemed "like a disease, a disability" (97), which he had to hide from everyone. Jaya pines for social communication but the society is impervious to her spiritual need. The society as a mirror "is always treacherous" (01) for it fails to show what we want to see beyond our visual perception.

There is hardly any communication between Jaya and Mohan, neither verbal nor emotional. Mohan wanted a well-educated and cultured wife, not a reciprocating and loving one. So he resolved to marry Jaya when he saw her speaking fluently:

> You know Jaya, the first day I met you at your Ramukaku's house, you were talking to your brother, Dinkar, and somehow you sounded so much like that girl. I think it was at that moment that I decided I would marry you. (90)

An intellectually idealised and cultural husband like Mohan, finds Jaya a square peg in a round hole. There develops disheartening silence between the husband and the wife. Mohan's queries remain unanswered by Jaya for she is unable to find a word of response: "I racked my brains trying to think of an answer" (31). Jaya's inner turmoils are so tense and acute that words fail her desire for articulation. She is unable to speak her trouble out for she is a woman who faces the suffering of her life and the opposition of the milieu in the true spirit of ideal Hindu womanhood where obedience and loyalty has degenerated to the state of dogged subservience. Hence, her life becomes chaotic. Temperamental incompatibility between Jaya and Mohan accounts for their incommunication and quizzical silence. Could a modern woman nestled in tradition like Jaya understand a traditionalist like Mohan who is rooted out and out in customs and whose repressive use of silence pressurises Jaya into conformity with his expectations? The discord in their temperamental outlook is so great that they fail time and again to understand each other. Deshpande presents here not a woman who has a desire to revolt but the one who ultimately reconciles to her hapless lot. Having failed to discover the truth, she remains silent and reticent revealing her most personal and private thoughts in her writings. Mohan wonders as to how could women be so rebellious and esoteric, so angry and recalcitrant. To him it is unwomanly to be angry for it is against the ideals of feminism (if by feminism we mean humanism and anti-fascism):

> A woman can never be angry; she can only be neurotic, hysterical, frustrated. There is no room for despair, either. There is only order and routine, today. I have to change the sheets tomorrow, scrub the bathrooms the day after, clean the fridge.... (147-48)

Marriage subjugates and enslaves women and it leads her to "aimless days indefinitely repeated, life that slips away gently toward death without questioning its purpose" (de Beauvoir 1974: 500). Women pay for their happiness at the cost of their freedom and de Beauvoir emphasised that such a sacrifice on the part of a woman is too high for anyone because the kind of self-contentment, serenity and security that marriage offers woman drains her soul of its capacity for greatness:

> She shuts behind her the doors of her new home, when she was a girl, the whole countryside was her homeland; the forests were hers. Now she is confined to a restricted space.... (*The Second Sex*: 502)

The role of a wife restricts rather circumscribes women's self-development. The role of a mother does it even more and "sometimes women play their roles not so much because they want to, as because they have to in order to survive economically and/or psychologically. Virtually all women engage in the feminine role playing" (Tong 1993: 208). It is against this encoded and pre-ordained role of a woman that Jaya revolts. For her, "in this life itself there are so many cross-roads, so many choices" (192) but a married woman has a few or practically no choice left to her save what her husband wills and desires. But Jaya's is a life of instincts and urges. Unlike other married women slavishly tagged to tradition, she has her own say. She unfurls and unburdens herself to activate the creative impulses smothered within her artistic self. "The act of unburdening herself through self-expression" observes Kamini Dinesh, "becomes for her a creative process. It is not merely a reliving of particular moments of the past but a coming to terms with herself..." (*Contemporary Indian Fiction in English*: 88). In reminiscing about the past Jaya succeeds in blotting out that long silence and making future life possible. With her traditionally muted voice she wobbles between the past and the present through her stream of thoughts which reveals "ten different faces emerging from ten different mirrors" (01). In keeping with the needs of the quality of consciousness, the flux of the stream of Jaya's thoughts is not tied down to a rigid clock progression. Through close-ups and flashbacks, Deshpande has laid bare the psyche of Jaya which is reluctantly responsive and passively secluded. The author's unrelieved stress on obliterating herself from the novel as a story-teller, giving full freedom to the protagonist to unveil herself using her resilient mind to document her vision of life has imparted an unquestionable credibility to the realism of the stream of Jaya's consciousness. Through the stream of consciousness technique Deshpande pictures Jaya's rejection of the patriarchal notion of a unitary self or identity. Jaya observes, "But what was that 'myself'? Trying to find oneself—what a cliche that has become. As if such a thing is possible. As if there is such a thing as oneself, intact and whole, waiting to be discovered" (69). On the contrary as has been pointed out earlier, there are so many selves, each attached to the other like a Siamese twin and "neither able to exist without the other" (*ibid.*). Thus, other people, other men and women occupy a place in Jaya's stream of thoughts and are linked to her own self. An individual's self does not exist in isolation but it coexists with other selves. Hence through Jaya's stream of thoughts we find references to many men and women. Jaya owns all. Disowns none. A veritable symbol of the Universal Mother.

The metaphor of silence under which the novel is organized helps to impose a quietude and discipline: the inner dynamics of a self cut off from human communication. That long silence is not an intrusion into the world of silence but a silent communion with the oppressed self-straining for articulation, for a voice.

Silence manifests in Jaya's discontent which is more personal and deeply sexual. Her romantic longing of adolescence are transformed into rigid rules and rituals by tradition. Jaya and Mohan hardly spoke to each other of love and sex. Love-making for them was a silent and inarticulate affair:

> God, how terrible it was to know a man so well. I could time it almost to the second, from the first devious wooing to the moment he turned away from me, offering me his hunched back. (85)

In the process of self-revelation through writing, Jaya comes to recognise herself as a failed writer because when she had continued writing, her stories had been rejected for lack of genuine feelings which she had laid aside. She had also kept away the clamouring voices of women who wanted to find expression therein, for fear that they may ruffle her domestic life. She comes to accept herself as a failed writer. She feels her identity effaced when she sees repeated images of herself as a person with variegated interlinked selves, all alike and without any uniqueness of their own. She says, "I was so exactly like the other. I was almost invisible" (142). In other words, she is self-alienated. Jaya's creative urge and artistic zeal frees her from her cramped and dubbed domestic and societal roles. It releases her from emotional turmoil. At length she resolves to break that long silence by putting down on paper all that she had suppressed in her seventeen years' silence—that long silence which had reduced her self to fragments:

> I am not afraid any more. The panic has gone. I am Mohan's wife, I had thought, and cut off the bits of me that had refused to be Mohan's wife. Now I know that kind of fragmentation is not possible. The child, hands in pocket, has been with me through the years. She is with me still. (191)

Such confessional statements like these manifestly show that the novel is a feminist critique disguised in the form of a novel. Through the image of a woman crawling into a hole, Deshpande describes the woeful plight of Jaya, unprotected and unshelled. Jaya says: "Distance from real life. Scared of writing. Scared of failing. Oh God, I had thought, I cannot take any more. Even a worm has hole it can crawl into. I had mine—as Mohan's wife, as Rahul's and Rati's mother" (148).

Towards the end of the novel Jaya consciously acknowledges her writing as a kind of fiction and quotes Defoe's description of fiction as a kind of "lying", which may make "a great hope in the heart". Hence, she decides to 'plug that hole' as said earlier by speaking and listening and erasing the silence between her and Mohan. It is this erasing of the silence that symbolises the assertion of her feminine voice, a voice with hope and promise, a voice that articulates her thoughts. The novel doesn't depict

Jaya's life as a totally dismal and hopeless struggle. It suggests "hope" and "change" for the better:

> We don't change overnight. It's possible that we may not change even over long periods of time. But we can always hope. Without that life would be impossible. (193)

Such an ending, suggests a new beginning for Jaya and Mohan.

Modern Indian writers like Deshpande tend to depict the oppression of women with greater self-consciousness, a deeper sense of involvement and often with a sense of outrage. Earlier writers had deified and eulogised women's suffering but the writers of the later part of the post-independent period have unpalliatively presented their suffering with much greater realism. But Shashi Deshpande "Overdose the theme of women suffering so that the novel is in some danger of turning into a sociological tract" (Gupta, *Indian Literature*: 184). William Walsh considers "the combination of the analytical and detached" (*Indian Literature* in *English*: 117), a particular and unusual quality of the novel. The noted critic further observes:

> A turmoil of feeling is conveyed in cool, idiomatic and sensitive prose. And it is served by a memory which is so rich and minutely specific and able to produce not just bright discrete images but rather a flow of naturally related scenes that it is a creative faculty making past life live again in the present. (*Indian Literature* in *English*: 117)

At once conversational and formal, the reminiscences of Jaya evoke a deeper and more tragic sense of vanished time, fleeting moments, personal losses recounted in a quiet and calm voice characterised by sobriety. It follows the natural movements of a mind experiencing, moments and expressions that become meaningful spots of time. Jaya's unruffled stream of consciousness symbolises the flow of mind that registers experience in a prose of recollection and nostalgia. Shashi Deshpande has made the story self-propelled without the novelist acting as a meddler and as an omniscient narrator. In fine, she has tentatively succeeded in introducing "the reader directly into the interior life of the characters without any intervention by way of comment or explanation on the part of the author" (Bowling 1950: 345).

WORKS CITED

Allen, Walter. "Introduction" to *Pilgrimage* (London, 1967).

Bowling, L.E. "What is the Stream of Consciousness Technique?" *PMLA*, Vol. LXV, No. 4 (June 1950).

Cunningham, John. "Indian Writer's Block", *The Indian Post*, March 6, 1988.

De Beauvoir, Simone. *The Second Sex*, trans. and edit. H.M. Parshley (New York: Vintage Books, 1974).

Deshpande, Shashi. *That Long Silence* (1988; New Delhi: Penguin Books, 1989). (All textual citations in the article kept in parentheses are from this edition of the novel.)

Dinesh, Kamini. "*That Long Silence*: The Narrator and the Narrative", *Contemporary Indian Fiction in English* (ed.) Avadesh K. Singh (New Delhi: Creative, 1993).

Freud, Sigmund. *Civilisation and Its Discontent* (London: Hogarth, 1939).

Gupta, R.K. "Feminism and Modern Indian Literature", *Indian Literature* (157), Sept.-Oct. '93.

King, Adele. "Effective Portrait", *Debonair*, June 1988.

Menon, Madhavi K. "The Crisis of the Feminine: Shashi Deshpande's *That Long Silence*", *Commonwealth Quarterly*, Vol. 18, No. 46, Dec.-Mar. 1993.

Sahgal, Nayantara. Interviewed by Nergis Dalal, *The Hindustan Times* (Sunday Magazine), Jan. 11, 1987.

Sheshadri, Veena. "*That Long Silence*", *Literature Alive*, II, 1 (1988).

Tong, Rosemarie. *Feminist Thought* (London: Routledge, 1993).

Walsh, William, *Indian Literature in English* (London: Longman, 1990).

8
Shreya of Sonagarh—A Sexist Approach

S.P. SWAIN

> Sexuality must not be thought of as a kind of natural given which power holds in check...it is the name that can be given to a historical construct: not a furtive reality that is difficult to grasp but a great surface network in which the stimulation of bodies, the intensification of pleasures, the incitement to discourse...are linked to one another. (Foucault 1984: 105-06)

Shreya of Sonagarh depicts the life of a middle-class women whose sexual urges lie covertly coiled behind the facades of innocence and submissiveness, of passivity and meek surrender. The novel deals with the theme of sex in relation to a woman's relationship with her husband as well as with her paramour. This paper intends to analyse Shreya's sexual relationship with her husband Brijesh and her paramour Anand from a feminist angle.

Unrequited sexual urges in a woman may lead to disastrous ends. A woman can acknowledge her sexual desires only if they have been gloriously satiated. Otherwise she vehemently repudiates them. And in case of Shreya, her emotional frigidity is due to her dislike of her husband. There seems to be hardly any sexual reciprocation between Shreya and Brijesh. This is because her husband lacks seductive power. He is cool, neglectful and awkward and fails to awaken her sexuality. He leaves her unsatisfied. Shreya fears his domination for she has

Anand in mind to whom she had already surrendered her body and got what she wanted. Anand thus remains in her psyche as an obsessive sexual presence which poses a barrier to her marital relationship with Brijesh. But Brijesh is no substitute in love for Anand. Hence, he stirs up bitterness and resentment in her mind and it is this resentment which becomes the source of Shreya's feminine frigidity and what she offers to Brijesh in bed is only an insulting coldness for she seems to be saying to him, "Since you don't love me, since I have defects that are displeasing (i.e. her ugly appearance), I shall no longer abandon myself to love, desire and pleasure".

Otto Weininger says that woman has "one, only one, quality: She is Sex. Her only interest in life is restricted to sexual activities either in herself or in other persons.... Sexuality is her only end and sense in the universe" (qtd. by Viola Klein in *The Feminine Character* 61). But Shreya of Sonagarh is a different woman. With her child-like ignorance and naivety, she wonders at the sexual union between the male and the female. She deems sexual intercourse as something crude and vulgar, an invasion of her unwilling body. It is something grotesque and detestable. Shreya says:

> ...do they enjoy the—the thing that produced a baby finally. She couldn't imagine such close contact to exist between two bodies. It seemed so, so improper somehow, even crude and vulgar I don't think I could ever bring my body invaded like that. It seemed so grotesque...I can't—never. (93)

Shreya seems to be a passive participant in sexual union with her husband. But why? Is she against the virile aggressiveness of the male (which she compares to an invasion of her body) that conspires to assert masculine sovereignty, reducing woman to a profoundly passive object in the sexual act? Or, is it because she is indifferent to Sex? Uma Vasudev has her answer to all these questions. She views Shreya as an introverted and ugly girl, an unambitious teenager who "hated people, entertainment, socializing, sex or politics" (45). As a woman, she is by nature passive and submissive and her female submission is the norm in something as fundamental as sexuality. The graphic description of sex in the novel centres round the character of Shreya. With the growth of her political character, there is a simultaneous change in her attitude towards sex. A typical middle-class girl with a puritanical and orthodox attitude towards sex, she views it as something dirty. Copulation to her is an animalistic and a filthy act and hence she does all her best to dodge any sort of sexual advances by Brijesh:

> No, please. I—I'm not fit. You know, not fit.
> She wished she could utter the word outright.
> Menses.... Even if She didn't have it. (93)

It seems that Shreya's escape from sexual union is due to her shy nature but this does not mean that she says "no" to sex. She simply conveys her dislike of it, or, of her husband Brijesh. But she forgets that sex is not solely for sex. On the other hand, it is the ultimate in the consummation of a relationship and it is a craving for wholeness, for totality.

Brijesh considers Shreya, a fool to think that sex was a horrible invasion of her body, and that it had wrecked her with pain and uneasiness. She is a child to think that sex has generated in her the feeling that made her oblivious of guilt. In an attempt at self-identification, she protects the physicality of her being on the city of Lucknow and finds it too physical, almost animalistic: "She didn't like to be touched by the physical. Not even after twelve years of marriage and three children" (102). Her married life is a sexual void. She had physical union with Brijesh without sexual pleasure for she loathed copulation and did her best to escape from it under the pretension that she had some sort of ache which hardly ever occurred:

> Did they really come, these aches in the stomach, the head, the liver, the kidney, the nose, the throat...! (89)

Even she doesn't hesitate to utter the word 'Menses' even if she didn't have it. This kind of pretension becomes a defence mechanism for her, a means to escape sexual intercourse with her husband which she calls a "dirty thing". But the paradox of such a remark is manifest when she thinks of her illicit sexual relationship with Anand, her lover, a pleasurable thing. With Brijesh, sex is a 'dirty thing' but with Anand, it is an 'enjoyable thing'. Her detestation of sex with Brijesh is because he does not love her and hence sex without love becomes wooden and sapless. She doesn't enjoy it but with Anand it is tempered with love and so she enjoys it. Sex with Anand makes her feel the ecstacy of orgasm and the throbbing quiver of the body. But Shreya fails to understand that such straying into forbidden pleasure of infidelity with Anand, may be looked down by the sanctimonious guardians of social morality and the orthodox middle-class society which she hails from. Like a sex robot, she carries on her amorous relationship with Anand, though married to Brijesh. Of course at times such a forbidden liaison breeds in her a feeling of disquiet, but she studiously ignores it since as a woman her duty is to satisfy her husband's sexual needs.

The novel begins with the description of an insipid and almost wooden act of copulation which observes Prabhat Kumar Pandeya "brings to our mind the typist girl in *The Waste Land* whose body is used like a public urinal" (*Indian Women Novelists*: 204).

Sex as depicted in the novel is related to Marxist Feminism. It is portrayed as a kind of domestic work that the wife discharges as a part of her obligation towards her husband. Male-female relation in marriage is as exploitative as the relation of a prostitute to a customer. Marriage, thus becomes a kind of prostitution where the wife who has sex with her husband feels almost alienated from her own self. This the Marxists call a women's sex-specific oppression. The female here suffers as an oppressed wife. Shreya is a wife-prostitute who does not act but is acted upon, an object of passivity, of self-surrender in sex without any participation in it:

> She lay under her husband's body that evening, like any other evening, staring at the ceiling. It was doing nothing to her, nothing, like every other evening. It was so exhausting, feeling nothing, like all the other evenings. (1)

An horrible invasion of her body indeed. Here we have an instance of "the hysterization of women's bodies, identifying them, in particular with a sexuality in need of surveillance and control (Waugh 1989: 173). Shreya lies down "with open legs, willing to let him have the only thing he could claim as his right, even if it was with a frigidity" (3). Such a type of sexual surrender to a man without any emotional participation is nothing but a 'literal rape' for in such a copulation there is no acquiescence of feelings or the intellect. It is just a surrender of the body before the male for he happens to be a husband to whose sexual advances, the wife is bound to condescend as a part of her conjugal duty. The unwilling body of Shreya here symbolises protest and rage. "Traditionally, women have always used their bodies as instruments of protest against their feminine positioning and identification" (Waugh 1989: 174). Hence, the radical dissatisfaction that Shreya feels with her cultural position as a housewife is a historical feminine construct. A woman like Shreya, denied the love and affection of her husband and mechanically yielding before his masculinity, becomes an object of sexual consumption and not sexual regeneration. This possessive love has the alienating effects of commodification. The body of the female is here identified with an inert consumer good and due to this self-alienation, women like Shreya experience their bodies as parts, 'objects', rather than integrated wholes. In Shreya, the psychical and sexual impulses and interests in relation to her husband do not exist independently. They are to be brought into existence only by and for others—controlled, defined and used. Hence, Shreya's extra-marital relationship with Anand. With Brijesh, she perceives herself as a shadow, a negative, an object but with Anand, she is a subjective being, very much involved in her female self, her feminity.

Lack of emotional rapport between the husband and the wife leads to their marital incompatibility. Both are sexual strangers to each other and both adopt a stand-offish attitude to each other. Each is a void to the other. Each a 'nothingness' that spawns an ineffable silence in their sexual relationship:

> How strange it was to be married...to find he meant nothing to her, that between their bodies—was a gap, and that she remained nothing, that they together,

> living, eating and fornicating, a husband and wife, were nothing to each other. Nothingness was joined to nothingness. (57)

In Shreya, we have the instance of a woman who has become a mother without ever having experienced the orgasm or even any sex excitement at all. Probably, marriage has destroyed her feminine eroticism. Her sexual urge is not spontaneous. It is artificial. She is chilled by the idea of sexual union and is ashamed to find herself given to someone who is administering a right over her. Fidelity is necessary for sexual love but this is missing in the conjugal life of Shreya. Due to the feeling of disgust and indifference between the husband and the wife, erotic attraction disappears, and the couple feel that the sexual act is no longer an inter-subjective experience in which each goes beyond self, "but rather a kind of joint masturbation" (de Beauvoir 1988: 465). Such brutish satisfying of the husband's sexual need is not enough to satisfy the wife's sexuality. The wife frequently resorts to erotic fantasies under such compelling conditions. Thus, we find Shreya visualising Anand's face in Brijesh when she is having sexual intercourse with him (Brijesh). Further, we also find Shreya's reluctance to participate in sex with Brijesh often ventilated through her pretension of pain. Even her phantasising pain in her private parts, though imaginary, at times assumes realistic dimensions: ·

> Take refuge in her pretensions again, feign the physical pain that had never been there. She looked up at him helplessly and slowly her face began to move to the contortions dictated by her imagination, with the stomach beginning to chum at the thought of those cold thrusts in her vagina she was afraid of...he must know that there was a mask there between her legs.... It was there, the pain was real. (132)

Shreya abhors sexual relationship with her husband to such an extent that she "wished her body were like those petals of flowers which fold up when the sun sets. She wished her body could set, like the sun, every evening" (52). Sexuality for Shreya is a pretension, an illusion. It is the absence of love in their conjugal life that fails to produce strong bodily movement during copulation. Lack of love also renders her sexuality a mere physical display suggestive of nudity. With Anand, her paramour, she has no such sexual thoughts related to the symbolic folding up of the petals of flowers with the setting of the sun. Shreya loves Anand so much that with him she feels herself a new being, not a domestic pet of Brijesh but the prettiest woman in the world. She has the real enjoyment of sexual tryst with Anand. During such sexual moments, she forgot that she was married and was the mother to three children. She felt untainted and untarnished, the white lotus of love, pure and virginal:

> She felt she was going as Shreya, virgin and free, even if she had a husband and three children.... Each time at the mere thought of what was happening her body would ripple like the suddenly excited waters of a tranquil pond. She would feel the tremors running like spirits all through her veins.... Was this love; or whatever it was?... Her eyes flew wide open, her mouth, her legs, her heart, were opened to receive, each pore an open receptacle for the showers of ecstasy that rained down upon her.... She had fallen asleep. For the first time in the arms of a man. (129-30)

But is Anand the man with whom a married woman like Shreya should sleep, even if it was the first time? Does Shreya carry out her feminine functions sincerely? In regard to the erotic fate of woman like Shreya de Beauvoir observes:

> ...two essential consequences follow: first she has no right to any sexual activity apart from marriage; sexual intercourse thus becoming an institution, desire and gratification are subordinated to the interest of society for both sexes; but man, being transcended towards the universal as worker and citizen, can enjoy contingent pleasures before marriage and extramaritally. (*The Second Sex*: 454-55)

But why do extra-marital affairs occur? Why does adultery take place? Psychologists believe that we ourselves create conditions for the secret flourishing of illicit amorous liaisons because of our childish emotional attachment to the monogamy myth.

One hardly finds any loving passion in the conjugal life of Brijesh and Shreya, though both had sexual tryst several times. Hence, it becomes very hard for them to understand each other both in relation to the self as well as the society. The paradox of marriage thus lies in the fact that it has at once an erotic and a social function. The wife's role in marriage is to unfold in her husband's shadow and share an experience that is often shameful and disgraceful, objectionable and upsetting. But Shreya does not feel any erotic sensation in her copulation with her husband but childishly caters to the sexual needs of Brijesh as a part of her social obligation as a wife. They have sexual involvement without sensual indulgence. Hence, the frustration in their married life. Since Shreya is sexually unsatisfied, her passions assume a possessive form which manifest in her illicit carnal love for Anand. Extra-marital sex is clearly and unforgivably bad and staying within the confines of a dead marriage considered decidedly the right thing to do. Shreya's fossilized marriage cannot hold out against the allure that adultery has. Both Brijesh and Anand live for sex but Shreya hates a life given solely to sex. She pines for emotional love which she doesn't get from either Brijesh or Anand. The sexual needs of Brijesh and Shreya's reluctance and failure to fulfil it becomes so obnoxious that "she could suffer it no more" (109), their "infructuous sex" (109) leads them nowhere. Shreya believes that she had acted "the way he had always wanted her to" (109) but still he pines for sex. "One can't have everything" (109) and "what did it matter if they did not have that infructuous bit of sex between them?... Nobody died for the lack of it..." (111). Such was her aversion towards sex that she was shocked to hear of loose sex talk by women in the clubs. Such women gossiping about illicit sexual relationships of gentle and sophisticated housewives and delighting themselves in dirty and vulgar jokes breeds irritation and scorn in Shreya:

> ...the jokes they exchanged were so raucous, vulgar and so, sexual.... They talked of women of the household having affairs with their Brahmin cooks...can you believe it, if the husband were impotent.... They talked of—of S-Sex, like about the weather.... They were so

> earthy, like animals, so unthinking, and full of sex, so disgusting. There is something so indecent, isn't there, so cheap.... (63)

This mental attitude, rather a typical orthodox Hindu feminine sensibility, accounts for Shreya's asexual and lack-lustre marital life with Brijesh. In such a context, we are to look upon her female sexuality as a negative construct with its concomitant feelings of guilt, hatred and jealousy. She is not only the 'second sex' but a 'weaker sex' too. Weaker in relation to her passivity to the patriarchal masculinist culture in India which considers women as the 'wrong' sex since a daughter in our country is unwanted and considered a burden on her parents.

Shreya's straying from the secure bonds of a staid marriage is to be perceived as outweighing the excitement of a rapturously thrilling and forbidden liaison with Anand with whom her sexual desire approximates a state of concupiscence. True indeed that human sexual behaviour is intricately tuned to the survival and happiness of the species but this does not mean that one should transgress the sanctimonious bonds of social morality. A married woman must know that satisfaction of her sexual appetite by adultery will only sever her from her roots, since her roots lie in her husband, her other self. Anand ultimately realises the futility of his illicit relationship with Shreya and advises her that she should remain with her husband and restrict herself to the familial set up. He says: "That's where you belong" (258). In fact, it is Anand who becomes instrumental in bringing about the sexual harmony between Brijesh and Shreya. It is he who awakens in Shreya her true possessive instinct. Shreya gains sexual possession over her husband, makes him act to her sexual needs. Now she attempts something which she had never attempted all her married life:

> That night in bed with Brijesh...she had made him respond to her...his passion rising, yielding, succumbing, reacting to her touch and her soft, low, cajoling murmurs of endearment.... She must get him back...he finally rolled over her...limp with open legs, all stoic but inviting, his wife. (308)

This sexual surrender to Brijesh's body and her sensual and physical participation in the act of copulation symbolises her final acceptance of Brijesh and also her submission to the aggressive male sexuality. Anand no longer obsesses her, no longer superimposes on her sexual life with Brijesh. A liberated Shreya now feels as if her sex-life is informed with higher values of love as distinct from mere carnality. Finally, Shreya is spiritually united with Brijesh—a union which makes their sexual life complete. The novel ends with an optimistic note, asserting the validity of true love which transgresses all mundane sexual values to attain a spiritual wholeness. Sex that destroys two souls also finally unites them. It serves as a catalytic agent in Shreya's marital life. The theme of sex also occupies a significant place in Uma Vasudev's novel *The Song of Anasuya* but in *Shreya of Sonagarh* it is given a more elaborate treatment. Shreya's quest for sexual identity culminates in her spiritual union with Brijesh.

In dealing with the theme of sex, Uma Vasudev does not exhibit an openness about sexuality as do Shouri Daniels and Kamala Das. She does not sound grisly vulgar or unbearably pornographic. We do not have here the erotic descriptions of the private parts of the body as we have in Shouri Daniels' *The Salt Doll*. Sexuality in *Shreya of Sonagarh* is real since it purports to "rationalise the invidious relationship between the sexes, ratify traditional roles, and validates temperamental differences" (Millett 1970: 178). Unlike Shouri Daniels and Kamala Das, Uma Vasudev portrays a sense of violence and protest in her description of sex:

> ...no please, not any more, not for another week, at least fifteen days, a month, a year, no, no, enough, her orgasm coming with such violent protests that Brijesh could have seen them...that night...there had been a violence about him...as if he had wanted to rip his body apart and tear out the compulsion which had drawn him again and again to a woman without love, a dutiful wife, with passive legs.... (113)

Sex has been given a very polished and gentle touch by Uma Vasudev and not too ingenuous and explicit, almost nauseating, as we find in Shouri Daniels:

> ...he slid in with her and into her and she swam again and again with him in a sea of receptivity. (142)

Uma Vasudev views Shreya's sexuality as the cumulative product of the conflict between her 'themistic self' (rationality and order) and her 'moiratic self' (irrationality and bestiality) symbolised by Anand and Brijesh.

The novel depicts Shreya's sexual odysseys her journey from self-alienation to self-identification, from rejection to acceptance. Uma Vasudev makes a sexist approach to the man-woman relationship in an informal and gentle manner. She has very adroitly exploited the unique nature of typically feminine modes of thought grounded on Shreya's sex experience.

WORKS CITED

De Beauvoir, Simone. *The Second Sex* (London: Pan Books Ltd., 1988).

Foucault, Michel. *The History of Sexuality*, Harmondsworth, 1984.

Klein, Viola. *The Feminine Character* (London: Routledge, 1971).

Millett, Kate. *Sexual Politics* (Garden City, New York: Doubleday, 1970).

Pandeya, Prabhat Kumar. "Married with Three Children Yet Virgin: Love and Sex in Uma Vasudev's *Shreya of Sonagarh*", in R.K. Dhawan (ed.), *Indian Women Novelists,* Set III, Vol. I (New Delhi: Prestige, 1995).

Vasudev, Uma. *Shreya of Sonagarh* (New Delhi: UBS, 1993).

(All textual citations in the paper are from this edition of the novel and are followed by page numbers in parentheses.)

Waugh, Patricia. *Feminine Fictions* (London: Routledge, 1989).

9

The Image of Woman in Uma Vasudevan's *The Song of Anasuya*—A Study

MALLIKARJUN PATIL

The Song of Anasuya is a novel of its own kind in Indian English fiction. It is written by Smt. Uma Vasudevan, a noted Indian woman novelist. Smt. Uma Vasudevan is a woman writer of a very rare talent. She is an authoress of many works. She has written the biography of the former Prime Minister late Smt. Indira Gandhi. She is a writer of many short stories that have appeared in *Short Stories International*, New York. She is also an editor of *Surge International*, a political and cultural magazine from New Delhi.

In the contemporary Indian fiction, Nergis Dalal, Ruth Prawer Jhubvala, Anita Desai and many others are well-known women novelists. To this list of women writers Uma Vasudevan, a young woman novelist may be added. Like the elder Indian women novelists, Uma Vasudevan deals with the practical problems of Indian women. Her portraiture of love or lust-stricken women of India is vivid and amusing. Uma Vasudevan, a novelist on feminism is, however, yet to be brought to light. Vasudevan's women as depicted in her maiden novel *The Song of Anasuya* and short stories have created an uproar in Indian literary circles. The reasons are crystal clear. According to some critics, Vasudevan's depiction of feminism is rather Western-biased. It is not firmly rooted in Indian soil. Therefore, critics are of the view that Vasudevan's feminist-attitude is not yet genuine, critical and comprehensive.

With all the passion and genius of a born story teller Uma Vasudevan tells us of the rapture and torment of a lust-stricken man who after many years of loveless sex, realizes the importance of love at the end of his futile existence. In her novel *The Song of Anasuya*, Uma Vasudevan handles the unusual and sensitive theme of sex and man's shameful emotional relationships with two women of entirely different natures. Priti, a woman of Platonic love, secure and firm, and the other, Anasuya, a woman of tenderly and erotic passion who torments him with her song are well depicted.

In this novel, there are three memorable characters: Priti Tandon, a goddess like figure, Anasuya, a lustful lady both warm and young and Jagat Sarin, a lust and grief-stricken man, a kind of anti-hero, always in search of sexual identity, joy and fulfilment. Jagat Sarin, the hero of this obscene novel, is a middle-aged man. He is full of life. He is a man of love and romance. No doubt, he stands for sex and sensationalism. He falls in love with many ladies—Shanti, a Marwari married woman, Priti Tandon, a separated woman and Anasuya, the admirer of his flesh and spirit.

Jagat, a worker in a firm, relates himself with Priti, who is a separated wife of a Punjabi, aged 30. She is a woman full of sex and desires. Since she is not satisfied by her former husband, she falls in love with a man by the name Gopal who, after all, deserts her. Then with no company of her's own, she lives with Jagat. She is very sexual, for she is adjusted to the Western style of life. She is very social too. Her charming sophistication believe complexion and love for social life lead her to live in the glory of Jagat's perpetual bloom. She avidly listens to men's speeches; cuts dirty jokes with them; and involves herself in hilarious fun and entertainment.

Jagat falls in love with Priti Tandon. In the very beginning his love for her seems to be very strong and inseparable. There is an intense physical bond between Jagat and Priti. The Platonic compulsions on their parts lead them to involve in love-affair, which to them, is a very genuine matter. In the company of Jagat's passionate sexuality Priti finds a sense of bodily relief. Jagat is also intensely in love with her. When he tells her the story of his love for a Marwari woman in Bombay she asks him; "Oh you ran after the woman". He says," O! Madly, I've told you" (p. 46). But the love-relationship between Jagat and Priti does not run smooth. The reason for this is that Priti lacks sex; while Jagat has no love which she is badly in need of. However, at the end, Priti decides to marry him, but he who is in love with Anasuya, does not like to marry her. So their love or lust relationship ends in failure.

Jagat also loves Anasuya, who is aged 20, quite pretty and charming. She has much warmth, beauty and laughter for vivid sensual life. She is an aristocratic lady of fair complexion and robust health. She is earnest in love-making. Like Priti, she is also a lady who wants to live with a variety of men. The reason for this, Anasuya says:

> But a woman can't be as a man in every strange, new encounter, unless there's the kind of sexual relationship which obviates the danger. (p. 119)

Jagat Sarin, being a man of loose morale, falls in love with Anasuya. His desire for Anasuya, a flower-like lady, creates a sense of musical melody in him. His love for Anasuya and the scene related to it is quite obscene. He tells Priti:

> I kissed her coolly and calmly and quickly over her face and her neck and down to the opening of her blouse in front, which was not very low. She too, sat still, as if she were quite detached from this steady attack upon her senses, as if, almost her body were not her own. (p. 101)

However, the things between Jagat and Anasuya go in a wrong way. Ana thinks that Jagat is loving her only for sexual gratification. So to teach him a lesson she pretends to have fallen in love with Saadat, a Muslim. This creates tension in Jagat's later life. As a result, he lands himself in a dilemma that he is unwilling to marry Priti who wants him, and desires to marry Ana who does not like him. He states:

> I was caught between a woman who denied me sex and gave her heart, and a woman who gave me her body loved another. (p. 124)

The feeling of emptiness dances in his mind and heart. Mentally sick, he tells himself: I hated My growing weakness, I hated her. All times, I just hated" (p. 126). He continues, "I lived in the absolute purity of physical impulse, physical experience and physical joy. I had been like an animal pure.... My moments of revelation were coming late, but among the force, shocks to the body" (p. 139). He becomes sick of love, sex and despair. He becomes sick of sex and sick of thinking of love too. The sense of sex haunt him hard until he feels that life is a farce. However, the song of Anasuya goes on in his heart forever. He tells, "This question of Anasuya, Anasuya, Anasuya, my love, An, Ana, the bloody refrain in my body, the song I would not hear, the song I could not forget. Yes, let's go to Anasuya, I thought why not?" (159). So the song of Anasuya goes on in Jagat's mind. It is an immortal touch. The touch of a strange song. *The Song of Anasuya* is full of sexless love and loveless sex. It is a picture of quest on the part of two passionate women and a man. The novel *The Song of Anasuya* has the theme of failure of harmonious love-relationship in the contemporary Indian society.

From the overall study of the novel *The Song of Anasuya*, it becomes clear that Smt. Vasudevan's understanding of Indian woman is not upto the mark. It merely reflects her biased opinion of woman picture based on Western style of luxurious life. She portrays Priti and Anasuya not in their Indian spirit but in a European atmosphere. In fact, the novel does not show a realistic delineation of man and woman in Indian soil.

However, Smt. Uma Vasudevan depicts the mental and moral tumults of woman, she fails to catch the real feminine grace of either Priti or Anasuya. What the novelist attempts is, she brings out the sexual crises between the two time-torn women and a man. The characterization of women protagonists is also imbalanced. Indeed, Vasudevan's women lack one or the other essential feminine features.

From another point of view, Vasudevan delineates modern Indian woman's liberation from the male-dominated society. In fact, Vasudevan sincerely tries to display two emancipated women's carefree life and their misuse of rights. Her depiction of feministic atmosphere is an indication of women's self-uplift for their enlightened growth and progress. Indeed, Uma Vasudevan's *The Song of Anasuya* brings out to the light an aspect of modern feminist movement which is depicted in the works of many Western women novelists.

This novel which is a haunting and bewitching tale of love and lust belongs to a genre all its own, and assures the novelist Smt. Uma Vasudevan, a permanent place among the great writers of Indian English fiction.

10

Yatra—A Journey Unto Self Accomplishment

A.G. KHAN

There are diverse opinions. While the blurb brings to our knowledge its success at the Algiers for begging the International Grand Prix for Literature in 1987 and the warm praise lavished in *London Literary Review* in which Lucy Ingram not only finds an ambitious and complex novel but also an ingenious and square attempt to "confront the issue of India's racially troubled past and present".[1] However, Ira Pande finds it unsuccessful in unfolding "the lotus of the East—making it look like an onion".[2] The Onion metaphor has been used by another reviewer also when she finds it to be "fascinating *pot-pourie*—a multi-layered Onion".[3]

Three women respond differently to a work by a woman writer. This paper is an attempt to examine how far it is an accomplishment by a woman and to what an extent it is Indian.

First, about the resemblances the protagonist bears to writer herself. While Shalini Gupta spots just one similarity, "half-Greek, half-Indian, like Ms. Sibal herself. Yet, there the resemblance ends".[4] This reviewer would like to add two more: both Krishna Chahal as well as Nina Sibal were teachers of English at Delhi and both had foreign visits—Krishna had here England visit while Nina an assignment at the U.N.O.

It is difficult to disagree with Shalini who finds it "complex, many stranded, dense-textured" and multi-layered as onion. Yes, it is an ambitious attempt to undertake portraying, so vast a canvas in one's debut. It is a pot-pouri in the sense that it is a hodge-podge of history, politics, whims, desires, sex, violence, war, partition, environment consciousness and so on. To quote Ira Pande again, "it includes all those masalas—make good Indian curry."[5] The bite was too large to swallow; a chunk she could not manage. Had she tried to curb her enthusiasm to include God's plenty, she could have done justice to her canvas. From the style point of view Shalini's charge is that it is a manque—her Achilles heel. There seems to be no justification for taxing the reader's patience and memory because most of the journeys into past or present contribute nothing to plot or characterisation—it turns out to be much ado about nothing. Her camera pans at Bombay, Greece, Delhi, Punjab, Dagra, Kohat, Hyderabad, Bangladesh "hurtling back and forth in time and space".[6] Probably, the recent wave of Post-Modernism to move ping-pong like in time and place, to undertake distant journeys, to traverse land and sea swept the writer off her feet and she tried to undertake what requires the calibre of a Margaret Atwood or a Robert Kroetsch.

While the protagonist in Atwood's "Surfacing" had just only one generation to explore and, therefore, she could manage; Sibal compounds (confounds) her task by probing several. While the Anna in 'Badlands' had only one desire to demonstrate how idiotic had been her father's quest for eternity; Krishna is all set to prove her father's innocence. In order to do so they had to undertake arduous journeys to distant places. The fathers in "Badlands" as well as in "Yatra" have no tender feelings for their wives—both pine for their husband's love all their lives. Naturally, both rely greatly on their paramours. Both male had their own illicit relations Dave his Anna, Paramjit his Dhiraj Kumari. While Anna's mother in "Badlands" has just one; Sonia in "Yatra" has two—the Greek one and the Indian one. In fact, this fact prompts us to realise that women in *Yatra* have extra-marital relations almost as habit (not an abnormal perversion), a poor reflection on women. Swaranjit Kaur, Prakash, Krishna, Anu's mother have lovers. And by what interpretation of the collective racial unconscious can one explain this unusual resonance in which generation gap simply evaporates: "Krishna went elsewhere into the past, straight into the arms of her aunt Kailash Kaur, everywhere that her green-eyed lover, Prakash had gone. She nosed up under heavy breasts, sprang through the shoots of her pubic hair, blindly felt the tender skin and fair young flesh of the body which lay under Prakash and the final bliss of her wet cunt with a sudden leap and arch of recognition..." (p. 37).

My male "sensitivity" fails to comprehend such a commonwealth of cunts!

Sibal begins with a traveller's guide how to approach India:

"Slowly, by sea, so that you have a sense of land coming to you with its arm held out, reaching for your life" (p. 7) because the landscape in India is horrible to an outsider:

"Sewage, sandalwood, spices, a dead pariah dog, burning gnats—when she had looked from her window she had seen a line of bare female bottoms defecating on the edge of a drain" (p. 9). Oh! what a landscape—welcome India, Salaam Bombay!

As pointed out earlier, the novel is more a work of fancy than of imagination applying Coleridgean distinction between the two; or is more like yoking together of diverse ideas and images through violence in terms of Dr. Johnson's notion of metaphysical poetry. There are excellent narratives, caravan of images, dreams and yet the unnecessary wanderings back to pre-partition period or emergence of Bangladesh are like jute patches in a velvet garment.

Time and again do we come across an experience in which a character identifies herself not only with her parents and grandparents but even with distant relatives as if it was something shared together simultaneously. Yes, the racial consciousness can explain it. But, how can a person foresee through her experience the ecstasy of her descendants in future generations?

"Horses were racing through Kailash Kaur's veins. They carried her outside the walled city, past the lawyer's houses, beyond the law courts—which would have pleased Swaranjit Kaur's heart. The horses were racing across the earth; they sent shudders through the wheat fields, connected Sonia Chahal's back, bedded by Surjit—to Kailash Kaur, drawing Prakash her nephew down upon her showing him how to enter" (p. 52).

Similarly, we find the riddle of Bibi Chinti something unpalatable. How can the same vicious figure haunt people belonging to different generations separated by time and space. Shalini Gupta tries to answer:

> "at Poonam's death, she weeps paradoxically for her dead buffalo,—In the final chapter, she is present when dogs tear apart Chaman Bajaj. She occurs as a false alarm earlier in the novel when Krishna and her lover visit Humayun's Tomb."[8] Should we infer that progenies share not only ambitions and fears but also hallucinations!

Tearing of Chaman Bajaj into pieces by *his* dogs. When they attack him they had been with him for pretty long and naturally should have allegiance to the *new* master, i.e. Bajaj himself. But instead, the dogs forgot their loyalty to the new master and "remembered" their loyalty to the old one.

"Chaman Bajaj kicked out at them viciously in his anger *and they turned upon him* (p. 311 emphasis mine).[9] This puts a serious doubt about the loyalty of dogs. Could a veterinary psychologist explain this "memory" which can dominate behaviour of dogs to such an extent?

Though there are several achetypal images and myths interwoven throughout—the two, Chinti Bibi and Chaman Bajaj are disguised versions of *Pootna* (who had tried to kill the child Krishna by poisoning her breast) and *Kansa*. So is the name Krishna borrowed from the Hindu mythology. The change in colour of her skin from "pretty white" to "blue" (black) in early childhood seems to be a plausible explanation. However, this change was quite perplexing to everyone, even to medical specialists. This assumes a symbolic meaning in terms of India, turning "black" during the partitions—a degeneration that also defies any rational explanation.

II

The discussion so far might provoke that "Yatra" can be dismissed as a novice's inept handling of theme and technique. Far from that—it has its merits too.

Firstly, it shows the rise of modern woman who has calm of mind and also perseverance and thus can meet any challenge and can emerge triumphant out of a crisis. Her crusade against Chaman Bajaj and her valiant bid to rescue her father from disgrace are two instances. In spite of her divorce (which was more because of his parents' wishes than because of personal disliking between the two) she is able to win the support and good will of her (ex) husband. The lover she takes is not merely a sensual or psychological necessity but a mature woman's capacity to take decisions at appropriate moment. It shows the growth of a teacher (whom everybody regarded a non-entity) into a crusader and champion of women rights.

The modern woman could achieve what her predecessors a few generations ago could not. While her mother Sonia belonged neither to Greece nor to India; neither to her Greek lover nor to Indian and all the time hostile to husband. Krishna, a witness to her suffering could tide over her own problems and thus escaped neurosis to which her mother sank in. We find Kailash Kaur and Krishna—two women who could find their salvation whereas Swaranjeet and Dhiren Kumari succumbed to restrictions imposed by society. The modern woman, instead of whining and weeping, can surmount her problems and assert herself. This is a positive aspect of the book.

The novel also presents women in non-traditional roles—Poonam as revolutionary, Shalini as a social worker unafraid of prison and fighting evils with a strong will, another social worker rescuing and helping refugees Pratibha Anand make an impression that women will no longer remain confined to kitchen and shall prove their mettle everywhere they go. The women associated with "Chipko movement"—illiterate yet strong also organise a movement that they are able to ensure final triumph.

It is not an instance of ecofeminism but also a strong verdict against male exploitation. Its non-violent character without the publicity stunt of "women lib" activists demonstrate that—they also serve who stand and wait.

In the list of defeated characters, apart from Sonia when have another tragic figure in Dr. Dhiraj Kumari—a victim of circumstances. Her suicide though unbecoming evokes pity.

There are moments of beauty, narratives of lyrical quality—images and metaphors charged with emotions and feelings. Strewn across the book are passages where probings into psyche of women bring pathos and induce compassion.

The tragedies of Swaranjeet and Poonam and their sordid end evokes sympathy but at the same has cathartic quality.

However, it must be added that the two sub-texts, Satinder and Poonam, similarly of Bangladesh forrays could be removed altogether without much injury to the text. That would have given the novel the much needed "compact" character.

Shalini Gupta notices in the text glimpses of Marquezian quality, Rushdien richness and Nayantara Sahgal's localization.[10] I would resist from so rich a compliment; yet would like to add that the writer has golden days ahead! It cannot be dismissed as "indifferently written."[11]

REFERENCES

1. Nina Sibal, *Yatra* (New Delhi: Roli Books, 1988), Blurb.
2. Ira Pande, "Literature of the baby-log," Seminar, 384 (1991), p. 39.
3. Shalini Gupta, "*Yatra*: Nina Sibal: A Rites of Passage Bildungsroman" In *Recent Commonwealth Literature,* ed. R.K. Dhawan *et al.* (New Delhi: Prestige Books, 1989), p. 124.
4. Shalini Gupta, p. 124.
5. Ira Pande, p. 39.
6. Shalini Gupta, p. 124.
7. Nina Sibai, *Yatra,* p. 37.
8. Nina Sibal, p. 52.
9. Shalini Gupta, *ibid.,* p. 129.
10. Shalini Gupta, p. 124.
11. Cover Story by team, Raj Reversal, in *Sunday* (4-10 Dec. 1988), p. 31.

❑❑❑

11

The God of Small Things—A Feminist Analysis

BIMALJIT SAINI

Arundhati Roy's novel *The God of Small Things*[1] unfurls a plethora of details regarding the changing political scene in Kerala, the problems besetting women in a male-dominated society, caste taboos, the lives of rudderless children of a broken home, and in the main, vivid descriptions of bees and birds, flowers and trees, sky and river, in a language that is immensely captivating. She narrates the pain and misery of a lonesome mother in an indifferent world as perceived through the eyes of her seven-year-old children—a world where the age-old subjugation of women and the indescribable humiliation of the underclass still persist. Despite the various forums focussing on the women's physical, financial and emotional exploitation together with their mental anguish, traces of oppression seem to have stayed. One cannot emphatically say that the women's unequal status in society is a legacy of the past or it is culture specific. But one can point that in Indian society the inequality is legitimized by the caste system which seems operative in the novel in 1969.

Though Roy states that "I don't want brownie points because I'm from India. My book doesn't trade on the currency of cultural specificity, even though the details are right...",[2] yet these details in the form of discrimination against women and the Paravans, a despised lot, seem to overpower and overwhelm the reader. The disparity between man and woman is a result of the complex operation of economic, political, social and other factors. In spite of the significant change in women's position in society in the post-Independence era, she is still not totally emancipated. These contradictions can best be understood by examining the Indian social structure which comprises institutions like caste, joint family and religious values and practices consolidating women's subordinate position. In this respect Maitreyi Mukhopadhyay says:

> It should be emphasized that the poor status of women, their oppression and exploitation, cannot be examined as an isolated problem in Indian society. Although the status of women constitutes a problem in most societies in the rigidly hierarchical and inequitable social structure which exists in India, the relative inferiority and superiority of various roles is much more clearly defined. The inequality and subordination of women is an instrument or function of the social structure.[3]

In *The God of Small Things*, Roy implicitly presses for greater social reform in the rigid positioning of women and the intolerable plight of the deprived class. The world of her novel is caught in a state of flux where the values of the patriarchal society are under attack from a new world in which self-interest and self-aggrandisement and social equality are forcing their way. Seen from a feminist perspective, the novel is about the violence inflicted on women and the paternal tyranny enveloping the unfortunate children. It exposes the double standards of morality in society regarding men and women, the passive, docile role of a wife in a man-woman relationship, and the malicious role of a woman in perpetuating the humiliation of another woman by a male.

Roy, has depicted the routine goings-on in an upper-class Syrian Christian family at Ayemenem, situated in the lush green area of Kerala abounding in natural beauty with the mysterious Meenachal cruising along its periphery. She deftly balances and eases the tensions accumulated from the cruel realities of life by shifting the attention to the dazzling delights of nature in an innocent, musical language structure that pours from the heart and mind of a child. It is through the play with words, coinage of new phrases that the children are able to lighten the dense and dark moments in a way providing some relief and simultaneously evoking pathos. While referring to Ammu's age when she died it is rationalized as: "Not old./Not young./But a viable die-able age" (*TGST*, p. 3). Then later on talking about Sophie Mol's special child-sized coffin, it is admired as: Satin-lined./Brass handle shined" (*TGST*, p. 4).

The two seven-year-old protagonists Estha and Rabel, male and female are dizygotic, two-egg twins. They are thirty-one now, the age their mother Ammu was when she died. Their being by themselves and not having established any permanent link with the outside world bespeaks of the negative impact the traumas of childhood have had on their development. When children, their apprehension "They knew that things could change in a day" (*TGST*, p. 339), rings true with the sudden death of their nine-year-old cousin Sophie Mol, on a Christmas vacation from England. This tragedy emotionally wrecked the entire family and signalled a nightmare for Ammu and her twins. It overturned their lives in a day that is why the urge to "Prepare to prepare to be prepared" (*TGST*, p. 200), had all along been so strong.

It all began with Ammu, accompanying her parents to Ayemenem after her father's retirement. Being denied a college education, marriage for her also became a difficult proposition as dowry could not be afforded. So she had to wait at home and become domesticated. Virginia Woolf sees domestic life as almost exclusively social without any privacy for women. "The son of the house may be granted freedom to develop his mind, he may have a room of his own, but the daughter is expected to be at everyone's back and call.... For domestic life cultivates the irrational side of a woman's nature; it is distinguished by the primacy of feeling as science is distinguished by the primacy of intellect. The domestic arts involve mainly, the fine discrimination of feelings and the ability to bring about adjustments in personal relations."[4]

Before long Ammu began to feel stifled by the restrictive atmosphere of the house. Worst of all were Pappachi's outbursts of physical violence inflicted on Mammachi from time to time. These irrational bouts were most unbecoming of a man who had been an Imperial Entomologist under the British and after Independence, a Joint Director of Entomology. His achievement of having discovered a rare moth with unusually dense dorsal tufts brought only partial fulfilment, as the moth was never named after him. He beat his wife with a brass flower vase every night till Chacko intervened and put a permanent stop. He, then smashed his favourite mahogany rocking chair with a plumber's monkey wrench because of deep-rooted frustrations emanating from an empty retired life, more so, because of Mammachi's success as a violinist and her popularity in the pickle-making business named later by Chacko as 'Paradise Pickles and Preserves'.

The only escape for Ammu, from the oppressive atmosphere was through marriage. While taking a break at an Aunt's place in Calcutta, she chanced upon a sober-looking Hindu Bengali from the tea-estates in Assam, and without looking back stepped into matrimony. Simone de Beauvoir again remarks, "There is a unanimous agreement that getting a husband—or in some cases a 'protector'—is for her (woman) the most important of undertakings.... She will free herself from the parental home, from her mother's hold, she will open up her future not by active conquest but by delivering herself up, passive and docile, into the hands of a new master...."[5] In no time the gloss wore off and she became a victim of her husband's drunken rages. When they began to spill over to the two-year-old twins, Ammu thought it time to pack up and go. Mr. Hollick, the employer had also sounded a warning and later advised him to go away for a while, for treatment perhaps, and send his wife to his premises to be 'looked after'. Finding no viable solution to his drunken stupor, and fearing her own vulnerability, Ammu returned reluctantly, to her parents home. Here, she was more of an intruder and less of a member of the house as she had been married, and according to Baby Kochamma, her Aunt "she had no position at all" (*TGST*, p. 45), as she had been divorced. With such a disqualification she had no choice but to suffer the fate of a wretched, man-less woman.

Baby Kochamma became Ammu's greatest rival as in Ammu she saw a potential threat to the safe niche she had created for herself over the years. Her fear of being dispossessed increased with the swelling up of numbers in the house and she made no bones about her displeasure:

> In the way that the unfortunate sometimes dislike the co-unfortunate, Baby Kochamma disliked the twins, for she considered them doomed, fatherless waifs. Worse still, they were Half-Hindu Hybrids whom no self-respecting Syrian Christian would ever marry. She was keen for them to realize that they (like herself) lived on sufferance in the Ayemenem House, their maternal grandmother's house, where they really had no right to be. (*TGST*, p. 45)

On her part Baby Kochamma, Navomi Ipe, underwent conversion, moved into a convent as a novice, just to win the heart of Father Mulligan an Irish Jesuit. When her hopes were belied, and the ennui of a confined life began to engulf her, she urged her father to retrieve her, even though marriage for her was completely ruled out. Thus, being an unfulfilled woman, she derived sadistic delight from distorting the facts and, with her sly machinations she searched for opportunities to trap Ammu. There is a note of harshness in her imposition of discipline on the poor twins. She made them write, "I will always speak in English" a hundred times and practise pronunciation through singing "Rej-Oice in the Lo-Ord Or-Orlways/And again I say re-jOice" (*TGST*, p. 154).

When seen as a sole survivor at the age of eighty-three at Ayemenem with Kochu Maria as her loyal lieutenant, Baby Kochamma's suppressed urges seem to surface. She adorns herself with Mammachi's jewelry, dresses like a young bride, shifts her interest from the front garden to the soap operas *The Bold and the Beautiful* and *Santa Barbara* and true to Rabel's words lives her life backwards in the bourgeois style.

Both Ammu and Chacko are in a similar position as far as their marital status is concerned. Ammu had been a victim of battering while Chacko had been discarded by his wife for his lethargic, unproductive ways. But in Ayemenem, Chacko holds the reins of control, being a male and Ammu is at his mercy for her and her children's subsistence. She works in the Pickles factory which Chacko claims as "my factory, my pineapples, my pickles" (*TGST*, p. 57). Legally, Ammu has no claim on the property as outdated and outmoded inheritance rights are weighted against her. Even Mammachi though actually blind, turns a blind eye to Ammu's needs and discomforts and her children's development. Instead, she looks up to Chacko, he being the only male support after her husband's death, tolerates his 'libertine relationships' with the women in the factory and in a way frees him of any kind of onus by quietly paying them off. She participates in the grand reception accorded to Margaret Kochamma, his English ex-wife and their daughter Sophie Mol, by playing the violin, but remains unconcerned about Ammu and her twins, being the least bothered about their inclusion or exclusion from the celebrations. Ammu's humiliation is the result of her marriage having gone wrong. Simone de Beauvoir asserts that:

> Marriage is not only an honourable career and one less tiring than many others: it alone permits a woman to keep her social dignity intact and at the same time to find sexual fulfilment as loved one and mother....[6]

Though Ammu quarrels with her fate, yet she does not achieve anything concrete. She has too many fronts to cope with—her personal misery and her children's upbringing. She has to love them double because they don't have a Baba and Chacko fails to meet their expectations even half-way. Sophie Mol, his nine-year-old daughter perceives his indifference to the twins within a few days of her arrival and suggests that he loves them instead. Ammu's fault is that she is too mild and docile to asset herself. Colette Dowling explains:

> It has to do with dependency: the need to lean on someone.... Those needs stay with us into adulthood, clamouring for fulfilment right alongside our need to be self-sufficient.... Any woman who looks within knows that she was never trained to feel comfortable with the idea of taking care of herself, standing up for herself, asserting herself.[7]

Thus, Ammu moves around without being heard. The male tyranny that is unleashed on her takes a cruel form in her parents' home—it is a battering that does not show but corrodes one from within. The arrival of Sophie Mol seems to ignite the so far contained and suppressed conflicts. The preferential treatment shown toward Chacko's widowed ex-wife and their daughter is openly displayed in front of all and sundry, throwing Ammu and her twins into complete isolation. This is too severe a blow for Ammu to bear, so she looks away only to find that Rabel has already escaped to the animated world of Velutha—a world of warmth and sincerity. She, while searching for an anchor catches the intent gaze of Velutha when he is tossing Rabel in the air, and both share a moment of intense desire for each other, the like of which they had never imagined or dreamt of before. Velutha noticed Ammu as a woman and felt that he had something to share with her and that she too had gifts to give him.

Not having any right on anything whatsoever, and constantly being made to feel dejected and low, Ammu is lured by Velutha's meaningful gaze. Unable to hold herself she breaks free of all the constraints and barriers and walks across to the life-infusing company of the despised Paravan. She did not stop to gauge the consequences, for nothing could be worse than what she had already faced. So, throwing all the cares to the wind, she allows herself to be drenched in the love of Velutha every night for two weeks. She ultimately is able to become a part of 'the sub-world' of her twins and Velutha from which she had earlier been excluded, 'a tactile world of smiles and laughter...' (*TGST*, p. 176).

Initially, she found her children's fondness for a man, who was subservient to the household somewhat odd. But he filled their days with a life they craved and hungered for. What their own father or Chacko could not give, Velutha gave in plenty. He played their games, satiated their thirst for stories, and above all gave them true love. Their moving across the river to set up their own independent unit in the History House, is symbolic of their rejection of the hostile, materialistic, shallow world of the well-to-do. Ammu also rejects a life of empty appearances and turns to Velutha for a fillip so desperately needed. Since she had no 'Locusts Stand I' in Ayemenem house and the Paravans had no locus standi in the class-conscious society, they both were thrown on a parallel plane:

> Virginia Woolf too, "frequently compared women to persecuted minorities, she could not, it would seem name any downtrodden group, and underdog without pointing out the parallel with women". She implied that women as a class "are comparable to the humblest domestic servants.... Finally, ironically, Virginia Woolf suggested that women may be likened the lowliest, and most familiar subject race of all."[8]

Though caste was more practised by the Hindus, some of its features had effected other religions too. The members of the Ayemenem house were Syrian Christians yet they followed the caste values of the Hindus, and likewise shirked from the Untouchables. The caste taboos were still prevalent and not a part of India's past history:

> Mammachi told Estha and Rabel that she could remember a time, in her girlhood, when Paravans were expected to crawl backwards with a broom, sweeping away their footprints so that Brahmins or Syrian Christians would not defile themselves by accidentally stepping into a Paravan's footprint. In Mammachi's time, Paravans, like other Untouchables, were not allowed to walk on public roads, not allowed to covet their upper bodies, not allowed to carry umbrellas. They had to put their hands over their mouths when they spoke, to divert their polluted breath away from those whom they addressed. (*TGST*, pp. 73-74)

The caste taboos were so deeply ingrained in the psyche of the people that such an act involving a respectable high-class lady and a Paravan was scandalous enough to take the entire area by storm and rouse widespread condemnation. Mammachi was furious with Vellya Paapen who brought the news. All along she had been kind and charitable toward him and in turn he was obliged to her for all her mercies. But her daughter, by crossing all the limits had now earned her cold contempt:

> She thought of her naked, coupling in the mud with a man who was nothing but a filthy *Coolie*. She imagined

> it in vivid detail: a Paravan's coarse black hand on her daughter's breast. His mouth on hers. His black hips jerking between her parted legs. The sound of their breathing. His particular Paravan smell. *Like Animals,* Mammachi thought and nearly vomited. *Like a dog with a bitch on heat.* (*TGST*, pp. 257-58)

For Mammachi Chacko's irregularities seemed trivial in comparison to Ammu's erotic involvement. She feared social ostracism from the surrounds and a blotch on the family honour. She felt disheartened to think that Ayemenem house would no longer be able to bask in the glory of its ancestral achievements.

Ammu was tricked into confinement, castigated vehemently and finally disowned and disinherited by the family. What she did and where she went was no one's concern. She was discouraged from visiting Rabel who was kept at Ayemenem, lest she have a bad influence on her. In death she was alone in a grimy, dingy room of Bharat Lodge in Allepey. She was denied dignity of a funeral as "The church refused to bury Ammu...". "So, Chacko had her wrapped in a dirty bedsheet and laid out on a stretcher" (*TGST*, p. 162), and cremated in an electric crematorium where beggars, derelicts, and the police custody were taken. And none from the family save Rabel attended.

According to Christianity, Jesus spared no occasion to denounce men for adultery, hypocrisy, pride or any other aberration. Throughout the Gospels he is seen as gentle, forgiving and understanding with women. But Paul more or less undid what Christ had done because long before the first century, belief in the inferiority of women had become embedded in the cultures in Europe, Asia and Africa, where he and the apostles preached the word. In fact, the early church theologians too suffered from the existing bias against women and in forming their thought systems they were influenced by the approach of Aristotle who placed women more or less next to slaves.[9]

Even the church did not spare Ammu on account of her grave sin. On the other side, Velutha was hounded by the police on charges of rape lodged against him by the malicious Baby Kochamma, and beaten black and blue till he bled to death. His one sin seemed to have been darker than Chacko's many sins of the same nature. The actual facts of the scandal were camouflaged and never established even after Ammu's confession to Inspector Thomas Mathew. Rahel was left in the care of Chacko who was disinterested in her affairs from the beginning. Estha, who was sent to his father and step mother was returned to Ayemenem owing to his abnormally quiet ways. He exhibited traits of an introvert, while Rahel was just the opposite—detached and aggressive. It seemed "That the emptiness in one twin was only a version of the quietness in the other. That the two things fitted together. Like stacked spoons. Like familiar lovers bodies" (*TGST*, p. 20).

Updike says that Estha and Rabel's sensibilities were "uncannily conjoined"[10] and that they found it difficult to relate to anything separately. When left to themselves they felt stranded and alone. Rahel had to shift from school to school because of her perverse behaviour. And, later she wound up her marriage in divorce because she was unable to relate completely with her indulgent, American husband. She then worked for several years as "a night clerk, in a bullet-proof cabin at a gas station outside Washington, where drunks occasionally vomited into the money tray, and pimps propositioned her with more lucrative job offers." One of the regular visitors, "a punctual drunk with sober eyes," invariably shouted "Hey, you! Black bitch! Suck my dick!" (*TGST*, p. 20). It was only Rahel who could manage to cope with such a job as no self-respecting, young Indian lady would dare to work in a such a degrading environment. She was shorn off the feminine virtues of sweetness, modesty, subservience and humility that were cultivated by women of cultured societies. To her nothing mattered and she did not bother of what people thought. Never having tasted a warm hearth of a stable home and being deprived of an adequate exposure, both Estha and Rahel were victims of a broken family. And, so they developed peculiar traits that were self-destructive, such as the abnormal withdrawal of Estha and the annihilating wrecklessness of Rahel. They could never make a success of their lives because of their inadequacies and lack of proper guidance.

Arundhati Roy has revealed how perceptive seven-year-old are at that tender age to their immediate surroundings—here to their mother's pain and misery. And, how they make adjustments and compromises in order to alleviate her suffering. Roy has "drawn the bare bones of the characters from the family" as her own mother faced "much trauma"[11] in her parental home for being separated from her husband. Even though her work has won wide appreciation for its "radical difference", for being unlike any other work and particularly for its "verbal exuberance"[12] yet in it are all the ingredients of a patriarchal world, where men remain more equal than women.

REFERENCES

1. Arundhati Roy, *The God of Small Things* (New Delhi: India Ink, 1997).

   Note: Subsequent references to this novel will be indicated by the abbreviation *TGST*.
2. Jason Cowley, "Why We Chose Arundhati". *India Today*, 27 October 1997, p. 28.
3. Neera Desai and Vibhuti Patel, *Indian Women: Change and Challenge in the International Decade 1975-85* (Bombay: Popular Prakashan, 1985), p. 82.
4. Herbert Marder, *Feminism and Art: A Study of Virginia Woolf* (Chicago: The University of Chicago Press, 1968), pp. 34-35.
5. Simone de Beauvoir, *The Second Sex* (London: Four Square Books, 1961), p. 352.
6. *Ibid.*, p. 62.
7. Colette Dowling, *The Cinderella Complex: Women's Hidden Fear of Independence* (U.S.A.: Fontana Paperbacks, 1982), p. 13.
8. Herbert Marder, *Feminism and Art: A Study of Virginia Woolf*, pp. 80-81.
9. T.C. Joseph, "The Church is still very much male dominated". *The Times of India*, 13 September 1988, p. 3.
10. John Updike, "Mother Tongues". *The New Yorker*, June 23-30, 1997, p. 156.
11. Mary Roy, "My Daughter and I". *India Today*, 27 Oct. 1997, p. 26.
12. Jason Cowley, *India Today*, p. 28.

❑❑❑

12

Fictional Treatment of the Neurotic Phenomenon—Indian Women Novelists in English and Psychoanalysis

M. RAJESHWAR

In some of their highly acclaimed works, the second generation Indian English women novelists have favourably responded to the changed psychological realities of Indian life after Independence. In doing so they seem to have been guided by the age-old experience of repression by Indian women. Ruth Prawer Jhabvala, Kamala Markandaya, Nayantara Sahgal, Anita Desai, Bharati Mukherjee, Shashi Deshpande and Nergis Dalal who constitute this group are emotionally and intellectually well equipped to give an authentic treatment of this situation.

The charge of narrowness and lack of vision is often brought against the women novelists as a whole. The second generation Indian women novelists, however, stand as a unique exception to this rather sweeping generalisation. The personal background and intellectual training of these novelists seem to have endowed the speciality which their fictional product bears. Their wide acquaintance with the vagaries and nuances of life, both in the East and the West, and their achievement of often high educational and intellectual standards have given a sharp edge to their observation. Their natural feminine sensibility and introspection have imparted to their observation a humane touch and a psychological depth.

According to an admission Anita Desai's purpose in writing is to discover for herself and then aesthetically convey the truth which for her is synonymous with art. Therefore, her endeavour is to discover the significance of reality by "plunging below the surface and plumbing the depths, then illuminating those depths till they become a more lucid, brilliant and explicable reflection of the visible world."[1] Kamala Markandaya believes that "the process of creative writing reveals depths in the mind which are of universal application."[2] Nergis Dalal incorporates "the essential loneliness of every human being and a sense of compassion"[3] into her writings. She is well-known for profitably employing the revolutionary findings of modern psychology for creative purposes.

Though stated in different words by different authors, an interesting preoccupation of these writers appears to be the delving into the labyrinthine depths of the Indian psyche and showing its relation to society. And nowhere is this concern more obvious than in the novels that figure neurotic characters. The characters are shown as grappling on the one hand with the changed realities of Indian life and the trauma they entail and on the other hand with the psychic conflicts of personal origin. These conflicts and traumas become too pronounced at a particular point of time in their life and their ability to hold their feelings under repression gives way. Anita Desai's *Cry, The Peacock* and *Where Shall We Go This Summer?*, Bharati Mukherjee's *Wife*, Kamala Markandaya's *A Silence of Desire*, Shashi Deshpande's *That Long Silence*, Ruth Prawer Jhabvala's *Get Ready for Battle*, Nayantara Sahgal's *The Day in Shadow* and Nergis Dalal's *The Inner Door* thus portray sensitive individuals in their moments of intense struggle and in their efforts to seek neurotic solutions to their problems. In the course of the ordeal called living the protagonists of these novels find themselves at odds with society and undergo various degrees of psychological transformation. Both as a physical reality outside and a psychic agent within, society which we take to mean the essence of one's relationships with others, plays a crucial role in bringing about this change for the worse forcing these sensitive people to seek neurotic solutions to their problems.

In their endeavour to come to terms with the reality of their situation and depending on the degree of their affectability and the pressure of the external circumstances these characters neurotically react in three different ways. The hyper-sensitive and deeply affectable Maya of *Cry, The Peacock* and Dimple of *Wife* get their psyches corroded by unhealthy introspection. In the process, they move too far away from the ordinary course of life, and at the end, nose-dive into the dark abysmal depths of psychosis. Sarla Devi of *Get Ready for Battle*, Simrit of *The Day in Shadow* and Rahul of *The Inner Door* follow almost an opposite neurotic course. On being compelled to silently suffer the strain of life they do not bite upon their heart but defy the social injunctions but only to become compulsive idealists. Their idealism is not born of their volition or of a genuine change of heart but of an attitude of revenge and necessitated by an inner compulsion to escape. Neurosis, however, has a sobering effect on the other group of characters. Sita of *Where Shall We Go This Summer?*, Sarojini of *A Silence of Desire* and Jaya of *That Long Silence* make important discoveries about themselves during their neurotic suffering and in the last analysis they find a measure of fulfilment in their relation to the world.

The women novelists in English have very ably treated the neurotic phenomenon in the Indian context by creating extremely interesting personages. Through this endeavour they have been able to lay bare the oppressive and anti-human value system of the society. Through the sensitive portrayal of the psychic conflicts and the psychological contours of helpless people the novelists seem to underline the importance of subverting the established values and replacing them with those values which are more amenable to human nature and which promote happiness. For this purpose the steely frame of the social machine, which forges and fosters these values, itself needs an overhaul. The women novelists bring home this point by subtly indicating that the society is often indifferent and vindictive towards sensitive and suffering people while actually it should be rushing to their help.

Our argument here is not to prove that the women novelists' concern has been exclusively with the inner life of their characters. They have dealt with cultural, political and social issues in a good number of their novels, but the focus has always been on the human condition and it has been artistically rendered with a deep sense of compassion for the characters. In the novels mentioned earlier this concern has reached its pinnacle, leading to the creation of the psychologically most interesting personages—neurotic characters. In this endeavour they have superbly succeeded because among other things they are *women.* Indian women, in view of their limited freedom and insular mode of life, have shown for ages a marked tendency towards growing introspective which is a prelude for neurotic reaction. This sort of feminine sensibility has a close relation to neurosis at least in the Indian context. Neurosis almost always results from a compulsion to repress one's feelings and desires because they are not in consonance with the accepted norms of society. Women are mercilessly denied opportunities for open expression of their true feelings in the tradition-bound Indian society. In this respect and in many other respects they are at great disadvantage when compared to men.

In spite of their privileged position the women novelists have gone through conflicts which are not at great variance with those of other Indian women. Conflicts of a qualitatively different nature have always characterized the life of every freedom-conscious woman in India, including the novelists. These novelists have therefore naturally created characters who are capable of close and sensitive experience of life as they themselves are.

The characters of the novels mentioned above, face problems of predominantly personal nature and they seek to resolve them at the personal level. The solution of Sarojini, Sarla Devi and Rahul is in keeping with the religious practices of India which, to certain extent, obscures their neurotic personalities. This religious element has been placed in proper perspective by the women novelists who are helped by an admirable understanding of the vagaries and travails of the human psyche.

Psychoanalytic thinkers from Freud onwards have not only viewed religion cynically but dubbed it as an instrument of oppression. Freud thinks religion to be "patently infantile, so foreign to reality."[4] As one with a friendly attitude to humanity he finds it painful that the great majority of people will continue to believe the falsehoods propagated in the name of religion. He therefore interprets it as a collective childhood neurosis of mankind. Erich Fromm puts it the other way round: "We can interpret *neurosis as a private form of religion*, more specifically, as a regression to primitive forms of religion conflicting with officially recognized patterns of religious thought"[5] (original emphasis). The women novelists have shown an almost uncanny awareness of the untenable claims of religion and exposed them by creating neurotic characters who seek religious solution. In the process neurosis and religion become indistinguishable, thus proving the contention of psychoanalysis without ever intending to do so.

Further the novelists' higher education has given them a deep insight into the human psyche and a clear critical perspective to re-examine tradition. They shed their inhibitions in a marvellous fashion and showed surprising frankness, boldness and honesty in the fictional treatment of the workings of the human psyche. Even the men novelists have not been so frank. They have instinctively shied away from such matters as sex, while the women have elaborately but artistically treated them.

Contrary to what one would expect in view of the oppressive, male-dominated social codes operative in India, feminist considerations do not appear prominently in the novels of these writers. While their foreign counterparts like Margaret Atwood and Lucette Finas have lent invaluable support to the feminist movement by their fictional endeavour, these writers seem to be content to render in fictional terms the human condition, barely discriminating between the sexes. Their characters are aware of themselves first as human beings and only then as women or men. One feels that more of great value emerges from such fictional endeavour than from the textbook demonstration of the degradation of women at the hands of men and the battle-cries against male domination which are so characteristic of the feminist writers of the West. In certain of Nayantara Sahgal's and Shashi Deshpande's novels feminist concerns do emerge but only incidentally. Their protagonists are acutely aware of themselves as women, so to say. Ironically, however, the elusive feminist concerns have been a point of much critical discussion. Although the apologists to feminism believe that "reading, as well as writing, is a gendered activity; and that the positioning of the reader, male or female, as a woman, is one of the most significant revisions in the gender-genre-modernism line,"[6] unbiased observers hold a different view. One of them, K.K. Ruthven,[7] is genuinely amused at such "gendering" of critical discourse which is supposed to be a purely intellectual activity. The feminist angle which most of these critics sought to give to the Indian women novelists appears to be forced and contrived. Their neurotic characters too have been often explained away in terms of feminism,[8] while the truth is that they suffer from enexplicable and deeply felt psychic conflicts. The application of feminist theories to the study of the neurotic characters in fact proves to be counter-productive. It helps neither in studying the characters at a deeper level nor in examining the real issues. Sahgal's Simrit has been often singled out to prove that feminism does form a significant strand in the fictional tapestry of the women novelists.[9] It can however be seen that Simrit is neurotically reacting to a particularly painful situation rather than consciously exercising her will to be independent and assertive. Significantly enough, it can be observed in the other characters that society is not blamed for their problems as it usually happens with those exhibiting a pronounced leaning towards feminism. However, society's rules, ideals and expectations are so firmly entrenched in their psyche and operate so subtly at that level that we can easily perceive how their actions are oriented towards obtaining only vicarious satisfaction out of their utter hopelessness. Our sympathy for them is fully activated only when we understand all these aspects of their enigmatic personalities for which psychoanalysis readily lends itself.

Although the women characters' urge for self-assertion is made to be felt, it is never properly articulated in these novels. It is expressed only symbolically through neurosis. The novelists themselves do not seem to be making an enthusiastic effort to espouse the cause of the women. They stop at the point of authenticating the human predicament. Feminism usually takes off from there. Bringing a feminist perspective to these writers is therefore very likely to lead one into a blind alley. On the contrary, these novelists have created very convincing male personages who are caught in the same kind of problems as, and sometimes because of, their women. Kamala Markandaya's Valmiki (*Possession*) fights a psychological battle to extricate himself from the soul-killing bondage to Lady Caroline. Her Ravi (*A Handful of Rice*) puts up a lifelong fight with his wily mother-in-law. Ruth Prawer Jhabvala's Esmond (*Esmond in India*) and Prem (*The Householder*) find themselves in an unenviable situation mainly as a result of the stupidity of their wives. Yet they do not invoke their traditional male authority. They suffer everything silently.

Feminist approach thus proves to be of little value to the study of these novelists, especially for the study of the neurotic characters. Another important theme that has been frequently harped upon is the cultural conflicts resulting from a character's exposure to a different culture. Again, the extent of cultural shock depends on the individual's susceptibility and the psychic conflicts he carries in his unconscious. Bharati Mukherjee's *Wife* is often chosen to demonstrate what devastation a hostile culture can cause in a sensitive individual (parenthetically it may be observed that neurosis is known to occur more frequently among immigrant population). A study of *Wife* shows Dimple in an entirely new light. The already existing neurotic picture in her is precipitated and aggravated by her American life. Her husband does not suffer from any of those conflicts because his psyche is structured entirely differently. What then ultimately interests us is not so much the cultural conflicts *per se* but the psychological suffering of the individual to which the cultural conflicts often contribute.

When these novels are studied in the light of the cultural or feminist themes the critical focus generally happens to be at the macro level. Such critical pursuit runs the risk of becoming a study of characters as cultural stereo-types or as abstractions of ideals or ideas. It further tends to blur the finer contours of the individual characters and thus overlooks the real achievement of the novelists because the novelists have here depicted generalities in terms of specifics. It is the particular individual who is the object of attention in every one of these novels. Cultural and feminist studies proceed from an idea and go on to hunt for evidence in the individual's reaction to prove a contention and tend to be reductionist in the process. The psychoanalytic approach is a centrifugal approach in the sense that it reverses the order by taking the individual character for closer examination at the micro level and then arrives at general themes concerning society, culture, politics, etc.

A comprehensive psychoanalytic approach to these novelists has been thus long overdue. The few studies that have already incorporated the formulations of depth psychology have concerned themselves only with the overtly neurotic characters such as Maya and Sita. The other important neurotic characters havė gone totally unnoticed or have been studied from totally irrelevant angles. One reason for this situation appears to be that the neurotic reaction of some of these characters coincides with the prevailing cultural practices of India. The neurotic picture behind the baffling actions of Sarojini, Sarla Devi and Rahul comes to light only when it is studied in the light of the depth psychology.

Psychoanalytic approach thus helps us with a better appreciation of the human situation of the characters of the women novelists and sharpens our understanding of and enhances our sympathy for them. At a time when the opinion that one has reached the limits of critical possibility in the field of Indian Writing in English is gradually settling, the endeavour to study the neurotic characters using psychoanalytic insights promises the reveal the new depths in the fiction of Indian English women writers. These depths need to be further fathomed and critically accounted for.

REFERENCES

1. Anita Desai, "Replies to the Questionnaire", *Kakatiya Journal of English Studies,* 3.1 (1978): 2.
2. Kamala Markandaya, "Replies to the Questionnaire," *Kakatiya Journal of English Studies*, 3.1 (1978): 83.

3. Atma Ram, "Interview with Nergis Dalal," *Interviews with Indian-English Writers* (Calcutta: Writers Workshop, 1983): 38.
4. Sigmund Freud, *Civilization and its Discontents* (Harmondsworth; Penguin, 1964): 261.
5. Erich Fromm, *Psychoanalysis and Religion* (New Haven: Yale University Press, 1950): 27.
6. Sandra Kemp, "But how describe a world seen without a Self? Feminism, fiction and modernism," *Critical Quarterly*, 32.1 (Spring 1990): 101.
7. K.K. Ruthven, "The gendering of critical discourse," *Feminist Literary Studies: An Introduction* (Cambridge: Cambridge University Press, 1988): 1-4.
8. J.G. Masilamani, "Feminism in Anita Desai," *Kakatiya Journal of English Studies*, 3.1 (1978): 25-33.

   Vimala Rao, "Anita Desai's *Where Shall We Go this Summer?*: An Analysis," *Commonwealth Quarterly*, 3.9 (1978): 44-50.
9. Jasbir Jain, "The Aesthetics of Morality: Sexual Relations in the Novels of Nayantara Sahgal," *The Journal a/Indian Writing in English*, 6.1 (January 1978): 41-48.

13

For a Story of My Own— The Female Quest for Identity: A Global Perspective

RAMA KUNDU

1

This paper proposes to examine the issue of the woman's quest for identity with reference to three different contexts: the creole woman's identity-crisis in the colonial context, the emerging woman's search for self-hood in the post-colonial third world, and the anguished quest of the 'free' woman of the first world for a meaningful life of her own. It is from this perspective that the paper will glance through the experiences of a creole woman of Jamaica, of two Indian women of two generations, and of one modern Canadian girl; these women—as depicted respectively by Jean Rhys, Anita Desai, Githa Hariharan, and Margaret Atwood—are apparently worlds apart from each other due to the situational-cultural-psychic disparities of their respective space-time continuum, and yet show a strange kinship.

2

Among the three cases mentioned above, perhaps the most intricate and complex case is that of the creole woman who seems to belong neither here nor there. As Christophine, the black woman in Rhys's *Wide Sargasso Sea*, fails to define Antoinette's socio-cultural identity: "She is not 'beke' like you (her British husband), but she is 'beke', and not like us either" (128). Being a white settler's daughter, she is held in suspicion by the colonized, to whom she is a 'white nigger', a 'white cockroach'; and to the white metropolitan British she is alien, strange, 'not one of us',—therefore, easy to suspect and unacceptable in the long run. Thrown into this situation, the woman is rendered particularly vulnerable, alienated as she is from any collective identity. Her attempt to relate herself to the metropolitan white ends up in a dislocating experience that frustrates and shatters her. As Antoinette, Rhys's heroine, sums up her position: "A white cockroach.... That's what they call all of us who were here before their own people in Africa sold them to the slave traders. And I have heard English women call us white niggers. So between you I often wonder who I am and where is my country and where do I belong and why was I ever born at all" (85). Ultimately, however, she finds it possible to identify with the colonized victims, the Christophines, rather than the victimizer; because she herself is also a victim of the imperialistic-androcentric power and ethos which had so ruthlessly exploited and victimized slave girls in the colonies. That situationally she is no better than those slave girls becomes apparent to her through suffering.

In *Wide Sargasso Sea*, the woman, whatever her origin or colour may be, is shown as the potential victim of all brands of male. Antoinette's mother Annette is a case in point. She had been the second wife of a planter who had, besides his two wives, "all those women". Annette bore no grudge either to the children of these exploits or their mothers. In a way, she provided for them and even arranged for Christmas gifts. She knew of their helplessness. Yet she is denigrated by people around for this very broadness on her part. They take this as evidence that she not only failed to keep her husband on the virtuous track, but even indulged his vice by her kindness to his women and their children. The onus for her husband's promiscuity falls on her. When the husband dies and a period of helpless poverty follows, she is supported only by a woman, her former slave girl Christophine. After some time Mason, a stranger from outside, comes to marry her and settle down in the island. But when she is broken by the shock of her son's death in the Coulibri fire and turns mad in consequence, Mason just leaves her in the hands of paid people. Being sure of Mason's indifference these people—of all colours—sexually exploit the helpless woman. The shadowy knowledge of this terrible ordeal was enough to undermine the child Antoinette psychically. The terrified child grows up a sad girl; and her husband, who marries her with a design, finds it easy to "break her up". She becomes the target of imperialist-patriarchal-racist assault, and the combine, as represented by her anonymous husband, shatters her completely; she ends up as "the madwoman in the attic". The anonymity of Antoinette's British husband helps him to emerge as an epitome, a paradigm of the ruling power's exploitative designs on the colony/on her daughter. Through her depiction of Antoinette Rhys gives a human face to the common legend about mad creole heiresses in the Caribs. She is deprived of her money, means, freedom and is forced to become dependent on an unloving stranger. As he confesses: "I did not love her...she was a stranger to me... who did not think or feel as I did" (78). The assumption stems from his fear/hatred of the 'other'. He admits later he hated the place, hated everything about it and "above all I hated her". He just makes a cynically calculated marriage through negotiations with a male relative, in which neither the girl nor her woman relative has any say. In spite of her aunt's protests the brother and the would-be husband secretly decide between themselves for the girl's deception, deprivation and subsequent shattering: "The thirty thousand pounds have been paid to me without question or condition. No provision made for her" (59). After having her completely within his power he systematically breaks her up when there is no one to defend except Christophine, her 'da' (nurse), the blackest woman. Once Christophine is scared away by the imperial police and their laws, Antoinette is left defenceless. Her husband follows the same path as treaded earlier by her father and so many male white settlers in the colony. Incidentally, the madness of the creole woman, a common syndrome of the region, may not have been unconnected with the veneral diseases that attended the male settler's sexual promiscuity. Antoinette's husband, after blaming her father for having "all those women", and her mother for failing to carry out the ridiculous responsibility of keeping the husband on the virtuous track, plays the same game; he has casual sex with a slave girl; he humiliates the wife in presence of servants: "What right have you to make promises in my name." As result she loses her mental balance, breaks down, and is smoothly carried over across the 'wide Sargasso Sea' to the cold prison of the English country mansion. So far it is the story of the steady dislocation of a woman's identity through systematic assault by insensitive, scheming male relatives, and finally through transplantation from her native place to an alien land. She loses her place, her name, her loved friends and people, her freedom, even her sense of time and comprehension of reality.

The story, however, does not end here. After years in her cold prison without mirror or calendar, one evening she suddenly recollects in a moment of epiphanic flash her entire life. Then she knows what she must do; she must get deprogrammed of all colonial and androcentric feedback forced down her throat. In the light of her fire she finds the darkened passage of her life illuminated, and in this light she rediscovers a mirror. Looking-glasses had been taken away from her attic prison. So she had forgotten what she looked like. Now in her last dream she recognises her childhood friend Tia in her dream-world looking-glass as she had done years ago during the Coulbri fire. From this mirror Tia, the black servant girl of the island looks back. Now the transplanted woman knows her identity; that she is not 'Bertha Mason' but Antoinette, and her self-hood is to be discovered by throwing her lot with the Tias of the island, the one-time colonial victims who had now risen to assertion. Slavery, for the woman means indignity-harassment multiplied through sexual exploitation. Rhys, however, suggests that it is from among them that the new woman may emerge. Christophine represents this collective entity,—self-assured, assuring, positive—who can hold her own unlike her one-time creole mistress and her daughter. Even before her complete breakdown Antoinette knew—actually she knew it since her childhood—that Christophine was her "only friend" (94). And in her last desperation she cries out only to Christophine for help. By then Christophine, if at all alive, is still thousands of miles away. But that does; not matter. Christophine, who had three children by three different fathers and no husband, who smelt of all the black women of Antoinette's childhood, emerges at this point as the epitome of the New Woman, who will surface through the ordeals of generations of the oppressed in the ex-colonies. Christophine in her embracing affection that can include a creole girl as her own '*doudou*', as also in her proud defiance that can dare the wrath of a masochist colonizer, represents this possibility of the dignified assertion of the underdog. Jean Rhys finds the creole woman an outsider among the metropolitan whites who can have her redemption only through an alliance and a recognition of identity with the coloured women, the worst sufferers among the underdogs in a remote colony. Antoinette's identity-crisis thus ultimately finds a solution, though through the immense sufferings of a shattered life.

The dirge-like tone governing the narration of the baffled, harassed woman desperately trying to reconstruct her past casts an overwhelming sadness over the brief novel. It is in tune with the lonely meaning of the Carribbean Sea lapping the desolate islands; and also in tune with an exhausted woman's last-ditch effort to attain to an identity by means of groping through the darkening passages of extremely painful and fragmented memories of a semi-forgotten past.

3

Post-colonialism is, in a way, an assertion of cultural nationalism, or the voice unheard so long, the voice of people who were formerly underdogs. Thus, it is a literature of the woman, of the black, and other formerly colonized ethnic segments. One of the paradoxical phenomena of this rise of cultural nationalism in the ex-colonies, however, is that the woman writers' attempt thereto give articulation to the woman's own unique agonies and quests also often involves challenging some basic tenets of their respective cultures.

Anita Desai, in *Fire on the Mountain* draws an extraordinary portrait of an Indian woman at the turn of the mid-twentieth century. Nanda Kaul is by no means the type, common, run-of the mill Indian woman. She is unique in her elegant isolation,—

thin and straight like the pines of Kasauli, high and empty like Carignano where she has retired alone after a long and busy life as wife and mother. Behind her facade of proud indifference, however, she hides a deep sense of futility, frustration and overpowering desolation in this last twilight of her life.

Nanda Kaul, the extremely beautiful dignified wife of the vice-chancellor, the perfect home-maker and admired hostess, had but led an empty life, devoid of any meaningful personal relationship, hardened by betrayal, withered under the demeaning indignity of having to carry on with a faithless husband. Her husband only gave her that much to keep her quiet, but had his real lifelong affair with another. Nanda's own children, demanding and bothersome, were alien to her. The too many guests and visitors in the house but annoyed her. The ironical smile with which she used to carry on the tiresome burden of these unending duties day in and day out indicated that her emotional withering had set in years before she had finally retired to Carignano. She used to preside over the frequent dinners at her husband's house, always the model of the perfect, glamorous hostess in silk sari; but mentally she remained distant, aloof. Nothing seemed to touch or stir within. In order to absorb the hurt, the indignity of being just a role, she needed to toughen herself, to get insensitized. This was part of her resilience, the lonely clenched fight she had to put up against the assaults of life. Coming to live at Carignano was but the logical culmination of her steeled withdrawal which had started long ago. The Carignano house and the surrounding Kasauli hill-scape are, as it were, extension of her drained inner self. The dignified old lady who proudly holds aloof from relatives, friends and society in general, has for her compeer only the fire-scorched nature scape around, and the weather-beaten house at the top of the steep incline, open to the bracings of rain, storm and cold. The persistent dirge-like sound of the pine and cicada, their "noise of silence" is appropriately in tune with the interior monologue of Nanda, carried on in a note of bitter, fragmented recapitulations of the past.

She is forced to turn to the present when Raka, her great-granddaughter, the child of a broken home (unlike Nanda, her granddaughter Tara had broken under marital pressure) is thrust upon her. She is annoyed at first as she had had enough of duties and responsibilities, and now wants only to be left in peace. But soon her resistance wall begins to show cracks. Once again, after years, she feels interest in a living thing; and this coincides with the sudden strong shower on the hills after a long draught and the burst of azure flowers next morning. Nanda tries to reach out to the strange child, to win her interest by fabricating stories about the houses of her father and husband (not hers), though her fragile myths do not carry with Raka who has already known the harsh reality that homes may not be that idyllic after all, and consequently finds her granny's tales too good to be real. Does Raka suggest the possibility of a future generation of girls who would evade the lure of false myths and would rather set the trappings of the old dreams—dreams of happy homes, perfect marriages, model parents and children-on fire.

With the brutal death of Ila Bose, Nanda's childhood friend, the violent world outside,—the obscene violence perpetrated by the male on the female in its crudest form—breaks into her carefully built-up shell. It is, as it were, behind her tall elegant stature there crouched one as humiliated, helpless, insignificant, vulnerable, small, pitiable as Ila. The rude shock of Ila's death forces her to review her own life and recognize in Ila's fate her own violation magnified, shorn of all the glittering travesties of status and property. The recognition kills her.

Ila's death, again, underscores the mean violence of vengeful male chauvinism when it feels threatened, even if by an innocent frail simple woman. As Ila tried to stop the marriage of a seven years' girl with an old man for a piece of land, the girl's father rapes and murders the tired old woman on her lonely way back home at the day's end. An extreme instance of the obscene violence of male assertion, perhaps not uncommon anywhere in the world.

Many a wife and mother of Nanda's generation in India may identify themselves with her; the sad emptiness of a so-called successful wife-mother-homemaker is but paradigmatic of the contemporary social situation, where even an extraordinary woman, once married, had to fit into certain roles and remain shackled therein; married life for a sensitive woman could be thus overwhelmingly demanding and also completely frustrating and withering in the long run. After playing her assigned roles, and fulfilling the exacting duties imposed by these roles, after being used up by the family and then thrown away,—Nanda refused to be pitied; so she assumed she chose this life. Like the scorched pines of the bare Carignano she continued to stand upright, proud-dignified-aloof, until the thunder struck in the form of Ila's murder.

Incidentally, Nanda's taking possession of Carignano and thus starting her new independent life is made to synchronize with India's independence, wrenched after a long trauma of exploitation and betrayal.

In a remarkably terse and evocative language Anita Desai tells the story of a pronouncedly individual woman who yet emerges a representative figure with her brave, though sad attempt to find an identity of her own. The narration, remarkable for its swift space as well as care for small details, acquires its special mood by means of the never-ceasing dirge of pines and cicadas that presides over the story.

4

Githa Hariharan in *The Thousand Faces of Night* relates a similar alienation of a modern Indian girl of today to her mythical heritage. Githa explores the continuing impact of age-old myths and lores about the women's roles and models which may still remain entrenched in the Indian woman's psyche, and thus make her vulnerable. Finally, however, the woman in her novel is shown to overthrow the heavy rock of heritage with its 'thousand faces of night'.

Devi, her mother, grandmother, mother-in-law and maid-servant, all are in a line, each epitomising the woman who is asked to play a role. Devi's grandmother, in her widowed old age, had at last asserted her feminine individuality through sheltering women who had been broken by marriage, or rendered homeless/helpless due to the norms of a chauvinist patriarchal society. Devi's mother-in-law Parvati had struck her own revolt by running away from the family to her god. Devi makes the same gesture with a minor variation. She elopes with a man. It is less for love than to show her rage of rejection of a demeaning marriage that had crushed dignity, individual aspiration and mocked her emotional-imaginative refinement. Devi's mother Sita also had to give up her individual pursuit after marriage and adapt to pre-fixed roles instead. Years afterwards, when she learns of Devi's escape that Sita stops to probe herself for the first time, and realizes how wrong she had been to give up the Veena for the society-approved self-effacing unfulfilling role of a model housewife.

Thus, Githa Hariharan sends different signal for the new woman of modern India,—that she must shake off the shackles of imposed notions which still haunt her life with their thousand faces of darkness. At the end Devi overcomes her 'night' to emerge in the light of the sun-bathed morning beach, and she is given a most appropriate home-coming by the caressing tune of the Veena. The freed daughter returns to the freed mother; both have now emerged as freed individuals,—daring, defiant—with enough self-assurance to seek their own fulfilment by themselves.

However, before this final release Devi had to go through her ordeals like just another woman in a traditional society. The relevance of her granny's tales and of Mayamma's recollections lies in suggesting the pervasive continuity of sexist values here across time and social layers. Devi had once asked her husband's housekeeper, old Mayamma, why had she put up with her miserable life; at this Mayamma laughed till tears rolled down her wrinkled cheeks. Then she told her about the only time she had screamed "Why?". It was when she had lost her first baby, conceived after ten years of longing and fear. The quack doctor's reflects the callous insensitivity still prevalent in large parts of rural India: "A woman must learn to bear some pain.... What can I do about the sins of your previous birth?" The mother-in-law's response is also characteristic. She beat the bleeding girl and shouted: "Do you need any more proof that this is not a woman? The barren witch has killed my grandson...." No. It is not melodrama or overstatement. Mayamma epitomises many a poor wives of Asia and Africa—used as producing machine, betrayed and exploited by husband, children, in-laws, used up, drained dry, robbed cheated by everybody around, and then thrown away to rot by herself. Even her responses are shrewdly controlled by an orthodox society through its imposed age-old superstitions and sexist values. The onus for all calamities falls on her. She is the target.

In spite of her American degree Devi agrees to negotiated marriage like a 'good' Indian girl; soon she realizes the emptiness of this life—two/three brief encounters a month when bodies stutter together in lazy lust, and two weeks a month when the shadowy stranger demands a smiling handmaiden. Mahesh's brazen self-assurance and total contempt for Devi's individuality shows the continuation (a common phenomenon) of the orthodox approach of the patriarchal *Manu-Shastra* that commands the woman only to serve her husband. The stuffed bird in Tara's room seems to be a grotesque reflection of Devi's marred life—its frustration, emptiness, death—the cruel draining of all life and hope,—"a hideous mockery of the winged creature that had soared high above the clouds in its untamed youth" (7).

In between his month-long tours Mahesh starts his "purposeful love-making" because, as he says, "I want to have my baby" (74). When she fails to get pregnant she has to undergo the torture of humiliating ordeal (though under the garb of clinical treatment); Mayamma's physical and mental torture at the hands of husband and in-laws for failing to get pregnant offers a parallel. Devi's mother too coaxes her to have a baby. The memory of her grandmother's tales about motherhood as also her of father-in-law's stories contributes its bit. Devi almost comes to believe that she needs baby. Then suddenly the realisation comes. This shows how the woman's response to issues may get programmed by the society,—the immediate human environment and age-old orthodox notions regarding her role. However, being a woman of the new generation she can have her realisation before it is too late. Through her "yawning emptiness" (68) Devi emerges with her bitter disillusionment about men; she decides to "learn to be a woman at last ... (to) walk on, seeking a goddess who is not yet made" (95). So she leaves her cage. After her initial experiment with love she leaves Gopal too, and goes ahead alone in her search for her identity.

All her life she has groped for an unknown goal, and now at last she feels: "I have stumbled on-stage alone (refusing to be a puppet any more), greedy for a story of my own". So she comes back to Sita with the conviction and confidence "To stay and fight, to make sense of it all" (139).

5

Atwood's heroine (*Surfacing*) apparently belongs to a different world. Here the woman is supposed to be free from the various social-cultural constraints inhibiting an Indian girl, even if with American degrees. However, the female subjugation through enticement or force and the subsequent panic and emptiness are still there. *Surfacing* depicts a lone woman's desperate struggle to attain the strength that would enable her "to refuse to be a victim". The novel evolves around a backward journey performed simultaneously at two levels: from city to forest and from present to past. The heroine undertakes the journey to trace her lost father. Soon it becomes apparent that the journey also involves for her a search for her own identity. In order to attain this, she feels, she must turn away from the society-dictated norms. The heroine's act of turning the mirror face downwards signifies her complete rejection of the ways of her society which traps a woman by means of its silent dictates. Her friend Anna, with her 'gold compact' has been trapped by this mirror. The heroine rejects this society and goes back to the ancient forest, takes her plunge in the glacial lake in order to resurface; surface with a new strength and self-knowledge that enables her "to refuse to be a victim".

As she journeys back to the island of her childhood, the heroine recognizes the wayside store that used to be run by a one-armed woman called 'Madam'. "None of the women had names then" (27). The heroine herself also, significantly, remains anonymous, thus becoming one in a crowd of anonymous women who carry on their fight in spite of the amputations and mutilations brought about on them.

The anonymity may also be seen as sign of the woman's powerlessness. Even the child she had conceived and nursed within her womb is not her own. As she remembers bitterly: "I never identified it as mine.... It was my husband's, he imposed it on me, all the time it was growing in me I felt like an incubator... he wanted a replica of himself; after it was born I was no more of use" (34). Doesn't this read like another version of Devi's tale or even Mayamma's? Mayamma's value, for her husband and in-laws, lies in her supposed potentiality as a producer of sons. When she fails she ceases to be of any worth to them, no matter how hard she works for them or how total her sacrifice is. And this may also recall to the reader's mind Mahesh's blunt demand: "I want to have *my* baby".

Atwood's heroine had divorced. Nevertheless, she feels, "a divorce is like an amputation, you survive but ther's less of you" (42). Even without being legally divorced Antoinette, Nanda Kaul, Mayamma, Sita, Devi, Parvati had all undergone this mental amputation, and had been rendered lonelier, more vulnerable, mauled by marriage.

After the separation she starts living with Joe. But it is a casual half-hearted relationship like Devi's affair with Gopal. Joe means very little to her; having him is little more than buying a gold-fish or a potted cactus plant (42) that might take one's fancy. She feels unhappy at the emotional inadequacy of this relationship. But who is there in this crude 'Americanized' world to understand her subtle emotional-imaginative yearnings?

She fails to understand what keeps a marriage ticking. Anna and David are supposed to be a happy couple; yet Anna cannot do without her make-up; even after long years of marriage she is afraid to show David her un-made-up face. So "she blends and mutes herself" to please David (47). This revolts the narrator; she refuses to blend and mute herself, to get disintegrated for another. This is what makes her so lonely. In the loneliness of her bitter disillusionment she knows even so-called 'love' could be used as an enticement to catch the inexperienced girl unaware. "He said he loved me" (7). So the magic word has lost all its meanings; she would never again trust that word. Thus, marriage had withered her emotionally. And even before the marriage had failed she had her apprehensions. All the time she was married she had a feeling of precariousness "like jumping off a cliff...in the air, going down, waiting for the smash at the bottom" (47-48). The smash came before long and she was left an emptied drained woman. Her child was taken away from her and with it a slice of her life. "A section of my own life, sliced off from me...I have to forget" (48).

The woman was made to feel that she was "a chemical slot machine" (80). It is too different from Mayamma's or Devi's position,—their humiliation under the male's purposeful love-making?

The girl feels that the male must score a victory over the female—marriage or no marriage, and she refuses to be an accomplice. So when David publicly humiliates and strips Anna, assuming the rights of a husband (135) she throws the film recording Anna's humiliation into the lake. This is her protest. Even in this so-called 'free' world there is humiliation and victimization of women. If Anna has sex with Joe, David must have Joe's girl as retaliation, whether she wants it or not. She is not an individual in his eye, but just a body with genital: "he needed me for an abstract principle" (152). Neither David nor the others can understand her; they can only reduce her to a formula: "She hates men or she wants to be one" (154). She sees in these males and their female counterparts 'the Americans',—a term used by Atwood to denote the imperialist lust for power; one of the various forms in which this lust gets manifest is the male's attempt to subjugate the woman to a mechanical role, to get his satisfaction out of her, nothing more.

At the end she looks for the last time "at the distorted glass face.... Not to see myself but to see. I reverse the mirror...it no longer traps me. Anna's soul closed in the gold compact, that and not the camera is what I should have broken" (175). She alone resumes her journey into nature and past; she seeks the power from her father and mother (one dead another lost) to relate herself meaningfully to life. This finally brings her through extreme hardship to the symbolic plunge and resurface, this time with the defiance never to be a victim any more.

6

The women in the four novels discussed above—from different places of the globe—represent the same constant, long struggle against the dictum of the society that the woman be perceived as object and not as subject. Here the epilogue to Ellison's *The Invisible Man* seems particularly relevant. In the epilogue the invisible man informs Mr. Norton: "If you don't know *where* you are, you probably don't know *who* you are". The authors of the above-mentioned novels precisely attempt this task; they shew the woman in relation to her place in order to enable her and the reader to realise *who* she is. Thus Rhys places her woman protagonist in *her* place—the Caribe islands, in order to project the "alienation within alienation" (Ramchand 231), to use Kenneth Ramchand's phrase for the incheate pain of the women writers from the English-speaking Caribbean. However, as Laura N. Abruna maintains, the strength of the Caribbean women writers is their concern with relational interaction; and in fiction, the women save themselves because of their strong connection with other women in their culture. Rhys is one of the most powerful of these writers, and "Rhys tells the story of the creolized West Indian women—a group whose confusion in identity is rarely explored.... Many of Rhys's characters identify with other oppressed groups such as the former slaves and the Caribbean Indians" (Abruna). Abruna also acknowledges in the context how "she (Antoinette) demonstrates that bonding is possible for white creole women and African-Caribbean women if the women can bracket the sexism, racism and imperialism that are thrust on them".

Anita Desai and Githa Hariharan place their women in the Indian scene. The position of women is necessarily an element in a total culture; and one cannot ignore the problem that altering an element may affect the traditional whole. Yet there is also the awareness, as Charles Ponnuthurai Sarvan says in the African context, that "change is not only inevitable but welcome, that societies and cultures should not be static but dynamic".

Atwood's heroine feels estranged from her own society and escapes into the ancient forests of Canada, looking for 'ghosts of the past', thus getting more profoundly restored to the place of her birth and childhood which she had abandoned during her seduction by the city, the technology, the male. Coral Ann Howells in her study of Canadian women novelists sensitively analyzes the similarities between the politics of imperialism and of gender. Howells even goes as far as to claim that "women's stories could provide models for the story of Canada's national identity".

Finally, it appears from the above discussion that what the earlier generations of creole and Indian women had achieved only partially and through much pain has been attained at last by modern women. Both the first world woman protagonist of Atwood and the modern woman of Hariharan have their ordeals of excruciating pain; but through this both emerge at the end, though mauled amputated, yet strong self-assured—one with the determination "not to see myself but to see" (rejecting the society/male-attributed image of herself); and the other to "walk on, seeking a goddess who is not yet made" (95), "to stay and fight, to make sense of it all, even if it means to start from the very beginning" (139).

WORKS CITED

Abruna, Laura Nn, "Twentieth Century Women Writers From English-Speaking Caribbeans", *Modern Fiction Studies*, 34: 1, 1986.

Atwood, M., *Surfacing* (1972) London: Virago Ltd., 1980.

Desai, A., *Fire on the Mountain*, London: Penguin Books, 1977.

Hariharan, G., *The Thousand Faces of Night*, New Delhi: Penguin Books, 1992.

Howells, Coral Ann, *Private and Fictional Words: Canadian Novelists of the 1970's and 1980's*, London: Methuen, 1987.

Ponnuthurai Sarvan, Charles, "Feminism and African Fiction: The Novels of Mariama Ba", *Modern Fiction Studies*, 34: 3, 1988.

Ramchand, K., *The West Indian Novel and Its Background.* London: Heinemann, 1983.

Rhys, Jean, *Wide Sargasso Sea* (1966), New York: Penguin Books, 1977.

❑❑❑

14

Shobha De's *Socialite Evenings*—A Feminist Study

S.P. SWAIN

Kate in Jane Wagner's *The Search for Signs* says:

> I am sick of being the victim
> of trends I reflect
> but don't even understand. (53)

Thus, she becomes painfully aware of her position in the system whose trends incarcerate her. But Karuna in *Socialite Evenings* is a different woman. She is all agog to break-out of such thralldom which "compel her to assume the status of the other" (Simone de Beauvoir 1974: 85). A problem child both at home and at school, she declines to dog the traditional path of etiquette and manners. At home, she refused to cower before elders and at school, she wore her sash hipster style. As she grows in age there develops in her the emotional urge to identify with the outside world, the modern crowd, the bewitching and fascinating world of affluent girls who had everything. Her slap-dash entry into all that is modern lands her in the lewd and clandestine world of modelling with her secret assignment as the Terkosa Girl (24). Throughout the novel Karuna figures as woman who asserts her feminine psyche through protest and defiance. She figures as a woman, not victim. Shobha De deals with the sullenly skewed power equation between the genders and its transformation into the stuff of art. We do not have here the stereotypes associated with male artistic representations of women. Karuna's initiation into the fashionable world of modern life begins at Anjali's fancy place in Malabar Hill. But Anjali accuses Karuna of bitchiness and lechery, her insatiable appetite for sex. This is borne out when she (Karuna) dates with the New Delhi and film-maker in London. Further her stay in the US gave her a feeling of superiority and made her assertive. Karuna with all her attempts at ego-assertion, refuses subscription to stereotypes, to succumb to the hegemony of the malist culture. Simone de Beauvoir finds man-woman nexus quite unsymmetrical and uncomplementary for

> ...man represents both the positive and the neutral, as is indicated by the common use of man to designate human beings in general; whereas woman represents only the negative, defined by limiting criteria, without reciprocity. (Selden 1988: 534)

A woman is never regarded as an autonomous being since she has always been assigned a subordinate and relative position:

> Man can think of himself without woman. She cannot think of herself without man. And she is simply what man decrees...she appears essentially to the male as a sexual being. For him she is sex—absolute sex, no less. She is defined and differentiated with reference to man and not he with reference to her; she is the incidental, the inessential as opposed to the essential. (Selden 1988: 534)

Socialite Evenings gives us the picture of the marginalisation of Indian women at the hands of their husbands. Shobha's is the picture of women not only as protagonist but also as motivating factors in society, initiating and regulating their own lives as well as the lives of others in the voluptuously fascinating world of Bombayites, its enticing glitter and glamour enamouring many a Karunas to its ensnaring and captivating gossamer. Karuna's marriage is a failure since it is loveless, joyless and bridgeless. There is no understanding between the husband and wife. She feels that she had married "the wrong man for the wrong reasons at the wrong time". Her husband was just the average Indian husband, "unexciting, uninspiring, untutored. He was not made for introspection" (65). The average Indian woman's conjugal life was to her "an exhausted generation of wives with no dreams left" and "marriage" was "like a skin allergy, an irritant". But she is not afraid to face this irritant, this allergy. She boldly and defiantly encounters it, for she realises "marriage is nothing to get excited or worried about. It is just something to get used to" (68) and she gets used to this stereotyped social institution in course of time. She detests the stand-offish and callous attitude of the husbands who often kept themselves busy in drab monotonous activities like reading the business pages of the *Times of India*. But despite these laxities, a husband was above all, a sheltering tree, a rock to the wife. They were not wholly bad or evil and the wife as a woman was only a peripheral being. Karuna says:

> We were reduced to being marginal people. Everything that mattered to us was trivialised. The message was "you don't really count, except in the context of my priorities". It was taken for granted that our needs were secondary to their. And that in some way we ought to be grateful for having a roof over our head and four square meals a day. (69)

In a patriarchal male-dominated society, it is the male who shout, hurl abuses, bully, reproach, criticise and it is the women who listen, tolerate and remain passive. But Shobha's women are different. Like Karuna they are not mere binding vine, "yes-persons" to bow down in meek subordination. They are the new women who fight back, who resist and shout back.

Subaltern attitude of women finds expression in the deletion from their mind of all thoughts of feminine liberty and equality. This is exemplified in the life of a qualified surgeon who was deliberately humiliated by her husband due to his repeated nagging that she married him for money. And what of the wife? She was "feeling humiliated and demoralised enough to actually half-believe what he was saying" (69). Look at the pitiable plight of such a woman as a housewife:

> He brainwashes me constantly. I'm made to feel obliged and in debt. It's awful, but even my insistence on working and contributing to the running expenses of

> the house has become a battleground. I don't know what to do—either way I'm stuck. (69)

The subordination of women as housewives stems from a castration—panic on the part of the husband. The Indian male is presented by Shobha De as a person "terribly threatened by self-sufficient women" (69). He is inadequate and incomplete as a husband since he lacks the traits of an ideal husband. Fear of the loss of domination and control over the self-affirming wife makes him resort to several defence mechanisms. One of this strategy is his male chauvinism and power-assertion ventilating in bullying and committing atrocities upon his wife. But his stupid self-conceit and ego restricts a free exchange of views among sexes. Karuna inquisitively wonders:

> ...how could we communicate anything at all to men who perpetually sat reading pages of the *Times of India* while concentratedly picking their noses? (68)

Karuna learns from Ritu, whom she chances upon, at a finance director's party that "men like dogs could be conditioned through reward and punishment" (87). But could she condition her husband in the like manner? She was fed up with her husband's compulsive socializing, his horrible safari suits and the gum he constantly chewed. She could not turn to anything in such a boring milieu save her books and her fantasies. Crosswords and newspaper chess were other alternatives to utter boredom. She realises that despite her little acts of protest, she is "a well-trained, Indian wife" (51) but she shares the same rational human nature as men do. Karuna is not "the toy of man, his rattle", which "must jingle in his ears whenever, dismissing reason, he chooses to be amused" (Wollstonecraft 1975: 34).

Rabindranath Tagore said in one of his early songs:

> O Woman, you are one-half woman
> and one-half dream.

So too with Karuna who combines in her both fact and fantasy. Her imaginary craving for the fulfilment of her physical desire finds reflection in her fantasies. Anjali's fancy place in Malabar Hill, the regular haunt of Karuna is symbolically the projection of her fancy, her dream which in reality is but a myth. A woman lives in a world of fancies, insignificant but profoundly imaginative. Talking of women, Virginia Woolf says:

> Imaginatively she is of the highest importance. Practically she is completely insignificant.... Some of the most inspired words, some of the most profound thoughts in literature fall from her lips; in real life she could hardly read, could hardly spell and was the property of her husband. (*A Room of One's Own*: 45-46)

In this context, it would be worthwhile to examine Karuna's views about the meaningless marriage in which she is trapped:

> I think our marriage was over the day our awful honey-moon started. We've got nothing going. I don't love you—never have. As for you—I really don't know to this day why you chose to marry me. I don't think you even know who you married. You don't have a clue what sort of woman I am. I'm tired of your smugness, your irritating mannerisms, the way you take me for granted and expect me to fall into your overall scheme of things—I was another one for your well-calculated deals. (185)

Locked up in a fragile and futile marital knot, Karuna was leading a life of emotional frigidity. There was no meaningful communication between the partners. No smiles and laughter, no free exchange of thoughts and ideas, no queries and questions but silence. Only silence. Karuna admits: "It wasn't that I never tried, but there was no question that my husband and I inhabited different planets" (68). But despite these emotional voids in her conjugal life, Karuna toed the track of an ideal housewife conforming to the demands of tradition. She did not protest but dutifully obeyed her husband. The house was kept in order, everything was well-trimmed, clean and tidy. Her husband is a compromising and forgiving type of person who is not a cruel and merciless individual to throw away her for her (Karuna's) sins, i.e. her affairs with Girish:

> I've thought over the whole thing carefully. I would've thrown you right now—but I'm prepared to give you one more chance. I'm not a mean man. You've been a

> good wife—I'm prepared to cancel this one black mark on your performance record and start with a clean slate. But you have to swear you'll never see or keep in touch with that man again...you have sinned but I must be generous and forgive you. (184)

I would rather call this act of forgiveness on the part of her husband as an act of his male ego, his assertion of superiority. What right has he to say that "I am not a mean man" when he himself has denied his wife the conjugal bliss of a marital life by often keeping himself at a distance from her? In what way is he "fair" which he in the course of his tirade admits to be? He is unable to look deep into the biological need of Karuna's female self. If she (Karuna) had any affair with Girish, it was only a means to fulfil her psychological and emotional need. It was her attempt to attend wholeness of personality for without a man, a woman is a fragment, a partial self. Such an involvement on the part of Karuna may also be a strategic escape from the claustrophobic and cloistered milieu of her marital life where they lived as two separate islands. Karuna says: "You never cared to understand me as a woman" (185). Basically, Karuna is pure for she is spiritually untainted and unsullied. The modern New Woman, independent in all respects, Karuna is a respectable, conservative Hindu housewife, wrapped in yards and yards of sari. The role of a wife restricts a woman's self-development. It circumscribes it. Rosemarie Tong maintains:

> Sometimes women play their roles not so much because they want to, as because they have to in order to survive psychologically. Virtually all women engage in the feminine role playing. (*Feminist Thought*: 200)

Karuna in *Socialite Evenings* plays different roles at different times to quench her emotional and psychic thirst. She is a model, a housewife, a society lady and an actor-writer and a paramour. Marriage subjugates and enslaves women. It leads her to "aimless days indefinitely repeated, life that slips away gently toward death without questioning its purpose" (de Beauvoir 1974: 500). But not so with the new women like Karuna. Unlike other married women who have practically no choice left to them save what their husband wills and desires, Karuna has independent thoughts. She has her own say and is free to choose her ways and means. The husband interferes but it is only by way of guidance and advice. There is no superimposition on her thoughts. Karuna's is a life of instincts and urges. Unlike other married women slavishly tagged to tradition, she has her own say. She unveils and unfurls herself to activate the creative urge stifled within herself and this act of unburdening herself is a compromise with herself. Like Shashi Deshpande, Shobha De does not overdo women's suffering. She transforms it into a creative principle of art and beauty.

The subordination of women in a malist culture is symptomatic of hierarchization of socio-moral values between the sexes. It symbolises the polarity between activity and passivity, between meek obedience and defiance. Helene Cixous observes:

> A male privilege can be seen in the opposition between activity and passivity. Traditionally, the question of sexual difference is coupled with the same opposition: activity/passivity. (Lodge 1989: 288)

Women are often the symbols of passivity. Cixous further maintains:

> Either the woman is passive; or she doesn't exist. What is left is unthinkable, unthought of. She does not enter into the opposition, she is not coupled with the father who is coupled with the son. (Lodge 1989: 288)

Woman is thus reduced to matter, a mere object. This reduction of woman to matter or a commodity is in the main a phallocentric pattern. Karuna's husband treats her as matter, a mere object subjected to his own will. Karuna's humorously sarcastic approach to her problems in the patriarchal male culture apparently deconstructs the traditional gender hostility used to elaborate the polarities of connubial ties. Karuna undermines male superiority. She loathes her husband's dwelling in "post-mortems" (186). She makes an ingenuous declaration about her inner urge to express herself through love:

> I love this friend of yours, and I want to be with him—in Venice. There is a good chance that I will feel thoroughly

> disillusioned after that. May be he will have some truly foul personal habits that will disenchant me. In which case it will really be *A Death in Venice*. You know by now that I'm not the flighty sort. I don't flirt at random like my other friends. I'm steady and grounded. It's the Taurean in me that's surfacing these days. Treat this as a short-term mania that will wear itself out. (186)

It appears that Karuna has just a formal relationship with her husband. Intimacy between the husband and wife is lacking for Karuna who never calls her husband by his name but derogatorily as 'Black Label'. Shobha De resorts to the technique of manipulating the language in order to deconstruct the male ego:

> ...the fact that his wife had taken a lover excited him. It seemed immoral that we should make love under the circumstances, but there was no point in resisting—it would have only consumed more time. (188)

She views woman not only as meekly/passively defiant but also as the embodiment of power. In Karuna this power (Shakti) syndrome assumes a positive figure but in Winnie it is a negative force, the destructive image, the image of Kali. Let us have a look at what Karuna's husband says about the bewitching Winnie:

> She is a very strange and powerful woman. I feel ashamed to admit this, but I'm scared of her. I can't do anything because I know she will destroy me. She has that power. (264)

Women in Shobha's novels symbolise the overpowering materialism and the lack of spirituality, that characterises modern age. With the crumbling of moral and ethical values there is an inner conflict which drives the modern Indian women to seek shelter in different identities for momentary solace. One of the most notable features of these women is they lack an identity. But we should not lay the whole blame on women only because in De's novels we do have the type of men who use and abuse women and then discard them. In *Socialite Evenings*, we do encounter a liberal Indian husband who allows his Indian wife to go abroad and get herself screwed once for all as the last gesture of goodwill! From the individual, let us come to the family. It is the family which is the centre of deviance. Subhash Chandra regards family's disintegration the instrument of degeneration in *Socialite Evenings.* The first tentative assay at the vamp ideology, Shobha's *Socialite Evenings* is a lust-laced work of sexploitation.

Anjali throws off the traditional conventions of moral values and seductively rises to the social status of the upper classes. She enacts a marriage of choice with Abe, "an experienced rake with a wild reputation" (12) and rejoices in orgastic acrobatics. Having a passion for illimitable sex, she has frequent sex encounters. Be he the die-hard rake Abe or the innocent Karan, she is after the desire of the body, the itchings of the sensations. Karuna too discards the dogmatic rules of a hackneyed and worn-out tradition for sustaining and cherishing her extra-marital relationship with Krish. Even she does not hesitate to restrain her husband from a week-long sexual orgy with Krish Kukherjee in Rome. Anjali, Karuna and Ritu are "the proverbial succubi who reign supreme in their world of licentious and unrestricted libido. In *Socialite Evenings*, Shobha articulates her own inclination towards vamp art and displays the troika of female characters who symbolise absolute freedom of womankind from all forms of patriarchal inhibitions. A housewife, Karuna encapsulates the plight of the Indian woman:

> I felt like an indifferent boarder in the house, going through the motions of house-keeping and playing wife but the resentment and rebellion remained just under the surface, ready to break out at the smallest provocation. (69)

Thus, De's novel shows the struggle of woman against the predatory male-dominated society. But her vamp ideology of feminism provides no redemption for the deviant and fallen women who in their frantic struggle to escape male-domination and attain individuality, meet with failure and are victimised in one way or the other. In enacting the drama of seduction and betrayal in her foray against patriarchal structures, the glamorous vamp in Shobha's novels "may end up being as seductively treacherous to women as to men" (Gilbert and Gubar: 145). In dealing with the problems of women in the androcentric society, she fails to provide viable solutions to the plight of the ailing woman. A woman in Indian society marries not just the man but also his family and subsequently loses her identity in marriage, relinquishes her freedom and sets about pleasing everybody. But the new generation of women with their new-found release from matrimonial bondage adopt different perspectives, and revolt against the old order. Shobha's women are such liberated individuals in search of a niche in their lives through escapades and sexcapades.

Karuna detests her husband's flattering nature, his duplicity and deviousness. He who had earlier rebuked and reproached her for having an illegal child is now satisfying her female ego by sly and base flattery, by saying that it was their legitimate child. But this is wrongly timed and too late for Karuna, for she has already undergone the protracted pangs of an abortion. Hence, her demolition of the male ego:

> ...you are even more of a worm than I thought. You deserve Winnie. I hope she's got a wax doll of yours. I'll send her some extra pins to stick into it. (264)

Karuna is a different Bombay Socialite. Unlike them, she defies the preconceptions and presumptions of a phallocentric patriarchal society, a world poles apart from her own rationale of life. Other women hardly defy the norms of the androcentric world. Anjali for instance has her own hangover following her separation from Abe. She is in search of a suitable life-partner. Hence, her amorous drift into the life of Kumar whom she chooses as her husband. As a woman she "projects her own sexual breakthroughs, energy, desire, onto a man (or sometimes another woman), as if such power has nothing to do with her" (Morgan: 143). Shobha's women like Anjali and Karuna project their passions onto others as a female power play in order to deconstruct the male ego. They like to be "eroticized as objects" and to view "themselves as erotic objects, not subjects" (Morgan: 143). But eroticism for these pervert women may either be a means to regain their sexuality or may be an expression of the confusion of their emotional and carnal urge. It may also be

"...a measure between the beginning of our sense of self, and the chaos of our strongest feelings...an internal sense of satisfaction to which we can aspire (Morgan 143).

Ritu exploits her sexual breakthrough, her female potentiality to keep her husband within her reach, within her control. Look, what she tells Karuna about her strategy:

> ...make them feel you have done them a favour by marrying them...make them feel insecure. Let them think you'll walk out on them if they don't toe the line. That's what keeps them in their place. (86)

Like Ritu, one has got to play the game, by flattering their male ego to suck anything out of them. Such an ideology of sexual power politics where the female is assigned a superior position and the male "a conditioned dog" has not been fully exploited and elucidated by Shobha's vamp feministic ideology culminating in cheap sexual encounters between the male and the female, almost a vile pornographic picture of man-woman relationship. But such a perspective does not promise one a safe life. Hence, Karuna's mother prefers the traditional way of life:

> A woman cannot live alone. It is not safe. We are here today—but who knows about tomorrow? A woman needs a man's protection. Society can be very cruel...a woman's real place is in her husband's house—not in her parents'—Take your time but marry. And marry the right one—that is important.... Before we die, we want to see you secure and at peace. (275-76)

But the mother's view is fraught with a lot of improbabilities and fallacies for is it possible for a girl to "marry the right one" and is it possible to attain 'security' and 'peace' in a modern society, especially in the urban milieu which forms the backdrop of Shobha's novels? No longer in the Indian society, the institution of marriage carries with it the traditional sense of security. Hence, Karuna questions:

> But, mother why does security rest with a man? I feel confident now that I can look after myself. I am earning as much money as any man, I have a roof over my head. I don't really have any responsibilities. I am at

> peace with myself. I'm not answerable to anyone...I can't make any "sacrifices"—not now. (276)

Thus, Karuna rejects the hierarchisation of male values where the female factor is reduced to a negative, and almost nullified. Her statements express her desire for the affirmation of her feminine self. It is in fact a search on her part for the genuine female self in a male-centred phallocentric world. But hers in not a traditional one. It is an esoteric quest, something weird and grotesque on the part of an Indian woman. But Karuna never bothers about the social repercussion her esoteric quest might entail. She is isolated from the traditional Indian heritage and its social implications. Taking up a non-conformist stance, she adopts a radical feminist point of view all agog to "destroy the sex/gender system—the real source of women's oppression—and to create a new society in which men and women are equals at every level of existence" (Millett 1970: 62). In order to avoid sexual exploitation or eroticisation of women as mere sex objects, Millett advocates a society having a single standard of "sex freedom" for boys and girls without which the equality between men and women will remain ephemeral. Shobha De has fully exposed the feminine world of the characters since for her humanness should be identified with "femininity" because as Marilyn French observes: "A masculine world is less fully human than a feminine one" (*Beyond Power*: 72). With dissident women like Karuna and Anjali oppressive gender roles will be deconstructed and women will take up a revolutionary role, flouting androgyny. A new generation of "wild", "lusty", and "wandering" women like those of Shobha's female protagonists will be created who would "prefer to identify themselves as radical lesbian feminist separatists" (Tong 1993: 102). Pornography in Shobha's novels becomes a symptom and symbol of the female's defiance of a male-regulated female sexuality. Shobha's women suffer in an androgynous world for they do not cherish genuine passions but only plastic passions which make them passive without a sense of purpose living in a frustrating world of anxiety, guilt, hostility, bitterness, boredom and resentment. These women cast off the conventional sense of morality, the old, tired and repressive sexual moves and revel in the erotic celebration of the body. Could we call Shobha, a pornographic and vulgar novelist since she depicts the naked sexual description in her novels? Then how should we justify the rationale of the people who patronise XXX porn films? The probable answer may be they do it to release or relieve their sexual tensions. And Shobha may be aiming to do the same thing when she describes the lusty sexual scenes. She may be aiming to provide the readers "with the mechanism that will, if all goes well, carry off the effluvia of socially banned sexual expressions into the realm of fantasy" (Deirdre 1980: 44). It seems that Shobha De views women as nothing but sex, a means to satisfy masculine lust.

The plight of women's present psychological situation is thus only one aspect of the problems involved in the growth of individual freedom. Viola Klein observes:

> Being in the position of outsiders, intruding into a finished system, and restricted by a century-old history of submissions, which had bred in them a sense of inferiority women's chief claim in their struggle was, as a natural result, to prove that in all respects they were just as good as men. (*Feminine Character*: 34)

These new women were like Shobha's Karuna "disgustingly self-assured and revoltingly self-sufficient" (305). Shobha De presents women with a lot of "pot passions". She exhibits the traits of neither the liberal feminists nor the radical feminists. At the most her novels are pulp-fiction, which sell well and read well but they fail to meet the aesthetics of feminism. Shobha's novels may simply be called as vamp feministic ideals of an experimenter in feminism. She has a long way to go in order to carve out a niche for herself as a genuine feminist novelist for what she most exhibits in her novels is gross pornography. She has yet to "prove her first commitment to feminism and shed off the popular stigma of being a mere peddler of pornographic fiction" (Sudhir Kumar: 124). A.G. Khan rightly regards "her entire acrobatics as an attempt to reduce 'fiction' to 'fucktion' (Shobha De "Vatsyayani": 78). Her novels portray her feelings of alienation from the traditional fictional craft of other women writers especially her predecessors. They are pieces of self-dramatization. They symbolise a woman writer's struggle for artistic self-definition, an attempt at self-differentiation from her male counterparts as well as an urgent sense of her need for a female audience coupled with her dread for the orthodox and traditional male readers. Shobha's *Socialite Evenings* fails to offer a viable strategy to the readers for socialisation though it may to some degree offer some panacea to the sex-starved unsociables.

WORKS CITED

Beauvoir, Simone de. *The Second Sex*. trans! and ed. H.M. Parshley (London: Penguin, 1974).

Chandra, Subhash. "Family and Marriage in Shobha De's *Socialite Evenings*", *Indian English Literature*, ed. K. Ayyappa Paniker (New Delhi: IAES, 1991).

De, Shobha. *Socialite Evenings* (New Delhi: Penguin Books, 1990).

(All citations in the paper are from this edition of the text, followed by page numbers in parentheses.)

Deirdre, English. "The Politics of Porn: Can Feminists Walk the Line?", *Mother Jones* (April 1980).

French, Marilyn. *Beyond Power: On Women. Men and Morals* (New York: Summit Books, 1985).

Gilbert, Sandra M. and Gubar, Susan. "The Mirror and the Vamp: Reflections on Feminist Criticism", *The Future of Literary Theory*, ed. Ralph Cohen (New York: Routledge).

Khan, A.G. "Shobha De 'Vatsyayani'", R.K. Dhawan (ed.), *Indian Women Novelists*, Vol. 1, Set. 3 (New Delhi: Prestige, 1995).

Klein, Viola. *The Feminine Character* (London: Routledge, 1989).

Kumar, Sudhir, "Artist as Vamp: A Feminist Approach to Shobha De's *Starry Nights*", R.K. Dhawan (ed.), *Indian Women Novelists*, Vol. 1, Set. 3 (New Delhi: Prestige, 1995).

Lodge, D. *Modern Criticism and Theory: A Reader* (London: Longman, 1989).

Millett, Kate. *Sexual Politics* (Garden City, N.Y.: Doubleday, 1970).

Morgan, R. *The Anatomy of Freedom: Feminism, Physics and Global Politics* (Oxford: Martin Robertson, 1983).

Selden, R. (ed.) *The Theory of Criticism: From Plato to the Present: A Reader* (London: Longman, 1988).

Tong, Rosemarie. *Feminist Thought* (London: Routledge, 1993).

Wagner, Jane. *The Search for Signs of Intelligent Life in the Universe* (New York: Harper and Row, 1987).

Wollstonecraft, Mary. *A Vindication of the Rights of Woman,* Carol H. Poston, ed. (New York: W.W. Norton, 1975).

Woolf, Virginia, *A Room of One's Own* (New York: Harcourt, Breace and World, 1929).

15

Elizabeth Bennet, Jane Austen's *Feminist Heroine*

SHARAD RAJIMWALE

Whether one finds Emma Woodhouse lovable or not, and reasons for doing so may be debated endlessly, there is little doubt that Jane Austen's other powerful character, Elizabeth Bennet (in *Pride and Prejudice*) has a universal and irresistible appeal. Even for those who do not find much to interest them in Jane Austen fiction, "dear Lizzy" stands out as one of the immortal in the gallery of fictional portraits alongside Dorothea Brooke and Isabel Archer, Tess and Ursula Brangwen. For a writer whose world doesn't have much by way of memorable events and sudden life-transforming quirks of destiny, even weddings, births and deaths are absent or overlooked as events of no consequence, creating a character like Elizabeth Bennet would demand the highest creative genius.

Jane Austen is not much given to external portrayal of character—at the end of the novel we hardly know what Anne Eliot looks like, or can barely conjure the precise physical attributes of Jane Fairfax or Eleanor. She builds up her characters by developing their qualities of mind, strengths or weaknesses of character and personality in their commonplace exchanges with other people in full view of everybody.

The novelist appears to have been particularly fond of Emma whom she knew at the outset 'no one but myself will much like'. But Elizabeth Bennet surpasses all other heroines in the sheer grit and strength she shows right from the opening pages. Overtly, heroines in Jane Austen's novels are seen as 'projection of certain moral forces moving the story in certain moral direction' and the comedy thus conceived as 'the medium of moral judgement'.

'Progress of enlightenment' is of course the substance of all the novels, through a merciless exposure of 'follies and nonsense, whims and inconsistencies', but out of all the conventional high humour, comic laughter, sharp duels of wit (again in strictly conventional mould) emerges something uncommon, something startlingly unconventional—the rebellious, highly self-willed and self-possessed Miss Elizabeth Bennet.

She may be read at two levels. On the surface, she follows the typical course charted for Jane Austen heroines, a comic instrument, an epitome of faults that lead her and everybody else to a crisis that can be resolved through a process of self-discovery, the correction being within herself. She must wait for the painful revelation.

> She grew absolutely ashamed of herself. Of neither Darcy nor Wickham could she think without feeling that she had been blind, partial, prejudicial, absurd.

This is how most of her heroines feel in the second half of the novels when the tide begins to turn and all must be set right for a joyous resolution. That part is, however, not significant. All that is distinctive and powerful in the character has already been presented in the highly strung first half of the novel. This is true both of *Pride and Prejudice* and *Emma.*

That a heroine has been presented in latter-half to submit to the power and persuasion of male protagonist, and cry to herself with self-admonitions and tearful repentance, may be taken (and have recently been taken) by many as Jane Austen's compliance to the conventional stereotype of a woman ever playing second fiddle to her male counterpart, and discovering the source of all the catastrophes in herself. This is all potentially inflammatory substance for the modern-day feminist enthusiasts.

Quite a great deal has been written on the subject and any further discussion would merely be repetitious. The angry protestations of the loud feminists have been too loud, one feels, to get a closer look at the other half of the characterization. Elizabeth Bennet and other female protagonists exist on two planes, the apparently conventional eighteenth-century social milieu of the English countryside upper-middle-class families, 'keeping close to common incidents, and to such characters as occupy the ordinary walks of life'.

On this plane "she suffers her reader by nothing vehement, disturbs him by nothing profound. The passions are perfectly unknown to her; she rejects even a speaking acquaintance with that stormy sisterwood".

It is this total agreement of the author with her times that irritates and infuriates the feminist critics of our times. Of course, their vision does not penetrate underneath. They cannot see that Jane Austen is both conventional and unconventional. Henry James appreciated it, and was prompted to express his deep indebtedness to her as much as to Turgenev. Because she was unconventional in more than one way. What we are concerned herewith, however, is the unconventional, non-stereotyped heroines she portrayed, and why.

That can best be understood by concentrating on the first half of the novel, where through a free play to their instincts, they show an independence of mind and power of judgement that is rarely found in the 18th and 19th century English fiction.

Perhaps the strongest of all Jane Austen's characters is Elizabeth Bennet. While her most towering male characters lead a kind of subdued life, emerging only as corrective voice, the full animation of living is conferred on the female protagonist. Elizabeth has many positive qualities that endear her to the readers.

> 'She has a powerful mind assisted by an instinctive understanding of the characters'
>
> 'Lizzy has something more of quickness than her sisters' as her father assesses her.

Darcy disturbs her emotions right from the beginning, that is why as a protective shell she builds a quick prejudice against him. Her prejudice is decided, firm and ever deepening. But how firmly does Elizabeth counter him in everything that provokes her sense of dignity and respect for her family!

> 'She is tolerable, but not handsome enough to tempt me', Darcy says to Bingley.

Elizabeth stands up defiantly to this attitude and decides to ignore him completely, and slight him publicly. Not only that, the Bingley sisters themselves are hostile to her as they are aware of the tremendous charm she exhudes and exerts on Darcy. "Eliza Bennet", said Miss Bingley, when the door was closed on her, "is one of those young ladies who seek to recommend themselves to the other sex by undervaluing their own; and with many men, I dare say, it succeeds".

Miss Bingley is anxious indeed to do everything to make Darcy despise Miss Bennet, and win his attention, but 'Darcy had never been so bewitched by any woman as he was by her' (Elizabeth). That she can spurn him easily and shock the entire party by her affirmations is a reflection of the strength of her character, qualities that we see in James' *Daisy Miller.* She runs all the way to see her sick sister, unmindful of 'her hair, so untidy, so blowsy!' and 'her petticoat, six inches deep in mud'—the appearance scandalised everyone, particularly the Bingley sisters, but Elizabeth was unshaken. Her concern for Janes well-being relegates all other considerations, even for herself, to the background. She is ready to undergo anything for her. This is a formidable strength of her character. This must be seen closely linked with her anxious perturbation at the 'total want of propriety, so frequently, so almost uniformly betrayed by...your three younger sisters, and occasionally even by your father', as Darcy points out in the letter to her. She knows what a disgrace her sisters are, and she feels sorry. But she counters manfully any assault on her family's honour. Darcy's behaviour in this respect is particularly resentful. He leads Miss Jane Bennet's suitor away precipitating the first major crisis.

Chapter 34 of the novel is a brilliant piece highlighting the courage and grit of the girl who is astonished to hear Darcy unexpectedly come into her room and announce,

> you must allow me to tell you how ardently I admire and love you.

This uncorks the pent-up anger and intense dislike Elizabeth nursed so long. She blasts him without any shred of regard or consideration with the withering words,

> I might as well enquire why with so evident a design of offending and insulting me, you chose to tell me that you like me against your will, against your reason, and even against your character? Was not this some excuse for incivility, if I was uncivil? But I have other provocations. You know I have....

'As she pronounced these words, Mr. Darcy changed colour'. Finally, she says,

> You are mistaken, Mr. Darcy, if you suppose that the mode of your declaration affected me in any other way than as it spared me the concern which I might have felt in refusing you, had you behaved in a more gentleman-like manner.

And then

> You couldn't have made me the offer of your hand in any possible way that would have tempted me to accept it.
>
> From the very beginning...of my acquaintance with you, your manners impressing me with the fullest belief of your arrogance, your conceit and your selfish disdain of the feelings of others, were such as to form that ground work of disapprobation on which succeeding events have built so immovable a dislike; and I had not known you a month before I felt you were the last man in the world whom I could ever be prevailed on to marry.

Critics often point out the tremendous irony couched in these words because later chapters bring about a reversal of situations and this obdurate, obstinate attitude transforms into the opposite of it. What is, however, striking in these utterances is the portrayal of an ordinary girl daring to speak her mind, refusing to succumb to the pressure which a 'superior' male thought would easily work. He had taken her acceptance of his offer for granted. He was unprepared for the kind of defiance and tongue-lash that she treats him to. It is difficult to know whether 'the best landlord, and the best master of Pemberley' had ever been spoken to in this manner, but Liza sure surpasses his worst fears. Jane Austen could not be more explicitly articulate about a woman's assertive power, her acute awareness that she is not to be manipulated around by a man simply because he is a man and belongs to the landed gentry. Her outraged sense of self-respect refuses to yield, though in doing so she may have been damaging beyond repair her brightest matrimonial chances. She comes to the defence of her wronged sister and jolts Darcy into consciousness that she or no other woman for that matter is to be taken for granted.

Another instance where Elizabeths' strength of character is asserted is presented by the way she mocks and spurns William Collins who is to inherit Longbourn, but can save the Bennet family by marrying one of the daughters. Upon hearing of this humiliating piece of intelligence Elizabeth reacts in a characteristic manner:

> I think it was very impertinent of him to write to you at all, and very hypocritical. I hate such false friends. Why could he not keep on quarrelling with you, as his father did before him?

But when Mrs. Bennet thrusts her determinedly into the presence of Collins, Elizabeth is ruthless and unrelenting in knocking him into understanding that neither she nor any one in her family is to be taken for granted.

> "You are too hasty, Sir," she cried, "you forget that I have made no answer. Let me do it without further loss of time. Accept my thanks for the compliment you are paying me. I am very sensible of the honour of your proposals, but it is impossible for me to do otherwise than decline them."

Collins's reply to this is highly offensive,

> I am not now to learn that it is usual with young ladies to reject the addresses of the man whom they secretly

> mean to accept, when he first applies for their favour.... I am, therefore, by no means discouraged by what you have just said, and shall hope to lead you to the altar ere long.

A fine example of condescending male attitude, which considers with blind confidence that any woman can be led along like sheep to the desired goal. Collins is silly, but he also harbours the typical masculine self-esteem, an over-weening high-handed approach that neither imagines nor brooks any feminine resistance. Jane Austen's projection of Elizabeths' strength of mind is simply superlative.

> I do assure you that I am not one of those young ladies (if such young ladies there are) who are so daring as to risk their happiness on the chance of being asked a second time. I am perfectly serious in my refusal. You could not make me happy, and I am convinced that I am the last woman in the world who would make you so....

But Collins is impervious to reason; he insists,

> When I do myself the honour of speaking to you next on the subject, I shall hope to receive a more favourable answer than you have given me. I know it to be the established custom of your sex to reject a man on the first application, and perhaps you have even now said as much to encourage my suit as would be consistent with the true delicacy of the female character.

That 'female character' is, obviously in the established conventional male estimation, pleasingly pliable, vulnerable, without a mind of its own and incapable of judging. With all the faulty sense of judgement, follies and prejudices, which critics make so much of, 'Cousin Elizabeth' is quite clear-sighted here, possessing the right degree of discretion, and unwavering constancy of faith in what she does.

> I do assure you, Sir, that I have no pretensions whatever to that kind of elegance which consists in tormenting a respectable man.... Can I speak plainer? Do not consider me now as an elegant female, intending to plague you,

> but as a rational creature, speaking the truth from her heart.

Elizabeth stands up to fight a type of mind-set, a kind of mentality which led the majority of menfolk along picking and choosing females for their partners as and when they willed without so much as consulting their mind. As we know already his fickleness had led him to consider Jane for future alliance, "for the first evening she was his settled choice". But Mrs. Bennet, fluttered at the suggestion, hinted to him 'that the eldest daughter was likely to be very soon engaged'.

'Mr. Collins had only to change from Jane to Elizabeth—and it was soon done—done while Mrs. Bennet was stirring the fire.' Later on, having been brought to his senses by 'Elizabeth, equally next to Jane in birth and beauty', we hear that Miss Charlotte Lucas sets his fancy on fire, and eventually marries him! Such is the fickleness of mind combined with an inflated form of masculine ego that Elizabeth has to contend with! She is not assisted by anyone in this fight, but cuts and pushes her way single-handed, first shocking Darcy then Collins into a better understanding of their own wrong headedness and her dour character Collins's stupidities are further to be exposed in later chapters.

Mr. Wickham is another person who tries and succeeds in winning her sympathies through preposterous means, blatant falsehoods and deceitful fabrications. This leads to complicated equations between the two and Darcy. For the first time we see Elizabeth being overwhelmed by the emotional out porings. She has been shown by the author totally taken in by Wickham's account of Darcy's injustice to him in the following manner,

> Whatever he said, was said well; and whatever he did, done gracefully. Elizabeth went away with her head full of him. She could think nothing but of Mr. Wickham, and of what he had told her, all the way home....

Complications arise because she is here deceived by Wickham, and she has erred in judging him. This makes her dislike of Darcy go deeper in her heart. She wonders, "How can Mr. Bingley, who seems good humour itself, and is, I really believe, truly amiable, be in friendship with such a man? How can they suit each other? Do you know Mr. Bingley?"

> "Not at all."
>
> "He is a sweet tempered, amiable, charming man. He cannot know what Darcy is."

For the first time we observe Elizabeth succumbing to the refined form of duplicity. But when she tried to fathom his real character, had information been in her power, she had never felt a wish of enquiry. His countenance, voice and manner had established him at once in the possession of every virtue. She tried to recollect some instance of goodness, some distinguished trait of integrity, of benevolence that might rescue him from the attacks of Mr. Darcy.... But no such recollection befriended her.

The mist seems to lift gradually and she feels she had been grievously wronged; "pleased with the preference of one, and offended by the neglect of the other, on the very beginning of our acquaintance, I have courted prepossession and ignorance, and driven reason away, where either were concerned".

So, we see here three different men of quite diverse characters, playing with her sentiments for different ends, seeking to manipulate her sentiments, desiring an easy, unresisting compliance. Each one of them, Darcy, Collins and Wickham takes her pliability for granted in the true self-opinionated frame of mind. The Tea-party at Rosings thrown by Lady Catherine de Bourgh (Chapter 29) occasions a fine encounter between Her Ladyship and our heroine with the former persistently probing the family background and upbringing of the latter. She is "a tall, large woman, with strongly-marked features, which might once have been handsome. Her air was not conciliating, nor was her manner of receiving them such as to make her visitors forget their inferior rank". Her Ladyship's questioning upon being introduced to Elizabeth progressed haughtily to cause the latter feel uneasy. But Elizabeth didn't lose her poise nor her wit. "Elizabeth felt all the impertinence of her questions, but answered them very composedly." She reacted vigorously and nothing seemed to scare her, neither Miss de Bourgh's position, nor her class, nor her domineering personality, nor the rank.

Once again we observe a decisive streak of character, a brief glimpse of how her self-respect steels her against the sneering undertones of Miss de Bourgh. "Upon my word", said her ladyship, "you give your opinion very decidedly for so young a person. Pray, what is your age?"

"With three younger sisters grown up", replied Elizabeth, smiling, "your ladyship can hardly expect me to own it". Lady Catherine seemed quite astounded at not receiving a direct answer; and Elizabeth suspected herself to be the first creature who had even dared to trifle with so much dignified impertinence.

None of the party there could have dared to speak to this aged member of the aristocracy so frankly—not even Darcy. Elizabeth comes forward quite manfully to prove she is not to be trifled with.

Elizabeth displays exceptional qualities of mind, a tough mould of intellect and a self-respecting, dignified free-willed personality in coming to terms with the formidable challenges thrown by hostile minds, both men and women. Perhaps only Jane and her father have sympathy for her. Rest of the other only create difficulties in her way. She is alone in this fight to save her honour and that of her family, amidst snooping Collinses, backbiting Wickhams, and jealous Miss Bingleys. She feels sorry about the complete inaction into which her father has fallen even when one crisis after another overtakes the poor family.

Elizabeth is more hero like in slicing her way through the crowding adversities than any female protagonists ever painted. We see the best of her in the first half of the novel; the second half moves quite predictably to underscore her miscalculations and bring the story to a well-established conventional conclusion. Jane Austen was born and writing long before the epithet 'feminism' came into being. But at least her two characters, Emma Woodhouse and Elizabeth Bennet, are endowed with the finest attributes of a sloganising feminist of latter-day European society. It is these characters and their powerful portrayal that makes us stop short and think when the loudest voices seem eager to brand Jane Austen 'a meek bourgeois conformist' whose heroines cannot think beyond ball room dances, picnic parties and an endless chase for a suitable husband. There is more to her world and especially to her heroines than these. One must only be prepared to go under the surface and see for oneself.

WORKS CONSULTED

1. *Pride and Prejudice*—Jane Austen Washington, Square Press Inc. 1965.
2. *Before Jane Austen—The Shaping of the English Novel in the Eighteenth Century*, Harrison R. Steeves Holt, Rinehart and Winston, New York, 1965.
3. "Narrative and Dialogue in Jane Austen", *Critical Quarterly*, Autunm, 1979.
4. *Jane Austen's Novels: A Study in Structure*—Andrew Wright, Penguin, 1965.
5. Sir Walter Scott's famous review published in *Quarterly Review*, Oct. 1815, quoted in *Emma* Casebook series, edited by David Lodge.
6. Charlotte Brontes celebrated letter to W.S. Williams, 1850 quoted in Andrew Wright's book mentioned earlier here.

16

The Concept of Perfect Man in *Between the Acts* of Virginia Woolf

NAJMA MAHMOOD

> Highest bliss of human beings be the personality.
>
> —*Goethe*
>
> I am the thing in which all this exists.
>
> —*Virginia Woolf*
>
> The universe is immersed within the Perfect Man.
>
> —*Iqbal*

Virginia Woolf's quest for wholeness led her to the idea of personality, to a cosmic vision which has great affinities with the concept of Perfect Man (*insan-e-kamil*) as presented by the Oriental Sufis. The idea of personality was with her since the very beginning of her literary career. In her novels she has "tunnelled out beautiful caves"[1] behind her characters. This process takes us to the past memories through which the present has been explained. Everyday events belong to the mundane. The world of memory belongs to the unconscious. Virginia Woolf has taken us to the "unconsciousness, the darkness, Amaa"[2] through which the present has been explained. Hers is a striving to examine the nature of "primal darkness which is the reality of realities".[3] She is able "to see into the life of things".[4] She is a "circle which stirs and whose harmony is complete".[5] Hers is a spiritual striving to attain the higher levels of perfection. She knows that life is an attainment of perfect self and death a failure in this regard.

Virginia Woolf's yearning for wholeness and perfection led her to realise that man in this modern world has lost his integrity, self-respect and wholeness, that he is fragmented and confronted by anxieties. She felt the need of an integrating force so that his wholeness may be restored. In *Between the Acts*, she addressed the modern man in the following words:

> All you can see of yourselves is scraps, orts and fragments.[6]

She has suggested that so long we remain 'orts and fragments' we shall never be able to rebuild civilization. She feels that corruption and ills of the world are due less to the bomb droppers, who do it openly, than to ourselves who do worse things slyly having lost our innocence, virtue, love and sincerity. Like *To the Lighthouse* and *The Waves*, etc. *Between the Acts* also, besides being a lyrical novel, is a sufi treatise presenting Virginia Woolf's own porous' personality. She has satirised in this novel vanity, selfishness, hypocrisy, greed, love of exploitation, and war—the vices which divide man from man. Real life, according to her is, the common life. We cannot be whole and entire unless we have faith in the oneness of the world and humanity, i.e. Universal Love. All the creation, according to her, is the same everywhere. There is a spirit that pervades everywhere. The "bellowing cows" presented in the pageant are symbolic of the basic unity of all life:

"Then suddenly as the illusion petered out, the cows took up the burden. One had lost her calf. In the very nick of time she lifted her great moon-eyed head and bellowed.... From cow after cow came the same dumb yearning bellow. The whole world was filled with dumb yearning. It was the primeval voice sounding loud in the ear of the present moment."[7]

As stated earlier, cow, according to Professor S.P. Singh's interpretation of Aurobindo's views, represents "Light", "consciousness" or the "Higher Consciousness".[8] The lines from *Between the Acts*, if read and assessed in the light of Sri Aurobindo's interpretation of the word cow, dawn their depths of meanings. Aurobindo, a mystic-seer, had presented an ideal of integrated personality or concept of Perfect Man who could save God's world, on whom is laid the burden of the past, the "burthen of the mystery, the heavy and the weary weight of all this unintelligible world which is lightened in the blessed mood"[9] (Tintern Abbey).

Isa, one of the Isiac personalities in *Between the Acts*, murmured:

"How am I burdened with what they drew from the earth, memories, possessions; this is the burden that the past has laid on me, last little donkey in the long caravanserai crossing the desert.... That was the burden, she mused, 'laid on me in the cradle; murmured by the waves; breathed by restless elm trees'."

By a close study of the passages quoted we reach the conclusion that there are parallelisms between the "murmuring waves" the "bellowing cows" and mothers ("sinking and falling mothers").

Professor Singh writes:

Among the followers of Sri Aurobindo the vision of the mother is most frequent. He regards mother as the direct embodiment of the consciousness force—the Supreme Creative power.... Being transcendent, if she is capable of assuming universal form on the one hand, no less should she be able to assume individual form on the other. For individuality as well as universality is implied in the transcendent.[10]

The mother is the prime force behind the spiritual development of her followers. Mother, according to Al-Jili as well is the origin. Search for origins is very characteristic of Virginia Woolf (Mrs. Swithin again and again enquires about the origin of words). During the World Wars, according to Virginia, the whole world was filled with "dumb yearnings" the "primeval voice sounding loud in the ear of the present moment", hence her deep interest in Pre-history, Egyptology and Isiscult whose symbol is cow representing Higher Consciousness.

Virginia Woolf's fascination with the sea and with the primeval has been related to her "search for a way out of sexual difference or equality for a continuity with lost origins".[11] She conceived mother as origin, the source of life as she had lost her mother at a very young age, hence "sinking and falling many mothers and behind them many more, endlessly sinking and falling" (*The Waves*, Halograph Draft 1, p. 64). Ms. Beer says: "Mothers, matrices, the acceptance of oblivion—these are connections crucial to Virginia Woolf."[12]

Both *The Waves* and *Between the Acts* are related with the ancient Egyptian religion. Ms. Beer further says:

Between the Acts is set in June 1939 before the coming of war. The present is pre-history in double sense. Whenever the action of the historical pageant falters it is saved by the unwilled resurgence of the primeval: the shower of rain, the idiot, the cows bellowing for their lost calves,... June 1939 is pre-history to a coming war which, the book makes clear, without hysteria, may mark the end of this society. The book is permeated with Lucy Swithin's reading of H.G. Wells. Virginia Woolf here amalgamates his *The Outline of History* with his *Short History of the World* and writes her own version rather than quoting Wells directly. Old Mrs. Swithin, so pious, repetitive and faithful, has an imaginative life swarming with sensual images of power and birth. During the book's twenty-four hours, she inhabits the repeated present of the day of pageant and the primeval worlds of her book's description.[13]

Virginia Woolf's reading of *Moses and Monotheism* while she worked on *Between the Acts* is an important fact revealed by Gillian Beer. Freud's observation that man has a pre-history which is unknown must have helped Virginia Woolf's ideas about pre-history.

Abdullah Yusuf Ali starts Appendix V of his translation of *The Holy Quran* with the title: "Egyptian Religion and Its Steps Towards Islam". He writes:

.... In the most fantastic forms of religion appear gleams of His Light of Unity, calls to Islam, i.e. man's submission to the Will of Allah. From that point of view the religious history of Egypt...is most interesting. The religious history of Israel is an earlier chapter of the history of Islam. It is a healthy sign that modern Egypt is showing much interest in it...it will in time recognise in it a valuable unfoldment of religious ideas leading to Islam. With the gifted and artistic people like the Egyptians their religious sense was led to a purer conception of man's eternal destiny until Mohammad's message was preached to them in the very language in which it was preached to them in Arabia. A process of unification was now consciously undertaken.... In addition to the symbolism of animals there was the worship of the phenomena of Nature, the Nile and the Sun which became the supreme God in Egypt. Then there was the myth of Osiris who came to the earth for the benefit of mankind.... His faithful wife Isis and his son Horus figure in mysteries.[14]

Abdullah Yusuf Ali's gradual perception of monotheism in Egyptian religion and its relation to Christianity and Islam is illuminating. According to him, Moses came in such conditions in order to direct his people to the Unity of Being, to one who had been Many but still One (all this is remindful) of Virginia's reading of *Moses and Monotheism.* Slowly, and gradually the soil of Egypt was made cosmopolitan in nature, culture and philosophy. In this appendix V, the author has discussed Christianity as well which began to displace the older Egyptian cults. The "new Christianity was evolved out of Christ's simple teaching". He says:

The Christian creed became narrower and narrower, less and less rational, more and more inclined to use earthly weapons to suppress the eternal truth of Allah.[15]

In the forthcoming lines, the author of the Appendix refers to the brutal murder of Hypatia, a beautiful, modest, eloquent philosopher and mathematician of Alexandria. It was for this reason, besides others, the inhabitants of Egypt generally welcomed the forces of Islam which was chiefly inclined towards justice to women (as Christianity had been in its original form which was rediscovered by Virginia Woolf at a later stage—the original Christianity which was hailed and wholeheartedly applauded by her in *Between the Acts*).

Abdullah Yusuf Ali has been just in his observations. Jesus was not a chauvinist (neither he was a rival to his mother, but was made so). As supported by the recently discovered and translated *Dead Sea Scrolls* (dated from 100? B.C. 70? A.D., discovered in 1947 in caves near the Dead Sea containing Scriptural writings), Jesus said:

Seek not the law in your scriptures, for law is not life, whereas the Scripture is dead. I tell you Moses received not his laws from God in writing but through the living word.[16]

There are to be found with the manuscripts of New Testament which exist in the library of the Vatican, in Rome, of the texts dating from early Christian centuries containing writings which refer to otherwise inaccessible words of Jesus:

"For I tell you truly, from one mother proceeds all that lives upon the earth. Therefore who kills, kills his brother and from him the Earthly Mother turn away...do the will of God...."[17]

The above information is given to us by a person who is deeply interested in spiritual truth. She writes:

"One wonders at all the great truth and wisdom contained within the Vatican Library, yet not spread to the multitudes. But one must be grateful at least for the access of truth permitted searching scholars.... It seems a non sequitur to teach falsehood while at the same time allowing suppressed truths to be researched."[18]

It is this Christianity (whose epitomes in Virginia's novel are Isa and Mrs. Swithin) that was dawned upon the author of *Between the Acts* while she had been antagonistic to its prevailing form throughout her life. Now the "dumb yearnings" of the bellowing cows and "sinking and falling mothers" become extremely, meaningful. The distressed primeval voice is sounding loud in the ear of the present moment while war and bloodshed and patriarchy as well as fascism are separating mothers from their sons, while men are mere 'orts, scraps and fragments' and the wall of civilization in ruins to be rebuilt.

Virginia Woolf's interest in roots and origins, in "digging and delving" had led her to Egyptology. Tiers of Isis and Horus in British Museum had influenced her. Besides that some strong minded women—Clara Peter and Janet Case, etc. also influenced her. She had read *Marius, the Epicurian* by Pater which contained eloquent descriptions of the rites of Isis. This book draws the reader to The *Golden Ass* by Apuleus—a major source of information about Isis. Isiac roles were very much loved by Virginia. Evellyn Haller writes:

"By placing aspects of Egyptian monumentality in her work, sphinxes, collasi, pyramids, donkey, sarcophagi, etc. Woolf builds an aesthetically Egyptian ambience into her novel that makes a cartouche surround the mythic figure of Isis, enabling her to make aesthetic war on imperialism, Christianity and patriarchy."[19]

Evellyn rightly feels that Virginia Woolf's choice of becoming a woman of letters intended to challenge the male-dominated systems of thought for one informed by most coherent female myth by emphasising Isiac roles of artists and peace-gatherers. Isis, says Haller, was the life-enhancing female factor in comparison to Phaeraohs and Osiris. Isis, with the flooding of the Nile remained the source of life. Images of Isis and Horus became models for Madonna and the Child. *Between the Acts* has "most perceptible Egyptian ambience".[20] Virginia Woolf in using the "mythical method"[21] chose "as referent the loving, maternal and beneficent Isis"[22] suggesting her name in that of the central character Isa. Another Isiac personality, according to Haller, is Mrs. Swithin who fondly reads Well's *An Outline of History* which discusses Isis in detail. Haller also refers to Virginia Woolf's acquaintance with Apulius' *Golden Ass* in which Isis speaks of her diversity of manifestations:

"I am she whose godhead, single in essence, but of many forms, with varied rites and under many names the whole world reveres" (Bk 11, Ch. V—tr. by Adlington Classical Library, London, pp. 546-47).

Egyptian symbols of the abundance of life abound in *Between the Acts* increasing the Isiac presence. Like Isis and Horus, Isa and George (her son) become the models for Madonna and the child. Isa refers to the loving, maternal and beneficent Isis. While the innocent world of her son was destroyed by cold and hard-hearted Oliver, her father-in-law (reminding us of Mr. Ramsay of *To the Lighthouse*) by terrifying him being masked, she felt extremely hurt. The child's world was the innocent world of grass, flower and tree full of sweet smells and lights at whose heart there was for George 'a flower complete'. Isa was teased by Oliver. He called her boy a cry baby and coward:

"She frowned. He was not a coward, her boy wasn't. And she loathed the domestic, the possessive and maternal."[23]

Isa "loves as well as hates" her husband who is the "father of her children" but is mere fragment being separated from her by Mrs. Manresa who is all lust. Her yearning for a husband (who may love her sincerely) is suggestive of her wholeness, a husband who may be whole and entire. For healing the wounds of her soul she was momentarily inclined towards the gentleman farmer, Rupert Haines, who was inaccessible to her. Out of her deep maternal love for her children she represses her desires and conquers her lower self—while her husband enjoys the company of Mrs. Manresa freely. While she comes to know that her husband had gone in front with Mrs. Manresa, she muttered, "the father of my children". Then, writes Virginia Woolf:

"The flesh poured over her, now lit up, now dark as the grave physical body. By way of healing the rusty fester of the passionate dart she sought the face that all day long she had been seeking.... Turning the comer there was Giles attached to Mrs. Manresa.... Did they perceive the arrows about to strike them?"[24]

Then both of them went away in a car leaving Isa in hiding with a bleeding heart—Isa the mother of Giles' children—the maternal Isis. Isa is the mother, direct embodiment of consciousness force, having "assumed individual form implicit in the transcendent". Mother is the prime force behind the spiritual development of her child (it reminds us of the mother who rose out of the waters of river Ganges). Isa, like Mrs. Ramsay, is the sinking and falling mother, the great Mother who "inspires and pervades everywhere".

Original Christianity, Islam as well as Sufism were inclined vehemently towards justice to women. Giles stands for narrower Christianity (which degrades women) inclined to use earthly weapons to suppress the eternal truth of the Absolute Being. Isa's are "dumb yearnings, the silent cries".

Moon is the main subject of Isa's poems which she hides from her husband. She is "burdened with what they drew from the earth, memories, possessions. That burden was laid on her by the past—the last little donkey in the long caravanserai crossing the desert". It was "laid on her in the cradle murmured by the waves...crooned by singing women".

The bellowing cows, who took up the burden (the "murmuring waves", the "sinking and falling mothers", the "individual embodiment of the higher consciousness", the supreme creative force), who saved the pageant (the world) at the crucial moment having great moon-eye heads, remind us of Isis' origin in Hathor, the ancient Egyptian cowgoddess (equally revered in India since the Vedic period). Isa's silent cries have parallelisms with the bellowing cows. She was capable of feeling deeply and expressing human sorrows poignantly. She laments the decline of the Universal Love and intuition which has fragmented man and divided the world.

With the ideal of integrated personality Virginia Woolf intended to challenge the male-dominated, patriarchal, Fascistic systems of thought by emphasising Isiac roles of artists. Isa is the life-enhancing female factor possessing a harmonious personality.

It is merciful wife, sister and mother nursing her child that Isis appealed to those who had faith in her. In *Between the Acts*, life is controlled by the figure of Isis—Isa and Mrs. Swithin, reminding us of the Oriental Sufis, especially Ibn'l Farid who had said "I am she" and "I am God" (aham "Brahmasmi" of *The Upanisads*). The myth of Isis, the Great Mother Goddess, has relation with Many and thus with that Christianity which has been eulogised in *Between the Acts*. Isis and Horus (so also Mary and Jesus—Madonna and the Child) were mysterious figures for Virginia Woolf hence the "bellowing cows" and the "murmuring waves"—symbols of "sinking and falling mothers", of the decline of intuitionism, of Universal Love, of the loss of the absoluteness of the Absolute Being resulting in ruin of the wall of civilization, of man becoming mere 'orts, scraps and fragments'.

Between the Acts was written during the outbreak of World War II in which Virginia Woolf's own house was ruined. Thakur feels surprised that this novel (which is very delightful according to him) does not reflect those hard times when Leonard Woolf kept enough petrol for suicide should Hitler win. There is not found any sense of insecurity or fear but "tranquil recollection and sober judgement"[25] which are suggestive of integrated and porous personality of a mystic seer and a perfect artist. In this novel, besides inner and historic time, pre-historic time also has been captured presenting a unified vision of life. The major personalities in this quintessential novel are of Mrs. Swithin and Isa like Mrs. Ramsay, Eleanor and Bernard, etc. Virginia Woolf felt the need for that integrating force that man needs today. Her vision of the Perfect Man is unique, fascinating and all-inclusive advocating the unity of life offering the divided self and the divided world a possibility to restore their identity, their personality by reuniting the fragmented aspects of life. This very concept of Unity of Being, being rooted in the antiquity, later presented by Ibn'l Arabi and Al-Jili, etc. is to be found at its best in this novel. Virginia Woolf has tried to cure the diseases, spiritual as well as moral, of modern man by Universal Love so that he could he whole and entire. At a time when there was a threat of war, when man was a mere fragment she promised a full-blooded life, an integrated personality, well-adjusted existence.

In *Between the Acts*, unlike her previous novels, Virginia Woolf is not against religion and Christianity. Her reverence for Mrs. Swithin's prayers, her crucifix, her compassion, Universal Love, her calm restoration, tolerance, moral courage and forgiveness, etc. indicate that she had by then understood the original Christianity, its very essence. This change of attitude was the outcome of her persistent study of religious writers, historians and interpreters of Egyptology and Christianity. She had always been inquisitive about the original meaning of Christianity, about such sayings, "God is Love", "Kingdom of Heaven is within us". She felt that man is in need of a God. The religious faith needed by the world today has been represented by the most integrated personality, i.e. Mrs. Swithin (who is a "unifier", is intuitive) in *Between the Acts*. In this materialistic age spirituality, faith and mysticism are vehemently needed for the survival of humanity, hence the concept of Perfect Man.

The Perfect Man, the integrated being, the origin of the universe, is the spirit of Divine Revelation inspired by the light of Mohammad (Speaking as the Logos—the doctrine which was common between the ancient Egyptian religion, *The Upanisads*, original Christianity and the great Oriental Sufis). Al-Jili treats the Perfect Man as the spirit whence all things have their origin. Mrs. Swithin and Isa of *Between the Acts* are such spirits whence all things have their origin, who are capable of seeing into the life of things. Iqbal, in his article "Al-Jili's doctrine of Absolute Unity" writes:

.... In the first stage of his spiritual progress he (the Perfect Man) meditates on the name, studies nature on which it is sealed; in the second stage he steps into the sphere of the attribute and in the third stage he enters the stage of the 'Zaat; the Essence. It is here that he becomes the God-man; his eye becomes the eye god, his life the life God, his word the word of God—participates in the general life of nature and sees into the life of things. It will appear how strikingly the author has anticipated the chief phase of Hegelian Dialectic and how greatly he has emphasised the doctrine of the Logos—a doctrine which has always found favour with almost all the profound thinkers of Islam.[26]

Like that of Iqbal the universe of Virginia Woolf's poetry is a God-oriented universe (*Between the Acts* is all poetry). Mrs. Swithin, an Isiac personality in this lyrical novel is a God-intoxicated personality, a real Christian, hence the following:

.... The stage remained empty. The cows moved in the field. The shadows were deeper under the trees.... Mrs. Swithin caressed her cross. She gazed vaguely at the view. She was off, they guessed, on a circular tour of imagination—one making—sheep, cow, grass, trees, ourselves, all are one. If discordant, producing harmony, if not to us, to a gigantic ear attached to a gigantic head. And thus she was smiling benignly. The agony of a particular sheep, cow or human being is necessary and so she was beaming seraphically at the gilt vane in the distance—we reach the conclusion that all is harmony could we wear it.... Her eye now rested on the white summit of a cloud. Well, if the thought gave her comfort William and Isa smiled across her, let her think it.[27]

Mrs. Swithin gives us an insight into Virginia Woolf's vision of life. She is the first major personality in her novels to carry a cross (which is ridiculed by her brother). She represents the simple religious faith which the world needs today. The pageant to collect funds for the village church is a significant device in this novel.

It would be appropriate here to throw light on the idea behind it. The pageant organised by Miss La Trobe attempts to give unity to history. The diverse elements of her audience are held together while her play is in progress. She had made the audience see (into the life of things), a vision giving relief from agony. The rustling breeze is heard in the branches. Her failure was that she could not make Mr. Oliver see the vision which was applauded by his sister Lucy Swithin. An autobiographical element is all prevailing. Throughout her life Virginia Woolf tried to make people see a world of values which was related with natural things—a world whole and entire. It was the outbreak of War and she had in her efforts to make the people see the whole truth. *Between the Acts* reflects the decadence of her age. Pointz Hall is a beautiful old house but in hollow. "Nature had provided a site for a house, man had built his house in a hollow. Nature had provided a stretch of turf half a mile in length and level till it suddenly dipped to the lily—pool".[28] Miss La Trobe's effort to unite her audience in a single vision is defeated by the feelings of lust, hatred and hypocrisy (of individuals who emerge and triumph in the intervals between the acts). They read in the morning paper about the rape of a girl. Europe is being raped by the dictators. At any moment that land would be raked by guns into furrows. Music plays the role of unifier, a synthesiser". It wakes us, makes us see the hidden, join the broken.[29] .... How can you deny that brave music, wafted from the bushes is expressive of some inner harmony.[30] Miss La Trobe signalled "music" whenever the audience split up in 'orts, scraps and fragments'. Music since ages has been a forceful device of healing. It was favoured by many saints and sufis (especially Rumi). Virginia Woolf wants to say that the fragmented personality of man may be made whole by the healing balm of music and harmony. Through the pageant she has ridiculed society very delightfully. She makes the children and elves expose the audience by mirrors. Like a saint she traces out the fall of glory and vanity. She shows the rise and fall of great houses and of golden ages evoking a sense of transitoriness of human life and vanity of individuals. This way she herself comes before us as a spirit of Divine Revelation. The pageant is the pageant of the world which is marvellous but which is vanity. She has suggested that Mrs. Swithin, a prayable being, is directing the pageant of life. Humanity, according to her, persists when the kings and Queens leave the stage of the world:

.... Digging and delving (they sang), hedging and ditching we pass.... Summer and winter, autumn and spring return.... All passes but we, all changes...but we remain for ever the same....

Palaces tumble down (they resumed), Babylon, Ninvevah. Troy.... And Caesar's great house...all fallen they lie.... Where the plover nests was the arch...through which the Romans trod.... Digging and delving we pass...and the Queen and the Watch Tower fall....[31]

Virginia Woolf's idea about time and change, about pre-historic time and the evolution of life are revealing. Mrs. Swithin's reading of *An Outline of History* in which Isis has been hailed, is suggestive of her own Isiac and integrated personality. After the description of the rise and fall of kingdoms the words died away. Only a "few great names Babylon, Nineveh", etc. floated across the great space.... The audience sat staring at the villager whose mouth opened but no sound came.... And the stage was empty: Miss La Trobe leant against the tree, paralysed.... Beads of perspiration broke on her forehead. Illusion had failed. This is death. She murmured 'death'.[32]

For Virginia Woolf, as for Iqbal and Aurobindo along with Rumi, life and death do not matter too much. While one is incapable of seeing into the life of things, of seeing the truth, it is death for him, death of his soul, of his self. Self dies when illusion fails Sri Aurobindo says in *The Life Divine*:

"Illusionism itself, even if we contest its ultimate conclusions, can still be accepted as the way in which the soul in mind, the mental being has to see things in a spiritual pragmatic experience when it cuts itself from the Becoming in order to approach and enter into the Absolute."[33]

The following is what Virginia Woolf says in *Between the Arts*:

".... Grating her fingers in the bark she damned the audience. Panic seized her. Blood seemed to pour from her shoes. This is death, death, she noted in the margin of her mind: when illusion fails. Unable to lift her hand, she stood facing the audience.

And then the shower fell, sudden, profuse. No one had seen the cloud coming. There it was black, swollen, on top of them. Down it poured like all the people in the world weeping Tears, Tears.

O that our human rain could here have ending, Isa murmured. Looking up she received two great blots of rain full on her face. They trickled down her cheeks as if they were her own tears. But they were all people's tears weeping for all people. Hands were raised.... The rain was sudden and universal. Then it stopped. From the grass rose a fresh earthy smell....

Nature once more had taken her part".[34]

Complete identification of Isa's tears with people's tears on the suffering humanity is suggestive of her Isiac and integrated personality possessing Universal Love. Here Virginia Woolf, along with Isa, becomes the God-intoxicated being, her eye becomes the eye of God, her life the life of God, her word the word of God. Iqbal says:

The hand of God is the hand of Perfect Man.

Isa's and Mrs. Swithin's "general participation in Nature" is exquisite. Their selves are alive as the self of Iqbal's Perfect Man is alive. Iqbal says:

Farishta maut ka choota hai go badan tera
Tere wujud ke markaz se door rahta hai.

Though death may lay its hands on thy body,
Access it has not to the centre of thy being.

Universal Love keeps the body alive, courageous and capable of defiance helping us realise the limitations of reason. "Love impels us to make a sudden leap in the dark and this ecstatic gesture discloses to us the secret depths of the unknowable...it enable us to establish between our consciousness and the object of perception an intimate relationship...love or 'ishq' helps us penetrate to the innermost recesses of the sanctuary. This reckless onrush into the unknown region by 'ishq' is juxtaposed to the calculated, prudential moves of reason.[35]

The absolute comes back within Mrs. Swithin who is epitome of Universal Love, Charity and absolution, peace and justice. She is motherly, protective; she creates, harmonizes and thus enhances life. Virginia Woolf's women, like the leading women of Shakespeare and Aurobindo (Rosalind and Savitri, etc.) possess androgynous and harmonious minds harbouring a "hidden man in their girlish hearts". Thus, sexes do not alienate. Today, intuitive aspects have to act more liberally within the individual and society. Love is to be prevailed for preserving man's soul.

Iqbal says about Universal Love:

Love is above thought of gain and loss
Life is being, but sometimes the surrender of being.

A man of Love is a "free man". Love is his guide and reason his slave. It is a way to self-realization—The basic trait of an integrated being. The intuitive process reveals the nature of Ultimate Reality.

According to Lucy Swithin reason cannot see beyond the Z. She is a "unifier", her brother Bart a "separatist". She has immense courage and defiance. She possesses Universal Love. When her brother attacks her faith, she does not lose heart:

"The forecast", said Mr. Oliver, "turning the pages till he found it," says variable winds; fair average temperature, rain at times.... He put down the paper and they all looked to the sky to see whether the sky obeyed the meteorologist. Certainly the weather was variable. It was green in the garden; grey the next. Here came the sun—an illimitable rapture of joy, embracing every flower, every leaf. Then in compassion it withdrew, covering its face, as if forebore to look on human suffering. There was a fecklessness, a lack of symmetry in the clouds, as they thinned and thickened. Was it their own law, or no law they obeyed? Some were wisps of white hair merely. One high up, very distant, had hardened to golden alabaster, was made of immortal marble. Beyond that was blue, pure blue, black blue, blue that had never filtered down; that had escaped registration. It never fell as sun, shadow or rain upon the world, but disregarded the little coloured ball of earth entirely. No flower felt it; no field, no garden.[36]

This kind of participation in the objects of Nature, this one-making, is an outstanding trait of an integrated personality. Mrs. Swithin "lives in others, in things. She is always herself". After the lines quoted above the novel reads:

Mrs. Swithin's eyes glazed as she looked at it. Isa thought her gaze was fixed because she saw God there, God on his throne. But as a shadow fell next moment on the garden Mrs. Swithin loosed and lowered her fixed look and said:

It's very unsettled. It'll rain. I'm afraid. We can only pray, she added and fingered her crucifix.

And provide 'umbrellas', said her brother. Lucy flushed. He had struck her faith. When she said 'pray', he said, 'umbrellas'. She half covered the cross with her fingers. She shrank; she cowered but next moment she exclaimed.

Oh there they are—the darlings.
The perambulator was passing across the lawn.[37]

Isa looked too. What an angel she was—the old woman. Thus to salute the children, to beat up against those immensities and the old man's irreverences, her skinny hands, her laughing eyes. How courageous to defy Bart and the weather.

Mrs. Swithin's Love of Nature, of God and of children is that of a mystic, a saint. She felt an illimitable rapture of joy on the visibility of the sun which seemed to embrace everything and then covering its face to forbear to look on human suffering. She saw God there. The sun was to be an embodiment of the wisdom and the spirit of the universe. The Sanskrit word 'Sutr' has been translated by Iqbal as Sun. Often ancient sages and sufis have interpreted God as light. According to Ibn'l Arabi God is light through which all objects are visible but He Himself is not visible. Iqbal has called the angels the children of light. Mrs. Swithin also has been called an angel by Isa. It is the typical Wordsworthian grasp of a relationship between the contemplative mind and the contemplated objects, an attempt to bring out the unique essence of items of observation.

Mrs. Swithin, unlike her brother, is capable of entering the world of a child (or see into the life of thing). Like Mrs. Ramsay she is a healer—an epitome of Universal Love which does not negate anything or anybody. She thinks not only of providing sandwiches, etc. for the people in the barn but also of feeding the fish in the lily pond:

"The fish had come to the surface.... 'Wait my darlings', she addressed them. She would trot into the house and ask Mrs. Sands for a biscuit."[38]

Loving both human being as well as animals, fish, etc. she represents an integrated being (possessing an androgynous vision) "who prayeth well, who loveth well, both man and bird and beast". She consoles William Dodges who says to her, "but you've healed me...."[39] Thakur says:

"He feels cleansed and healed as would a sick man before the grotto of the Virgin Mary at Lourdes. He feels purified. He becomes able to see the beauty of the visible world which took his breath away."[40]

Like Iqbal's Perfect Man both Mrs. Swithin and Isa are "boundless oceans" consisting of an universe within themselves—dynamic, merciful, loving and courageous. Like Jili's Perfect Man, they are capable of seeing into the life of things. They possess Higher Reason or 'Ishq'.

Miss La Trobe, "the queerest mixture of them all", organises the pageant and attempts to give a unity to history and in the end shows the present time and its scattered individualities. All the diverse elements of her audience are held together for creating synthesis. Those diverse individualities, "orts and fragments", are "collected together into one Miss La Trobe"[41] (or Virginia)—as we are extension of one another. Virginia's was an effort to 'make people see' so that they could save the pageant of the world, to save God's world like Aurobindo's and Iqbal's Perfect Man on whom "is laid the burden of past, the burden of mystery, the heavy and weary weight of this unintelligible world". Like Isa, she is a poet possessing an androgynous vision and is burdened "with what they drew from the earth, memories, possessions".[42] The "burden was laid on her in the cradle murmured by the waves"[43] or by the "sinking and falling mothers". Like the "bellowing cows" who had taken up the burden she represents "Light", Consciousness or "Higher Consciousness". The supreme creative power assumed individual form—the peace-gatherer, the creative artist—an epitome of Universal Love. Virginia Woolf's Perfect Man, the origin of the Universe, is the spirit of Divine Revelation, the Light of the Logos (the doctrine common between all the Scriptures). In *Between the Acts*, Isa and Mrs. Swithin are the spirits whence all things have their origin, who participate in the general life of Nature and "see into the life of things" like Wordsworth, the mystic seer and Al-Jili's Perfect Man. Virginia Woolf's concept of Perfect Man is fascinating and all-inclusive offering the divided self and the divided world a possibility to restore their identity reuniting the fragmented aspects of life. This very concept of Unity of Being, rooted in antiquity and presented later on by great mystics and sufis, is to be found at its best in this novel. Virginia Woolf has tried to heal the diseases (spiritual as well as moral) of the modern man by Universal Love or 'Ishq' so that he could be whole and entire.

Thus speaks Virginia: "I am a circle. It stirs. The circle is unbroken. The harmony complete."

And thus speaks Iqbal:

Hamah affaq ki geeram ki banigahe oo ra
Halqua-e-hast kiaz gardish-e-purkar manast.

The Universe that I comprehend at a glance
It is the circle by the campus of my being.

NOTES AND REFERENCES

1. Virginia Woolf, *Mrs. Dalloway*, Introduction. Modern Library Edition, p. 2.

2. Dr. Mohammad Iqbal, "The Doctrine of Absolute Unity as Expounded by Abd-al-Karim Al-Jili" in *Three Articles of Iqbal* (Pub. by Iqbal Academy Hyderabad, 1979), p. 9.
3. *Ibid.*
4. William Wordsworth, "Tintern Abbey", in *The Poetical Works of William Wordsworth,* ed. E. de. Selincourt (Oxford University Press, 1994), p. 259.
5. Virginia Woolf, *The Waves* (Penguin Books Ltd., Harmondsworth, England, Reprint, 1966), p. 120.
6. Virginia Woolf, *Between the Acts* (Triad and Panther Books Ltd., Granada Publishing), 1978, p. 316.
7. *Ibid.*, p. 103.
8. Professor S.P. Singh, *Sri Aurobindo and Jung* (Madhuchandandas Publications, 86), p. 65.
9. William Wordsworth, *The Poetical Works of William Wordsworth,* E. de. Selincourt (Oxford University Press, 1994), p. 259.
10. Professor S.P. Singh, *Sri Aurobindo and Jung*, pp. 62-63.
11. Gillian Beer, 'Virginia Woolf and Pre-History' in *Virginia Woolf—A Centenary Perspective*, ed. Eric Warner (Macmillan Press, London, 84), p. 111.
12. *Ibid.*
13. *Ibid.*, pp. 112-13.
14. Abdullah Yusuf Ali, Translation of *The Holy Quran*, Amana Corporation U.S.A., 1989 (New Rev. Edition), pp. 408-09.
15. *Ibid.*
16. This quotation has been extracted by Ms. Goodman from *Dead Sea Scrolls* and included in her book *A New Approach to Human Heart* (Macmillan, London), p. 1124.
17. *Ibid.*
18. *Ibid.*, p. 1125.
19. Evellyn Haller, "Isis Unveiled" in *Virginia Woolf and the Feminist Slant*, p. 113.
20. *Ibid.*, p. 118.
21. *Ibid.*
22. *Ibid.*
23. Virginia Woolf, *Between the Acts*, p. 25.
24. *Ibid.*, p. 151.

25. N.C. Thakur, *The Symbolism of Virginia Woolf,* London (Oxford University Press, New York, Toronto, 1965), p. 141.
26. Dr. Mohammad Iqbal, "The Doctrine of Absolute Unity", p. 5.
27. Virginia Woolf, *Between the Acts*, p. 127.
28. *Ibid.,* p. 12.
29. *Ibid.,* p. 89.
30. *Ibid.*
31. Virginia Woolf, *Between the Acts*, p. 103.
32. *Ibid.*
33. Sir Aurobindo, *The Life Divine*, Vol. II (Calcutta, Arya Publishing House, 1919), p. 557.
34. Virginia Woolf, *Between the Acts*, p. 131.
35. Professor A.A. Ansari, "An Existential Approach to Iqbal" in *Iqbal Essays and Studies*, ed. by Prof. A.A. Ansari (Ghalib Academy, New Delhi, 1978), p. 127.
36. Virginia Woolf, *Between the Acts*, p. 21.
37. *Ibid.*, p. 95.
38. *Ibid.*, p. 149.
39. *Ibid.*
40. N.C. Thamur, *The Symbolism of Virginia Woolf*, p. 146.
41. *Ibid.,* p. 136.
42. *Ibid.,* p. 114.
43. *Ibid.*

❑❑❑

17

Atwood's 'I' and 'Thou'

PADMA SRINIVASAN

Atwood practises a totally unconventional style in her poetry to initiate the reader into a new perception. Her early poems exhibit her distrust of the everyday world loaded with deceptive appearances and emotional shallowness. Opposed to this world of gossamer, she desires to show to her readers the necessity of conducting a 'journey of the interior'. She also believes that "It is only through descents into the psyche and the rediscovery of the primitive and mythick dimension of both mind and world that one can experience wholeness."[1] Atwood then, is willing to take up a hazardous quest for self-identity. The poems, hence, yield to philosophical dimensions, with the poet's concern to carry on a 'I-thou' relationship within herself.

This paper is an attempt to see the various facets of this relationship and the progression of the interior journey of the poet.

Mikhail Bakhtin, while constructing his 'Philosophical anthropology', attempts to elaborate a coherent aesthetic theory, and more specifically a description of the creative act. To do so, he is compelled to posit a general conception of human existence, where the 'other' plays a decisive role. Bakhtin affirms that it is impossible to conceive of any being which does not have relations to the 'other'. He says:

> In life, we do this at every moment; we appraise ourselves from the point of view of others, we attempt to understand the transgredient moments of our very consciousness and to take them into account through

> the other...in a word, constantly and intensely, we oversee and apprehend the reflections of our life in the plane of consciousness of other men.[2] There are elements of consciousness external to it but nonetheless absolutely necessary for its totalization. Bakhtin asserts that we can never see ourselves as a whole; the 'other' is inevitable, even for a while, to have the perception of the self, Bakhtin's concept of the 'other' can be well applied to Atwood's poem to understand the underlying dialogic principle.

Atwood's first major book of poetry, the *Circle Gam*[3] shows her maturity, "the authority and control, now recognized as integral to the Atwood voice...as well as the distinctive aural-visual dynamic of the style, and [her] intense preoccupation with the double aspect of life".[4]

The opening poem of the collection, 'This is a Photograph of me' points to the key factor of the 'I-thou' relationship that of adjustment of perceptions; the photograph has been taken some time ago, and so has lost its lustre and figures. The poet herself scans for us and takes us through the blurred contours of photograph, identifying the landmarks for us, until she arrives at a lake bordered with low hills, and then, there is the sudden reversal in the poem; the next twelve lines given within the parentheses, at once shift our sight from the familiar to the unfamiliar and offer a different perception altogether. The poet who has conducted the tour in the photograph, suddenly turns eerie and says:

> The photograph was taken the day after I drowned. I am in the lake, in the centre of the picture, Just under the surface.

The reader is jolted to reality, as he is compelled, like the poet, to identify the Jungian 'shadow', by staring into the lake of unconscious. The reader is exposed to yet another perception that the 'you' in the poem is not after all the reader, but the 'other' of the 'I' of the poem; the blurred landscape in the photograph is the 'mindscape' and the photograph itself is not a physical, ordinary photograph, but the self's photograph with its ever-changing contours. The poem challenges our perception immediately, says Sherril Grace, "asking us to adjust our sight, to find out where this particular voice is coming from.... The ironic double structure of this poem, its emphasis on seeing and its sharp visual imagery, urges us to rediscover our senses and our relationship with the world."[5] The adjustment is not merely with the outside world; it is an adjustment within, to adjust without. In other words, identification of the 'other' eventually leads to a circle game.

'The Circle Game' juxtaposes the innocent children's game of the outside world and the deceitful inner game played by the 'I' and 'you'. While the children lose themselves in their circle game, unmindful of what is around them, the 'I' and 'you' seem to be caught in a "Claustrophobic entrampment," neither willing to adapt with each other nor ready to separate from each other. The poet wonders at the concentration of the children-in-play:

> ...their eyes fixed on
> the empty moving spaces just in
> front of them.

Their movement seems to move the space before them in which they could easily adjust themselves. On the contrary, the egocentric selves, the 'I' and 'you' continue to watch each other with "Taut curiosity",

> ...caught
> in the monotony of wandering
> from room to room, shifting the place of
> our defences....

The congestion is too much and the 'I' wants to have its freedom by breaking the circle game. It would do anything to get release from this ever-watchful 'Other'. As Sherrill Grace rightly says: "the growing sense of defeat and impasse climax in this title poem. The poem portrays the misperception of the roles one assumes and also the games one plays with his own self, which is tantamount to deceiving his own being."[6] The images of rooms, mirrors and circles convey the idea of the indispensable Jungian 'Shadow'.

'Camers' once again exploits the photograph—image, with the difference. The 'I' is maturing and it now knows only too well that the 'other' is going for its 'Organized moment'; its glassy eye can nevermore cheat the 'I'. The remnants of the confused, earlier 'I' are still visible. But, the 'I' has learnt some escape-routes. Moreover, an unknown gush of spirit, like that of the wind of the 'elgonyi', tribe,[7] sweeps away the 'I' from the mad, monotonous circle game. The 'I' is carried away in a great speed to some destination unseen.

> that small black speck
> travelling towards the horizon
> at almost the speed of light
> is me

The 'I' at a last has got its freedom; its journey has begun. The poem ends without a period, suggesting the timeless endless travel of the 'I'. Nevertheless, a speck in the cosmic wilderness means the loss of total identity. However, it cannot afford to lose its identity now, as it has to conduct the journey of the interior.

'Journey to the Interior' expands the landscape metaphor suggested in the first poem. The 'other' as a cosmic expansion seems to be too much and the poet finds it easier to withdraw herself and conduct and interior journey with its steep ways and pitfalls. The speaker "explores the labyrinth of the self...only to discover that she is enclosed in the final, most dangerous circle".[8] However, dangerous it might be, it is her own land whose geography she may not know; but, it gives her an extremely comfortable feeling, as she commences her meandering route. Small details and irrelevant information distract her. At times, she is afraid that she is once again caught in the limbo; whoever enters he has to abandon hope. There is no guarantee of safe return; there is no aid to lead her aright. But, in spite of all the handicaps, the 'I' is sure of itself:

> Whatever I do I must keep my head. I know it is easier for me to lose my way forever here, than in other landscapes

The periodless end again is suggestive of the continuous dangerous, journey. Most of the poems in the collection focus upon the tension between the opposites and the poet "explores the fallibility of human perception and the concomitant changer of the egocentric self. Man distorts and delimits life and makes it as an endless circle game".[9] Freedom from this monotonous wheel is necessary, but it is dangerous also. But, one has to start an interior journey to find "a place of absolute unformed beginning,"[10] to be an Amphibian, to wade in the Saltish waters and touch the shores of our own land. To become a child once again is to receive a sense of reassurance, which 'The Settlers' offers.

> Now horses graze
> inside this fence of ribs, and
> children run, with green smiles (not
> knowing where) across
> the fields of our open hands:

What Sherrill Grace says is true: "These simple images of happy children at once with nature offer an alternative vision to the earlier traps of self and reason."[11] But at the same time, one cannot forget that the songs of innocence have to become necessarily the songs of experience, which means once again the claustrophobic entrampment of the limbo-game. "The ring-o, ring-o roses", the action-song of the I-Thou has to go on, so long as the misconception and unadaptability between the two continues.

The 'I-Thou' pattern is continued in the 'Nine to Untitled poems'[12] which make audible the mind's inaudible conversations, and define the psychopathology of everyday life and convert space as a function of time. Uncertainty seems to be the only certain thing. 'Relationship' is the 'leit-motif' of these poems. Relationships range from the familiar to the intimate, expressing all shades of emotions such as love, friendliness, disgust, wonder and even awe. The explorations of the relationship between the 'I' and the 'other' sometimes tend to become rhetorically obscure on account of excessive condensation of thought; however, even this obscurity appears to be functional in the sense that it underscores both the complexity of human relationship and subtlety of poetic expressions. In short, they register an interior journey towards self-identity.

The first poem of the series opens with a sort of prufrockian pronouncement. The mood is one of irritation. Existence is impossible without relationship and relationships, formal or intimate, are never free from friction or frustration. The poem seems to explore an intimate relationship the 'I' of the external world and the 'you' of the internal world. The 'you' is the 'other' of the 'I'. The attempt to change the 'other' seems to have ultimately failed. Though the nature of the change desired is not specific in the poem, the tone and the urge point to something important. The poet would rather change herself into the impossible, say a bark or a shrub, rather than try to change the 'other' any more. The cataloguing of the impossible indicates the extent of efforts taken by the poet, to change the 'other'. She is even prepared, as she puts it:

> ...collapse across our
> bed clutching my heart
> and pull the nostalgic sheet up over
> my waxed farewell smile
> which would be inconvenient but final.

In spite of the disgust and frustration revealed, the point to ponder about is the 'love', in the ultimate analysis, is the underlying factor to accept the 'other' as it is. This should not be misconstrued as the Narcissistic self-consuming Love; but a love that accepts the demands of the 'other' and effect at best, a half-hearted reconciliation. The tough, daring 'I', conducts a duel with the tougher 'other', resulting in an irritating acceptance. The 'other', says Bakhtin, is the elementary principle of cosmos. A person had to recognise his 'Other' and engage himself with it in a dialogue. This dialogical mode ultimately leads one to self-scrutiny and recognition of the 'Being'. It is a never ending process. To engage in a dialogue means to enter in conflict and without conflict, progress is impossible. Acceptance in the beginning leads to surrender, and this surrender is to the supreme, 'I'. Needless to say, that this is what is said in *Bhagavad Gita*. A significant point to note in the first poem is the poet's gender-consciousness. Only when she comes out of this inhabitation, she enjoys a transcendental bliss as expressed in the ninth poem. For a moment, the poet is released from the agonising compulsion of her 'other' self which refuses to acknowledge the yearnings of the 'I'. The 'I' meekly confesses that 'This is not something I wanted'. But there extends a vast incredible unlimited 'Sky', with all its threats and promises, luring the 'I' to enjoy the sheer expanse. The entire inner space seems to be grown with hard boulders of which, the poet has realized only a 'Precipice'. Once again, the poet is in a confusion whether to accept the freedom of the 'other' or the joy offered by the precipice. Her entire voice is now absorbed in the expanse; the experience creates an inner strength, an indomitable will in her. This is the time of her release, her awakening, since her 'other' is now asleep. She now decides to enter the vastness offered, the moment of her transcendental awakening and here her inner journey begins. As in *The Circle Game* poems, the last line of the poem is not punctuated with full-stop. The suggestion is that her real journey, from innocence to experience has just commenced and she has miles to go. Atwood's image for 'expanse' with all its boulders is suggestive of the need to put the 'other' into sleep and thus escape its demonic clutches. The warning is that the demon is asleep only for a while, and is likely to wake up with greater force and vigour.

The seven poems in between these two records the conflict between the 'I' and its 'other'. Their different facets are presented in a verbal idiom, totally feminine. Atwood's claim is to create a psychic space, a space equivalent to the cosmic space. One who sets in this breath-taking process, is baffled and bewildered. Atwood rightly puts it. "Stranded in the midst of a vast space which nobody has made sense out of for you, you settle down to map making, charting the territory, the discovery of where things are in relation to each other, the extraction of meaning."[13] In brief, the confrontation between the 'I' and 'you' is irksome and painful, but the dialogue has to continue, to effect a merger, to conduct the journey towards the Higher Reality.

NOTES

1. Margaret Atwood, *An Anthology of Canadian Literature in English*, Vol. I (ed.), Russell Brown & Bonna Bennett (Toronto: OUP, 1982), p. 454.

2. Quoted by Tzvetan Todorov, Mikhail Bakhtin: The Dialogical Principal, tr. Wlad Godzich (Minnesota: University Press, 1984), p. 94.
3. *The Circle Game* (Toronto: House of Annansi Press Limited, 1978). Hereafter called *CG*.
4. Sherrill E. Grace, "Introduction", *The Circle Game,* p. 10.
5. *Ibid.*, p. 11.
6. *Ibid.*
7. Referred to by G.G. Jung, "Archetypes of the Collective Unconscious," *Twentieth Century Criticism*, ed. William J. Handy and Max Westbrook (New Delhi: Light and Life Publishers, 1974), p. 215.
8. Sherrill Grace, *Circle Game,* p. 12.
9. *Ibid.*, p. 14.
10. 'Migration: C.P.R.' *Circle Game*, p. 65.
11. *Ibid.*, p. 14.
12. *New American and Canadian Poetry.* ed. John Gill (Boston: Beacon Press, 1971), pp. 9-16.
13. *Second Words.* Quoted in *An Anthology of Canadian Literature in English,* Vol. I, ed. Russell Brown and Donna Bennett (Toronto: OUP, 1982), p. 455.

❑❑❑

18

The Feminine Predicament in Margaret Atwood's *The Edible Woman*

F.A. INAMDAR

In the introduction to Atwood's novel, *The Edible Woman*,[1] she says: "it is pro-feminist rather than feminist: there was no women's movement in sight when I was composing the book in 1965." We need not remind Atwood that women's movement proper started with Hardy's *Jude the Obscure* with Sue Bridehead as a feminist. Marian in *The Edible Woman* is a further step towards such a trend. Women like Marian and Ainsley are in search of a destiny that should transcend and replace, the domestic round. They are dissatisfied with man-made values. They are reluctant to be mere wives to be that is to be lose ones existence. It is to become a commodity for consumption. Therefore, they are in search of their freedom and liberty. They are eager to break the balance between their public and private lives. They are bewitched by the lure of a distinct identity and worldly fame by a secure and lucrative job. They have an instinctive dislike for their home and hearth. They hardly recognize what women have to bring into the world of men to make their lives whole and meaningful. They are eager to achieve their goals by sacrificing their nature. For them autonomy is the hallmark of their psychic health. To get married is to invite subordination and obligation. To get children by marriage is to make a mess of one's life. For them fear of divorce does not have heavily over their heads but they voluntarily intend to enjoy that liberty. As Virginia Woolf said that she had to kill the Angel of the house before it killed her. Thus, they are portrayed as rebels of established norms.

Atwood's masculine characters in the novel are Peter, Trigger, Len Slank, Joe, Dick, the underwear Man, Fischer Smythe and Trevor. Atwood's interest pieces to the author's thesis of antimarriage, antihusband and antifamily motifs. Her feminine portraits in the novel are Marian, Ainsley, Emmy, Lucy, Millie, Mrs Grot, Mrs Bogue, Mrs Dodge, and Clara. They are used to evoke women's painful realities; their suffering and endurance of life's perversities. They are skeptics and hardly have any ideals. Their feminine views tend to reveal an undercurrent of egoism, self-involvement, self-centeredness. These tensions are represented through psychological dimensions. These psychic tensions are also expressed through zoological, claustrophobic, atmospheric and food imagery. My aim in this paper is to explore these.

I

Sex in Atwood's *The Edible Woman* is used to evoke masculine blindness to the women's point of view. Peter takes Marian into his bathroom because he desires love under the shower. Complying with Peter's wish for a showery sex, she suddenly feels that perhaps Peter really "thought of me as a lavatory fixture" (pp. 59-62). It is most degrading for Marian to call the "Palace of love" a lavatory fixture. Marian would have easily refused to make love in that place. Putting the blame on Peter like this is not consistent with Marian's character, through it represents a strong antisex and antiman example. It represents forcefully Atwood's thesis that woman is important to man not because she is herself but because she is useful, usable. As Clara in *Sons and Lovers* makes it clear: "But is it me you want, or is it It?" (357). It makes Paul Morel feel guilty. He thinks whether he left Clara out of count, and take simply women? (357).[2] Peter's reaction at Trigger's wedding is that the bride is predatory and malicious. She has "sucked" poor trigger into the domestic void. This reaction is Atwood's rather than Peter's. Had it been so, he would not have gone after Marian to coax her into marrying him. In this context, Marian rightly thinks of the bride as a "vacuum cleaner" (64).

Len Slank is a "self-consciously lecherous skirt-chaser" (87). Yet he is an "inverted moralist". Atwood uses him for her point of view in making him a cynic and an idealist. The pure and unobtainable girl was attractive to this idealist and the cynic viewed her as spoiled and threw her away. For the thematic intent of the novel, he is portrayed as a beast enjoying and discarding its prey. When he is received into fathering a baby for Ainsley he shouts like a frenzied spaniel: "All you clawed scaly bloody predatory whoring fucking bitches can go straight to hell" (215). It is antifeminist comment in a feminist fiction.

Joe is a little short of the American Dependent husband. We see him busy cooking food and serving, and changing the kids dipers. His philosophy is Atwood's. According to him, getting married attacks a woman's personality and spoils the image of herself.

Joe, the wifely husband is appropriate for the feminist novel, but getting married is in no way attacking the personality of the women. It is, on the contrary, making life meaningful. It is wrong on Atwood's part to make him say that after marriage woman's core, her personality, her own self is useless to her. Children alone know what mother is to them. Her status and value in the family circle is usually higher than that of her husband. Had Atwood known it from the Indian mothers, she would not have had such philosophy. Wedding is a matter of adjustment. It is a give and take. Here wife is a complement to the husband.

Dick used in the novel as a foil to Peter. He is a neurotic. It is brought out through his obsession for ironing and breaking and smashing the things to satisfy his male ego. He too is a mouth piece for Atwood's views on anti-marriage. For him, Marian's marriage would be "another substitute for the laundromat." Fitting to the theme of the novel, Dick has "the gaunt shape of a starved animal in time of famine" (17). This novel has no place for robust and sexy men who can be proper matches to women. Therefore, Duncan is more dead than alive. Significantly, he likes museums and relishes to mediate on immortality. This indicates his fossilized self. It is his "favourite mummy-case" (186), "the shrivelled figures inside". He is in two minds to decide whether he is a homosexual or heterosexual. His interest in immortality and museum Mummy-cases make him say that his friends would turn him into an "amoeba" (201). For him being a person is getting too complicated. Such a person is suitably warning a freedom loving Marian with "I'm not letting you into this bed until you go in there and peel that junk off your face. Fornication may be all very well in its way, but if I am going to come out looking like a piece of flowered wallpaper I reject it" (253). This rejection is intended as an antisexual intention much to the liking of Marian. He adds another dimension to his important love making:

> I feel like some kind of little stunted creature crawling over the surface of a huge mass of flesh. There's just altogether too much flesh around here. It's suffocating. (253)

Fischer's views on population, birth control and the wiping of human beings from the surface with the process beginning again is not in keeping with the theme of the book. It reminds us of Anthony Burgess's *Wanting Seed*:

> Another black death...civilization as we known it all but obliterated, then birth would be essential again, then we could return to...the old gods, the earth goddess, the goddess of waters, the goddess of birth and growth and death. (200)

II

Marian is a major figure carrying the burden of Atwood's thesis. She is a psychic case. Peter and Len consider her as a "hysterical type" (74). At the hotel Plaza, since she is ignored by Peter and Len, she displays one of her psychic gimmicks:

> I was running along the sidewalk. I looked back over my shoulder as I ran.... Each lamp port as I passed it became a distance-marker on my course: it seemed an achievement and accomplishment of some kind to

> put them one by one behind me.... I grinned at them and waved at some as I went by...I was filled with the exhilaration of speed.... (72)

Probably, it is Marian's way of showing her superiority over Peter and Len. In fact, a very annoying and an eccentric feat at that. Again at Len's department, she feels neglected and "felt deflated...but there was no outlet for it" (71). She seeks an escape in some strange and curious action and finds shelter under the bed where she is forced to lie absolutely flat against the floor. She thinks she "had dug herself a private burrow" (76). This is a psychic activity. Her escape under the dark bed is entering into the subconscious and her emergence from it is her realization of her status in the male-dominated world:

> There would be no dignity at all in crawling out from under the bedspread, trailing dust, like a weevil coming out of a flour barrel. (76)

With similar psychic implications are used her cake, dolls, and mirror image. Robert Lecker[3] says that her rejection of food is a rejection of male-dominated culture. The preparation of the cake and eating it is a form of reconciliation. She herself is a mixture of consumer and consumed. Moreover, her cake is a celebration. She is born again in eating it; as her ignorant self is dead and the self with awareness is reborn. It is re-enactment of a ritual feast. It is coming together of human and divine, individual with the others, a woman with her own body and feelings. Like the cake-doll, Marain thinks of herself as a kind of a doll. The two dolls—one blonde and the other dark represent two sides of her personality. Her world is divided into eater and eaten, into the good and evil. The doll is her symbolic child. She rejects her childish doll-like feminity of her former self and affirms her adult, enlightened self. During the engagement party, she looks into the mirror and finds: "...a vague damp form in a rumpled dressing gown...the blonde eyes nothing...the dark one looking deeper...the two overlapping images drawing further and further away from each other.... By the strength of their separate visions they were trying to pull her apart" (219). In a mirror scene previous to this Marian has refused to grow up. Now it is a reflection of oneself, a perception of truth not seen before. In Indian society, we have girls like Marian who have willingly gate-crashed into spinster-hood and have chosen to sacrifice their marital status for their liberty and freedom.

Through Ansley's activities Atwood probably predicts the direction into which the femininity would take in future. Her image in cocacola glass and her contemplation of her own reflection in it reveals a truth that she herself is a hypocrite. She sees the reflection of her real self in it. In Indian society fortunately, we don't have Ainsley type girls. It would have ruined our image.

Clara is Atwood's anti-marriage and anti-children character. Though she married for love, she has made a mess of her domestic life. To Marian she appears "like a strange vegetable growth" (32). Clara greets her pregnancy first with astonishment; second with dismay and third with inert fatalism. Atwood takes pleasure in decrying motherhood by showing Clara's pregnant body bulgingly obvious, looking like "a boa-constrictor that has swallowed a watermelon" (36). The novelist comes heavily on children through Clara's metaphors for them as barnacles encrusting a ship and limpets clinging to a rock (36). Had Atwood seen Indian mother-hood, she would have created different Clara. We are not short of Indian Sitas and Savitris. But the only thing that we lack is that the career-women should get enough time to rear children. Three should be different leave arrangements for women to not to sacrifice their domestic duties for the pursuit of their careers.

III

Atwood has attempted to convey the theme of woman as an edible commodity for man through her image sequences. The zoological imagery predominates; the thematic nexus of the novel is either to eat or be eaten. In this context, it is a fitting image for Len to term him as a whale to virginity (119). Ainsley sitting on the wicker basket chair reminds Marian of "a pitcher-plant in a swamp waiting for some insect to be attracted, drowned and digested" (75). While Marian's empty mind is "as though someone had scooped out the inside of my skull like a cantaloupe..." (83). The office virgins "...squatted at their desks, load-like and sluggish, blinking and opening and closing their mouths" (18). For Marian the simple activities like drinking and sitting are expressed through animal imagery. She drinks tomato juice "blood thirstily" (83). She sits like "escaping from a giant squid" (84). The men looking at Lucy are "ravenous as pike" (112). Ainsley's baby is not going to be a chicken but a lovely nice baby (160). Marian is frightened as a sea anemone to look at the yolk of an egg. Atwood's imagery is local and particular. It does not have deeper layers of meaning; it is situational. With this dimension we have atmospheric images. The inner struggle of Marian's mind is evoked in description of her skin being "stifled"; in her being "enclosed in a layer of moist dough" (37). Marian's dull and suffocating day is predicated by nature: "This day...was windless and oppressive...the air hung heavily like invisible steam, so that the colours and outlines of objects were blurred" (44). "The invisible steam" and the blurred distance adequately convey her mental confusion and her dubious future. Such prefigurative imagery indicates the break between Peter and Marian: "In the distance the thunder was beginning" (79). Immediately after Marian is husked into the car, as if to indicate the emotional releases the rain lashes. Similarly, Peter's proposal.... "How do you think we'd be, married? 'Corresponds with a tremendous electric flash'...it reflects the one for the other: '...I could see myself, small and oval, mirrored in his eyes'" (83). Food images convey woman as a commodity for consumption; Marian's dream makes her feet "like melting jelly" (43).

Lucy has "confectionery eyes" and "delicious dresses" (112). With similar implication Marian tells her doll: "you look delicious. Very appetizing: And that's what will happen to you; that is what you get for being food" (270). Claustrophobic images express one's psychic impasse and cul-de-sac. After trigger's wedding, Peter thinks that here his "...pacing up and down in the kitchen, but it was too narrow, so he sat down again" (64). With this implication objects such as a tray are used to indicate Marian's mind. There are samples *per se* and not an exhaustive image pattern in the novel. A great deal can be explored in this direction.

Margaret Atwood has forgotten her points raised in *Survival*.[4] For her Australian woman is an ice-woman. She has to be kneaded to respond to the male's demands. 'A Stone Angel' is shown an emblem of Australian Woman-hood. Women in Australian literature are shown to be either dying during delivery, aborting or giving birth to still-born babies. Against her thesis in *Survival* we have in this novel babies born just for the asking. Clara is shown as a baby producing machine. This view of women in *The Edible Woman* is opposed to Australian background. Such antithetical evocation of Canadian women-hood is not in keeping with the Canadian ethos.

NOTES

1. Margaret Atwood, *The Edible Woman* (London: Virago Press, 1980). All subsequent quotations are from this text.
2. D.H. Lawrence, *Sons and Lovers* (Madras: Macmillan, India), 1989.
3. Robert Lecker, "Janus through the looking glass: Atwood's First three Novels," *The Art of Margaret Atwood: Essays in Criticism*, eds. Arnold E. Davidson and Cathy N. Davidson (Toronto: Anansi Press, 1981), pp. 179-80.
4. Atwood Margaret, *Survival: A Thematic Guide to Canadian Literature* (Toronto: Anansi, 1972).

❑❑❑

19

A Doll's House—A Reassessment

NAJMA MAHMOOD

Ibsen in *A Doll's House* has dealt with a universal and eternal theme—the conflict between the individual and society, between reality and illusion, between true and false idealism and between innocence and experience. This play, which was created by a visionary, a mystic, a philosopher, an idealist, an individualist, shook the whole Europe. Ibsen, a moral and social rebel, is acknowledged to be an ardent supporter of women's rights. But he was not a feminist in the traditional sense as his objective was to depict life and its problems realistically and objectively. He was against all those aspects of contemporary living that obstructed the free self-realization of an individual's personality—hypocrisies, conventions, fear of social criticism, rigidities, bigotries of institutionalized religion and all those factors, which, under the guise of duty and loyalty or moral obligation, stop the growth of the personality and inhibit the natural development of the individual and shut him off from genuine living. Ibsen was interested in freedom which is something personal—a matter of individual responsibility. He disliked outdated attitudes and opinions which he found inappropriate for the new individual. He was anxious to revise current thinking about what one owed to oneself. He clearly pointed out that a concern for himself was one of the supreme duties of a person. Again and again he returns to the idea that our society is essentially false, that it lives by a set of traditional lies and carefully hushes up everything that might reveal their falsity. It is a society which has no real principle except that appearances must be saved at any cost. He stood vehemently for freedom from all instruments of human servitude, the codifications of law and the dogmas.

Ibsen, a philosopher, has used drama to ask questions rather than supply answers to them. He had faith in man's capacity for good (a Wordsworthian influence). He had belief in human perfectibility and possibility of improvement. Being an individualist and an idealist, he had faith in potential integrity of man's dignity and self-respect. His plays insist that marriage is a union of souls, an association by free choice and held together by mutual trust.

The highest aim of Feminist Movement, as Virginia Woolf, the great 20th century artist-seer, perceived it, "was to create favourable, adjustment in the inner lives of the sexes." It reminds us of Ibsen's philosophy as presented in *A Doll's House.* Virginia Woolf was undoubtedly the most genuine, positive and humanistic interpretation of the Feminist Movement. A marriage had to be consummated within the mind itself of every individual, a union of the feminine and masculine principles.

Ibsen has tried to interpret the unwritten laws of the mind. Ibsen's humanism was thus based on not only his faith in the equality of the sexes but also on prefect understanding between them. Like Virginia Woolf he contributed something original to the cause of women's emancipation and their rights. He felt that it was desirable to solve the problems of women's rights along with others but that had not been the whole truth. His task had been the description of humanity.

A Doll's House, after its first presentation was celebrated most for its social theme—the emancipation of woman. Men felt ashamed of themselves. Selfish, egocentric males felt hurt. Any discussion about this play was strictly prohibited at parties and social gatherings. Females naturally felt elated.

Ibsen and the modern audiences of *A Doll's House* consider its importance to lie in its concern for the true basis of wider human relationships. Whether Nora Helmer has the right, whether she is justified as a woman to leave her husband, home and children, is of secondary importance to the significance of leaving them as a seriously thinking individual human being.

Ibsen considers it to be humiliating and degrading for a woman to live together when one refuses to accept the other as a socially responsible individual with independent ideas. That Nora could have some serious thought was something unbelievable for Torvald Helmer. For him independent action was undesirable in wife.

Nora had been a doll-wife living in A Doll's House playing with her doll-children. When the "wonderful thing"[1] (the words which are symbolic and ironical) did not happen, when her husband failed to support her in a crisis and turned against her as an "unscrupulous", "irresponsible"[2] woman, she realized that her whole life with her father and husband had been a doll-life. Her own personality had been subjugated and her worth as an individual completely ignored. The revelation that "before all else I am a reasonable human being" required decisive step. So Nora left her husband and children in order to learn for herself the conditions of the world: "to see who is right, the world or I".[3]

Ibsen uses the word "home" symbolically for the home-country, the home town, the family, etc. *A Doll's House* analyzes such "home conditions" of the conventional organizations of domestic and legal affairs. Leaving home, for a bright lad, is an essential part of the process of self-assertion, a necessary step on the way of self-reliance. To escape from home is to win release from the place that stunts one's growth, stifles one's breath, distorts one's values and ruins one's opportunities.

Ibsen himself was in this special sense a homeless person, a voluntary exile. He insists that contact with the outside broadens the mind and liberates the spirit. The domestic aspects of "home" are thus taken up and scrutinized in *A Doll's House*. Here "home" is seen as an institution tending to inhibit the development of the authentic self. For a child to be treated by his or her father as Nora, was to suffer a complete eclipse of personality. As the title echoes, it is to endure becoming a doll for the gratification of others. For the married woman of Nora's day the home could be as disabling as it is for the child. For Nora finds herself to just a home-comfort, a luxury, something flattering the male-ego of the husband at the cost of destroying hers. She becomes a possession, a property. A self-respecting woman has no other options to advance on her way to self-reliance but to quit her home.

"For a man", Helmer says, "there's something indescribably moving and very satisfying in knowing that he has forgiven his wife".[4] It is as though it made her his property in a double sense. He has given her a new life and she becomes in a way, both his wife and at the same time his child. So immediately marriage becomes a microcosm (a miniature representation of the system of the male-dominated society at large, at which a woman cannot be herself. It is male-society with laws drafted by men and with male counsels and justices judging feminine conduct from male point of view. Nora's inbred faith in authority and in male-domination clashes with her natural instincts making it a drama of inner conflict. Ibsen, by such devices builds up his case against the 'home' as the source of hypocrisy, bigotry, blurred vision, and possessiveness, the place that confines. Strange things happen to truth in such surroundings—perversions, the garbling and dissembling and pretence.

Suppression, Nora's "big secret,"[5] is of course the pivot about which the action turns. Exploited by Krogstad, shared with Mrs. Lynde and withheld in terror from Torvald's and Rank's mortal secret is similarly a matter to share with some and withhold from others. Secondly, both Torvald and Nora need the opiate of day dreaming to help them to bear the reality of their lives, Torvald indulges himself with the pretence that he and Nora are secretly in love, newly-wed and Nora dreams of a rich admirer who will leave her all his money. While they knowingly daydream, they also unknowingly deceive themselves. Torvald with the image of himself as the broad-shouldered courageous male longing only for the opportunity to save his wife from distress; and Nora with a belief that her marriage is a source of genuine happiness when in reality it is nothing but a hollow sham. All the time she is acting a part up to the role of an irresponsible scatterbrained that her marriage seems to have cast her for, masquerading as the helpless little doll so utterly dependent on her strong-willed husband.

The entire menage (domestic establishment) is based on misrepresentation, deception and falsehood in small thing as well as big. It was a fraud that had to be exposed. Nora's crime is sublime one as she wants to transgress the insensate and unsympathetic laws created by male-dominated society. Her deeper motives are admirable and honourable.

Ibsen's grasp of the intricacies of female psychology is miraculous. The mystic in him gave him a sensitive understanding of the mysterious invisible life of woman. His knowledge of woman is intricate and accurate. Women, he opined, should not be judged by man's laws as their psyche is different from that of men (they are more intuitive than men). Thus like John Stuart Mill, Ibsen was a moral and social rebel, a great humanist, a critic of traditional morality, social laws and institutions. He felt the need of a revolution in human psyche, and was a psychiatrist curing the diseases of the soul. He was a dramatic poet of the individualistic side of man's nature. Individual, according to him, could try to become an admirable human being without the help of society. He felt that woman had not been considered to be an individual possessing a soul. Therefore, he defended her cause vehemently. The quality of fearless individualism makes Ibsen's women strange and distasteful to many people. Such fallacies have been built about women particularly in plays and novels. In most of the fiction, women were either good or bad. But to treat woman as a rounded human being was not in vogue. Ibsen has presented rounded women. Being a man of learning and knowledge he knew the mysteries of woman's inner self.

The women of saga, their wild, deep nature, fascinated him. Sharpness, warmth, strength crept into many plays of Ibsen a combination of ice and flame. Susanna, Ibsen's wife was an embodiment of saga womanhood. In *A Doll's House*, Nora reminds us of saga women. She is wild and deep, possessing warmth, strength and intuitive bent of mind. She asserts her independence by finally leaving her husband. This bold step stirred up such controversy that Ibsen felt called upon to suggest an alternative ending.

A Doll's House is a true story of Laura Keiter who had borrowed money for her husband's treatment and had kept it a mystery. Ibsen persuaded her to tell it to her husband. She was divorced as borrowing was considered to be unwomanly and illegal. It annoyed Ibsen to the extent of fury. Thus was created *A Doll's House* which shook the whole Europe. "Everything", Ibsen says, "that I have written, has the closest possible connection with what I have lived through even though it has been my personal experience". He derived his intensity from his dreaming and solitary self. The theme chosen by him has a close connection with the adventures of his soul.

Nora has been called an infantile doll-wife who has failed to grow up. She has been condemned to be childish and immature. She has been misunderstood due to the lack of visionary insight. Children can be more than mere puppets. They are individuals. "Child", to Wordsworth, is "father of man" and may prove to be astonishingly brave and devoted. Children are innocent and unwordly capable of loving much more intensely than the elders. There dwells God in their hearts. There is that innocence in Nora which has been eulogised both by Blake and Wordsworth.

When Torvald's health and life depends on a journey South, Nora finds the money by forging her father's signature. To her eyes, with a woman's commonsense and directness, a feigned signature seems in such circumstances a mere formality for her father would surely have signed had he not been at death-bed. For repaying that debt she copies documents in secret and saves half her dress money. Is this immaturity and childishness? Some critics have wrongly suggested that Nora really wanted a Mediterranean holiday for herself and was merely romancing her husband's illness.

Children's direct clear vision is not necessarily foolish. The Greeks, said the old Egyptian priest, are always children. Yet the Greeks were no fools. Wise simplicity of children has been admired in the Gospels. The ideal is not for either partner to keep the other as pet nor for both to become competitors. True marriage, something sacred, is partnership and companionship.

The drama ends with Nora's departure. Whether she succeeds in finding the answers to her questions and becoming the individual she feels she is meant to be is not revealed to us.

Ibsen once said: "A dramatist's business is not to answer questions but merely to ask them."

A Doll's House is one of the best examples of question asking. Are duties to husband and children more sacred than duties to oneself? Does the individual have the right and freedom to do what Nora did? The answer must come from the audience.

Ibsen used the language which could reveal the inner recesses of human mind—the depths and mysteries which are unrevealed even to characters themselves. The action of *A Doll's House* is tense, exciting and fast. Both a fine sense of action and a careful character development are combined in this play to make it one of the most popular of Ibsen's plays.

A Doll's House is a remarkable play because there has been presented in it a remarkable saga woman with wild, deep nature possessing warmth, strength, sharpness, innocence, and self-respect who awakens her responsibility as an individual; and as a result throws off the yoke of subjugation imposed on her by her selfish, shallow and egotistical husband. She had a self which combined in it reason and intuition. Nora is an emblem of love and sympathy and therefore of light. Her heart is pure in which a lamp shines. Purity and sincerity of heart is a light which God introduces into the heart. It has been said by a great saint:

> Knowledge is not the multiplicity of information, it is a light which God introduces into the hearts of his servants.

This "light" is the key to most of the secrets, i.e. the secrets of Self and of the Universe. It is the "inward light". Gnostics regard it as the essential reality of man. They say that 'the refined element' (called heart) is the essential reality of man. Nora's self-respect born out of this light—the purity of heart—makes her sublime her moral strength and courage enhance that sublimity.

A Doll's House has a great relevance in the present age when man has lost his intuitive, feminine self hence the increasing materialism and masculinity in today's modern world. Man has lost his intuitive self, his soul. Humankind is oblivious of this fact nowadays that woman is the creator of life upon this earth (as it has been said in the Mahabharata), that womanhood and motherhood ought to be respected and revered deeply and sincerely. The real aim of Ibsen in writing this play was to teach a lesson to the egotist, self-centred, shallow, ignorant, narrow-minded, uncultured men, the humane lesson of equality, liberty and fraternity. Helmer, being one-sided, and egotist, could not at all identify himself with his wife whom he pretended to love. His was not a balanced and integrated personality. While Nora comes to know about the lack of balance, of moral courage and strength, of the power and capability to protect, she gets disillusioned and disheartened. Her heart breaks. Then in moments of distress it became impossible for a woman like Nora (who possessed a harmonious personality, was a pure soul) to live any more with a weak, fragmented, disbalanced man as Helmer was. She yearned for a whole man, an entire man who could love her deeply and sincerely and who could be strong enough to protect her, to defend and save her in moments of crisis. Helmer was incapable of supporting her. When she realized and reached the conclusion that Helmer was not a protective master, an ideal husband, she left him, his home and children and she was right. That was the only way she could save her soul and preserve her sanity, equilibrium, peace and serenity of her mind.

Ibsen, through this play emerges as a great Humanist, a visionary, trying to establish a relationship of his own soul to society. He loved humanity immensely, possessed a balanced personality and yearned for the deliverance of mankind. His message took the form of *A Doll's House* which has been having a great impact on the minds of people since it was created.

NOTES AND REFERENCES

1. From *A Doll's House, The Wild Duck & Lady From the Sea* ed. and tr. by Farqularson Sharp, Eleanor Marx (London: J.M. Dent and Sons Ltd., New York), 1910, 1958, p. 47.
2. *Ibid.*, p. 68.
3. *Ibid.*, p. 69.
4. *Ibid.*, p. 65.
5. *Ibid.*, p. 14.

❑❑❑

20

Ellen Glasgow's *The Miller of Old Church*—A Vision of a Changing Woman

SUREKHA DANGWAL

Ellen Glasgow liked to write about women because their complexity fascinated her. And she was able to portray, define and then redefine the essential female qualities. She was amused by the differences between the traditional concepts of woman and vividly described the common plight of women:

> Women, waiting for the first word of love from their lovers, women waiting, with all the inherited belief in the omnipotence of love, for the birth of their sons, women waiting, during the civil war, for news of their sons, and husbands, women, waiting beside the beds of the sick and dying-waiting-waiting.[1]

Glasgow was able to portray both the condition of woman during the late 1800's and the most desirable position of the ambitious modern woman. She knew about the traditional woman because she had witnessed the comparatively unfulfilled lives of her mother and several of her sisters. Glasgow's mother after bearing ten children, had discovered her husband's black mistress.[2]

The Miller of Old Church was written when Glasgow was disturbed by her brother's suicide and her sister's incurable illness. Despite humourous elements in the book, it is predominantly grave in tone. It combines her feeling for the soil and her interest in woman's problems. This novel deals with a woman, like

Molly Merryweather, the heroine of the novel. Like Glasgow's other heroines, she does not change according to circumstances. She is the master of her own circumstances.

The story centres around the Revercombs who inhabit the area near the Mill. Heredity and environment play a vital role in the formation of the major characters. Abel, the young Miller, and Molly, his beloved, are the primary characters, whereas there are several others of equal importance. The Miller's family consists of Sarah Revercomb, his mother, Abner, his elder brother, Archie, his younger one and his old grandparents. Abner's daughter Blossome too lives there. And at a little distance, reside the influential and affluent Gays. Old Jonathan Gay is no longer alive, but exerts a vital influence throughout the novel. Angela, Old Jonathan Gay's sister-in-law and the young Jonathan's mother, is a powerful character, who symbolises the inherent forces of destruction. The other important character is Molly Merryweather. Molly, however, around whom the plot revolves, is the illegitimate child of old Jonathan Gay and Janet Merryweather, upon whom grave injustice has been wrought. Molly lives with Angelica Gay and Kesiah Blount, the plain Old-Maid sister of Janet Merryweather, after her grandfather Reuben Merryweather's death.

Molly is the central character of the book. She has been brought up as a heartless flirt because of taking her mother's revenge upon men for betrayal, just like Estella's upbringing in *Great Expectations*. Molly has captured the hearts of the young Miller, the Reverend Mullen and the farmer, Jim Halloween, and plays them off against each other. Her kindness is reserved for the old, the children and the animals, but she is self-appointed scourge for the menfolk. The dead Janet Merryweather, whose mental wandering, social impediments and final demise crippled young Molly's attitude towards men and distort her normal life.

In this novel, religion has been shown as a powerful source in the mental make-up of women. The church is obviously the centre of the women's social life. Ladies auxiliaries, Sunday School and making of garments for the poster take up such time and conservation among the rural women. The question of the role of woman is here debated in the rural area and becomes a link for Glasgow's next two novels directed specially for this theme, *Virginia* and *Life and Gabriella*. In *The Miller of Old Church*, Mrs. Angela Gay represents the ideal Virginia lady of the earlier Virginia tradition. She is noble, delicate, refined and beautiful. Dependent upon other for all the necessities and comforts of life. She is served by everyone with pleasure, because she represents an ideal that is quickly disappearing, a weak existence, which can be shaken too easily. Kesiah Blount, the ugly and utilitarian old maid, is ignored or tolerated by those around. She gives up her ambitions to study art in Europe and her desire for independence to devote herself to her family. Of the rural women, Mrs. Ming of Bottom's ordinary commands respect for her outspokenness and cynical independence. She is the arbiter of her customers and of her husband. Molly draws down criticism for her flirting and her spirited independence. In this way, she disqualifies her for marriage in the conventional society. The plot of *The Miller of Old Church* revolves round the mystery of Jonathan Gay's murder and his will, acknowledging the illegitimate Molly on her twenty-first birthday. Gay romantically tied the money to the obligation for Molly to live with the Gay family, including the nephew Jonathan, in hopes that a new romance would flourish and a marriage would right the wrong to Janet Merryweather. But plans from the grave are seldom practical. Molly does not want to surrender her personal freedom to marriage and is really in love with the Miller, Abel Revercomb. Young Jonathan who is eventually attracted to his spirited cousin, Molly, had already made a secret and unacknowledged marriage to Blossome Revercomb. Abel reacts from this situation of Molly and Jonathan and gets married with the dutiful and unattractive Judy Hatch, who cherishes a hopeless passion for the pastor, Mr. Mullen. This situation provides much material for the comparison of love and duty like Shakespeare's *Antony and Cleopatra*.

The question of class is nicely bridged by Molly, who has a mixed breed and quickly learns the customs of those with whom she lives. Molly goes through a great crisis with her grandfather's death. She voices to Abel her feelings upon Reuben's death: "All the feeling I had went out of me when grandfather died—I've been benumbed ever since and I don't want to feel ever again that's the worst of it."[3] After returning from Europe Molly realizes the importance of love:

> Love, which filled the world, was not the beginning and end, as it ought to be, of every mortal existence. Substract it from the universe and there was nothing left but a void; yet in this void, life seemed to move and feed and have its being just as if it were really alive.[4]

This is before Molly discovers that Abel is no longer waiting for her. But it is his tenderness, that Judy scorns and Molly loves, Molly left him because of his angry jealousy. She is like most Glasgow's heroines struggles against the captivity of marriage 'like a bird in a net'. Abel is now married but promises her that if she needs him, he will gladly die for him. It is this spiritual devotion alone that Molly can trust, and Blossome is hurt by Jonathan's coldness, it is Molly who must comfort her because "the relation of woman to man was dwarfed suddenly by an understanding of the relation of woman to woman".[5] As they have temperamental differences, their relationship emerges as one, full of conflicts and pitfalls, particularly because two strong natures are juxtaposed against each other, each forceful in one's own way.

Ellen Glasgow, by virtue of her understanding of human nature, discusses at length, man's compulsion to possess, and woman's resistance to such domination. Molly is thus, not the submissive, clinging southern lady who existed namely "to win love or to bestow it". Molly has a "distinct will" of her own, and this differentiates her from the other dependent counterparts of her sex. A mixture of ardent passion and rationality, she hates the norms of society which have stood in her way of achieving identity. She is of the firm opinion that she cannot be confined in a cage, and resists her lover's advances. She knows that "once surrendered, the very strength and singleness of love would bring to cage".[6]

Molly's aversion to man is also justifiable in the context that she is bitter when she thinks of her mother's agony—"I'm all hard and bitter inside",[7] she says. Molly rebels because she feels that her identity as an authentic human being has to emerge, and she automatically revolts against, "the masculine foke".[8] Thus, Glasgow felt, as Livermore did in one of her articles:

> When women are trained and self-poised, they will not be in bondage to ignorance; nor will they be as liable to become dupes on the prey of others. A wife and mother should be mistress of herself and of her department and never a slave of another—not even when that other is her husband, and the slavery is founded on her undying love.[9]

The conversation that ensures between Abel and Molly again reveals the fact that the average male generally takes a woman for granted, and the result is that the male pursues, whereas the woman is diffident. The following dialogue proves the point:

> "Have you ever loved me, I wonders"? He asked little bitterly. For an instant she hesitated, trying in some fierce self-reproach to be honest. "I thought so once... once. So much less...me than to others."[10]

Molly cannot be categorised as the totally stereotyped woman, nor does she remain completely free from the dictates of norms. She plays the role of the active participant as well as of the passive recipient. She learns to control her life rather than passively be controlled.

Abel is, comparatively restricted in his attitude towards women. In his set up where chastity was the criterion of judging a woman's character, he felt that:

> She possessed a thousand virtues, he was aware; she was generous, honourable according to her lights, loyal, brave, charitable, and unselfish. But it is the woman of a single virtue, not a thousand, that a man exalts.[11]

Molly Merryweather, however, is the focus of the action. She has in her, the royal blood of the Gay's, and the undistinguished blood of the oppressed Janet Merryweather. She abhors the very fact of her dependence on the Gays, hates Jonathan, and as a result, all men. She alternates thus, between varied needs of love, tenderness and passion, as opposed to hatred, contempt and scorn. At the end of the novel, however, she is united with Abel, the Miller, and her former lover and realizes that with him lies her happiness. She neither conforms to the category of the angel nor the bitch. She does not wish to remain "as a queen in the eyes of all mankind, unrivalled and unsurpassed as will enshrine her forever in the hearts of the father, the husband and the son".[12]

The image of the priestess, wife or mother does not fit her, and she feels she can remain a true woman without completely surrendering herself. She is a different individual, unlike most women of her time who "did with themselves nothing at all; they waited, in attitudes more or less gracefully passive, for a man to come that way and furnished their destiny".[13] She does not yield before the circumstances. She turns circumstances according to herself. She has a power to face every impediment of her way and struggles for her individuality. She has a vision of a changing woman. She has paved a way for a liberated woman of a contemporary American society.

REFERENCES

1. Ellen Glasgow, *The Woman Within* (Autobiography), New York: Doubleday, 1954, p. 37.
2. *Ibid.*
3. Ellen Glasgow, *The Miller of Old Church*, Garden City, New York: Doubleday, p. 232.
4. *Ibid.*, p. 308.
5. *Ibid.*, p. 375.
6. *Ibid.*, p. 256.
7. *Ibid.*
8. *Ibid.*
9. Livermore, "Our Daughters", pp. 3, 132, 149, Mary A. Livermore, "Supertfours Woman", an undated article found in the ECTU papers of the Sophia Smith Collection, pp. 216-17.
10. *The Miller of Old Church*, p. 253.
11. *Ibid.*, 254.
12. Quoted in Allen S. Kraditor, ed., *Up From the Pedestal: Selected Writings in the History of American Feminism*, Chicago: Quadrangle Books, 1968, p. 197.
13. Henry James, *The Portrait of a Lady*, New York: Signet, 1963, p. 59.

❑❑❑

21
Female Characters in F. Scott Fitzgerald

ATTIA ABID

American fiction had long ignored woman and her rights of existence on equal terms with man. However, in the wake of the feminine movement in Europe a new consciousness during the beginning of the present century emerged which somehow remained confined to sex. It was Theodore Dreiser, Scott Fitzgerald and Ernest Hemingway who paid serious attention to feminist issues in their fictional works.

The Fitzgeralds, Scott and his wife, Zelda, found themselves cast as models for the new worship of youth. They soon accepted their roles as pioneers. But though they regarded themselves as eponymic figures which they did become, it will be erroneous to blame them for the excesses of The Twenties. In the conflicting manners and aspirations that was going on, Scott Fitzgerald was not only the leading actor but the audience as well; he had lived in great moments and stood apart and reckoned the causes as well. He lived more intimately than any writer the life of his times, and it became the material he dealt with in his works.

He was a social historian who chronicled the manners of an age, the mood of a people, the psychological conditions of a decade, the history of a consciousness. In fact, in his writings he "epitomised 'all the sad young men' of the post-war generation, and captured the essence of a period when 'flappers and gin and the beautiful and the damned' were symbols of the carefree madness of an age."[1]

He wrote plot stories with fresh characters not magazine types. What differentiated his writing from others was that he treated the concerns of youth more seriously than some of his contemporaries. But soon he complained that he would go mad if he had to do "another debutante". Hence, the stories are in two groups, success in wooing and rejection. For Fitzgerald's girls marriage is the only future and they are determined to make the best possible matches because they are deciding for their children as well. The early stories have a Jane Austen like beginning: "It is a truth universally acknowledged that a single man in possession of a good fortune must be in want of a wife."[2]

This good fortune becomes the glitter or the halo for which the person is pursued. The girl wastes herself on these trivial romances that provide no preparation for a responsible life and make her emotionally bankrupt, having nothing to offer the person she will finally marry. *Little Women* came to be considered a book about "inane females" who had been models for the mothers of the "emergent Amazons" who knew little about their daughters' problems, the problems that centred round how they could have three, four or even more men in love with them and be cut in on every feet at dance. There was cut-throat competition and every girl had to think of herself. Those that thought her gay and fickle saying she would come to a bad end were just indulging in the sour-grapes syndrome. They were playing for very high stakes so indulging in a little cheap popularity or cheaping themselves a bit were all part of the game. Gone were the days of the "womanly woman" when all young ladies from good families had glorious times; feminine qualities came to be considered "ghastly inefficiencies". In "Bernice Bobs Her Hair", as long as Bernice had talked of the weather or Eau Claire, from where she came, or automobiles or her school, she was considered dull and unbearable, and had a "bum time" at parties. Warren Mc Intyre made a remark that he sometimes made to girls at College Proms; she blushed and became clumsy with her fan, and annoyed him by an unexpected response: "You've got an awefully kissable mouth." He had said, "'Fresh!' The word had slipped out of her mouth."[3]

Her cousin, Marjorie, gives her flapperly advice, and she learns the tricks of the trade only to outwit the "sphinx of sphinxes".

There was no flight from love, and it was pursued for its own sake, the experience being more important than the identity of any particular beloved. Girls and boys were in no hurry to get married, often remained engaged and had affairs with others. In "Ice Palace", Sally Carrol wants to go places and see people, wants her mind to grow, wants to live where things happen on a large scale. She leaves the somnolent South with its "ineffectual, sad failures" (men) and goes North only to be disappointed and nearly killed in the Ice Palace. In "The Sensible Thing" though Jonquil Cary loves George O'Kelly with all her heart, marrying him doesn't seem the sensible thing because she was nervous at the prospect of marrying into a life of poverty and that was putting too much strain upon her love.

These girls were callous, much like Keats' La Belle Dame Sans Merci, but for some inexplicable reasons had the knights enthralled by their serpentine beauty. Love was far more consistently a source of misery. The boy was almost frustrated in his need for love and was driven into miserable situations from which there was no escape. He was often made vulnerable to exploitation by unscrupulous characters. The enjoyments he got from love were transitory. Worst of all, his needs and fears defied reason and control, and knowing that the object was not worthy of his love, he was in the grip of deep irrational forces. Generally, love was depicted as a selfish emotion, the lovers not making concessions to the beloved. Whether it is Judy Jones in "Winter Dreams" or Anson Hunter in "The Rich Boy", they were never happy unless someone was in love with them, responding "like filing to a magnet". Thus, romantic exhilaration varies: sometimes it is a sense of mystery and remoteness, sometimes it resides in glittering associations of wealth, sometimes in the quest for excitement of adventure and novelty of experience. Whatever form it takes, this romanticising motive is a compelling force in many lovers who find it necessary to transform or uplift their homelier motives.

However, after all the dancing cheek to jowl in the dark, petting and kissing, what became of the selfish, spoiled, uncontrolled, disagreeable, impossible girls and young fools that spent "their vacuous hours pursuing them round the country"? In "The Last of the Belles", Lt. Canby climbed up 6000 ft. in his plane and shut off the motor; in "May Day" Gordon Sterret married Jewel Hudson, "the spectre of womanhood", and shot himself when he realised what he had done; Dexter Green joined the war, welcoming the liberation from the webs of tangled emotion; some joined the ecclesiastical order, and suppression of the need to love and be loved erupted in madness; some got married but didn't "possess their wives" because they realised that they had married a mere "bundle of clothes", a weak, cowardly mass of affectations; some retaliated in a peculiar and ominous way: in "The Cut-Glass Bowl" Carleton Canby sent Evelyn a big cut-glass bowl as a wedding present and it assumed the proportions of fate when ominous things happened and were associated with it; in "Diamond As Big As The Ritz", Braddock Washington, the richest man in the world, had encouraged his children to have visitors and had them drugged and murdered so that they wouldn't reveal things about his illegal empire to outsiders; his daughter, Kismine, acknowledges that she too would harden upto it.

In the volatile and bizarre world of flappers, philosophers and sad young men, it was a question of survival of the fittest. A man had to have the courage of his convictions and imagination to win the heart of the flapper who, in going from man to man, had become restless, less acquiescent and more dissatisfied, a "husk of herself". Tony Moreland in "The Offshore Pirate" impresses Ardita Farnam with his ingenuity when he passes as a pirate and fugitive with a reward of $2000 on him and abducts her. In "The Bridal Party", Hamilton Rutherford explains that with a girl of commonsense one has to play squarely and tell her what is right at the very start; his fiancee, Caroline Cary seems to appreciate that: "I'm pretty flighty, and I need somebody like Hamilton to decide things. It was that more than the question of—of [money]".[4]

In "The Ice Palace", Sally Carrol talks along similar lines:

> "I'm the sort of person who wants to be taken care of after a certain point and I feel sure I will be".
>
> "It's encouraging to find a girl who knows what she's marrying for nine-tenths of them think of it as a sort of walking into a moving picture sunset", said Roger Patton.[5]

When girls feel sorry for boys and get all sentimental over them, it's a marriage only in name and the man is "gobbled up", "made a monkey of" and reduced to the lowest level. The outcome is adulteries, extra marital affairs and divorce. Couples remained restless or chained to their antagonism even when love had died or was mixed with hostility so that there was persistent suffering.

The day can be saved and thereby the family by tolerance, sacrifice and conformity to social norms. In "Four Fists", Samuel Meredith is made to realise: "The man's strength, his rest, was then protection of his family."[6]

In the case of women too, what ultimately counted and was responsible for a stable family and happy married life was not just "dainty looks" but the immutable qualities of head and heart, a sense of commitment, commonsense, hope, emotional strength, sincerity, loyalty, faithfulness and stability. In other words, it was all right to have a "gaudy spree", but: "Character is the greatest thing in the world".[7]

As opposed to the flappers there are girls like Thea Singleton of "One Interne". The anaesthetist and assistant of the surgeon Howard Durfree, she is like a goddess symbolising the glory and devotion of the medical profession. Her singleness of purpose and determination are also seen in Emily in "Majesty"; she was an American and became Queen of a small Middle European Kingdom, realising the twin dreams of from log cabin to the White House and aristocracy. Thus, the ideal of the quest was changing from "personalities", i.e. immature debutantes to "personages", i.e. matured professionals and aristocrats.

Love could also bring out the latent qualities and uplift an individual as can be seen in "Head and Shoulders" and "The Rich Boy". Of course, there were men like Dexter Green and George O'Kelly who lost all for love and won, reaching the pinnacle of success, realising the ideal for the one they worshipped and adored.

Fitzgerald's love stories were based on his own experiences with Genevra King and Zelda Sayre, but it must be remembered that they reflect his double vision. The former matched his dreams of the perfect girl, beautiful, rich, socially secure and sought after. She later remarked that Fitzgerald thought she knew the way up. In 1916, when he went to visit her, he was no longer her number one suitor, and the competition included sons of wealth. It was pointedly remarked within his hearing that poor boys should not think of marrying rich girls. Zelda, the golden girl from the South would not have him till he succeeded in life. They married only after his first novel, *This Side of Paradise* was published. Later they started having marital problems, and accused each other of all kinds of things related to an unsatisfactory conjugal relationship. These conflicts are reflected in the stories also. Then Zelda had a short affair with a French pilot, Jozan Eduord, and that was the time Fitzgerald was working on his masterpiece, *The Great Gatsby*.

In the stories a galaxy of female characters is presented but that in not surprising because the stories number around 160-178. The novels being just five, the number is restricted. However, between the novels collections of his stories were published, and some of them cluster round the novels. In the novels too women are presented as mothers, girlfriends, wives and mistresses, but as compared to the short stories they are weak and colourless personalities; none of them are mature enough to be elevated to the status of a "personage". However, besides that, the heroines of the novels assume symbolic proportions.

In *This Side of Paradise*, there are five women in the life of Amory Blaine: his mother who insists that he call here Beatrice, and the golden girls Isabelle, Eleanor, Rosalind and Clara. Beatrice is a product of "those days when the great gardener clipped the inferior roses to produce one perfect bud". She is placed in a gilded era, a distanced age when a tutelage was measured by the number of things and people one could be contemptuous and charming about. She is beautiful young, sad, disengaged, aristocratic, surpassing the upper middle-class values. She symbioses the shaping hand of society that must mould his "aristocratic egotism" and self-awareness but he perceives the futility of her affectations. She sends him to Monsignor Thayer Darcy who represents Catholicism because she feels he could be a great help to her son. The golden girl attains a generic role. She is set with a surface froth of emotions but lacks depth and cannot form a meaningful permanent relationship. Amory like the young Siddhartha was searching for a meaning in life. The girl of his dreams, Isabelle, is a match for his "narcissistic poses" and vanity. For him the "orgy of sociability" is an initiation into the new ambience of his ideal contentment but he became aware of the "vast juvenile intrigue" which had inflicted the youth's morale. Her spoilt-child behaviour seems undoubtedly outrageous when as the "baby" she embarks upon the adventures of a "vamp", but her seductive designs fail to entice or sway Amory and the relationship ends. Thus, revulsion and horror at the reversal of values in the emerging American city are expressed in the portrayal of the Popular Dame (P.D.) Rosalind, in spite of her "fresh enthusiasm, her will to grow and learn, her endless faith in the inexhaustibility of romance, her courage and fundamental honesty", bears the fangs of evil. She was "Rosalind Unlimited", and her social preferences put premium on the value of man. Her passionate love epitomises her desire for a "male to gratify ones artistic taste". She is a creature of moments and Amory is important for the future of "next things", only. She thinks she would fail if she married him; she hates the "narrow atmosphere shut away from the large world". She gives him up for someone floating in money. She represents The Twenties that had lost their moorings: the traditional home had been washed away, and with it the lasting riches of "love and spiritual communion which transcends all human passions and ephemeral allurements". In his romance with Eleanor Savage it was "the last time that evil crept close to Amory under the mask of beauty". She is contemptuous of mere innocence, and had insisted on being a debutante at 17, had a wild winter, shocked her relatives into fiery protest and "led many innocents...into the paths of Bohemian naughtiness". She was not only a manifestation of the malaise of the age but assumes the contemporary symbol of detachment, and with her blasphemy tears to shreds the thick cloak of materialism. Clara did not fit into this fabric of evil; her angelic image made her different. Moreover, Monsignor had asked Amory to meet her. She was alone in the world with two small children and a little money. She could do the most prosy things and had "a latent strength; realism"; she symbolises the moral standpoint from which others can be measured in a world of flux. That compels Amory to confess in a trembling voice "I think...that if I lost faith in you I'd lose faith in God". She is an embodiment of the anti-vamp, a perfection unrealised in a materialistic world. Thus, women of whom Amory had expected much had only contributed a "sick heart and a page of puzzled words to write".

Gloria Gilbert, the heroine of *The Beautiful and Damned*, is Fitzgerald's most complete and energetic debutante, the post-war female apotheosis, the Jazz Baby, "the beauty of succulent illusions". She is no shadow like Isabelle, Rosalind and Eleanor who impinge on Amory's consciousness. Fitzgerald admitted to Edmund Wilson that the most enormous influence on him in the creation of Gloria was Zelda's "fine and full-hearted selfishness and chill-mindedness". Zelda didn't want to be famous and feted but "very young always and very irresponsible", and that is what Gloria is. She is pampered and childish to the extent of demanding absurd things to satisfy her whimsicalities. She has the qualities of life-giving sunshine, though they turn to infertility. She considers pregnancy to be a "crowning indignity". Thus, beauty becomes unproductive and sterile, evil and immoral like Isabelle, Rosalind and Eleanor, all beautiful and damned. Like the others she hates the bourgeoise, middle-class life and continues to search for novel means of pleasure. With money and financial security she hopes to achieve identity. Obsessive attention to her beauty and appearance keep her alive and happy, and with the fading of youth and beauty, the golden splendour grows dimmer, fades into futility, and there is no alternative except isolation and lowliness.

In *The Great Gatsby*, Daisy is no better than Myrtle Wilson, the garage owner's wife living in the Valley of Ashes. Gatsy "forever wed his unutterable vision to her perishable breath", and "at his lips touch she blossomed for him like a flower and the incarnation was complete". But she wed Tom Buchanan's pearl necklace and hereditary wealth. Gatsby hopes that she will go to Tom and put an end to their years of marriage and return to him. From his house he keeps watching the green light at the end of her dock, and stretching his arms towards it. He throws lavish parties and people attend without even knowing who the host is. Then, in their cadillacs Daisy, Tom, Gatsby, Jordan Baker and Nick Carraway rush around escaping from boredom. In one such spree Daisy runs over Tom's mistress Myrtle, and her angry husband shoots Gatsby: "They were a careless people, Tom and Daisy.... They smashed up things and creatures and then retreated back into their money or whatever it was that kept them together, and let other people clean up the mess they had made."[8]

In her betrayal, Daisy has lost all credibility. Her moral cheapness bludgeons Gatsby's love and devotion. She was as absent from his life as from his death, while alive he had heaped flowers on her but she had not even sent a single flower or message when he died.

Tender is the Night presents a host of women "never seen before". Nicole is a victim of incest, raped by her father. She is a schizophrenic for whom they buy a doctor, Dick Diver. She is the fictional portrait of Zelda. The association gains in importance in the merging specifics of the personality of Zelda through her mental illness. The novel is about breakdown of human relationships and marriages. Dick was destroyed by the romantic charm when he dissipated his talents and his precious possession of self-discipline and cultivation of old virtues and graces in pandering them to satisfy the egos of Nicole Warren and others of his charmed circle who came within the spell of his magic. In the world of the golden girl and her vain self-indulgence, sexual identities are lost; women use up all the energies of men which destroys them both. Nicole's shopping forays, gorgeous and interminable, are symbolic of her wasting male energies. What she does with her apparently innocuous spending becomes essentially what Fitzgerald saw the entire national effort being geared toward—pandering the "bitch goddess" of moneyed success. Rosemary, the innocent, still unspoilt girl, too in time imitates Nicole, and becomes the very being, the very personage who contains all the destructiveness concealed within the surface gloss of glittering, fascinating life with its implicit destructiveness. It is the perfect beatitude, the gorgeous beauty of the American moneyed imagination, alluring and attractive, brutish and energetic, voluptuously enticing, but what simultaneously destroys the male and female, and is hence predatory. Rosemary Hoyt is encouraged by her mother in her affair with Dick, a married man. Her youthful innocence permits her to be gay and careless, free and irresponsible. She is not burdened with what might be the possible consequences of the Dick-Nicole relationship: "You were brought up to work... not especially to marry. Now you've your first nut to crack, and it's a good nut...go ahead and put whatever happens down to experience. Wound yourself or him...whatever happens it can't spoil you because economically you're a boy, not a girl."[9] She is an actress, and reminds one of the effervescence of Hollywood, unreal and dreamlike, a symbol of what is tawdry, shallow, inane, almost dehumanised yet having the radiance of a gorgeous illusion, perfect but brittle at the touch of reality as Fitzgerald would depict in his last novel which remained incomplete. Dick had told her, "you're the only girl I've seen for a long time that actually did look like something blooming". However, with surrender to lust they destroy for themselves what a dependable relationship might have been in nursing old dreams of life in a new world. Nicole goes back to the incestuous Warren world where she feels she belongs. She leaves the security, shared discipline and dependable personal identity offered by Dick. He had been owned by the "emergent Amazons", and he became embittered. He couldn't make Nicole human and sensitive. She throws him as she threw the rare and unavailable camphor rub. She resembles Rosemary and Mary North, and all three of them differ from many American women in that: "They were happy to exist in a man's world...preserved their individuality through men and through opposition to them. They would all three have made alternatively good courtesans or good wives not by the accident of birth, through the greater accident of finding their man or not finding him."[10] Mary North changes altogether after the controlling brakes have been removed once her husband dies. Her symbolic role can be seen in her relationship with Lady Caroline who is the liberated woman with the strength of evil, incarnate of the new gilded world of hot pursuits. Baby Warren makes her attitude harden into a cool, calculating, experimental gesture almost like her grandfather. She conceived human relations only in terms of "usefulness". She is unaware of the cause of her sister's schizophrenia just as she is ignorant of the extra Dick had put into his marriage. Even when she bails him out "Daddy's girl" is satisfied that now they possessed a moral superiority over him. It was her moment of triumph since it gave her a sense of socially acceptable appearance which was her concept of morality. When Nicole's "white crooks eyes" are ironically noticed by Tommy Barban she expressed the complex moral dilemma: "So I have white crooks eyes, have I. Very well then, better a sane crook than a mad puritan". It sums up the two worlds the old and dying, outmoded puritan morality and the emerging eager, youthful new generation. The scene of Nicole's adulterous liaison with Tommy Barban and the cacophony of turmoil and confusion outside show the whorish betrayal of the American dream. Wealth, leisure, restlessness, all lead to different experiments in pleasure, be it incest, homosexuality or lesbianism. Towards the end Gausse sighed forth: "I have never seen this sort of woman. I have known many of the great courtesans of the world and for them I have much respect often, but women like these I have never seen before."[11]

To Fitzgerald's mind Hollywood had become symbolically associated with the unfulfilled dreams, desires and the possibility of their being ever attained. Hollywood was the only dream of America left to the seeker, and in Monroe Stahr, the hero of *The Last Tycoon* the historical perspective comes out in a wider cultural and social context. The narrator-commentator, Cecillia, with her background and heritage adequately provides the moral point of view and exercises an honest, evaluative judgement to bring to the highly inflated picture of Hollywood a point of view both involved and distant. The affair of Stahr and Kathleen, the emotional centre of the novel, is rather blurred and patchy. Maybe she was to symbolise the restorative powers of love that he would lose as a result of his energies being completely absorbed in his career. He has a choice to opt out of his doomed fate into the love of Kathleen, leaving his care and career behind, but temperamentally and perhaps burdened with a stricken conscience he cannot abandon himself to a life of unshared responsibilities. Maybe it was Fitzgerald's personal involvement with Sheila Graham who was the model for the fading apparition of Kathleen Moore that could not be crystalised into moments of deep and lasting passions.

The literary traditions for Fitzgerald's male lovers may be traced to the code of courtly love and to Keats' "La Belle dame sans Merci". His heroes are betrayed or destroyed by women who lack the capacity for total commitment; the men deliberately choose the destructive women; it's like a death-wish, the love of the moth for the flame. Referring to this major theme of Fitzgerald's fiction, i.e. the gifted man being ruined by a selfish woman, the effect of Irish-Catholic Jansenism is suggested which maintains the doctrine of total depravity, misogyny and puritanical concepts of sex. However, Fitzgerald was not a misogynist or Puritan. In his world, the golden girl never stands for sexual triumph. She symbolises status and being. His novels are conspicuously free from erotic fantasies. This is remarkable in an age which was celebrating sexual freedom with great exuberance and he was its most vocal spokesman. She lures her lovers on, like America itself, with a "voice...full of money". She is the "phallic woman with a phallus of gold". Even though her fairy glamour is illusory she remains magical to entice and lure. She is the golden idol, the soul of wealth as well as of America, and both are no longer innocent. This lost innocence is what leads to corruption and ultimate destruction. Possession of wealth makes her aggressive for like the wealthy she can retreat into her money once the devastation is complete. The moment of beauty and illusion can be kept alive, and indefinitely extended because wealth gives a sense of "raw ostentation...of privilege existing outside the reach of moral responsibility and confers freedom beyond any moral calculations". Such are the implications of the pursuit and wooing of the golden girl, of the charisma of love, beauty and youthful innocence. The quest and the attainment are imperative even when the winning becomes a destructive triumph, the efforts reduced to ashes, the absorption of the seeker into the ideal, the ritual must be undergone for winning of the golden girl is symbolic of winning American. It a symbol of the Golden West, the Frontier, the receding ideal, though to Fitzgerald's generation the 'Westward Ho' had begun to absorb the Eastern cities as well, New York with its desiccated streets, pallour of death and destruction housing the Eastern Princess of the golden American West.

REFERENCES

1. Quoted, Mathew Bruccoli, *Some Epic Grandeur*, p. 4.
2. Jane Austen, *Pride and Prejudice*, p. 5.
3. F. Scott Fitzgerald, "Bernice Bobs Hair", *The Short Stories of F. Scott Fitzgerald*, ed: Malcolm Cowley, p. 42.
4. F. Scott Fitzgerald, "The Off Shore Pirate", *Flappers and Philosophers*, p. 48.
5. F. Scott Fitzgerald, "The Bridal Party", *The Short Stories of F. Scott Fitzgerald*, ed. Malcolm Cowley, p. 276.
6. F. Scott Fitzgerald, "The Four Fists", *Flappers and Philosophers*, p. 256.
7. F. Scott Fitzgerald, "Two Wrongs", *Taps at Reveille*, p. 200.
8. F. Scott Fitzgerald, *The Great Gatsby*, p. 136.
9. F. Scott Fitzgerald, *Tender is the Night*, p. 98.
10. *Ibid.*, pp. 111-12.
11. *Ibid.*, p. 325.

❑❑❑

22

A Critique of Toni Morrison's Feminism

SHRUTI DAS

Toni Morrison is the 1993 Nobel laureate for literature. She was born as Chole Anthony Wofford in 1931, the second of four children, in Lorain, a small town in Northern Ohio. Morrison went to school in Lorain. She was the only black child in her first-grade class and also the only one who could read. Morrison's natural inclination for literature drew her to the treasury of world classics in her adolescence. *Madame Bovary* and characters from Jane Austen's novels seemed to speak to her from the pages. They inspired her and built in her a desire to write about her own culture, the culture she had grown up in.

She graduated with honours from High School and then attended Howard University. It is here that she changed her name to Toni. At Howard, she met stars like Leroi Jones and Andrew Young. She did her M.A. at Cornell. Here she wrote a thesis on the theme of suicide in William Faulkner and Virginia Woolf.

Toni Morrison returned to Howard University as an instructor in 1957. During her Howard days, she married the Jamaican architect Harold Morrison. But her marriage dissolved even before her second son was born. On one of her foreign trips with her husband, she had conceived of "The Bluest Eye" in the form of a short story, which after her divorce, she developed into a novel. In 1970, she published her much acclaimed first novel *The Bluest Eye.*

In 1964, after her divorce, Morrison moved back to New York and began working as an editor for Random House, first in textbooks in Syracuse, then in trade in New York city. Here she published many black, especially female writers such as Toni Cade Bambara and Gayle Jones. She published autobiographies of Angela Davis and Muhammad Ali. She also edited *The Black Book*, a scrap-book of 300 years of Black American life. *The Bluest Eye*, 1970, brought Morrison many respectful reviews. She has not looked back since then. Her second novel, *Sula*, published in 1973, gained her national recognition. *Song of Solomon*, 1977, became a best-seller and paved a path for its authors entry into the list of noted contemporary novelists. It became the second black novel since Richard Wright's *Native Son* to become a Book-of-the-Month Club selection. It also won the National Book Critics Circle Award. The fourth novel the best-selling *Tar Baby*, was published in 1981 and was the recipient of the Bookers Award. Her fifth novel *Beloved* (1987) won the Pulitzer Prize in 1988. Her sixth novel, *Jazz*, published in 1992, catapulted her to Nobel Prize fame. Morrison frequently lectures on African-American literature, has written a play "Dreaming Emmett" and a book of criticism: *Playing in the Dark: Whiteness and Literary Imagination.*

Her continuous successes made *The New York Times* call Morrison "the nearest thing America has to a national novelist". Her unbeatable reputation has made her return from the editorial chair to the lecture hall. She is now a Professor of Humanities at Princeton University. Morrison won the Nobel Prize for literature on October 7, 1993 and became the first Black American woman to win the literature prize and the eighth woman to win it since it was first awarded in 1901. She is also the eleventh American to win it. Pearl S. Buck was the first American woman to win this prize in 1938. Morrison is the only other lady who has won this prize and has reached what is considered to be the pinnacle of literary success.

The black-power movement of the 60s and 70s wielded the weapons of protest. Black writers like Wright, Howe, Ellison, Hurston, et al., chronicled sagas of protest. But Morrison does not merely do so. Conscious as she is of the dilemmas of the black people, her novels reflect the tension between protest and transcendence; between suffering and strength, and between collective and individual identity. Morrison was brought up in a basically racist household, where both her grandparents and also her parents were a politically conscious people. They inducted into her their contempt for while people. She was taught that 'resistance, excellence and integrity' were very much a part of their rich African past.

Exotic, fantastical worlds from Morrison's childhood are woven intricately into the tapestry of her work. They appear larger than life linged as they are with folklore, magic, superstition, fable, poetry, song and myth. The characters are uniquely named from the Bible or colourfully nicknamed. Morrison presents the trauma of black life. She universalizes oppression—where blacks torment blacks, whites oppress blacks, women are against women, parents torture their children, etc. The picture of black life that emerges from her novels is indeed harrowing.

The Bluest Eye is the story of a young black girl Pecola, her inability to either understand or adjust to the ways of the world around her and the consequences thereof. She is pitted against two hostile worlds: one, the white world that entices her with values unnatural to her, viz. blue eyes, and then ruthlessly rejects her; the other, her own people, her own culture. Pecola's family ironically named Breedlove, breed hatred and neglect for their own children. Her own family being full of quarrel and violence the child seeks and gets love from prostitutes. She associates herself with many wrong kind of people to acquire what she imagines to be the symbol of beauty, love and security, that is the Shirley Temple blue eyes. Morrison in the course of the narrative shows how Pecola's obsession with blue eyes degenerate her and make her lose her mind in the process. Further the social order in black society is shown to be in shambles—Cholly Breedlove, the father, rapes his daughter, Pecola; obscenities are common household happenings; mothers neglect their own family and children to shower their love either on white children or on non-human creatures like cats.

The sultry and horrowing tale of the blacks, especially that of Pecola Breedlove appears mere miserable in contrast with the warmth, love and security of the MacTer household who though poor are able to give their offsprings love. Claudia's innocence and childlike comments offer a breath of fresh air in the novel. Both Claudia and her sister Frieda are brought up in positive circumstances and hence have positive psychological reactions to situations. Whereas Pecola brought up in a confused and negative situation shows an absolutely confused and negative attitude to life. Towards the end of the novel Claudia, now a more mature person, blames the entire black society for having failed to love Pecola. Instead they have merely hated her for her ugliness and intense poverty. She even holds the black community responsible for Pecola's plight. *The Bluest Eye* through its strong narrative voice gives a sensitive delineation of the miseries of black life.

Sula carries the theme of dual oppression still further. In their effort to run after and adapt the value system of the whites, the blacks suffer intolerable psychological trauma. Nel's mother dons the garb of white middle class respectability and looks down on her own kind. Yet she is rejected and insulted by black policemen on the train. Nel suffers as she is not able to completely identify herself with her own cultural values. Sula's journey in quest of trans-cultural knowledge only results in negative behaviour and frustration. She is a libertine. She feels men are simply to be used and discarded. She doesn't even spare her best friend Nel's husband. She threatens the peaceful existence of the black community, and they identify her with the devil. Her return to the community is marked symbolically by the epidemic of birds. She removes her grandmother, Eva, to an old age home and thereby consecrates her malevolence.

Sula's nature does not spring any surprise on us because Morrison has very carefully and meticulously built up her character. Sula had been as innocent and playful as a child could be. One can only blame the environment and the pseudo values for channelizing the artist in Sula in a negative direction. The grandmother, Eva, the head of the family, allows her daughter Hannah, promiscuity, and even burns her own son to death in his bed to save him from becoming an imbecile, a drug addict. The structure of the household is completely loose as compared with the tightness and rigid orderliness of Nel Wright's household. Sula envies the middle class respectability that Nel's mother has cultivated. Nel and Sula had once playfully drowned a small boy and Sula had taken the blame on herself. She had also undergone terrible mental agony when she overheard her mother confess to a friend that she did not like Sula. Many such incidents add up to make Sula what she is.

The novel appears to criticize the feminist doctrine of unconditioned freedom. Sula's frustration results from such unattachment. She looks for her moorings in her relationship with Ajax. She sinks and is mutilated when she ultimately finds herself loveless and friendless.

The theme of universal oppression is reiterated in *Song of Solomon.* There is hardly any obvious aggressive protest against such oppression except for Guitar and his gang's meaningless militancy against the whites. Tension is created in the novel, between the characters due to Guitar's terrorist actions. In the vast scope of the novel, Morrison has clandestinely harped on one thing—that the loss of identity, the feeling of insecurity and above all susceptibility to any kind of oppression arises from the rootlessness of the people themselves.

Macon Dead attempts to copy and don the middle class respectability of the white society. The family's weekly outing in a car is a parody of such pseudo-sophistication. Macon Dead's rigidity in denying both himself and his family the richness of his own culture, almost forcing them to accept the values of a culture not their own brings about a disintegration in the family. Milkman, Macon's son revolts against the rigidity, cruelty and perversion in his family. Rather, he sways towards his father's sister, the bohemian Pilate. Pilate is the diametric opposite of Macon Dead. She lives in the outskirts of the town with her daughter and granddaughter and sells wine. The members of the Pilate household love each other dearly and are very protective about one another. It is with the help of Pilate that Milkman sets out on the ultimate guest—in search of his roots. They are proud of their African ancestry and are liberated through the song of Solomon, their African ancestor.

Morrison uses the epic scope of her novel to full advantage. Here she successfully experiments with myths and fantasies. She makes profuse use of rich Afro-American folklore and also skilfully adapts myths from the Bible. The name of the book *Song of Solomon* itself has been taken from the Old Testament. The names Pilate, Hannah, Ruth, Corinthians, Magdalene, etc. are purely biblical. Morrison's lyrical language and balanced expression make even the wildest of fantasies seem possible: Pilate is unique. She does not have a novel. She denies the birth myth and stands apart. In that she refers to the primordial woman—free, original, authentic and strongly rooted. Morrison's mission of bringing about a cultural awareness in the Afro-Americans that, in rejecting the mutilating identification with white values would make them more authentic and respectable is just about served in *Song of Solomon.*

The Eurocentric mythic patterns give way to a popular and mystifying Afro-American folktale in *Tar Baby.* The tar baby folktale becomes a motif in the novel. Each fictional character is examined in keeping with the roles of Tempter, Tar Baby, and Trickster and consequently these determine their relationships. For example, Jadine is groomed by her patron/oppression Valerian Street. He uses her like the former to tempt Brer Rabbit Son, an innocent black man, who is authentic and true to his own cultural values. Son is attracted to the frigid raven haired Jadine, who is a jet set Parisian model. In his pursuit of Jadine Son is faced with many a dilemma whether to surrender to the white-tainted temptress or whether to return to his primitive black past.

In *Tar Baby*, there is a lack of mutual comprehension and communication between the characters; each being a captive of his own private myth. Son holds on to the image of the pie ladies, Jadine casts herself as the queen of warrior ants; Valerian Cherishes the delusion that he reigns over a private Eden; Margaret spins a fantasy around her about the return of there persecuted son; Therese explains Son's destiny in terms of the legend of the chevaliers. Each one is ensconced within his personal mythical shell and thus denies any genuine relationship with the others. *Tar Baby* is based on contradictions. The central couple lack common ground. At the end Son opts for his mythical past, running like Brer Rabbit to join the blinded slaves in the Isle des Chevaliers, while Jadine is pulled into the quicksand of destructive white values as unseen women watch her.

Contemporary life has been finely delineated in *Tar Baby.* Here Morrison has effectively shown that relationship between the genders has reached an impasse. Not only that but also the novel denounces the possibility of a White and Black cultural amalgamations. Even the prospects of an alternative seems to be quite bleak to Toni Morrison.

In her fifth novel *Beloved,* Morrison again turns back to the history of slavery. Here Morrison delineates the psychological and emotional effects of slavery. There is no sense of self; a fear to trust or to love when anything can be taken away at any time. The painful slow growth of the slaves and ex-slaves towards a damaged self-awareness is quite effective. The novel collects and synthesizes myths for the black community. *Beloved* chronicles the fortunes of Sethe, once a slave on the Sweet Home plantation in Kentucky. Sethe and her husband serve under a good master but upon his death are subjected to untellable cruelty by the new master. Some of the slaves decide to escape the bondage. Sethe sends her three children to freedom and herself, manages to escape later. On the way a child is born to her. She names her Denver after the poor white woman who helps her with her delivery. Her husband had been shattered after secretly witnessing his wife being forced to give her milk to grown white boys. Sethe has the support of her husband's mother Baby Suggs. Baby Suggs is strong and bighearted. She preaches her fellow blacks that they must learn to love themselves in a world where no one else does. Baby Suggs succumbs to her grief one day announcing that "there was no bad luck in the world but white folks".

Here Morrison make use of Gothic fantastic elements of African culture, viz. ghosts. The house of Sethe had killed one ghost of "Beloved" a baby daughter that Sethe had killed one month previous to her freedom fearing that this child of hers would also be forced into slavery. The ghost is exorcised by Paul D. and Sethe, Denver and Paul D. are about to settle back into a happy family life when the ghost returns—now in the form of a grown girl apparently around the age Beloved would be. At this point the world of the dead and the living converge. This impossibility seems natural within the Morrisonian plot structure. As should be expected the ghost Beloved turns malevolent and destroys any kind of happiness or life Sethe and Denver would have expected. Denver tries to control the situation. She with the help of other women now exorcises Beloved. Paul D. returns and the Sethe household seem to breathe freely again.

In *Jazz*, Morrison continues with her examination of gender relationship; of relationships between individual and community; of the theme of multiple oppression. Here her treatment of the themes seem a little different. The characters are all based in a city and are no longer mere dreamers. They have graduated to respond in kind to any violence against them. The sparkle of the city is corrosive in that it is white-tainted and destroys the internal morality of the characters. For the first time Morrison places couple Joe and Violet, at center stage. Their relationship is again spoilt by the entry of Dorcas, Joe's young lover. Dorcas is young enough to be Joe's daughter. One day she ditches this father-figure for a young man. She prefers the violence and uncertainty in her relationship with the young boy to the tenderness of the elderly man. Joe reacts to the loss by violence. He murders Dorcas. Violet reacts to the relationship by going a step further, she interrupts the funeral of Dorcas and attempts to knife her dead body.

In keeping with modern city life most of the characters are commercial in their relationship with one another. The stability of his marriage to violet is seen by Joe as a commercial proposition. He uses it to get access to his customer's houses to sell cosmetics. Violet goes around straightening the hair of black women. Relationships between the genders in *Jazz* are either strained by exploitation or are broken by breach of trust. But at the end of the novel Morrison offers a small hope by reuniting Joe and Violet.

Jazz justifies the music referred to in the novel's title. Jazz music represents an original Afro-American response to the need for community cohesion. It is instantaneous, collective improvisational and cumulative. It involves the acts of anonymous individuals. It expresses and emphasizes difference in collectivity.

The black community's natural and spontaneous response to this music is hindered by the world view of the dominant while culture. Alice Manfred represents this worldview. She is confused in the distinction she makes between the Fifth Avenue marchers and the lowdown blues. Each kind of music brings to focus different dimensions of life in the new urban community, i.e. the anger, the violence, the desire, or the sweetness. It is for the community members to find the proper response to the different kind of music, be it that of the Fifth Avenue protestors or the dance of the reunited Joe and Violet.

Toni Morrison in her novels has explored various possibilities for the Afro-Americans. The fabric of her texts do not show any loud protest against the manifold oppression of society nor do they offer any radical solution to the multiple problems of the blacks. Her lyrical language softly persuades us to accept her camouflaged suggestions. Through her novels she clearly says that the multiple oppression is not confined to only one class or community it is universal and largely due to the individual and community's lack of response to and participation in its own native culture. This soft but firm voice of Toni Morrison has forced the world to recognise her, not as a marginalized Afro-American woman writer but as an important voice in the mainstream of world literature.

23

The Alienated Self—A Study of Anita Desai's *Clear Light of Day*

S.P. SWAIN

From fire to light, *Clear Light of Day* dwells on existentialist theme of time in relation to eternity. Existentialism which is basically concerned with the enduring human predicament in relation to unchanging human destiny has been the sole concern of Anita Desai. Desai quotes on the last page of the novel a very significant line from Eliot's *Four Quartets*: "Time the destroyer is time the preserver". It is 'time' which brings about a change in the lives of the characters in the novel. The childhood intimacy of the four children—Tara, Bim, Raja and Baba is gradually lost as they grow older and become aware of their variegated dreams and aspirations. In their pursuit of individual aims they reckon the loss of a wider-based, socially integrated deep rootedness. Anita Desai presents their polarities of personalities through images of sounds and silence. The despair and isolation of Bim is projected through the image of the mosquito (zoological image of sound):

> Tara and Bakul, and behind them the Misras, and somewhere in the distance, Raja and Benazir, only to torment her and mosequito-like sip her blood. All of them fed on her blood.... Now when they were full, they rose in swarms, humming away, turning their backs upon her. (153)

The zoological image of a "snail slowly, resignedly making its way from under the flower up a clod of earth only to tumble off the top onto its side—an eternal, miniature Sisyphus" (2), symbolically stands for the silence of Bim who withdraws herself from the El Dorado of life to shoulder all alone the responsibility of looking after her mentally retarded, dumb brother, Baba, and her widowed Aunt Mira. Then again, we have the image of the morning sun that instead of providing inspiration and zeal for existence shuts Tara out from the general go of life. Tara bows her head to "the morning sun that came slicing down, like a blade of steel onto the back of her neck" (1). The morning sun repels and isolates Tara. It is not homely but alien that acquires a brutal and harsh nature which "slices down like a blade of steel" (1). It is not a playful and cheerful sun. It is formidable and intimidating which triggers off the feel of alienation in Tara, who drops the screen and remains isolated from its ghastly sight:

> She actually got up and went to the door and lifted the bamboo screen that hung there, but the blank white glare of afternoon slanted in and slashed at her with its flashing knives so that she quickly dropped the screen. (21)

Desai evokes, through Tara's reactions to the light of the full-moon, a sense of the eerie: "...like snow, its touch was cold, marmoreal and made Tara shiver.... She could not free herself of them, of this shabby old house" (158-59). The most striking and powerful image projecting isolation and estrangement in the novel is the image of the cow drowned in the well. The cow can drown but was never taken out. It becomes the symbol of nausea, nausea generating isolation. Tara "seemed to fly apart in rejection and agitation" (159) from the house that "looked like a tomb in the moonlight, a whitewashed tomb rising in the midst of the inky shadows of trees and hedges, so silent—everyone asleep, or stunned by moonlight" (*ibid.*). The children continually broke apart into violent eruptions of emotion, seemed rigid, encased in separate silences like larvae in stiff-spun cocoons.

In this fourth dimensional novel, Desai endeavours to fathom the depths of time as destroyer and as preserver, mirroring the vicissitudes, distortions and manifestations that the two realities—past and present—bring about in the identity of the characters. In an interview with Sunil Sethi, Desai elaborates upon the theme of the novel:

> My novel is set in Old Delhi and records the tremendous change that a Hindu family goes through since 1947: Basically my pre-occupation was with recording the passage of time: I was trying to write a four-dimensional piece on how a family's life moves backwards and forwards in a period of time. My novel is about time as a destroyer, as a preserver and about what the bondage of time does to people. I have tried to tunnel under the mundane surface of domesticity. (Desai interviewed, *India Today*: 142)

The novel does not have a tangible story in the true sense of the term. There are some sharp, interlinked, episodic splinters of a disrupted family life, discussed or recollected after a long lapse of time by the two leading characters—Bim and Tara. Their recollection forms a new pattern, a transformed design within the old and the common, the unusual and the familiar, thereby revealing an enervating scenario of passions and personal traumas, love and sacrifice, death and betrayal, anger and accusation. The novel revolves round two brothers and two sisters who grew up in a house in old Delhi. The mental agony of a delicate young woman trapped in the pattern of movement and stillness has been musically orchestrated in this novel. Points and counterpoints, to and fro movement of the story bring about a sequential harmony to the entire piece. Thus, the novel carries the pattern of a musical composition. It sets off with the song of the koel and concludes with the song of the old master, thus suggesting a fusion of the rhythms of life, both natural and human. Time-bound existence is juxtaposed with timeless existence. Here again there is a creative tension between polarites, between death-themes and life-themes, between creation and destruction. It has the "pattern of a *raga* with harmonious *arohas* (rises) and *avarohas* (falls)" (Sharma 1981: 131). The four sections of the novel, suggesting "the four dimensions" of time, document the transitions in identity that take place in a New Delhi family. Prof. R.S. Pathak opines that "the novel throws some significant light on discords at various levels" (*The Fiction of Anita Desai*: 44).

The young girls, Bim and Tara, growing up with their callous and disinterested parents have to cope with a diabetic mother, a father who is nothing but "a master of entrance and exist" (131) and a mentally retarded brother. The novel describes the emotional affinity between the two main characters, Bim and her younger sister Tara, who are haunted by the memories of the past. The two epigraphs, one by Emily Dickinson:

> Memory is a strange bell—
> Jubilee and Knell

and other by T.S. Eliot:

> See, now they vanish
> The faces and places, with the self which,
> as it could, loved them, To become
> renewed, transfigured, in another pattern

which preface the novel highlight the theme of the effect of the remembrance of things past on the chief protagonist. While to Tara, the memories are a "jubilee", a source of wistful joy, to Bim, they strike the "knell" of sorrow, thus suggesting their temperamental alienation. The former wants to retain and cling to her past identity and enjoy it, while the latter is wearied of it and is in search of a new identity. Hence, the meeting of these two chief characters implies a clash of identities—the past and the present. By delineating their present identity, Anita Desai links it with their past and shows the inherent tie between the two. Here again, she comes back to the theme of polarisation and temperamental disaffinity. The two sisters differ in their attitudes to memories of childhood. The circumstances of their lives differ. The identity of each enacts and articulates the past in its own pattern. Tara, wife of Bakul, a diplomat posted abroad, is home after many years. Her homecoming is a return to the pleasant and unpleasant memories of childhood. Tara is a girl of modest ambitions "physically smaller and weaker than Bim", she lacks Bim's "vigour, her stamina" (123) and is a nonentity at school. Bim has an ambition to shape herself in the image of Florence Nightingale and Joan of Arc. Tara rejoices in the sheltered and cloistered life of her home in the company of Aunt Mira. In fact, Aunt Mira is her other identity. The marriage with Bakul and her stay abroad bring about a great change in the identity of Tara. Her life turns over a new leaf. When Tara returns to old Delhi, her old love for home revives and she wishes to fade away, to dissolve in the reminiscences of the past and to lose herself in order to recover her past identity. She feels "a part of her was sinking languidly down into the passive pleasure of having returned to the familiar" (12). The "old rose walk" (2), the sight of the snail, "an eternal, miniature Sisyphus" (*ibid.*) kindle her memory ablaze. But "I had not meant to go anywhere", she exclaims, when her husband invites her to his uncle's house, "I only wanted to stay at home". Tara opts for a home-bound life. Bakul is annoyed at her relapse into her childhood frivolities. On the other hand, Bim's reactions to her adolescent days have nothing of the romantic glamour of Tara's passionate musings about them. Bim is a victim of circumstances. Contrary to Bakul's expectations, she leads a different life. Usable to take decisions, face challenges and be strong, she revels in her childhood fancies. The abrupt change in the circumstances of her life and her family not only poses a threat to her high aspirations but simultaneously breeds identity crisis. She is unable to reconcile her aspirations to the circumstantial changes around her. After her parents' death and Tara's marriage, she is left alone to nurse her ailing brother Raja, attend to the aged, alcoholic and invalid aunt and look after her mentally retarded brother, Baba. It is these burdens and responsibilities that shatter her marital bliss and destroy her conjugal identity. With the passing away of Aunt Mira, she feels forlorn. She is left alone in the company of her helpless younger brother. The said and dismal experiences she passed through and the alienation from those she so fondly cherished, drain all her enthusiasm for the past.

Tara was fed on romances, and in reading them she would be "dragged helplessly into the underworld of semi-consciousness of the romances", while "Bim was often irritated and would toss them aside in dissatisfaction" (121). The polarities of temperament and imagination between Tara and Bim has been very lucidly portrayed by Anita Desai:

> Physically smaller and weaker than Bim, Tara lacked her vigour, her stamina. The noise, the dense populace, the hustle and jostle of school made her shrink into a still smaller, paler creature.... Whereas school brought out Bim's natural energy and vivacity that was kept damped down at home, school to Tara was a terror, a blight.... To Bim, school and its teachers and lessons were a challenge to her natural intelligence and mental curiosity. Tara, on the other hand, wilted when confronted by a challenge, shrank back into a knot of horrified stupor.... (123)

Both Tara and Bim realise the tremendous transformation brought about by time, altering their relations and attitudes. They recall the period of childhood as an age of love and intimacy with each other, the four of them forming a complete whole. But cracks begin to appear as they grow up and acquire more individual personalities. The partition of India and Pakistan creates a fissure in their familial ties. It disintegrates their family, becoming a powerful image of their feeling of estrangement. The partition brought barriers between people who had lived together for centuries in an atmosphere of mutual social and cultural understanding. Tara, Bim and Raja face a severe identity crisis. They are unable to relate their present to the past—their adulthood to childhood. Santosh Gupta observes:

> The period that lies inbetween—the growing consciousness and search for individuality of adolescence—fails to provide a continuity from the early period of childhood to the later stage of adulthood, causing deep psychological trauma and stress. (*The Fiction of Anita Desai*: 122)

Tara wistfully yearns for her childhood days, but all in vain. She is unable to resurrect the past. Her old home—the abandoned and moribund house symbolises the frustrated life of the aging Bim. The house is her identity. She too, is abandoned and in decay. Her realisation of her suffering, her dedication for others and her self-sacrifice intensify her feeling of loneliness. She thinks all her relations—Tara, Bakul, Raja and Benazir... came brutal invaders into her life only to torture her. In this cantankerous mood of agony, she wishes to get rid of the responsibility of her helpless brother Baba: "...but I might have to send you to live with Raja. I come to ask you...what would you think of that? Are you willing to go and live with Raja in Hyderabad" (183). But Bim is not without the milk of human kindness. As her rage is spent, she feels sorry for having chosen "Baba to vent her heart and pain and frustration on" (*ibid.*). She gradually regains her calm, and her heart is filled with love for "Raja and Tara and all of them who had lived in the house with her." So far she was living in a dark, dismal world where she could hardly get a glimpse of the clear light of day, where she experienced again and again, "the spider fear that lurked at the centre of the web-world" (135). But with her redeeming realisation and penitence, she is able to see this clear light:

> Although it was shadowy and dark, Bim could see as well as by the clear light of day that she felt only love and yearning for them all, and if there were hurts, these gashes and wounds in her side that bled, then it was only because her love was imperfect and did not encompass them thoroughly enough, and because it had flaws and inadequacies and did not extend to all equally. (165)

The vision of childhood dominates the novel. The adult world of the characters is seen as a projection of their childhood identity. The contrast between time past and time present, between childhood and adulthood is crucial to the aesthetic get-up of the novel. The moonlit dream-world of childhood is seen against the passage of time. Thus, the adult life of the characters is beclouded and bedimmed by their childhood identity. The novelist visualises the reality of childhood with a feminine and poetic-sensibility. The pestilent-stricken, violent world of the adults is contrasted with the boisterous and carefree world of the children. The images of sickness, disease and violence suggest the adult world, whereas images of joy, enthusiasm, curiosity and carelessness characterise childhood. This is the only Desai novel in which the domestic drama of absurdity is harmoniously juxtaposed against the backdrop of the partition of the country. Tara discovers her tender sensibility and her feminine identity in her adolescent infatuation with her teacher and even Baba is able to decipher the identity of his inarticulate world in the sounds of the gramophone he had collected from the abandoned house of Hyder Ali. The children in this novel pass through different levels of awareness. They are alienated from the external world which intrudes upon their consciousness, breeding anguish in their unruffled existence. Lost in their fairy world, they are attracted by forces, beyond their control, which bring about a change in their identity. Time acts as a catalytic agent in their lives. Tara seems to have lost her identity in marriage. But she gains in terms of family and motherhood. She assumes a new identity with her marriage, the identity of a mother and a housewife. Raja, too, seems to have lost his own. He relinquishes his Byronic longings in marriage, but experiences a new kind of freedom and a new kind of awareness linked with his marital and conjugal life. Both Bim and Tara admire Raja but Bim alone is able to keep pace with him. Tara finds it difficult to learn passages of poetry and recite them. She feels left out of the orbit of the companionship in which Raja and Bim stood together. Raja, Bim and Tara realise the dullness of their household and the strange distance between the world of adults and children. The adults, with their separate world of club and card-games, remain away from the children who are very close to each other in search of love and security.

Bim seems to have lost love, marriage and domesticity and is eagerly waiting for new experiences, new livers and new roots. Bim symbolises forces that have strengthened the foundation of all family life. She is the archetypal mother, a metaphor that Anita Desai subtly employs to reaffirm and reassert the life-themes in the novel. The sustaining presence of the maternal identity has been referred to in a number of ways. Mira Masi acts as a mother substitute and when she is gone, Bim plays the foster mother to her brothers and sisters. Thus, the three facets of the mother identity have been fictionalised in the novel—the mother who bears, the mother who cares and the mother who shares. But not the mother who destroys, as in *Voice in the City.*

Bim is a mother and a housewife. She embodies not only the katabolic impulses but also the forces which ensure permanence and continuity in a dynamic and transient world. Bim reflects Desai's vision of the identity of the new Indian woman, the dim stirrings of which we see in her desire to dress and smoke like men. She revolts against the traditional image of the Indian woman in words and deeds. Unlike most Indian girls, she opts out of marriage for the life of a spinster. She is reluctant to play the conventional role of a sex-object and a yoked-wife. In a sense, she is the symbol of the emancipated woman, the forerunner of the emerging Indian woman with her liberated womanhood.

Both Bim and Tara represent two aspects of the maternal identity—begetting and upbringing, breeding and nursing. Characters are brought together by the marriage of Moyna, Raja's daughter. Thus, marriage which, in Desai's earlier novels, was a destructive institution, breeding alienation assumes a positive significance. It is a source of movement in stillness, of continuity in change, of permanence in transience. Desai discovers the ultimate truth of life in an intuitive apprehension and a human acceptance of the polarities and paradoxes of life. The existential angst acquires a new dimension. Bim achieves her 'feminine self' in fusion, not in fission, in association, not in alienation, in affirmation, not in negation. Her deep commitment to her past as a maternal symbol, a feminine principle sustains her against the ravages of time. Her quest, positively affiliated to others, goes beyond her introvert self. Both Bim and Tara admire Raja's love for Urdu poetry but Bim alone is able to keep pace with him. "Tara finds it difficult to learn passages of poetry and recite them. She feels left out of the circle of companionship in which Raja and Bim stand together" [Gupta, *The Fiction of Anita Desai* (ed.), Dhawan, 1989: 119].

Unable to communicated and conceptualise, Baba lives in a vacuum of silence. Forced to live on the margins of the lives of others, he becomes a centrifugal force moving on the periphery of the lives of Tara and Bim. His withdrawal from the world of human Voices to the artificial sounds of the gramophone records makes him an eerie presence in the Mishra household.

In the shaded darkness of the house "silence had the quality of a looming dragon" (13) and Baba overcomes this oppressive and oneirodynic silence by playing the records on the gramophone "so endlessly, so obsessively" (*ibid.*). In associating himself with the world of the gramophones, Baba moves from a state of alienation to a state of identification. But Baba's fondness for music is confined to the traditional music, that of the 1940s. He dislikes contemporary music. Even the musical notes of the birds calling out in the garden and the sounds of the life outside his window do not move him. He finds solace in mechanical music: "...a mechanical bird had replaced the koels and pigeons of daylight" (30).

The theme of movement and stillness which figures prominently in *Fire on the Mountain*, is suggested in this novel through metaphors of the stagnant pool and the ever-growing tree. The theme of fusion or contact is indicated through reiterative allusions to the balustrade, the supporting railing. The balustrade exists only in relation to the individual balusters supporting it. After this revealing realisation, Bim forgets all her bitterness—she forgets the objects that had alienated her—from Raja and Tara. She is gradually relieved of the trauma of alienation.

The alienated anguish of a thwarted motherhood and the searing pangs of a widowed existence are most powerfully evoked in Mira Masi. The anguish of Bim's marital life is transformed beyond the limitations of traditional motherhood so as to give a new form to her marital identity. Her presence is a 'maternal presence', and it is this aspect of her character that renders a new dimension to her personal identity. She is the consummate symbol of a mother. Patterns of contrast in themes, characters and incidents besides adding to the textural density of the novel highlight the alienated life of the characters and their identity crisis. Bim's father leads an insensitive and callous life. Shanta Acharya observes:

> Quite contrary to expectations, Bim's parents are both portrayed as remote and far removed from the world of their children. They are both noted by their absence, they do not influence the lives of their children in any

> significant why. The father seeks refuge in the club playing bridge, unable to cope with the twin horrors of a diabetic wife and a retarded child. [Acharya, *Explorations* (ed.), Dhawan, 1982: 250]

The action of the novel is divided between the house and the garden. The characters are found either moving into the house from the garden or are going out from the house into the garden. This to and for shuttling of the characters between the house and the garden suggests their human and natural identity. Their inability to harmonise these two aspects generates identity crisis. The alliance of the human characters with the natural world is seen in the snail, the koel, the cat and the dog—all partaking in the drama of human experience. The bizarre translations of Raja and the profound lines of Eliot keep reverberating in Bim's mind. These 'poetic presences', skin to the calls of the koel outside, bring in the infinite dramas of self-identity into the action of the novel and refer to the affinity between art and life, between the human identity of the characters and their fictional identity. Bim becomes symbolic of Mother India that accommodates all and accepts all, disowns and shuns none. The Mishra sisters represent a clash of values. They cannot wholly get rid of the past nor can they completely accept the present. The past and the present accentuates their isolation and self-estrangement.

The renewal of self-identity in another mould and pattern is the theme of the novel. The attempt of Bim to transcend her past identity is suggested when she mockingly enquires of Tara: "Do you know anyone who would...secretly, sincerely, in his innermost self...really prefer to return to childhood?" (4). Both sisters are afraid to face their past identity. The book divides itself into two parts—first, Tara's visit to the filthy and unkempt mansion on the banks of Jamuna in Old Delhi and the two sisters' memories of the past. This reminiscence unveils a past quite alien to the present, to the cheerful, chaotic childhood that one finds in a joint-family. Bim and Tara are the artistic equivalents and projections of all other Desai protagonists. Tara is a foil to Bim. The identity of the one is a passport to the identity of the other. Tara's weakness reveals Bim's strength but

Tara's sensitivity to weakness also throws Bim's character in perspective. The novel reveals itself through the consciousness of Bim who is disgusted with her cloistered presence in the family. She feels she is unwanted, since she fails to get any response from anyone around. Bitterly lonely, she develops signs of nausea. Illness, both mental and physical, seems to infect the novels of Anita Desai. Caught in the contradictions within herself, Bim is unable to relate with her brothers and sisters. She feels split within and torn apart in "loving them and not loving them, accepting them and not accepting them. Understanding them and not understanding them" (166). Her emotional estrangement and turbulence is symbolised by the violent dust-storm raging outside. She longs to come out of the cocoon of herself to discover her true being and form viable relationship with others, and to make her fragmented existence "a whole, a perfect pattern" (*ibid.*).

Bim's separation from her brothers and sisters accelerates in her the feeling of fragmentation and incompleteness, of the disintegration of herself. She feels isolated from her domestic milieu and is unable to co-ordinate and relate herself with others. Bim, who and felt herself to be the centre and had "stayed and become part of the pattern, inseparable" (56), now has the feeling of isolation and forlornness. Even when her own self is concerned, Bim is unable to relate it with its past life which symbolically suggests the estrangement of the modern individual in a transitional society.

The cruel, intolerant, puritanic and power-hungry life of Aurangzeb becomes a mirror in which Bim reckons the growth of her own self. She rejects Aurangzeb as an apathetic, ego-centric power-maniac. This symbolises her transition from hatred to love, from alienation to accommodation and from egotism to altruism. The life of Aurangzeb holds an epiphany to Bim's life. In moments of awakening, she becomes aware of the forces that hindered her quest for a truly emancipated self, and moves towards a new, genuine and authentic identity which she discovers in the embraces and kisses of her nieces. There is sunshine. The twitter of pigeons brings a note of joy. The air is reverberating with the excitement of the anticipated marriage, of release from staticity. The novel closes like *Where Shall We Go This Summer?* with hope. Anita Desai seems to dwell upon the theme of hope-despair-hope. The novel moves zig-zag. This optimistic atmosphere relieves the pervading gloom in the earlier parts. The identity of the resurrected and rejuvenated Bim, becomes the symbol of a resurrected and rejuvenated India—a nation having shunned her violent, bitter and eventful past is on the verge of a new beginning, a nation in search of a new identity. The last words of Aurangzeb bring to Bim a searing realization of the fundamental alienation of man: "Many were around me when I was born but now I am going alone" (167).

Alienation of the self in *Clear Light of Day* unlike Desai's other novels is not related to psychic illness but to emotional callousness operating within the domestic ambience of silence and staticity. Alienation here finds expression in the to and fro shuttling of the characters between the past and the present, tradition and modernity. In this novel, alienation leads to identification which is symbolised by the "clear light of day". The novel, nevertheless, ends in a positive note. Like the other novels of Desai, here, alienation does not lead to the annihilation and immolation of the self but to its rejuvenation and reidentification with the milieu. Ultimately, all "opposing needs" and discords "seemed to mingle and meet at the very roots" (110) and Bim could see the clear light of day.

REFERENCES

Acharya, Shanta. "The Problems of the Self in the Novels of Anita Desai" in R.K. Dhawan (ed.), *Explorations in Modern Indo-English Fiction* (New Delhi: Bahri, 1982).

Desai, Anita. *Clear Light of Day* (New Delhi: Allied, 1980). (All citations from the text followed by page numbers in parentheses are from this edition of the novel.)

Gupta, Santosh. "Polarities of Imagination", in R.K. Dhawan (ed.), *The Fiction of Anita Desai* (New Delhi: Bahri, 1989).

Interview, Anita Desai, *India Today*, December 1-15, 1980.

Pathak, R.S. "The Alienated Self in the Novels of Anita Desai" in R.K. Dhawan (ed.), *The Fiction of Anita Desai* (New Delhi: Bahri, 1989).

Sharma, R.S. *Anita Desai* (New Delhi: Amold-Heinemann, 1981).

❑❑❑

24

T.S. Eliot and Hinduism

SUREKHA DANGWAL

Born in a Unitarian family of Henry Ware Eliot and Charlotte Eliot, on 26 September 1888, in Massachusetts, U.S.A., Eliot graduated from the University of Harvard with Sanskrit, Philosophy, English Literature and History as one of his chief subjects. He inherited the intellectual as well as the religious traits from his grandfather, William Greenleaf Eliot, one of the leading social and educational reformers of Boston. Where his mother's puritan ideals moulded the 'tet-et-face' character of Eliot, his study of Sanskrit, and also the influence of his favourite teachers, like Irving Babbit and George Santyana, imbibed a philosophical nature in both his thinking and behaviour. He visited Paris for soliciting Bergson's views on the concept of his 'duree'. His fellowship for research on F.H. Bradley made his visit possible to Germany, wherefrom he had to shift to England in view of the ongoing World War I.

He stayed with Bertrand Russell in England, once his teacher at Harvard. He met Vivienne Haigh-Wood in 1914-15, and married her in the same year against the approval of his parents. He wrote tremendous poetry between 1915-27, including "The Waste" and the "Hollow Men". The period proved to be a making-phase in his career, contributing his early criticism, like *The Sacred Wood* and several of his essays on metaphysical poets. The "Rock" inaugurated a shift to drama, with a background of several of his conversions. The period from 1935 to 1965 consists of his plays as well as the philosophical poetry. The conferment of the Nobel Prize, in 1948, is the significant event associated with the duration. He completed his popular critical theories during this period, before his death in 1965.

Oriental influences, particularly the Vedic philosophy, bears a tremendous influence in Eliot's works. The Western world is degenerated in respect of both moral and spiritual values to the extent of an animal society. Eliot finds the reason behind the sterility in contemporaneity as the lack of discipline and restraint among its citizens. The crux of the problem in the *Waste* contains the dismay, caused due to the negative culture in sex and society. Eliot proposes the solution through the myth of the Lord Bhagirath, and also the way suggested by *Brihadaranyaka Upanishad,* in its three commands of 'datta', 'dayadhvam', and 'damyata'. Eliot makes vedic philosophy more apparent than the Christian conditions itself. If Lord Buddha has been elemental in inspiring Eliot's view of salvation, the Hindu Upanishads make the oriental metaphysics easily realizable down the lines of the *Waste.*

T.S. Eliot is essentially an environmentalist, one who has worked upon the stage, exhibiting the balance through a philosophical atmosphere. Among other givings of the environmental theatre, Eliot establishes that death is a natural source of balancing ecology. Unlike Science, he shows that metaphysical reality has a better correspondence to the physical environment, balancing the air, water, and population on a natural accord. The idea of destruction emanates both the ideas of creation and preservation. Thomas is one whose sense of sacrifice, martyrdom, salvation, and also destruction have been presented on vedic information of the entities of death as well as rebirth. He is treated in a Christian condition, but developed through the knowledge available in comparable situations in *Ramcharitmanas* and *Rig Veda.* It is in view of Eliot's imitation of vedic situations, and also atmosphere, that Thomas talks of a universal consciousness, and not a Christian martyrdom. Death, in itself, is a renewing agent and not a dreadful reality. The idea is not Christian but Hindu. The vedic atmosphere, from both *Rig Veda* and *Athar Veda,* helps in making Thomas' advancement from the physical to the spiritual possible. The 'Action Suffering Formulae' is not a Greek 'epiphany' but an imitation of the following discourse, reflected in the atmosphere of *Athar Veda*,

> Penance and also action were within the great sea (Arnava); those were the groomsmen; those the wooers,

and followed by,

> Both penance namely an action were within the great sea; penance was born from action, that did they worship a chief.

Among the popular vedic scripture, to have been imitated by Eliot in respect of its form and content, is the *Bhagavad Gita.* At least, in general making of *The Family Reunion* and *The Cocktail Party*, it has a vital role to play. Eliot borrows both situations and atmosphere from *Bhagavad Gita*, and befits his Christian character to it. *The Family Reunion* carries a similar problem to Arjuna, in *Gita*. Harry has a problem which he really does not understands. He is confused, susceptible of himself and remains in a perennial tension. His problem is not the sin and expiation, incorporating his wife's ghost, but the whereabouts of his father, which he repeatedly interrogates to Warburton. Arjuna puts questions regarding human relations in his denial to the Lord when he disagrees to kill his own kiths and kins on the battlefield. The confusion and also frustration of the two, i.e. Harry and Arjuna are common and commonly have these been responded to by Agatha and Lord Krsna, respectively. The Lord, in *Bhagavad Gita*, admonishes Arjuna about 'Karma' and divine knowledge through four yogas, preparing him for his participation in the war between Pandavas and the Kauravas. The essence of *Bhagavad Gita* is the development of Arjuna from the bonds of time, 'maya' (allusions) and successive births. This actually has he described as a right choice for salvation. In *The Family Reunion*, Harry is treated by Agatha into a spiritual plane, both from the physical and the religions levels. Harry's advancement, from one to another level of salvation, is vedic, to which, Agatha has played as a substitute of Lord Krsna, admonishing the disciple for the spiritual upliftment.

Harry has been taken for Arjuna, and Agatha replaces Lord Krsna. Similar are the compatriots of *The Cocktail Party* both in theme and characterization. Celia is detached on a negative path of spiritual realization through the mystic knowledge provided by *Bhagavad Gita*. Harcourt Reilly works like another Krsna, admonishing Celia in a perfect mood of Arjuna's dullness, melancholy and frustration. She follows a similar situation to *Bhagavad Gita,* in her escapism into the world of epidemics, as a substitute for self-realization, or salvation as told by the Lord. Even Eliot's dramaturgy, in these two plays, feeds and grows upon the incantation of *Gita*. The plot of *The Cocktail Party* is dependent upon its dialogue. The pattern of developing the plot through the rhetoric is vedic, especially, imitated upon *Bhagavad Gita*. The most illustrative aspect of *Bhagavad Gita*, in Eliot's plays, is the idea of reconciliation, which, ultimately, means as the salvation itself. The two odds of the East and the West, and also the Christian and the vedic, have been enjoined for exacting the spiritual reconciliation.

The *Four Quartets* is spread over into four quartets, consisting of "Burnt Norton", "East Coker", "Dry Salvages", and the "Little Gidding", corresponding to the four separate elements of air, water, earth and fire. The scheme of the quartets is to justify the four yogas, enunciated by the Lord, representing *Dhyanyoga* (meditation-air), *Karmayoga* (action-water), *Jnanyoga* (wisdom-earth), and *Bhaktiyoga* (devotion-fire). The metaphysics of *Gita* has been reproduced as a matter of detachment, working upon salvation through right action.

Eliot is a romantic in theme and a classicist in treatment. His theory of impersonality proves paradoxical in regard to the text of the *Four Quartets*. Eliot, in the poem, is initially autobiographical, as the four different places described as Burnt Norton, East Coker, Dry Salvages and Little Gidding relate his personal experiences, because of which he appears to be more sentimental than a pre-romantic poet. He is essentially a pre-romantic poet, at least, in view of his love of the past, medievalism, the melancholic and the estranged sensibility, 'dull and barren fields' and 'empty pool'. It is a purely romantic characteristic, when he becomes nostalgic with his aloofness in England, and also the memories of his childhood. The contents of the poem, which work in its background, are, thus, romantic.

He is a classicist as a philosopher, making for himself an atmosphere in which the teachings of the Lord, reverberate in its full echo. The metaphysical knowledge, given by the Lord to Arjuna, makes Eliot to understand that the soul has some day to depart to its original abode, and so, the attachment of the worldly relation is not meaningful. He accepts the sermons of the Lord, and reproduces there in his text with perfect faith and confidence. He realizes peace for himself by understanding that, whether it is England, or America, one has to pass away from this earth. *Bhagavad Gita* has best suited to his need in detaching himself from the realities of the temporal world, finding a perfect mode of resignation and renunciation for himself.

Eliot's works show an arrangement in individual's advancement from one level to another. *Murder in the Cathedral* exhibits the advancement from the religious to the spiritual; and in *The Family Reunion*, the levels are of both the physical and the religious; the planes have been shifted to pure psychology in his later plays. The reconciliation is the self-realization, or a salvation, which cannot become feasible, unless the physical itself is not elevated to the spiritual. That is to say, not only salvation, even heaven is not possible without death, or detachment. Eliot affirms the belief that all human problems are solvable. He suggests that a human malady should first be tried psychologically, because a human illness basically belongs to psychology. If the cure on psychological ways does not become possible, so, instead of leaving the character in a perfect insanity like Hamlet, the person should be tried philosophically, by changing his medium completely. As Carl Jung believes that "all saints and sea fearers have an element of crime in them", saints, like Thomas and Harry, consist of a previous life changed to a new medium in their present. That is to say that all roaming saints are characters transformed from one physical medium to another of the spiritual. Eliot cent per cent treats himself in this technique of the 'Philosophical psychology', which helps him in trancendenting himself from an atmosphere of intense emotionalism to a metaphysical detachment of renunciation. This is how Eliot believes that one action does fructify the lives of others. The admonition of *Bhagavad Gita* is to be nicely acknowledged in this respect,

> So Krishna, as when he admonished Arjuna
> on the field of battle.
> Not fare well,
> But fare forward, voyagers.

The oriental mysticism is the chord of Eliot's works. The remaining, unpublished portion of the *Waste Land* could be more helpful in authenticating Eliot's sources in the Vedas. There is still ample opportunities to work on Indian inferences in Eliot's minor poetry, including the "Ash Wednesday" and "The Unfinished Poem". Eliot's critics are many more, and the comments, thereupon Indian inferences, are less commanding. Need is there to evaluate the Western critics on Indian influences in Eliot's works, so that the Sanskrit metaphysics is not misinterpreted, and Eliot is not condemned for his philosophical taste and talent. There is still more to be searched than doing research on Eliot's treatment of the oriental, particularly, vedic mysticism.

❑❑❑

25

Superstition and Psyche in Anita Desai's *Cry, The Peacock*

M. RAJESHWAR

Maya, the central character of Anita Desai's *Cry, The Peacock*, is obsessed almost from the beginning of the novel with the gloomy prophecy of an albino astrologer. According to the prophecy, she or her husband would die during the fourth year of her marriage. Her father dismisses the prophecy as nonsense and orders that it should be forgotten. Obeying his wish Maya keeps the prophecy rigorously repressed in her unconscious until her marriage with Gautama enters the fourth year. Now triggered off by the death of her pet dog, Toto, it assumes during the course of the novel the shape of an obsessional neurosis and keeps gnawing at the core of her being like an oversized pest feeding on a tender leaf.

It is strange that Maya should so superstitiously believe in the veracity of the prophecy, although she knows that Gautama and his family "hoot with derision at the mention of superstition."[1] In the beginning of her neurotic affliction she frequently tells herself that it was she herself who was fated to die. But she is in ardent love with life and so she soon begins to wonder whether it was not "Gautama's life that was threatened" (164). Taking this line of reasoning further she fears for her life and would keep the secret for herself at any cost.

> He must not know, not even guess. Never, never, never. If he guessed, new dangers would arise like sudden fires out of the cracked earth.... Ah, if Gautama found out,

> would he, might he not put me in peril of my life? Did he not love life too.... (151)

Not very long after she is almost convinced that Gautama is certainly fated to die and the thought makes her more and more secretive.

> I glanced at him now, slyly, for sly I had grown with such a load of secrets that had to be hidden from him, such evil and awful secrets. (165)

It has been suggested in the novel and later harped on by critics that Maya is obsessed with the prophecy because of the romance involved in it. But the knowledge of depth psychology holds the promise of examining her irrational and superstitious belief from an entirely new angle. Freud attributes superstitious beliefs to suppressed hostility.

> It can be recognized most clearly in neurotics suffering from obsessional thinking...that superstition derives from suppressed hostile and cruel impulses. Superstition is in large part the expectation of trouble; and a person who has harboured frequent evil wishes against others, but has been brought up to be good and has therefore repressed such wishes into the unconscious, will be especially ready to expect punishment for his unconscious wickedness in the form of trouble threatening him from without.[2]

Does Maya's superstition too originate in her suppressed hostile and cruel impulses? To all appearances she has been an absolutely submissive and obedient daughter, sister and wife and so it may sound outrageous to accuse her of harbouring cruel impulses. But probing into her unconscious would reveal that there is immense suppressed hostility in her unconscious against her husband and to an extent against her father.[3] Being a "creature of instinct" (16) she seems to hold Gautama responsible for her unfulfilled instinctuality in the marital relationship. She is also angry with him because after four years of life together she is compelled to come to the sad conclusion that she would soon lose her already rudimentary self. She grows anxious on account of the threats to her self-preservation and neurotically perceives Gautama's death as a solution. The prophecy comes as a convenient external justification to her unconscious wish and for that reason she tenaciously clings to it. I will dwell at some length on Maya's reasons for wishing Gautama dead and then return to her superstitious belief.

Maya is extremely faithful to her instincts which, as is their nature, crave for unqualified and wild satisfaction. According to Freudian tenets normal people in her circumstances would have effected a withdrawal by influencing the instinctual urges at the psychic level. But tragically for Maya, her very life appears to be intricately woven with and highly dependent on her instincts. Given her instinctuality Maya expects some emotional and physical satisfaction in married life but both of them are denied her, one by Gautama's cold intellectuality and the other by his age. Maya's longing for the sensuous enjoyment of life is dampened by liberal doses of the *Gita* philosophy of non-attachment. Her effusive emotionality is always counter-balanced by Gautama's analytical mind. While he views "nothing subjectively, nothing with passion" (150) she is "flooded with tenderness and gratitude" (11) when he merely touches her hair, falls "into the soft, velvet well of the primordium of original instinct, of first-formed love" (11) when he draws a finger down her cheek, and takes to hating her own pretty face for failing to make any impact on him. She has to thus continually contend with unreciprocated emotionality and feels terrible on that score.

Sex is not only an intensely and intrinsically pleasurable experience but it can act as a revitalising force in an otherwise sterile life. Freud, in fact, views sex as the prototype of all pleasurable experiences of life. Maya's earth-bound nature makes her well-inclined to derive the fullest satisfaction from this intimate experience. It is difficult to conjecture what course her psyche would have taken if she were married to a much younger man and has been satisfied sexually. But because of Gautama's age and attitude to sex she remains a much disappointed woman. Even when they do make love the act is utterly devoid of passion. Several passages in the novel have been devoted to the portrayal of her disillusionment in sex. At the beginning of the novel itself Maya makes a frank admission of her sexual dissatisfaction born of Gautama's unpardonable negligence.

> Telling me to go to sleep while he worked at his papers, he did not give another thought to me, to either the soft, willing body or the lonely, wanting mind that waited near his bed. (9)

Frustrated by his coldness she gives herself up to a fit of pillow-beating! As her disillusionment becomes a routine experience she increasingly sexualises her surroundings, perhaps by way of displacement. The papaya trees in the courtyard, for example, assume a new sexual significance for her.

> I contemplated that, smiling with pleasure at the thought of those long streamers of bridal flowers that flow out of the core of the female papaya tree and twine about her slim trunk, and the firm, wax-petalled blossoms that leap directly out of the solid trunk of the male.... (92)

As her grip over herself begins to slacken she begins to experience hallucinatory visions of lizards and birds coupulating in weird settings.

> Of lizards, the lizards that come upon you, stalking you silently, upon clawed toes, slipping their clublike tongues in and out, in and out with an audible hiss... they have struck you to a pillar of salt which, when it is motionless they will mount and lash with their slime-dripping tongues, lash and lash again, as they grip you with curled claws, rubbing their cold bellies upon yours, rubbing and grinding, rubbing and grinding. (127)

What Maya experiences here seems to be a symbolic gratification of the sexual desire which remains unfulfilled in actual life.

The image of fighting and mating peacocks, apart from being the central motif of the novel, underlines Maya's sexual frustration too. The memory of her innocent enjoyment of their call in her childhood becomes a foil to her present over-crowded mind, full of bird and animal imagery.

> But sleep was rent by the frenzied cries of peacocks pacing the rocks at night—peacocks searching for mates, peacocks tearing themselves to bleeding shreds in the act of love, peacocks screaming with agony at the death of love. The night sky turned to a flurry of peacocks' tails, each star a staring eye. (175)

In spite of her total frustration, Maya's moral scrupulosity does not allow her to cross the bounds of marital morality. Nor is she able to sublimate this powerful biological urge in the manner of her friend Leila who selflessly serves her tuberculous husband. Her married life ends up being emotionally and socially sterile.

A continuous frustration of the body's sexual needs can be disastrous to somebody like Maya, given her fierce instinctuality. A healthy emotional and sexual life would have given her a sense of security and stopped her psyche from decaying. This view acquires validation from Freud's observation:

> experience shows...that women, who, as being the actual vehicles of the sexual interests of mankind, are only endowed in a small measure, with the gift of sublimating their instincts, and who...when they are subjected to the disillusionments of marriage, fall ill of severe neuroses which permanently darken their lives.[4]

Freud attributes neurosis of women to sexual dissatisfaction resulting from the rigours of civilized sexual morality. Biologically speaking, marital unfaithfulness could be a viable cure for the ailment. However, such a thing entails perhaps the most severe indictment in the rigidly organised Indian society. Freud continues:

> the more strictly a woman has been brought up and the more sternly she has submitted to the demands of civilization, the more she is afraid of taking this way out; and in the conflict between her desires and her sense of duty, she once more seeks refuge in a neurosis. Nothing protects her virtue as securely as illness.[5]

Maya too seeks a neurotic solution but only to find it inadequate. Something more drastic than neurosis needs to be considered by her psyche.

Secondly, Maya perceives that eventually she will lose herself as a result of a long experience of eventlessness. Her life appears to her as an endless tedium with nothing significant taking place at any time. She is never the centre of importance nor is she instrumental in any event. The sphere of her social activities is so severely restricted that she seems to feel suffocated within it. But by Indian standards her life situation appears to be ideal. She has a secure home, earning husband and well-defined future. These seemingly ideal external conditions are however not acceptable to her unconscious where her desire for unbridled freedom is hidden.

The novel abounds in incidents that show how her longing for outdoor life is constantly frustrated mainly by Gautama. As a child she had enjoyed the scenic beauty and cool weather of Darjeeling and now she longs to go there with Gautama. When she timidly suggests the possibility to Gautama he replies in a cold astringent tone, "Why don't you?... Your father would take you wherever you wanted to go. He *can*" (40). The Kathakali ballets performed at night in parts of South India, hold great attraction to Maya.

> 'I want—I want,'...'to see the Kathakali dances. I have heard of the ballets they have in their villages.... And the dancers are all men,....' The masks they wear—you must have seen them? And their costumes. And the special kind of music. And it is all out in the open, at night, by starlight—and perhaps they have torches. (42-43)

To her imploration to take her to the South, Gautama coolly suggests that she wait till a Kathakali troupe comes to Delhi. He apparently sees no strong reason to undertake a tiresome journey down South in the sweltering summer.

The fact of Maya's constricted life comes most vividly alive in the scene of Gautama's all male party. Charmed by the vibratingly rich Urdu poetry recited by these cultured wine-drinking gentlemen, Maya breaks an age old rule and joins them. While the other men politely, but uneasily, respond to her presence Gautama not only shatters her hope of participating in the pulsating and poetry-charged atmosphere but also subtly drives home to her the truth that she does not belong there.

> Turning his back to me, he stood talking to a friend, a glass in his hand, and his voice rose, in order that I might hear, when he said, 'Blissful, yes, because it is unrelated to our day, unclouded by the vulgarity of ill-educated men, or of overbearing women...'. (104)

To add to her problems stemming from inactivity she remains childless. The birth of a child would have given her a sense of achievement and her creative urge would have got focussed on a helplessly dependent human being instead of getting diffused over nature and spread outside human interest.

Three plus years of married life and the prospect of a passionless and unchallenging life for the next forty or fifty years, during which she would continue to be obedient to her husband and face neither choices nor challenges, comes as a shocking revelation to her hyperactive mind. Her repeated confession that she or Gautama will surely die, in a way, indicates that the opposite would be true—that especially Gautama will not die before her. So according to this logic if she is to live and find the happiness that is her due Gautama will have to go. And the focal point of her thought, day in and day out, becomes the albino's prophecy which appears to justify and dramatise her wish. But she allows herself considerable time before she does anything drastic. All through the novel she keeps her wish hidden in her unconscious and the prophecy itself shrouded in secrecy. This is because as a neurotic she is still aware of the moral sanctions against such wishes. Indoctrinated to be faithful to her husband, she feels her hand held back by an invisible force. The neurotic defence mechanisms such as sleep rituals, hallucinatory visions and nightmares (where her secret longings come alive to her), experience of split personality, adverse somatic symptoms and religious avoidance of violence woefully fail to blunt the edge of her unconscious wish. At most places she appears to reel under the pressure and break to pieces as a result of the struggle within. Yet she hesitates. She is aware of the unseemly consequences and she is scared of not only society but her own conscience. In order to be done with Gautama without antagonising the social imperatives and her own super-ego the only way that is still open to her is psychosis. Once a human organism is entrusted to psychosis nature takes its own course. The preservation of its physical integrity becomes more important than the protection of its social image. In fact, in psychotics the super-ego, the moral agency, becomes completely inactive. Psychosis would thus help Maya to carry out her wish without earning disapproval. She therefore progressively moves towards a psychotic solution to her struggle.

Her transition from neurosis to psychosis is powerfully underscored in the scene of the dust-storm in which she is shown as running "on and on, from room to room, laughing as maniacs laugh once the world gives them up and surrenders them to their freedom" (190). Maya's shutting herself in as a measure of protection from the raging dust-storm is symbolic of her total withdrawal from the world of purposeful action and meaningful relationships. The exact point of her plunging into the abysmal depths of psychosis, however, is her act of violence itself. Maya's pushing Gautama off the parapet of their house is not fortuitous. There are simply no accidents in psychic life. Behind Maya's final indulgence in violence there has been a prolonged psychic struggle which she has not known herself. Having done the deed and having taken recourse to psychosis she relaxes and openly declares that unlike her, Gautama has not been in love with life and so according to the prophecy he had to die.

> It had to be one of us, you see, and it was so clear that it was I who was meant to live. You see, to Gautama it didn't really matter. He didn't care, and I did. (215-16)

Governed by the primary process thinking she does not camouflage her thoughts by drawing on her linguistic resources any more. Her adult life with all its responsibilities and anxieties has become a sealed book for her. She is faithful to herself and the social and moral consequences of her actions do not matter to her any more now.

Her superstitious belief thus helped her immensely in the process of unconsciously identifying her problems and their source. From a shadowy figure the albino sprang to life and has come to mean much to her during her neurotic struggle. After she embraced psychosis what the charlatan said years ago has become gospel truth to her. But for him she would not have perceived Gautama as her foremost enemy and would not have considered the possibility of violently working out her equation with him.

NOTES AND REFERENCES

1. Anita Desai, *Cry, The Peacock* (Delhi: Orient Paperbacks, 1980, rpt. 1988), pp. 75-76.
2. Sigmund Freud, "Determinism, Belief in Chance and Superstition—Some Points of View", *The Psychopathology of Everyday Life*, tr. Alan Tyson (Harmondsworth: Penguin, 1960), p. 232.
3. In an earlier article while playing down the father fixation theory I argued that Maya nursed a grouse against her father Raisahib for impeding the development of her individuality with his over-protective attitude all through her childhood and adolescence, then for throwing her into the fetters of marriage with a passionless and cold intellectual and finally for callously neglecting her thereafter. I concluded that Maya unconsciously took her revenge against him by creating a scandal which she knew he dreaded. But in psychological life things are 'over determined.' Every significant psychological event in a person's life has a multiplicity of reasons. Maya's wish to avenge herself on her father could be only one of the many reasons for her to want to kill Gautama.

   "Anita Desai's *Cry, The Peacock*: The Father's Unconscious," *Indian English Literature Since Independence*. IAES Golden Jubilee Volume, ed. Ayyappa Paniker (New Delhi: The Indian Association for English Studies, 1991), pp. 44-48.
4. Sigmund Freud, *Civilized Sexual Morality and Modern Nervous Illness*, tr. James Strachey (Harmondsworth: Penguin, 1985), p. 47.
5. *Ibid.*

26

Where Shall We Go This Summer?—Sita's Incarcerated Self

S.P. SWAIN

Anita Desai's *Where Shall We Go This Summer?* (1975) dwells on the theme of incertitude, alienation and incommunication in married life. It is the alienation of a woman, a wife and a mother, an alienation conditioned by society and family. The childless Maya's angst in *Cry, The Peacock* is existential and psychic, but Sita's anguish in this novel is domestic and mundane.

Desai dramatises the conflict between two irreconcilable temperaments and two diametrically opposed attitudes to life. Sita, the protagonist, is a nervous, sensitive, middle-aged woman who finds herself isolated from her husband and children because of her emotional reactions to many things that happen to her. She is an introverted character, whose suffering springs from her constitutional inability to accept the authority of the society. Hence, her alienation is natural and dispositional. Unable to put up with her in-laws, she withdraws herself from the milieu into her own protective shell. She withdraws herself from her husband which is suggested through the crows preying on the eagle. Thus, her alienation is biological and physical.

Raman, Sita's husband, like Gautama in *Cry, The Peacock*, fails to understand her violence and passion. Raman is sane, rational and passive. Sita is irrational and hysteromaniac. Through Sita, Anita Desai voices the awe of facing all alone "the ferocious assaults of existence".[1] The conflict between two polarised temperaments and two discordant viewpoints represented by Sita and Raman, sets up marital discord and conjugal misunderstanding as the *leit-motif* of Desai's novels. The interrogative and inquisitive title of the novel is a pointer to the ennui of Sita's anguished soul. Her introversion, like Maya's in *Cry, The Peacock*, leads to her psychic odyssey. Fed up with the dreary metropolitan life in Bombay and tormented by the 'paranoic' fear of her fifth and reluctant pregnancy, she leaves for Manori islet off the Marve mainland. Sita's father-fixation hinders her contact with her husband. Here, once again Desai returns to the elusive father-figure. She demonstrates Sita's temperamental disaffinity with Raman through the scene where they talk about the stranger encountered *en route* from Ajanta and Ellora: "He seemed to be brave," she observed when Raman asked her why she had once more brought up the subject of the hitch-hiking foreigner months later.

> "Brave? Him?", Raman was honestly amused. "He was a fool.... He did not even know which side of the road to wait on".

"Perhaps that was only innocence," Sita faltered, "and it made him seem more brave, not knowing anything but going on nevertheless" (p. 52).

Sita's unconscious recognition of the irrationality of the stranger is illustrative of her own longing for "a life of primitive reality" (p. 152) and the distance she had travelled away from her husband. She feels a frog out of water in her father-in-law's "age-rotted flat" where they all live like pariahs "a life of sub-human placidity, calmness, and sluggishness" disinclined to introspection and introversion. She regards their soulless existence as a menace to her own marital and conjugal identity and boldly flouts the dehumanising and destabilising norms and values of a society whose stranglehold it is difficult to escape. The disintegration of their human identity is emphasised through the recurrent images of prey and predator. Sita says:

> They are nothing...nothing but appetite and sex. Only food, sex and money matter. Animals. (p. 47)

The first section of the novel is profusely loaded with images of brutality and violence. Raman's sadistic delight in Sita's failure to protect the eagle, Menaka's indifference to the vegetable life or even her senseless destruction of her dilettante paintings are all symbolic of a subterranean fury. Unable to reconcile herself to this violence, Sita leaves for the islet of Manori where her father had created enchantment out of emptiness. Sita, in fact, wants to escape the tyrannous grips of a cannibalistic urban milieu. She wants to escape the forces of fear and destruction which breed archetypal urges. Her alienation from all experience is due to her love for life and her reluctance to accept violence in any form. Thus, her flight to the island forms the focus of the novel.

Sita deems the flight a holy pilgrimage, a journey for spiritual purification, a search for identity. The theme of estrangement and violence is projected in terms of social and psychic forces moulding individual identities. As a result, the novel is based on a very narrow canvas, too narrow to reflect the intricacies of Sita's aloofness. Yet had Desai probed deeper into the sources of Sita's alienation, much of the fictional value of the novel would have been lost. Sita is an uprooted woman who wants to regain her primitive self. Her escape to the island is a biological, not an existential necessity. Ironically, Sita's pilgrimage with its promise of renewal and regeneration is the result of her social alienation. There comes a change in Sita's identity. But the children refuse to share the life of primitive reality which is the very identity of the island. Hence, their alienation has very little or no impact on their individual identities. The island forms the core of Sita's conscious existence. The sea and the island which suggest two different polarities of existence provide a picture in contrast in the symbolic design and movement of the novel. Sita's other identity finds expression on this island. It represents that part of herself which she had failed to realise earlier. The islet is a projection of her other self, her other identity. She knows there exists a close tie between herself and the island, but she knows too it is the island that alienates her from her instinctive drives. The parallel existence of these two levels of awareness in her mind gives rise to her identity crisis. It keeps on tormenting her till she discovers that undifferentiated life is like a jelly fish, live and objective, but without form, without definite identity.

Through the objective correlative of the jelly fish, Desai depicts Sita's amoebic and shapeless life. Through this, Sita realises the existential nature of all reality. From now onwards, she cuts herself off the deceptive, elusive and quasi-mystical world of her father. Sita's escape to the island is an escape from the 'madding crowd', from the dictates of her social conscience: "He who refuses does not repent. Should he be asked again, he would say No again. And yet No...the right No...crushes him for the rest of life" (p. 47). Sita's refusal to live life as it comes motivates her journey to the islet for the second time after a lapse of twenty years, a self-conscious journey made to revive and recreate the past. But this quest for the forfeited charm and simplicity of her past identity is an illusion. Her frequent return to her childhood days impedes her refusal to grow up and accept the responsibilities of adult life, and her inability to comprehend the past conspires against her marital harmony.

Sita's unconscious identification with the stranger's irrationality is expressive not only of her own quest for a life of primitive reality, but also of her alienation from Raman who regards it practically as an act of infidelity. Sita knows that since the 'infidelity was only psychic', it was so much more immeasurable for that.

Desai delineates the physical and psychic states of her characters through objective correlatives. For instance, the pathetic sight of an old man and a fatally anaemic or fatally tubercular but beautiful woman looking lovingly at one another suggests the alienated plight of Sita in a hard, harsh world beaming with lust and violence. Sita's return to Manori is, like the withdrawal of Monisha and Nirode in *Voices in the City*, an act of alienation. To the father, the island has the identity of an ashram; to the daughter it has the identity of a magician, a necromancer. The father lives a non-committed life, indifferent to the milieu. Sita feels that her father's daylight-pragmatic wisdom and charisma had its nocturnal aspect. Her envy of Rekha gives an uncertain clue to a possible incestuous link between Rekha and her father. We, however, miss the true identity of the man. The shifting point of view suggests the transience of human experience and the impracticability and implausibility of a permanent illusion or a permanent reality. Sita's alienation from her father blurs her vision about his identity. She is able to decipher only a fragment bridge between her own emotional life and the life on the island. She is unable to recover the true identity of the geographical milieu. Hence, the island eludes her imaginative vision. These implicit contrasts between the lives of the father and the daughter show that Sita merely serves as a foil to her father. The horrors she experiences on the island are shadowy and unreal. They resemble the illusory snakes Karan had seen.

Desai describes the tension between illusion and reality through the use of irony and the shifting of focus. Sita's reversion to the past, to her childhood identity is but a continuity of her present identity that persists despite transformation. The island figures as a haunting and obsessive presence in her psyche. She is conscious of the isolation not only between her and the island but also between the island and the sea. The pervasive presence of the sea in her psyche forms a mystic backdrop to the setting of the novel. She is able to recover her natural affinity with the soil through a ritualised mud bath. Through Desai's predilection for mythopoeic reality we see Sita's maiden contact with the soil. The concomitant change in her behaviour is objectively correlated with the change in natural phenomena.

Sita stands surrounded by the island, the sea and the palm trees. She merely participates in their awfully majestic splendour; she is not much involved with them. There is just the sea; it drowns them or detains them on the sandbar, and there is the island. That is all.

Everything linked to her twilight existence seems ambiguous and ambivalent. Her marital life is a series of emotional chiaroscuro. She is uncertain of her own self. How could she tell, how decide which half of her life is real and which unreal? Which of her selves was true, which false? All she knew was that there were two periods in her life, each in direct opposition to the other... (p. 153). Moses traces the temperamental alienation between Sita and her father: "After all,...she is not like her father. She is 'plain' compared to him who was like a god...a magic man" (p. 156). Madhusudan Prasad in his book *Anita Desai: The*

Novelist, finds Sita a square peg on a round hole in her father-in-law's. But he fails to consider Sita's biological and physiological urges. He only takes into account the temperamental drives which are but a part of an individual's identity. Sita is the symbolic equivalent of the modern housewife whose sensibility is perpetually under stress. Her mental agony is the outcome of her inability to cope with the modern society. The conclusion carries the focus of the novel beyond the resolution of Sita's obsessive identity crisis. It points to a transcendental reality.

Desai's heroines often act violently, but here, is a positive change. Sita reconciles herself to her lot. She strikes a balance between her inner self and the outer world, her prosaic self and her poetic sensibility, her individual self and the societal consciousness. Unlike Maya's, her alienation is bio-psychic, not temperamental or environmental. Rightly does B. Ramachandra Rao observe: "The novel may, thus, be seen as a parable on the inability of human beings, to relate the inner with the outer, the individual with the society...."[2] "Only connect", says Desai recalling Margaret Wilcox, in Forster's *Howard's End*. Wilcox remarks, "Only connect the prose and the passion, and both will be exalted, and human love will be seen at its highest. Live in fragments no longer. Only connect, and the beast and the monk, robbed of the isolation that is life to either, will die."[3]

Thus, *Where Shall We Go This Summer?* is an answer to temperamental incompatibility and the resultant alienation. Sita's hope for consolation from the island is but a frantic and desperate bid to relieve the boredom and hypocrisy of her bourgeois existence. All she gets from the island is a cold welcome and, thus, remains an island on the island. In the words of Madhusudan Prasad, "...it is a memorable piece of fiction which provides us proudly with a panacea for an endemic existentialist predicament, threatening to assume epidemic proportions in our country".[4] It is a testament of psychic turbulence, the very image of poetry and parturition which Ezra Pound could have called "an intellectual and emotional complex in an instant of time".[5] Unlike the other works of Desai, here is a novel where the quest for identity does not end in death and desolation; it closes with compromise and conciliation.

NOTES AND REFERENCES

1. Yasodhara Dalmia, "An Interview with Anita Desai," *The Times of India*, April 24, 1979, p. 13.
2. B. Ramachandra Rao, *The Novels of Anita Desai* (Ludhiana: Kalyani, 1977), p. 59.
3. E.M. Forster, *Howard's End* (London: Penguin Books, 1976), p. 188.
4. Madhusudan Prasad, *Anita Desai: The Novelist* (Allahabad: New Horizon, 1981), p. 77.
5. Anita Desai, *Where Shall We Go This Summer?* (New Delhi: Orient Paperback, 1982). (All quotations from the novel are from this edition and are followed by page numbers in parentheses.)

27

Tradition and Deviation—A Study of Anita Desai's Novels

S.P. SWAIN

In dealing with the interior landscape and the psychic odyssey of the characters, Desai has extended and enlarged the thematic horizon of the Indo-Anglian novel. Her major novels tend to disappoint the reader due to their one-dimensionality, turning the characters wooden and insensitive. They are not kaleidoscopic in their thematic projection. In most of them there is a repeated and droll harping on the isolation of the self. However, they are deeply moving in their existential and socio-psychic import. Microcosm of man's endless struggle for survival, they voice the anguished ennui of the caged bird that symbolises the modern man. Emblems of remonstrance and psychic protest, they strive for the protection and preservation of their dignity and self-esteem in a patriarchal society. Indignantly promiscuous and inordinately self-conscious, they long for mutual understanding and reciprocation of love and respect.

Anita Desai speaks to us not only of the tumult of the human soul but also of its depth, its poetry and pathos, its beauty and compassions. It is through "the quality of mind and soul alone" (Iyengar 1962: 343), that Anita Desai's novels would be a major contribution to literature. That is why the existential predicament in her novels has the unique touch of the universal. Her tender, flexible, malleable and moribund sensibility whipping inanities into awe and wonder becomes at times, as in *Fire on the Mountain*, too melodramatic to make the story artistically coherent and aesthetically satisfying. The "fire" in *Fire on the Mountain* and the "light" in *Clear Light of Day*, have an insignificant and trivial link with the central plot and as such have a dim symbolical and metaphorical relevance, which, instead of ennobling and satisfying the artistic sensibility of the readers often bewilders them. Her hold on the reader's mind loosens. The readers instead of identifying themselves with her artistic sensibility, get alienated from it. Desai endeavours to offer the reader a slice of life but fails to impart the required voltage. The action at times detonates to poetic and philosophical speculations on existence and essence which the readers find too arduous to grapple with. The readers are so much repelled by the peculiar psychic set-up of her novels that they fail to take stock of the gravity of the alienated self's existential plight.

Dealing with the thoughts, emotions, and sensations at various levels of consciousness, Anita Desai found the technique used by D.H. Lawrence, Virginia Woolf, William Faulkner and Henry James quite suitable for her purpose of character delineation. Hence, we have the use of flashbacks and the stream of consciousness technique in some of her novels, mainly in her first novel, *Cry, The Peacock* which to R.S. Sharma, is "the first step in the direction of psychological fiction in English" (Anita Desai 127). Very few Indo-Anglian novelists have paid so much attention to form and technique. Prof. Srinivasa Iyengar rightly observes:

> Since her pre-occupation is with the inner world of sensibility rather than the outer world of action, she has tried to forge a style supple and suggestive enough to convey the fever and fretfulness of the stream-of-consciousness of her principal characters. (*Indian Writing in English* 1973: 16)

This inner world of sensibility rendered through splendid poetic prose gives a "peculiar poetic quality" (Sharma 1981: 14) to Desai novels.

Alienation is basically a Western concept and in imitating this idea in her novels, Anita Desai remained at heart no less traditional than Western. To her, alienation is more related to the emotional and mental moods and attitudes of her characters than to their spiritual, moral or ethical temperaments. The alienated self in Desai experiences the pangs of emotional isolation, not the spiritual and intellectual angst of a Raskolnikov or a Roquentin. The struggle of the alienated self in Desai is more similar to the Kafka protagonist than to the Camus hero. The Camus hero is nauseated and stifled. He seldom delights in his alienated existence but a Kafka hero does. Anita Desai's protagonists never dodge the harsh reality of existence. They encounter it single-handedly. They delight in despair. Nirode in *Voices in the City* longs to move from failure to failure. The Desai protagonist is not an instance of bureaucratic alienation of Kafka's "K".

Alienation in Nathaniel Hawthorne suggests not only physical isolation but also psychic imperviousness. To him alienation is insulation. But in Desai, alienation seldom manifests in imperviousness. Desai protagonists are not like the Hawthorne hero who basks in the sunshine but is as cold as death. Hawthorne's treatment of alienation unlike that of Desai's, has moral and religious concerns. There is some similarity between the solitary self in Hawthorne and the sequestered self in Desai. Both undergo a gradual disintegration of their personality and both are the pictures of suffering arising from a sense of deep gloom sometimes thrown over their mind (monodic self) by morbid reflections on death and despair. Both are the manifestations of thanatophobia and both frantically long to break out of their cocooned self in quest of something more real and more palpable than their shadowy and hollow existence. But Desai protagonists in no way contribute to the tradition of the romantic hero as a sad clown as does the Hawthorne hero.

Like the Kafka protagonist, Desai heroes too, encounter the distressing conflict between external and internal obligations. Maya's conflict in *Cry, The Peacock* is between her obligations to the dead Toto and her biological obligations to her husband; Nanda's in *Fire on the Mountain* is between her filial obligations to Raka, her granddaughter and to her unrequited psycho-emotional urges for self-isolation; Sita's in *Where Shall We Go*

This Summer? is between her external life on the island and her emotional life as a housewife.

The Alienated self as portrayed in the novels of Anita Desai is not an instance of total alienation. The lone self in Desai novels does not undergo the pangs of alienation as does Hemingway's Santiago, who stands isolated from every entity and group. Even from God.

Anita Desai portrays women as not totally cut off from familial and social ties but women who remain within these orbits and protest against monotony, injustice and humiliation. Woman in her novels is not a mere goddess or a robot but a self-actualising and self-realising individual. The names of Desai women like Maya, Sita and Raka are suggestive of their epic and mythic parallels to them (*i.e.* their names). They are ideals rather than facts. Maya says: "As a child, I enjoyed, princes like, a sumptuous fare of the fantasies of the Arabian Nights.... Indian mythology...lovely English and Irish fairy tales..." (*Cry, The Peacock* 89). Even Nirode's attitudes are also partly governed by the Greek Myths and contemporary Western philosophy. Thus, Anita Desai imparts a fancifully mythopoeic colouring to the alienation of her characters. Save R.K. Narayan and Raja Rao, no other Indo-Anglian novelist has resorted to this strategy. To Raja Rao, myth is a legend, to Narayan it is a social reality, but to Anita Desai, it is a psycho-emotional reality. Unlike Raja Rao and R.K. Narayan but like Arun Joshi, Anita Desai resorts to the stream-of-consciousness technique which serves as an experience of the private inner world. Desai adopts the special narrative technique of setting apart from the main fictional narrative, the fragmentary passages which imply the theme of alienation.

In Bharati Mukherjee and V.S. Naipaul, it is the sense of "exile" that leads to the alienation of the characters. But, in Desai, it is not so. Anita Desai's novels do not deal with the theme of exile: "...exile has never been my theme" (Desai Interviewed, Rajasthan University Studies in English 69), says Anita Desai. Her main thematic concern is how people cope with society, alien or not alien, without losing their sense of self-identity and individuality. In Mukherjee, it is people and cultures in collision but in Desai, it is people and people in collision, in Mukherjee, it is cultural confrontation but in Desai, it is psychic confrontation. Desai protagonists are emotional orphans. Emotionally maimed, they hail from fractured families. Their parents are either dead physically or psycho-emotionally (i.e. absent and uninvolved in their life). Jasbir Jain observes:

> ...they (the protagonists) either disown or are disowned by their families. Maya's only memory of her mother in *Cry, The Peacock* is the photograph on her father's desk (134); the Ray children in *Voices in the City*, all four of them, are alienated in different degrees from their mother, their only surviving parent, as well as from their father, who is now dead, Sita's mother in *Where Shall We Go This Summer?* had run away from home leaving her children to the care of a father whose concerns lie outside the family, Sita had imagined she came into world motherless. A similar withdrawal, from her parents, is there on part of Sarah in *Bye-Bye Blackbird*, who by marrying an Indian, has at one stroke, placed herself outside the family and the cultural situation. The children in *Clear Light of Day* resent the long absences of their parents and are aware only of their exists and entrances... (*Stairs to the Attic* 113-14)

Like the novelist herself making a bold deviation from tradition in her approach to the fictionalisation of artistic ideas and ideals, Desai characters "carry very little of their parents in them; it is as if they were consciously rejecting whatever little they may have inherited. They prefer to go in the opposite direction" (*ibid.*, p. 116). But heredity figures only marginally in her novels. In tracing the positive and negative effects of heredity on her characters, Anita Desai fails to supply the required voltage. Hence, it is not as strong as in the novels of Emile Bronte, George Eliot or Thomas Hardy.

Delineating in novel after novel the pitiable and awful plight of the alienated self, especially of housewives, facing single-handed the torments and tortures of their insensitive and temperamentally callous husbands, Anita Desai has rendered a new dimension to Indo-Anglian fiction. This is further enlivened by her unconventional concern with the inner reality of the characters and their psychic topography. Desai denies the importance of theories in the shaping of artistic imagination. A work of art should grow from within, from the writer's inner beckonings and compulsions:

> I think theories of the novel are held by those of an academic or critical turn of mind, not the creative. A writer does not create a novel by observing a given set of theories...he follows flashes of individual vision, and relies on a kind of instinct that tells him what to follow and what to avoid, how to veer away from what would be destructive to his vision. It is these flashes of vision, and a kind of trained instinct that leads him...not any theories. (Atma Ram, "An Interview with Anita Desai", *World Literature Written in English* 100)

Thus, Anita Desai eschews traditional practices and gives free reins to her individual vision. Edgar Allan Poe, Henry James, E.M. Forster are at once critics and creative writers. Not Desai. She propounds no systematic theory of the novel against which to gauge the merit of her literary creations. Most of the Indo-Anglian novels are the result of a deliberate planning and plotting. In the case of Desai, they are an instinctive outcome of her inner motivations and compulsions—her desire to show as well as to see. It is a natural and vegetative growth. The object that triggers her imagination could be very trivial and insignificant—"a leaf dipping under a rain drop, a face seen on the bus, or a scrap of news read in the papers" (Ram, *op. cit.*, p. 99). Her fictional world witnesses the chaotic strife between the self and the society. Society here is a conscious entity, perpetually administering its gravitating influence and grip over the despairing self, which is enmeshed in the bewildering texture of the social gossamer and struggles unsuccessfully for an escape. The self struggles and falters, falters and struggles again. In almost all her works, save a few meant for the gratification of the puerile adolescent taste, this bold and chaotic tussle of the self for a release from the stranglehold of a pandemonic and hollow society is conspicuous. In her interview with Yasodhara

Dalmia, Desai speaks of "the terror of facing single-handed, the ferocious assaults of existence" (Desai interviewed, *The Times of India* 13). These assaults of existence are the outcome of a society in which norms and values have degenerated. Her protagonists are socio-psychic rebels, recalcitrant selves, who find it difficult to compromise with the milieu. The self frantically endeavours to escape but in the process enters another world equally disturbing and disheartening. Thus, it lies cloistered in a world, where there is a perpetual and persistent struggle between the physical and the psychic, leading to the triumph of the latter over the former. The temporal existence of the self in contrast to the eternity of the soul is the crux on which the fictional tapestry of Desai rests. The flux of recollections and ruminations that perpetually keep haunting the psyche of the characters is an aspect of the individual self which is at loggerheads with the socio-psychic reality. Desai mirrors the mythic reality of our life through the complex interaction of the self and the society. The reader is lost among some dark forgotten city streets where the sunlight seldom falls, streets pull of shadows, phantoms and skeletal beings, anaemic and cadaverous: streets smelling of generations of anticipated death and regretted birth, dread and desolation, worn-out clothes, cold and damp wood. And as one walks through, the street usually ends in cul de sac. Desai seldom offers any acceptable solution or clear-cut conclusion. There are hardly any abrupt revelations or surprises. Not even much overt anguish or vivid emotions. There is a kind of aerial drowsiness and an awful equanimity. There seems no noticeable effort at carrying the narrative forward. The novelist prefers to meander from episode to episode in a dubious wilfulness. The impression, thus generated, is very deceptive. Desai creates a hazy and blurred landscape, slotting in a story here and a suggestion there. The jigsaw puzzle she presents is incomplete and fragmentary, and the final picture that emerges is anything but impoverished and dull. Unlike R.K. Narayan, Mulk Raj Anand and Bhabani Bhattacharya, Anita Desai is chiefly concerned with the portrayal of inward or psychic reality of the characters. To use her own words, not "the one-tenth visible section of the ice-berg that one sees above the surface of the ocean..." but "the remaining nine-tenths of it that lie below the surface" (Desai, "Replies to the Questionnaire", *Kakatiya Journal of English Studies* 01). She "probes deep into the inner recesses of the psyche of the character and delves deeper and deeper in a character or a scene rather than going round about it" (Jain, "Desai Interviewed", Rajasthan University Studies in English 68). She prefers the private to the public world. For her, literature is neither a means of escaping reality nor a vehicle for parading political, social, religious and moral ideas. It is an exploration and an enquiry. Desai imparts no messages, preaches no morals. Like Jane Austen, she works on a narrow canvas, her "two inches of ivory". Narayan, Anand and Bhattacharya have opulence of subject matter, richness of experience. But a woman novelist, has her limits. Yet her novels have intensity, though not variety. Unlike Raja Rao's, they are occasionally abstruse and abstract. Since Desai believes that literature should deal with most enduring matters, less temporary and less temporal than politics, she is opposed to the art of delineating contemporaneity or documenting socio-economic reality. There are occasional allusions to contemporaneity but they are not deliberately or elaborately dealt with. Only in *Clear Light of Day*, we find a reference to the partition riots and the assassination of Mahatma Gandhi.

In dealing with the problem of the alienated self, Anita Desai has adopted a realistic/metonymic mode of writing. Dr. Madhusudan Prasad attributes alienation in Desai's novels to temperamental incompatibility of the characters. But the feeling of alienation in most of her characters is psychotic and psycho-neurotic. It is neither the alienation of Savithri in R.K. Narayan's *The Dark Room* nor that of Madeleine in Raja Rao's *The Serpent and the Rope*. It is the alienation of a psychically malformed character in quest of an authentic selfhood.

Unlike Narayan and Malgonkar, Anita Desai does not believe in a pre-conceived plot. She does not believe in its linear movement in terms of exposition, conflict and resolution. For her, the plot is just an idea occupying one's subconscious mind, a fragment of her imagination and a flash of her vision. Desai prefers pattern and rhythm, which is natural, to plot, which is artificial and mechanical, something superimposed upon the aesthetic vision of the artist. In such an organic whole, fragments are so integrated and interrelated that together they lend artistic unity and picturesque intelligibility to the work of art: "the perfect novel achieves the perfect balance, with just as much story or as much fantasy as its structure can bear, no more" (Ram, "Desai Interviewed", *WLWE* 100).

In *Cry, The Peacock*, it is the character of Maya and in *Voices in the City*, the voice of the metropolis Calcutta that smothers other voices and lends organic unity to the novel and sensitivity to the caged isolation of the characters. Anand, Narayan and Bhattacharya wrote for social documentation, and hence they selected characters from amongst socio-economic preys and predators. Anita Desai, on the other hand, is concerned with the delineation of psychological reality, and hence prefers such characters who are peculiar and eccentric rather than general and commonplace. Most of her major characters do not have fixed personalities. They are either entirely imaginary or an amalgam of several different characters. Desai conceives each character as a riddle and a mystery and believes that it is the duty of the novelist to solve this riddle and unravel this mystery. Her characters are almost sick of life and listless playthings of their morbid psychic longings. Most of her female protagonists are abnormally sensitive and unusually solitary to the point of being neurotic: Maya in *Cry, The Peacock*, Monisha in *Voices in the City*, Sita in *Where Shall We Go This Summer?* and Nanda in *Fire on the Mountain*. This is conveyed through her stream of consciousness technique, her use of flashbacks and lyrical language. To Dr. Brijraj Singh, her novels are "an extended piece of music, subtle, sensitive, sensuous...complex and richly integrated in its total effect" ("The Fiction of Anita Desai", *The Humanities Review* 43). English in the hands of Anita Desai becomes so flexible and tractable that it not only yields to the steerings and chumings of her intellect and the movement of her pen but also rises to such poetic heights so as to mirror and manifest her visions and views. In dealing with the psyche of the characters, their motivations and compulsions, she moves along the labyrinthine and dimly-lit corridors of inner reality.

The English novelists before Anita Desai studies man and his world in relation to the objective social reality. They used their art as a powerful "public instrument" (Daiches 1965: 01) to present social problems but Desai walks out on such a traditional approach to fiction. She writes neither for providing entertainment nor for the dissemination and propagation of social ideas. Her main pre-occupation is to study human existence and human predicament, her exploration being a quest for self. She is the novelist of psycho-emotional situations and her theme is the individual against himself and against the milieu. Like Joseph Conrad, she has a double function—to pull away the individual from the social milieu, so that "he can be put in extremis, and to act as an agent of self-confrontation" (Allen 1954: 303).

The Indo-Anglian novel till 1970s treated themes of political and social import. It exhibited a splendid array of limited, contrarious items: princes and paupers, saints and sinners, whitemen and babus, farmers and labourers, untouchables and coolies, prosperity and adversity, cities and villages. Mulk Raj Anand, Bhabani Bhattacharya were pioneers in this field. Writers like Raja Rao, Kamala Markandaya and Khushwant Singh dealt with more impressive and sophisticated themes like the country's independence movement, East-West encounter, tradition and modernity, materialism and spiritualism. The very notion of gauging the unexplored recesses or an individual's mind, of transcending the narrow and shallow conscriptions of the physical self was alien to them. It is only with the arrival of Anita Desai that such long-neglected themes were given an emotionally poetic treatment. She paraded them in sophisticated poetic cut-outs. Thus, by shifting the realm of her novels from outer to inner reality and fathoming the nocturnal recesses of the human psyche, she brought the Indo-Anglian novel into the mainstream of European and American fiction. An important phase in the growth of fiction in India, as elsewhere, is the gradual shifting of focus from the external world to the inner world of the individual, capturing the atmosphere of the mind, and directly involving the reader "in the flow of a particular consciousness" [Lawrence, "Morality and Novel", Lodge (ed.),

20th Century Literature Criticism 130]. A housewife with selected family ties, Anita Desai, George Eliot and Virginia Woolf resemble one another. Solely concerned with the inner weather of the characters, Desai is a painter of their kaleidoscopic and prismatic moods, their wills and conflicting choices. Her predecessors dealt with political turmoils and social evils. She discusses problems of temperamental incompatibility, conjugal chaos and inharmonious man-woman relationship. "The great relationship for humanity", says D.H. Lawrence, "will always be the relation between man and woman. The relation between man and man, woman and woman, parent and child will always be subsidiary" (Dalmia, "Desai Interviewed", *The Times of India* 13). Due to rapid industrialisation, growing awareness among women of their rights and the westernisation of our attitudes, man-woman relationship has become a popular concern for R.K. Narayan in *The Dark Room* and *The Guide*, Raja Rao in *The Serpent and the Rope*, Mulk Raj Anand in *Gouri*, Bhabani Bhattacharya in *Music for Mohini*, Manohar Malgonkar in *A Bend in the Ganges*, Arun Joshi in *The Foreigner* and *The Strange Case of Billy Biswas* and Kamala Markandaya in *The Nowhere Man*. Anita Desai, on the other hand, has given this theme a unique treatment. In her novels, most protagonists are alienated from the world, from society, from families, from parents and even from their own selves, because they are not average people but individuals who are unable to communicate with the people around. Unable to relate themselves with the milieu, they drift into their own sequestered world where they spin their dreams which never materialise. Mrs. Desai elaborates upon this aspect of her protagonists in her interview with Yasodhara Dalmia:

> I am interested in characters who are not average but have retreated, or been driven into some extremity of despair and so turned against, or made a stand against, the general current, it makes no demands, it costs no effort. But those who cannot follow it, whose heart cries out 'the great No', who fight the current and struggle against it, know what the demands are and what it costs to meet them. ("Desai Interviewed", *The Times of India* 13)

Unlike the other Indo-Anglian novelists, Anita Desai's predominant concern is not with society or social forces but the individual psyche and its interaction with social values. While the other Indian Novelists in English "have been content to record and document" (Desai, Quest 43), she is solely interested in the psychological aspect of the characters. In her review of Amitav Ghosh's *The Circle of Reason*, she shows her discontent for the novelists who prefer the "outer" aspect of an individual to the "inner" aspect and prefer the social to the psychological novels (*India Today* 149).

Anita Desai dealt though on a subjective plane, with the theme of East-West encounter, "the conflicts and reconciliations or two cultures" (Mukherjee 1947: 64), Indian and Eurasian in matters of love, sex and marriage. Look at Raja Rao in *The Serpent and the Rope*, Kamala Markandaya in *Nectar in a Sieve*, *Some Inner Fury and Possession*, Bhattacharya in *A Dream in Hawaii*, Manohar Malgonkar in *Distant Drum and Combat of Shadows*, Nayantara Sahgal in *A Time to be Happy*, Arun Joshi in *The Foreigner* and Anita Desai in *Bye-Bye Blackbird*.

In Indo-Anglian writings, the theme of violence and death has been dealt both emotionally and spiritually. Leslie Fiedler refers to two stages in the treatment of violence in fiction: the urbanisation of violence and the ennobling of violence. In the first stage, "violence is transferred from nature to society, from the given world that man must endure to the artificial world he has made, presumably to protect himself from ravages of the first" (*Love and Death in the American Novel* 489). Thus, we find the association of large metropolitan cities like Paris and London with the elements of crime, violence and poverty. In Desai, we hardly find any such association. Only in *The Voices in the City*, is Calcutta associated with sinister and demoniac elements. In Indian writing in English, there are virtually no war novels and the only acts of violence and death that recur are either around the freedom movement and partition of the country or around famine, flood and poverty. Hence, violence in Markandaya's novels is due to poverty, in Anand and Bhattacharya to economic disparities and exploitation, in Raja Rao, Manohar Malgonkar and Chaman Nahal to independence movement and the country's partition, in Nayantara Sahgal, to the bickerings of politicians and in Arun Joshi, to the conflict between tradition and modernity, primitivism and civilisation, or to incommunication and insubordination. Anita Desai says Darshan Singh Maini "is a disturbing and demanding presence in Indo-Anglian Fiction" [K.K. Sharma (ed.), *Indo-English Literature* 216].

The treatment of violence and death in Anita Desai's novels is quite different. Now it is psycho-emotional, now hysterical projections and symbols of her own contrite and sensitive psyche. Desai's protagonists are moved by the muffled whisper of individuals, leaking of taps, creaking of shoes, chattering of birds, ticking of clocks, rattle of vehicles and the thumping of pedestrians. They stand apart. They are highly poetic and nervy. "Anita Desai", says R.S. Sharma, "seems to be struggling towards the mastery of a violence which seems to threaten not only her protagonists but also her own introvert self. Right from *Cry, The Peacock*, this violence has persisted and permeated in her works as a kind of inevitability, forcing one to conclude that it has some kind of inevitability,...metaphysical or psychological significance, not yet explored or analysed" (Anita Desai 167). This violence is psychical end clinical. *Cry, The Peacock* begins with the death of Toto, the pet dog and ends with the death of Gautama. Maya, the protagonist, is deeply moved by the astrologer's prediction of the death of one of them. She associates herself with the peacocks and their knowledge of life and death. She is obsessed by death and her death-wish issues out of her frustrations and dejections in life. In *Voices in the City*, violence and death are largely due to the 'demoniac' and 'death city' of Calcutta. Violence has been poetically and symbolically represented through the images of birds and animals who act as preys and predators. In *Bye-Bye Blackbird*, violence has been sarcastically portrayed through jeers, taunts, sarcasms and aspersions of the white towards the blackbirds. Sarah, for instance, is the victim of individual and social violence, the victim of derisions of her countrymen for having married an Indian. In *Where Shall We Go This Summer?*, Sita is so much horrified by the violence rampant in our society that she is reluctant to deliver her fifth child. She undergoes fits or depression in her lone struggle to assert her identity. She is a split self and it is her desire to 'stay whole' (107-08) that evokes in her the urge to escape to the island of Manori. She looks at the raucous and greedy crows attacking a young eagle and reflects: "There was much black drama in this crow theatre... murder, infanticide, incest, theft and robbery" (*Where Shall We Go This Summer?* 38).

Nanda Kaul in *Fire on the Mountain* withdraws into the secluded world of Carignano for peace and tranquility but is upset by the rape and murder of Ila Das—a scene too horrific and ghastly to bear. In keeping with her theme and technique, Anita Desai makes a liberal use of symbols, though instinctively and subconsciously. What matters to her is the movement of the object, not the object itself, the quintessence and not the essence. The reiterative use of symbols not only enriches her work of art, it elevates it to aesthetic and transcendental heights. Even the title of some of her novels, like *Cry, The Peacock*, are highly symbolic. Her symbols lend docility, flexibility, richness and pliability to her works. They add to their mythopoeic beauty.

Concerned mainly with the nocturnal and nebulous atmosphere of the psyche, Anita Desai is a psychological novelist whose characters are different from those of Raja Rao, Sahgal, Narayan, Bhattacharya, Markandaya and Malgonkar, who deal with the socio-economic or political or philosophical aspects of a character. What matters for Desai is the motivation, the conscience, the psychic tension of these characters. Unlike the other Indo-Anglian novelists, Anita Desai creates an opulent gallery of characters, though dominated by the female. Most of her protagonists are hypersensitive females. They are hypochondriacs. Each is presented, as an inscrutable individual, enigmatic and eccentric. Neither are they chosen from the common rung of the society nor are their problems related to food, clothing and shelter. They are rebels and their rebellion is not so much directed against society as against individuals. Their problems are neither physical nor social. They are psychical and emotional.

In dealing with psychic maladies, Anita Desai strikes a new note. Her characters suffer from various complexes and mental diseases, which impede the healthy growth of their personality. A particular trait in a character, a tragic flaw develops into a psychic malady making the character neurotic and hysterical which in turn breeds a morbid and contrite temperament. Maya suffers from father-fixation, Nirode from claustrophobia and Dev, from Caliban complex.

A unique feature of Desai's characterisation is her dexterous handling of objective correlatives. These objective correlatives project the alienation and identity of the characters. It is, in fact, their state of alienation that motivates them in their quest for identity. For the first time in Indo-Anglian literature, Anita Desai makes an associative use of landscapes and myths, symbols and images (esp. of birds and animals) for characterisation. This animal imagery shows that we still retain in our nature a portion of that primitive animal identity. In the words of Dr. B. Ramachandra Rao, "Anita Desai evokes the necessary mood and elicits the right emotion from the reader through a series of objective descriptions" (*The Novels of Anita Desai* 10). Since she belongs to the upper middle class and has a limited or no access to the infernal and filthy lanes of power-hankering politicians and diehard criminals, her characters are polished and sophisticated and are verily an imitation of life. Yet her feminine and domestic sensibility seldom strays beyond the narrow confines of family life. Working on such a limited canvas, she has been able to create masterpieces in Indo-Anglian literature that have won her the coveted Sahitya Akademic Award.

Desai records the psychic oscillations and tensions of her near-neurotic characters and articulates them through hints and suggestions, symbols and images. Albeit, there have been many women writers before Desai, such as Kamala Markandaya, Nayantara Sahgal and Ruth Prawer Jhabvala, yet none has her exotic feminine sensibility of depicting love as an ennobling ideal in man-woman relationship.

As has been pointed out, Desai's fiction tends to conform to both American and English tradition. It takes its form and tone from polarities and irreconcilables. Oddities and eccentricities of character, disintegration of personality and morbidity or temperament, the prose of order and the poetry of disorder, alienation and depersonalisation of identity constitute the tradition she draws upon. One remembers Virginia Woolf for whom.... "Life is not a series of gig-lamps symmetrically arranged; life is a luminous halo, a semi-transparent envelope surrounding us from the beginning of consciousness to the end" (*The Common Reader* 177).

Desai prefers 'pattern' to plot, Hopkinsian 'inscape' to external incident, cubist composition to cumulative accumulation of facts. Unlike R.K. Narayan and Mulk Raj Anand, she employs 'the language of the interior' to portray the compulsions and tensions of her characters, most of whom suffer from 'emotional and intellectual consumption'.

The theme of immigration and consequent alienation of the self has been the thematic pre-occupation of Indo-Anglian novelists like Naipaul, Kamala Markandaya and Bharati Mukherjee, but they are chiefly concerned with cross-cultural and racist encounters between the characters on socio-cultural plane. Seldom do they deeply and punctiliously probe into the psyche of the characters like Anita Desai. What differentiates Anita Desai from them is her capacity to transform such alienational experiences into the monument of living art. It is neither the concern of an absurdist nor the enigma faced by an existentialist but the simple, homely rendering of emotions of individuals who face abnormal situations in living and partly living every moment of life on an alien soil in a strangely fascinating way.

S. Sujatha maintains that Anita Desai's protagonist faces the predicament of the tragic isolation of the individual and consequent sense of the absurdity of human life ("The Theme of Disintegration", *The Commonwealth Review* 49) but to me the Desai protagonist is confronted with the very reality of existence. It is never absurd, for, Maya, Monisha, Sarah, Sita, Nanda and Tara, all battle with a reality hard to bear, a workaday reality. Their problem is our problem, their plight is everyone's plight. What is absurd is real and it is the reality of absurdity that the Desai protagonists are confronted with. Hugo Baumgartner's alliance with the cats might sound absurd but it is real. Hugo the kitten is isolated from the mother cat (i.e. his mother). Hence, his transference of love to the cats in whom he possibly sees the 'maternal image'. Kai Nicholson rightly opines that the life and death of this German Jew, a refugee from Nazi terror, is close to reality ("Are We Expatriates", *The Commonwealth Review* 14).

Historical themes like partition dealing with alienation have found an important place in the novels of Mulk Raj Anand, Manohar Malgonkar, Khushwant Singh, Attia, Hosain, Chaman Nahal and Nayantara Sahgal. In Desai too, there are allusions to historical incidents in *Clear Light of Day* but it is patchy and sketchy. Such references only serve as a foil to the alienation of the protagonist. Like R.K. Narayan (with reference to *Waiting for the Mahatma*), he remains silent about the horrors of the partition. She builds her novels round the struggle within the self, the dismal and morbid moods of men and women. Like Arun Joshi, she explores the depths of human psyche against the muddling social backdrop.

To Desai, writing is a means of discovering one's identity, of unravelling the hidden truth of life. Narayan's use of irony, Raja Rao's acceptance of Indian metaphysics is irrelevant to Mrs. Desai's fictional needs. Even the doctrinaire humanism of Mulk Raj Anand and the sanguine exploits of Kushwant Singh and Malgonkar are alien to her art of fiction. On a small canvas, she weaves the web of the protagonist's anguished odyssey.

Anita Desai's works clearly indicate the direction Indian fiction was taking in the hands of the third generation of urban writers. It is the turning inward of Indian fiction from the romantic tryst in gardens or on river banks to a more meaningful exploration of the world of reality. What matters to her is the character and not the tale, the situation and not the environment, the depth and not the dimension. Esoteric and secret passions and tensions occupy her interest.

Desai's novels are autobiographical, in the sense they mirror her 'quiet' temperament. Her novels exude the feeling of gentle isolation. In the words of Dr. Atma Ram, "Whereas a man is concerned with action, experience and achievement, a woman writer is more concerned with thought, emotion and sensation" ('Desai Interviewed', *WLWE* 102).

Prof. Jasbir Jain rightly points out:

> The world of Anita Desai's novels is an ambivalent one; it is a world where the central harmony is aspired to but not arrived at, and the desire to love and live clashes—at times violently—with the desire to withdraw and achieve harmony. Involvement and stillness are incompatible by their nature, yet they strive to exist together. (*Stairs to the Attic* 16)

Desai's novels plumb man's perennial dilemmas: love versus hate; action versus inaction; possessiveness versus renunciation. They are mainly concerned about things that every individual longs for—the courage to live and the capacity to love as well as be loved. Most of the characters in her novels are characters without roots. It is their alienated state that propels them from crisis to crisis, sucking in its wake several other characters. They are presented mostly as seekers—questers through love—questers for identity. Emotionally and psychically perturbed, they are relentlessly and maniacally driven by undefined hunger and feverish lust which bring about their own fall. Incapable of silent submission and ungrudging suffering, they somehow pull the load of life. The Desai heroines are 'Pativratas', and yet are unhappy and gloomy, for they do not have the mental strength to be Nora (Heroine of Ibsen's play, *A Doll's House*). Desai's Monisha, Sita, Maya and Nanda Kaul—all aspire for a socio-psychic emancipation. They crave for the liberation of their feminine self from the shackles of a socio-psychically maladjusted environ. They desire to stay whole but when offered the choice, they retrace and retract.

Desai's concern for violence and conflict, for isolation and guilt link her with Camus, Hemingway and Sartre, rather than with her Indo-Anglian contemporaries. Despite these continental affiliations, she is unique in her own way in dealing with the past and its haunting obsession; death and its grim horror; love with its anguish and alienation, now savage, now still.

Anita Desai has made the landscape not just a backdrop but an environment reflecting the isolation and nostalgia of the alienated self. She uses memory, in a series of internal monologues to give us an access to the characters' minds. Through the psychology of association, the reader is made to participate triumphantly in the characters' movements back and forth in time. The world outside reason appears to be the major dimension of her work, where she probes the manifestations of the irrational in human relationships.

In *Cry, The Peacock*, Maya's abortive marriage to Gautama with its lack of emotional attachment stands in sharp contrast to her jolly and love-laden infancy. Maya's childhood remembrances overshadow her present with gloom and foreboding and bring about her alienation from her time-bound present. Time, that had preserved and ensconced her past, destroys her present. Desai admits that her novel is about 'time as a destroyer, as a preserver and about what the bondage of time does to people' ('Desai Interviewed', *India Today* 142). The mind's time occupies a more prominent place in Desai's novels than clock-time, and sometimes the passage of clock-time is transcended by the characters in moments of vision. Desai's intention is to portray the moment 'whole', so that the very texture of life is revealed. In her novels mind's time is not shown in conflict with linear time, but is depicted as one unified whole that is central to human experience. Like Virginia Woolf, Desai is obsessively involved with the characters' past as a key to their consciousness, their psycho-emotional life. Her pre-occupation with reminiscential thoughts takes the form of nostalgia. Like Virginia Woolf, she makes use of the stream of consciousness as an integral part of her fictional craft. But while Virginia Woolf uses parentheses to ensure the continuity of thought, Anita Desai uses dashes to the same effect:

> He notices a dead branch on one of the silver oaks and, with a small muscle at the comer of his mouth twitching—for he is particular about garden—he complains of the laziness of the gardener. (*Cry, The Peacock* 39)

Reality, for Desai, is neither metaphysical nor socio-political. She has given an existential dimension to the three most vital human predicaments—anguish, alienation and despair. Plot development in her novels is not a spatio-temporal progression. It leads to the protagonist's self-discovery. A letter, a telephone call, and a forest fire triggers off a chain of situations and incidents that intricate and complicate the plot. "My novels are no reflection of Indian society, politics or character. They are a part of my private effort to seize upon the raw material of life—its shapelessness, its meaninglessness" ("Desai's Comments", *Contemporary Novelists* 348).

D.F. Karaka is one of the first novelists to depict the plight of the alienated self in *There Lay the City* (1942). The narrator-protagonist here lives an insulated life with an expatriate sensibility. Karaka portrays the impact of the urban milieu on the psyche of the stranged self, a theme which Desai chooses for her novel, *Bye-Bye Blackbird.* While alienation of the protagonist in Karaka is self-imposed, in Desai, the alienation of Sarah, Adit and Dev is due to their inability to adopt an alien culture. Karaka gives physico-spiritual dimension to the alienation of the protagonist, whereas Desai treats the problem psychologically. The alienation of Karaka's protagonist is physical, spiritual and social, whereas Desai's is temperamental.

In R.K. Narayan, the serio-comic and hapless plight of the 'lone self' assumes an ironic and sarcastic dimension. In *Swami and Friends*, alienation of Swaminathan's father from his son and his mother is the outcome of the generation gap between the son and the father. This alienation may be called socio-historical or socio-biological. Chandran, in *The Bachelor of Arts*, finds his friends 'scattered like spray', but unlike him, they were 'at grips with life, like a buffalo' caught in the coils of a python (154). Desai's protagonists, too, are at grips with life, but their encounter is psycho-emotional and psycho-physical, not socio-economic and socio-political. In Narayan, the characters remain alienated, without losing their intrinsic hold on the comic perception of life. Raja Rao's alienated individuals like Govindan Nair and Ramakrishna Pai in *The Cat and Shakespeare and Ramaswamy* and Madeleine in *The Serpent and the Rope* face the pull of the transition in society from the old to the new, they face the emerging realities of Indian life. They set out on a quest for self-awareness and self-fulfilment in a world replete with social anomalies and incertitudes. Rao's protagonists experience alienation mainly on the metaphysical and mythical plane, occasionally on the mystical. Sarah and Maya in *Bye-Bye Blackbird* and *Cry, The Peacock*, share an alienation, purely emotional and psychic, while Rosie and Marco in Narayan's *The Guide* pass through an intellectual alienation. Narayan's protagonists face alienation with compromise and conciliation, Desai's with defiance and combat. Narayan's heroes remain humorously alienated from the milieu. This alienation is ironic and comic, while Desai's is hysteric and oneiric. Alienation in Narayan chiefly operates on the domestic and social plane. His protagonists, like Jagan, flee from the milieu. Their alienation is socio-religious and socio-cultural. In Naipaul, alienation leads to the forging of a new identity and a new life. It leads to the transformation of the native into an expatriate sensibility. Such transformation of identity hardly occurs in Anita Desai. Her characters alienate in order to involve themselves in a frantic quest for their identity. Alienation leads them into a blind alley, where they decay and decompose. In Desai, the alienated self is a 'mind forged manacle'. The earlier Indo-English novelists like R.K. Narayan, Mulk Raj Anand and Raja Rao were concerned with the dilemma emanating from alienation, whereas their successors, Arun Joshi and Kamala Markandaya dealt with the impulse behind alienation and its harrowing effect upon the individual. In Mulk Raj Anand, alienation is solely limited to the socio-political milieu. The 'lone self' in his novels is an underdog and a downtrodden.

Manohar Malgonkar, unlike Anita Desai, seems aware of the problems and predicaments of the alienated self in all their magnitude. The alienation of the Eurasian young woman in his novel, *Combat of Shadows*, represents the feeling of the rootless and the spineless, who oscillate and waver between their choices and wills, like O'Neill's *Yank*. In *Ruby Miranda*, the novelist portrays "the awareness of rootlessness, of not belonging, of not being wanted, even being despised..." (Malgonkar, *Combat of Shadows* 103).

Ruby is a lonely lady leading a de trop existence. The feel of alienation in Ruby and her English lover, Henry Winton, has been polarised. Winton does not feel it so deeply as Ruby, who deems it a problem of life and death, of bitter survival in the threatening milieu. Gian Talwar in *A Bend in the Ganges* peevishly shies away from reality, but in Anita Desai, the protagonist encounters it single-handed. Malgonkar depicts his protagonist, a bewildered wanderer between two worlds...the Indian and the English in the midst of cross-cultural contacts. In Desai, we have it in *Bye-Bye Blackbird* and, to some extent in her latest novel, *Baumgartner's Bombay.* But she does not deal with the problem so overtly, so revealingly.

In Kamala Markandaya, the alienated individual is portrayed against Indian socio-ethnic scene with 'a particular contemporary relevance' (Kumar, "Tradition and Change" Books Abroad 508) which we do not find in Desai's 'lone outsider'. Helen of *The Coffer Dams* and Saroja of the *Two Virgins* feel cut off from their heritage, forgetting what they knew. It is a case of alienation from nature as well as from the self. However, alienation in Markandaya, is only superficial and skin-deep, since it neglects the psychic aspect. Kit, in *Some Inner Fury* clings to the British Raj and apes Western culture only superficially. In *Possession*, it is the possessive and mundane love which alienates Val from the milieu and unites him with Lady Caroline. The alienation of Srinivas in *The Nowhere Man* is no doubt, instinctive but it lacks penetration and finesse. Srinivas is rooted in his cultural ethos. The psychic and the temperamental factor hardly counts. Uma Parameswaran believes that Markandaya's portrayal of the alienated self in her novels is without any authorial commentary. She has artistic instinct to know where the roots of the protagonists are, but she does not possess sufficient artistic care to do full justice to her subject ("India for the Western Reader", *Texas Quarterly* 123). In Raja Rao and Markandaya the alienated self's quest for identity takes a social-phisophical direction but in Anita Desai it is socio-psychic.

Balachandra Rajan, too, deals with the dilemma of the rootless individual. Though Rajan's approach is searching, he fails to capture the essence of Indianness. He misses the Indian topography and ethos on account of his mixed sensibility. Alienation of Krishnan in *The Dark Dancer* is social and of Nalini in *Too Long in the West*, cultural and environmental. Krishnan's callousness and apathy towards his family and his cynical view of the society drives him to a state of rootlessness. Alienation in Rajan does not end up in gloom and despair, while in Desai's major novels it does. It brings about self-recognition and self-restoration in the protagonist. In Rajan, the phenomenon of alienation is all-pervasive. It is diffused in the entire atmosphere, but in Desai, it is confined to the psyche only.

Nayantara Sahgal handles alienation more persistently and resolutely. The solitude of Sanad Shivpal in *A Time to be Happy* is the outcome of a clash of values. It is the outcome of his upbringing in an anglicized atmosphere. Moral disorder and cultural chaos breed alienation in Sanad which is not the case with Desai's protagonists. In Sahgal's *This Time of Morning*, Rashmi's estrangement from her husband is due to her unfulfilled 'freedom of sex'. Her desire to be ultra-modern alienates her from the emerging socio-cultural scenario. Her approach to life alienates her from the society. In Desai, the protagonist does not look at life from the surface. He is committed and involved. Communication gap between man and man and the disintegration of social values in a culture-ridden society bring about the alienation of her protagonists. Sahgal uses political background to focus marital alienation of three young couples—Inder and Saroj, Jit and Mara and Dubey and Leela, in her novel *Storm in Chandigarh*. Dubey's longing for companionship with his wife Leela reminds one of Gautama's alienation from Maya in Desai, *Cry, The Peacock*. But while in Desai, alienation is set against a socio-psychic background, in Sahgal we see it against a socio-political backdrop. In Desai, it is the disintegration of human values and the emotional and psychic void in characters that alienates them from the milieu.

Arun Joshi's treatment of alienation is unvarnished and ingenuous. It takes on an eternal dimension. Sindi Oberoi in

The Foreigner is 'a perennial outsider' (Quest 101). Forever forlorn in the world, he shirks even ordinary responsibilities. His alienation is a projection of his self, it is within himself, it is spiritual: "My foreignness lay within me..." (Joshi 1974: 61). Sindi is alienated from everything save himself. His alienation is not geographical. It is spiritual. Joshi's Billy in *The Strange Case of Billy Biswas* escapes into the saal forests of Maikal Hills to be suckled in a creed outworn. There is a heathen and a pagan element in Billy's alienation from society. But the alienation of Naipaul's *Billy in a House* for Mr. Biswas is unreal and superficial. In Joshi, the lonely self encounters the void both within and without. In Desai, it sees the void within. Joshi's execution of the outsiders' point of view is verily engaging and impressive. In Desai, it is diffusive and distracting. In Joshi, the protagonists are always alone. In Desai of the later novels like *Clear Light of Day*, *The Village by the Sea* and *In Custody*, they move from a state of alienation to that of 'mythic acceptance' [Sivaramakrishna, *KJES* 3 (1), 1978] and stoic resignation. In her treatment of alienation, Anita Desai is different from Arun Joshi. In Desai, alienation is psycho emotional and intellectual but in Joshi, it is spiritual. It is the alienation of the soul.

The protagonists of many Indo-Anglian novelists are 'alienated from nature and society' (Glicksberg 1963: 128). Desai's protagonists are torn from their socio-psychic self, and psycho-emotional milieu. In Joshi and Raja Rao, alienation leads to cultural schizophrenia, in Desai, it results in a psycho-emotionally oriented identity crisis. Desai paves the way for a new kind of novel—the novel of psychic sensibility. Desai protagonist is a lone individual, and not a social man. In most other novelists the hero is country-bred, but in Desai, he is an urbanite. "No other writer, it is said, is so much concerned with the life of young men and women in Indian cities as Anita Desai is" (Kohli, *Times Weekly* 3). Alienation in Desai, at times, assumes schizophrenic dimensions, where the character loses all contact with reality. Maya, in *Cry, The Peacock* says, "I strolled with him slowly across the lawn, feeling that an unreal ghost stalked beside me—a body without a heart, a heart without a body—what was he?" (196). Anita Desai and Raja Rao deal with the philosophic detachment of the hero, what Raja Rao renders in prose, Desai does in poetry. Raja Rao is concerned with dry facts, Desai with the mellifluous outpourings of the lone individual. Rao renders his philosophical speculations through dull, monotonous prose, whereas Desai ventilates her lyrical thoughts through soothing and poetic prose. Desai uses depth psychology in her study of women. She expertly explores the psychic reverberations of her female characters: Maya's masochism, Monisha's neurosis, Sarah's expatriation and Sita's regression. In Desai, the conflict is not so much between society and the lone outsider, as between 'Yes' and 'No', between two polarised and ambivalent choices and wills of the human psyche in the crisis of a transitional society.

Like Karen Horney, Anita Desai believes that childhood experiences determine conditions for neurosis but they are not the sole cause of trouble in adult life. In her interview with Jasbir Jain, she agrees that experiences of childhood are no doubt vivid, yet adult life has its traumatic experiences. Desai does not fully expose the childhood of her protagonists, but whatever flashbacks she provides are enough. Her characters tend to lose their 'vital self' in the course of their growth from infancy to adulthood. Sita struggles to 'connect'. Nirode 'spurns' everything. Bim, Nanda and Raka wish to 'forget'. Each wants to guard his/her identity but fails. Most of them are estranged women in quest of a new self, a new identity.

In Carson McCullers, grotesquerie serves to symbolise the disordered and the fragmented society, in Anita Desai it projects the demented, derailed and disintegrated self in the face of antagonistic and apathetic socio-psychic forces. If McCullers anatomises the malady of the emotionally disturbed society, Desai probes the psyche of the emotionally disturbed self. Man's search for a God, his desire for a harmonious world is the basis of McCullers' work, while in Desai, it is man's search for his roots, his desire to belong. Grotesquerie in McCullers is organically integrated into the mosaic of her work, it serves as an objective correlative, which lays bare the wounded psyche of the alienated self. The search for identity in McCullers ends in integration, whereas in Desai, it ends in frustration and misery heightening the individual's feel of alienation. The protagonist in McCullers fails to reciprocate or respond in love. He cannot communicate, since he is either physically or spiritually maimed. But in Desai, lack of response in love and failure in communication arise from some psychic malady or trauma. McCullers' is grounded upon spiritual alienation, Desai's vision upon socio-psychic alienation.

Like Edward Albee's dramatic personages, Desai protagonists face the problem of incommunication. They want to articulate their human problems. Against the forces of isolation, they strive to assert themselves. Albee's heroes realise the presence of an in-built sense of alienation in the very fabric of the society, with everyone separated from everyone else. Desai protagonists too, arrive at such an awareness but only at the unconscious plane of their existence. Jerry in Albee's play *The Zoo Story* suffers the pangs of alienation and experiences the utter lack of communication. But there, the concern of the dramatist "is unavoidingly metaphysical while Anita Desai has noticeably confined herself to the mundane reality of life. Transcendental American concern is missing here" [Singh, in Prasad (ed.), *Response* 236].

In Conrad, the alienation of Lord Jim leads to his immoral 'jump' from the Patna. His alienation is spiritually stultifying and annihilating. It is deep-rooted and death-like. Such alienation is foreign to Anita Desai. It does not propel one into such nocturnal and ghastly corridors of life. Alienation in Desai is neither moral nor spiritual, it is intellectual and emotional. The death of Lord Jim reminds us of Monisha in *Voices in the City*, who asserts her identity by committing suicide. But in Monisha, the 'death-wish' springs from her psychic maladjustment and not from moral or spiritual vacillation as is the case with Lord Jim.

Unlike Conrad, Desai does not make the individual's alienated plight spiritually baffling and morally humiliating and ridiculous. Conrad projects the theme of estrangement and isolation of the self through marine and spiritual images, Desai through animal and stellar images, the images of prey and predator and at times through natural images like day and fire. The existential dilemma of the sequestered self is more profound and intense in Conrad than in Desai. In Conrad, it extends beyond psychology to philosophy and, in a sense, to the socio-political subjective milieu. In Desai, it touches the cloistered socio-psychic world. The despair of her protagonists is the despair of a Yank or an emperor Jones. It is the despair and derangement, of not belonging. Anita Desai's narrative like Shouri Daniels' fictional plot, moves from emotional outbursts to philosophical musings. In Daniels, the problem of alienation assumes a comic and extravagant dimension through the disjointed and loose extravaganza of its structure, but in Desai, it functions within the family save in *In Custody* and *Baumgartner's Bombay.* It lacks the element of humour and comedy. Shouri Daniels' novels are a conglomeration of the elements of fantasy, absurdity, irony, sarcasm, philosophy, comedy, lofty wisdom and nostalgic reminiscences. They are an extravaganza of creative ingenuity. The alienation between Mira and her husband Nanjundan is religious. It is an alienation of two cultures—East and West—which result in a clash, the clash between tradition and modernity, generating identity crisis. The novels of Desai, like those of Daniels, explore the bedimmed and beguiled psyche of the protagonist who has gone through intense and fiery moments of conflict. The protagonist is a 'lone explorer' of his identity.

Anita Desai's novels are a blending and binding of both exterior landscape and interior vision. In *Clear Light of Day* and *Baumgartner's Bombay*, there are allusions to communal disharmony and political turmoil and in *Bye-Bye Blackbird*, there are notes of East-West encounter. But here these allusions are peripheral and incidental, in Raja Rao, Arun Joshi, Kamala Markandaya, and B. Rajan, they are central and functional.

In dealing with the problem of alienation, Anita Desai makes abrupt change in the narrative focus. The scene rolls on from character to character and we have "the rhetoric of characters in opposition which causes them to reveal each other's values as well as the values in the situations" (Springer 1978: 32).

Anita Desai simply skims over the surface of a character's life without making deep psychological probing without graphically portraying the inner turmoil of the alienated self. Artistic devices of monologue and soliloquy have not been fully exploited to analyze the alienation of the self. Hence, the reader fails to get a comprehensive picture of the psychic malady of the solitary self and simply left to wander from one speculation to another. Kalpana Wandrekar has very aptly pointed out this defect in relation to the character of Sarah in *Bye-Bye Blackbird*:

> When Sarah refuses to play with her childhood toys, we are kept ignorant about the emotions felt by her at that time.... At the tea party we are told that she is relieved but we are not told what exactly she feels, the turmoil in her mind.... None of the vehicles of monologue and soliloquy is fully exploited to analyze Sarah's character.... The outer reactions we see, but what goes on within is often known only to the character and its creator. ("The Ailing Aliens", *Image of India in the Indian Novel in English* 48)

In *In Custody* and *Baumgartner's Bombay*, Desai explores, the psyche of a male protagonist outside the circumscriptions of familial ties and obligations. She makes a departure from her earlier obsessive pre-occupation with the interior landscape of hypersensitive and neurotic women. In *In Custody*, the artist protagonist, Deven, is endowed with a different kind of sensibility. He is not an alienated self, in the sense the female protagonists of Desai's earlier novels are. For Desai was "conscious of the need to write outside oneself, to be able to feel oneself into completely different personalities from one's own" (Sheth, "Desai Interviewed", Imprint 84). Suresh Saxena maintains that *Baumgartner's Bombay* is "a complete departure from her earlier writings" (*Commonwealth Literature* 237). But it is not. The alien plight of Hugo has an apparent similarity with that of the blackbirds in *Bye-Bye Blackbird*. From the nostalgia of the blackbirds, Desai shifts her focus to the estrangement of the exiles. Each of her novels is a step forward in the growth of her fictional self, where the immured spirit passes through spontaneous self-realisation and self-discovery.

In the novels of Anita Desai, the theme of disharmony and discord is confined to the family and at times to the maladjusted or ill-adjusted self. Loneliness and unrequited love drives Desai heroines to the jaws of death, often manifesting in madness or suicide. Desai deals with the alienation of upper-middle class people of society. Her protagonists, like the characters in Charlotte Bronte's novels, suffer from lack of parental love, disturbed infancy, broken homes and Oedipus or Electra Complex. Disgruntled with their existence, they often opt out of the mainstream of life. Alienation in Desai characters often manifests in immoral ties and activities which we hardly find in any other Indian Women Novelist save Shobha De. Alienated from their selves, Desai protagonists search for their identity in the milieu through self-discovery and self-identification.

WORKS CITED

Allen, Walter, 1954. *The English Novel*, London: Penguin.

Daiches, David, 1965. *The Novel and the Modern World*, Chicago: Phoenix Books, University of Chicago Press.

Dalmia, Yasodhara, "An Interview with Anita Desai", *The Times of India*, April 29, 1979.

Desai, Anita, "Reply to the Questionnaire", *Kakatiya Journal of English Studies*, 3 (1978).

——, "Comments", *Contemporary Novelists*, ed. James Vinson, New York: St. Martin's Press, 1972.

——, 1980. *Cry, The Peacock*, New Delhi: Orient Paperbacks.

——, 1982. *Voices in the City*, New Delhi: Orient Paperbacks.

——, 1982. *Where Shall We Go This Summer?*, New Delhi: Orient Paperbacks.

——, 1985. *Bye-Bye Blackbird*, New Delhi: Orient Paperbacks.

——, 1977. *Fire on the Mountain*, New Delhi: Allied Publishers.

——, 1980. *Clear Light of Day*, New Delhi: Allied Publishers.

——, 1983. *The Village by the Sea*, New Delhi: Allied Publishers.

——, 1984. *In Custody*, London: Heinemann.

——, 1988. *Baumgartner's Bombay*, Harmondsworth: Penguin.

(Textual citations, if any, are from these editions of Anita Desai's novels.)

Fiedler, Leslie, 1966. *Love and Death in the American Novel*, New York: Dell Publishing Co.

Glicksberg, Charles, 1963. *Tragic Vision in Twentieth Century Literature*, South Illinois University Press.

Iyengar, K.R. Srinivasa, 1962. *Indian Writing in English*, Bombay: Asia Publishing House.

——, 1973. —(Second Revised Edition)—.

Jain, Jasbir, "Interview with Anita Desai", Rajasthan University Studies in English, Vol. XII (1979).

——, 1987. *Stairs to the Attic: The Novels of Anita Desai,* Jaipur: Printwell.

Joshi, Arun. 1974. *The Foreigner*, Bombay: Asia Publishing House.

Kohli, Suresh. "Indian Women Novelists in English", *Times Weekly* (8 November 1970).

Kumar, Shiv K. "Tradition and Change in the Novels of Kamala Markandaya", Books Abroad, 43/4 (Autumn 1969).

Lawrence, D.H. "Morality and Novel", in David Lodge, ed. *Twentieth Century Literary Criticism*, London: Longman, 1971.

Maini, D.S. "The Achievement of Anita Desai" in K.K. Sharma (ed.) *Indo-English Literature,* Ghaziabad: Vimal), 1977.

Malgonkar, Manohar, 1964. *Combat of Shadows,* London: Hamish Hamilton.

Mukherjee, Meenakshi, "A Review of the Foreigner", *Quest*, 60 (Jan.-March 1969).

Nicholson, Kai, "Are We Expatriates", *The Commonwealth Review*, Vol. IV, 1992-93, No. 2.

Parameswaran, Uma, "India for the Western Reader: A Study of Kamala Markandaya's Novels", *Texas Quarterly*, Summer 1968.

Rao, B. Ramachandra, 1977. "The Novels of Anita Desai: A Study", Ludhiana: Kalyani.

Saxena, Suresh, "Anita Desai's Search for Roots in Baumgartner's Bombay", *Recent Commonwealth Literature*, ed. Dhawan et al., New Delhi: Prestige, 1989.

Seth, Ketaki, "It is fatal to write with an Audience in Mind: An Interview with Anita Desai", Imprint (June 1984).

Seth, Sunil, "Interview with Anita Desai", *India Today*, December 1-15, 1980.

Sharma, R.S., 1981 *Anita Desai,* New Delhi: Arnold-Heinemann.

Singh, Brijraj, "The Fiction of Anita Desai", *The Humanities Review*, III, 2, July-December 1981.

Singh, C.P. "The Visitor and the Exile: A Study in Anita Desai's *Bye-Bye Blackbird*", in Prasad (ed.), *Response: Recent Revelations of Indian Fiction in English*, Bareilly: Prakash, 1983.

Sivaramakrishna, M. "From Alienation to Mythic Acceptance: The Ordeal of Consciousness in Anita Desai's Fiction", *Kakatiya Journal of English Studies*, 3/1 (1978).

Springer, Mary Doyle, 1978. "A Rhetoric of Literary Character: Some Women of Henry James", Chicago: The Univ. of Chicago Press.

Sujatha, S. "The Theme of Disintegration: A Comparative Study of Anita Desai's *Cry, The Peacock* and Bharati Mukherjee's Wife", *The Commonwealth Review*, Vol. IV, 1992-93, No. 2.

Wandrekar, Kalpana. "The Ailing Aliens: Anita Desai's *Bye-Bye Blackbird* as a Symptomatic Study in Schizophrenia", in Pandey and Rao (ed.), *Image of India in the Indian Novel in English 1960-1985,* Bombay: Orient Longman, 1993.

Woolf, Virginia, 1953. *The Common Reader* (First Series), London: Hogarth Press.

28

Feminism Jettisoned in Pinter's Plays

SANJAY KUMAR

Feminism refers to the belief that women should have the same rights, power and opportunity that men have. Of late, it has come to mean a movement in support of the idea that the present situation should be changed to give women equality with men.

Obviously, believing that women have been denied their real status in the society and personal relationship by men, many playwrights like G.B. Shaw, Shelagh Delaney, Ann Jellicoe, Pam Gems, Tennessee Williams, Caryl Churchill, etc. have turned into feminists, directly or indirectly. These authors try to bring about a change in the social mileau so that women are accepted as equal or better than the males in all social as well as familial responsibilities, rights and situations. In fact, they attempt to remove the persisting gender discrimination in all its manifestations.

Harold Pinter, the greatest living British playwright, however, propels a different point of view. In a typically Pinteresque tongue-in-cheek manner, he seems to be suggestively discarding the popular view that women are inferior to men and, hence, are tortured by them. He seems to be breaching the dead wall of complacency as his plays set up the situations which involve the male-female contention. Mostly, the contention in his plays is for superiority, dominance and possession and almost, invariably, it is the female in his plays who imposes her authority over fellow males and assumes the position of superiority and dominance. The discussion that follows attempts to observe this pattern which is recurrent in many of Pinter's plays.

Though much of the battle in Pinter's plays is due to the territorial struggles of the characters which they indulge in but what, generally, escapes the eye of the audience is the contention between males and females. Thus, the popular struggle in Pinter's characters is for getting a foothold inside the cozy, warm room from a dark, hostile outside but in "many of Pinter's plays, the key struggle for power is between male and female".[1] Quite often, we find the home turning into a battlefield and the men and women in his plays try to sweep each other aside to capture power and security and assert dominance over one another. In this male-female contention, the victory, generally, lies with Pinter's female characters as they move strategically with a better knowledge of their own desires as well as that of their male counterparts. But as Pinter's women appear to be nagging, unfaithful and somewhat libertine, the critics tend to disparage Pinter's portraits of women. One representative view is voiced by Alrene Sykes: "Does Pinter say anything more about women than that they are mothers, wives and whores? Not, I think, a great deal".[2]

This paper attempts to present an altogether different view about the playwright which suggests that rather than disparaging women, Pinter finds them more strategic, subtle and superior when compared to men. In fact, like many of his views contrary to the established canons, Pinter chooses to believe that females are better poised. To him, they appear in control in their contention with their male counterparts and always outclass them with their poise, mental toughness and an uncanny handling of the complex situations around. The study of Pinter's characters like Flora, Ruth, Kate and Anna, which follows, provides enough of the evidences to believe this impression.

Flora of *A Slight Ache* is one of the most feminine of Pinter's heroines. She is soft and delicate as well as intuitive and the way she finally decides to take up the old Matchseller, her nurturant attitude is also confirmed. But, besides showing these natural feminine traits, she exhibits a mental toughness and remains enigmatic for her husband, Edward. She first allows Edward to kill the wasp that hovers around their breakfast table as

Edward's question: "You want to kill it?"[3] is answered in the affirmative: "Yes" (I, 173). But she quickly shifts her stance and grumbles philosophically at the bizarre nature of the execution: "What an awful experience!" (I, 174). Flora remains elusive and complex for Edward as she continues to show an interest in the Matchseller, who is a source of constant torture to her husband.

In fact, throughout the play we find Edward to be terribly disquieted as he is unable to understand his wife's attraction for the Matchseller. He fails to understand why Flora takes interest in the mysterious Matchseller standing outside their gate and does not know how exactly to stop her. Flora quite clearly understands her husband's perplexity and torments him for she subtly reveals her liking for the Matchseller as she finds him to be a "quiet and harmless old man" (I, 176).

She continues to refer to the Matchseller with positive remarks: "He looks bigger.... He looks like a bullock" (I, 177). The implications of these remarks are obviously sexual. The fact that she finds the Matchseller to be "bigger" (than Edward) is enough to perplex Edward and that she takes the Matchseller to be a potential sex symbol, compounds her husband's misery. Witnessing Flora's growing desire for the Matchseller, Edward breaks from within and slips into verbal incoherence in his pursuit to disarm his opponent with his marathon speeches.

He starts giving unnecessary details about the squire and tries to assert authority: "they look upon me with some regard" (I, 182). But, gradually, he sinks into stale, jargonistic expressions: "Now and again I jot down a few observations on certain tropical phenomena not from the same standpoint, of course [Silent pause]. Yes, Africa now. Africa's always been my happy hunting ground. Fascinating country. Do you know it?... Most extraordinary diversity of flora and fauna. Especially fauna" (I, 183).

It is interesting to note how quickly he gets away from the expression of "flora and fauna" and likes to concentrate only on "fauna" as the word "flora" happens to be a strange allusion to his wife's name. This confirms his uneasiness even with Flora's name and that he jumps quickly away from it, confirms his escapist tendencies.

Flora intuits this weakness of her husband and attacks her vigorously: "You are frightened of a poor old man. Why?" (I, 178). Edward grimaces, fumes and hisses and commits the blunder of inviting the Matchseller inside his house assuming that he would be able to overpower him with the help of his aggression and communicative skills. From here on, Edward never recovers. He lets himself loose on the Matchseller as he opens a disguised verbal attack on him but derails down miserably as the Matchseller's immaculate silence becomes the source of constant and multiplying worries. So, Edward becomes terribly incoherent and fragmented in his speech and action. Though the barrier of silence seems to be working against Edward, what frustrates him more is the feeling that the Matchseller is an opponent only to him and not to his wife. He, in fact, can very much be the object of her liking and may even snatch her away from him! Under this fear of a prospective betrayal, Edward groans and appears disjointed even from his own ambitious task of bludgeoning the mysterious Matchseller. He becomes utterly meaningless in the series of questions that he shoots at the Matchseller to extract an answer.

Edward's desperateness exhibits a spirit that has been dented from within and the otherwise effective speaker sounds discordant and disjuncted from his own speech and sound. Edward is the man victimised not by the outward circumstances; he is a man hunched from the inside. That he receives the mysterious outsider with trepidation is due to his feelings of insecurity which he constantly experiences in Flora's company. The fear of desertion looms large on him and Flora to him always appears too complex and elusive a person to be understood ever. His inability to understand female behaviour puts him under a constant uncertainty about his relationship with Flora. He tries to overpower Flora by subjugating her to his desires with his tyrannical attitudes. He thus attempts to possess by force what he cannot win with wisdom, love and intellect.

Understandably then, Edward's supposed calculated assault turns into a blind slog. He chips and charges, but is always defeated by the impregnable silence of the Matchseller. The gap between his expectations and results widens up monstrously and he finally gives up groaning under the weight of an unfulfilled desire. Flora quickly substitutes him with the Matchseller, the befitting answer to her husband's incapacities and weaknesses.

Thus, the frustration of failure finally catches-up with Edward. But rather than being the frustration of failure in knocking out the outside menace, projected by Pinter through the Matchseller, it is the frustration of failure in love. That Flora always remains on the borderline of desertion, weakens Edward and that eventually leads to his ouster from her life.

By projecting the complex nature of male-female relationship and attributing an obvious victory to his female character Flora, Pinter makes his stance clear. It is the women who hold the key to the decision when to accept and discard their male partners in Pinter's plays. They thus enjoy a better status than their male counterparts as the males in his plays are less convincing and easily subdued.

In *A Slight Ache* thus the man-woman contest of wills looks one sided as Flora defeats her husband Edward with a huge margin and looks all powerful. Though Flora is thus capable of outplaying her male counterpart successfully, yet she is no match to Ruth of *The Homecoming*. In one of Pinter's most controversial and successful play, Ruth becomes the most important and powerful figure as she not only invades the household but also stamps her superiority on all her male pursuers. In this play, the male characters are shown to be torn between their contempt for female guiles and an awful fascination towards a feeling of sexual satisfaction and fulfilment that only a woman can provide them.

The males then attempt desperately to define their females with mutually contradictory remarks. The old and cynical Max shows a similarly bewildering attitude when he remembers Jessie, his wife: "Mind you, she wasn't such a bad woman. Even though it made me sick just to look at her rotten stinking face, she wasn't such a bad bitch. I gave her the best bleeding years of my wife".[4] The inability to define woman with certainty spreads the entire male household of Max. This confusion about male behaviour is most obvious in his philosopher son Teddy who is a university professor in America. Like Edward, Teddy too anticipates a desertion from Ruth. He walks back to his father Max and brothers Lenny and Joey after seven years expecting to instil a sense of family and belonging in his wife Ruth who, otherwise, appears displeased with his philosopher husband.

Ruth's superiority is explicit to us right from her first appearance on stage with Teddy. She looks composed and disinterested as Teddy tries to seek reassurance. When Teddy asks if Ruth is cold, her answer is cold enough: "No" (III, 37). She also declines to drink anything while Teddy attempts to comfort Ruth, his superior partner:

> What do you think of the room? Big isn't it? It's a big house. I mean, it's a fine room, don't you think? Actually there was a wall, across here... With a door we knocked it down...years ago... to make an open living area. The structure wasn't affected, you see. My mother was dead. (III, 37)

Clearly, the power lies with Ruth as Teddy fumbles and sounds discordant while explaining. He, further, rambles: "Look, it's all-right. I'm here. I mean...I'm with you. There is no need to be nervous. Are you nervous?" (III, 39). Ruth's answer "No" (III, 39) is again more pointed than Teddy's question. The statement "I'm with you" looks ironical as it appears to mock Teddy's male assertion as his remark seems to be more of an attempt to align himself with Ruth than to offer her any solace.

Teddy is nervous like Edward about a possible betrayal as he gets panicky at Ruth's announcement that she is going to take a walk. He sounds hollow and helpless as he tries to stop her: "But what I am going to do?" (III, 40). Obviously, Teddy exercises no control over Ruth; he can only plead with her that she remains with him. He too, like Edward, wants to possess Ruth as both of these males are isolated and in need of emotional help from their females. As both Edward and

Teddy exhibit a rigid and cerebral attitude of mind, their female counterparts are more flexible and fun-loving and they hold their existence with ease than their males. In an article "What's in a Name", Bernard Dukore compares both Edward and Teddy and points out: "Although suppositions are not certainties, the intellectual Teddy seems to be another side of the intellectual Edward: more controlled, more cunning, more successful".[5] Though both Teddy and Edward possess intellectual powers, they lack the knack to cope-up with their wives and have to act with detachment, yet their latent frustration is explicit when they visualise their women's crossing their defined territories to be an act of their refusal.

Their fears become understandable as Flora replaces Edward with the Matchseller and Ruth begins to work as a prostitute for Teddy's father and brothers. But Ruth's acceptance to serve the entire household as well as the stranger as a prostitute is more of an act of choice rather than a compulsion. In fact, she tightens the grip on the entire household as she first outplays Lenny in their verbal duel and then mesmerises both Max and Joey to position herself at the top.

In the superb scene between Lenny and Ruth, both compete verbally for power. Lenny's need to talk, suggests his weakness while Ruth's equanimity is a manifestation of her strength. She performs with precision at language throughout her encounter with Lenny. In answer to Lenny's casually platitudinous remark: "Good evening", she shoots right back: "Morning, I think" (III, 43). Ruth thus indicates her placidity as she exhibits no qualms at having seen a stranger like Lenny. Quite subdued in the very beginning itself, Lenny brings Ruth a glass of water as a gesture of intimacy.

But, as Ruth refuses to acknowledge his hospitality with gratitude, it blunts his proposal. Deeply feeling humiliated, Lenny launches himself to assert his masculine bravado while describing himself as a soldier in Venice and follows up with his erotic proposition: "Do you mind if I hold your hand?" (III, 46). Ruth still shows no surprise and calmly asks: "Why?" (III, 46). Again, in order to assert his superiority, Lenny indulges in an extended monologue: "One night not too long ago, one night down by docks..." (III, 46). From an apparently romantic start, Lenny goes on to describe his potential violence towards women and announces that he contemplated killing the woman who can to him and made him a "certain proposal" (III, 46). Lenny intends the story to communicate power over women, his right to attack a woman he disapproves. This implicitly suggests that he can make a proposal to whom he likes and that once such proposal is made, it should be gracefully accepted. But Ruth deflects his assertion with a timely question: "How did you know she was diseased?" (III, 47).

To diminish the advantage built up by Ruth, Lenny launches another anecdote in which he describes how he beat and kicked an old woman:

> So after a few minutes I said to her, now look here, why don't you stuff this iron mangle up your arse? Anyway, I said, they're out of date, you want to get a spin driver. I had a good mind to give her a workover there and then, but as I was feeling jubilant and snow-clearing I just gave her a short-arm jab to the belly and jumped on a bus outside. (III, 49)

The purpose of both these anecdotes is to indicate Ruth that he holds an upperhand in his relation with women. But the implications are that even in narratives he conquers women violently and not sexually. The final suggestions that he jumped on a bus outside indicates his tendency to escape and a possible impotence. Ruth penetrates this weakness of Lenny. She assumes dominant position as she first refuses Lenny's request for taking away the glass out of her way and then warns him: "If you take the glass...I'll take you" (III, 50). Ruth advances dauntlessly as her offers become more and more blatant: "Sit on my lap. Take a long cool sip.... Put your head back and open your mouth" (III, 50). Lenny retreats with an expression which suggests his defeat at the hand of Ruth as he seems paralysed with the feelings of anger, defeat and humiliation. "Take that glass away from me" (III, 50).

Thus, Ruth imposes her authority on Lenny after having already subdued his elder brother Teddy. Her victory over Lenny is, however, of greater importance than that of the one over Teddy as Lenny himself is a master manipulator of language. So, Ruth's victory over him certainly places her right at the top. Ruth goes on to win the entire household as she mesmerises all her male onlookers with the help of her analogy that is full of sexual overtones and the suggestions that she possesses better perception, greater intellect and more authority than any of her male counterparts. Her attack on the fossilized forms of words confirms that she rips through the male complacency of philosophical debaters, Lenny and Teddy:

> Look at me...I move my leg. That's all it is. But I wear...underwear...which moves with me...it...captures your attention. Perhaps, you misinterpret. The action is simple. It's a leg...moving. My lips move. Why don't you restrict...your observations to that? Perhaps, the fact that they move is more significant...than the words which come through them. You must bear that... possibility...in mind. (III, 68-69)

By challenging both the intellectual as well as the physical supremacy of her male pursuers, Ruth imposes her authority over the entire household. So, when she accepts to sell herself for money through Lenny & Co., she is not the victim but the "queen bee the conqueror of the swarm and the hive".[6]

The dominance of Pinter's female characters continues even in his later works like *Old Times*. However, in contrast to the pattern of *The Homecoming*, wherein we saw many men fighting for one women, here we find one woman and man fighting for another woman. The object of contention here is Kate and those who fight over her are her husband Deeley and her friend Anna. The play, however, achieves greater amount of mendacity, guile and complexity as the characters move more deviously than they did in *The Homecoming*. The characters here attempt to invent and "rearrange the past to suit their own ends".[7] Nevertheless, the core of the play lies in the battle for possession, supremacy and dominance among Pinter's males and females and quite like *A Slight Ache* and *The Homecoming*, the victory lies with his female characters.

In the beginning itself, Deeley, the only male in the play, is shown to be "slumped in arm chair",[8] which, in itself suggests his defeat even before the struggle begins. Kate is "curled on a sofa" while Anna is "standing at the window, looking out" (IV, 3).

Clearly, the posture of Kate indicates her security and repose, whereas that of Anna suggests her emotional detachment. But surely both these ladies are introduced by Pinter in a much more commanding posture than their male counterpart—Deeley.

Whey the dialogue unfolds it confirms the view as Deeley seems too inquisitive to know everything about Kate's past relationship with Anna. His "repeated attempts to clarify the bond the two women shared reveals his jealousy, his doubts about his wife's fidelity, and, perhaps, his fears about his masculinity".[9] Thus, in the beginning itself, Deeley has gone on his defensive and has allowed Kate to take the initiative. Kate takes advantage of this and begins to dominate. She is deliberately vague in her meaning of the word "friend" (IV, 4). She first refers to Anna as "my only friend" (IV, 5) but changes it quickly to "my one and only friend" (IV, 5). She then goes on to add that Anna used to "steal things" (IV, 6) and seems to vividly remember that these things used to be "Bits and pieces, underwear" (IV, 6). But soon she quashes the entire information stating: "I hardly remember her. I've almost forgotten her" (IV, 8).

Kate's mixed strategy of affiliation and detachment from Anna's memory is a source of confusion for Deeley. Kate confounds the confusions as she confirms that they used to live together for: "How else she would steal my underwear from me? In the street?" (IV, 13). Obviously, the nature of Kate's answers is quite complex and the depth of her relations with Anna appears to be unfathomable for Deeley. However, whatever little information Kate gives Deepley about Anna is enough to alienate him. By referring to the stealing of her underwears by Anna, she indicates their sexual intimacy but more than that, it proves that "women, by their very nature, share an understanding of one another's physical and emotional needs that men cannot fathom and certainly cannot duplicate".[10] Thus, by juxtaposing her views and giving intimate details about Anna, she implies that the very womanliness of Kate and Anna isolates Deeley from both of them. Deeley never recovers from this subtle exile and throughout the play, he seems to be struggling so as to find a foothold in the togetherness of Anna and Kate.

Nevertheless, Deeley continues to fight. He tries to nullify Kate's relation with Anna by confirming the existence of Anna's husband with a strategic question: "Why isn't she married? I mean, why isn't she bringing her husband?" (IV, 8). Kate first deflects her question while saying: "Ask her" (IV, 9) and then gives an irritatingly vague answer: "Everyone is married" (IV, 9). Deeley continues to force the existence of Anna's husband into light implying that since Anna is a married woman, Kate can no longer live with her. But his very necessity to ask questions and seek clarifications indicates his weakness and the consequent superiority of Kate over him.

Anna is quick to gauge this weakness of Deeley. Sensing very much his possible alienation from Kate, she starts staking her claims for her and immediately relates herself to Kate with an intimate recollection of their escapade in London: "We sat hardly breathing with our coffee, heads bent, so as not to be seen, so as not to disturb, so as not to distract and listened to all those words" (IV, 14). Deeley tries to belittle the importance of their relationship by derogating the place itself: "We rarely get to London" (IV, 14). But Kate aligns herself with Anna as she confirms her recollection: "Yes, I remember" (IV, 14).

From this moment onwards, Deeley and Anna continue to fight bitterly for the possession of Kate. The strategy chosen is to recall images of the past and prove the mutual intimacy with the object of their contention—Kate. In this subtle memory game, Anna outplays Deeley.

It is Deeley who first tries to prove that he understands Kate's present likings as he reflects: "She likes taking long walks. All that you know. Raincoat on. Off down the lane, hands deep in pocket. All that kind of thing" (IV, 20). But his choppy prose makes far less conviction. Moreover, Anna takes this image of Kate's walking and turns it into a more intimate experience: "Sometimes, walking in the park, I'd say to her, you're dreaming, you're dreaming, wake up, what are you dreaming? and she'd look round at me, flicking her hair, and look at me as if I were part of her dream" (IV, 20-21). Thus, Deeley loses the advantage early on to Anna who appears more poetic and deep in her relation with Kate than Deeley whose experience with his wife appears to be prosaic and stale.

Anna begins to fortify her advantage as Deeley starts singing songs which rather than indicating his intimacy with Kate, confirm his alienation from her. He first sings a song in Kate's praise: "Blue moon, I see you standing alone..." (IV, 23). The implications are that he can only admire Kate distantly without ever understanding her. Anna retorts with a much more intimate observation: "The way you comb your hair" (IV, 23). The observation suggests the realistic and close relation of Anna with Kate in contrast to that of Deeley which indicates his isolation and too romantic an approach for his wife.

Deeley's next line: "Oh no they can't take that away from me..." (IV, 23) suggests his desperation and Anna pushes her advantage further with another expression which exhibits her intimacy with Kate: "Oh, you're lovely, with your smile so warm" (IV, 23). Deeley finally gives up complaining: "They don't make them like that any more" (IV, 25). As we know that the contest of songs is, in fact, a way to stake claims over Ruth, Deeley's resignation underlines his inability to create images to challenge Anna's claims to Kate.

Like Lenny of *The Homecoming*, Teddy tries to rally back with an anecdote which is meant to spoil the grace of the relation between Kate and Anna. In this anecdote, he recalls attending a show of a film and tells how he saw too usherettes in the foyer: "One of them was stroking her breast and the other one was saying 'dirty bitch' and the one stroking her breasts was saying 'mmnnn' with a very sexual relish and smiling at her fellow usherette..." (IV, 25). The main purpose of Deeley's narrative is to equate the crude relation of the usherettes with that of Kate and Anna. He wants to spoil the grace of Anna's feelings for Kate and expose its grossness.

Quickly afterwards, Deeley narrates his sexual intercourse with Kate implying thereby the naturalness of his relationship with Kate: "Our naked bodies met, hers cool, warm, highly agreeable" (IV, 27). Anna, however, dismisses this image with a remark which constitutes the core of the play: "There are some things one remembers even though they may never have happened. There are things I remember which may never have happened but as I recall them so they take place" (IV, 27-28). Anna's statement is clearly meant to undercut the assertion of Deeley's narrative. She punctuates Deeley's claims altogether as she goes on to describe how she once discovered a man in the apartment of Kate. It means Kate was not only attached to Anna, she had relations with other men before marriage and that Deeley offers nothing new to Kate when he boasts of his sexual relation with her.

As the play progresses, Deeley's alienation increases from both Kate and Anna. He fails to relate to either of the two as Anna and Kate seem to settle down in a domestic bliss in the second act of the play and thus isolate Deeley completely.

Tension mounts up for Deeley much in the same manner as it did for Edward of *A Slight Ache*. He resorts to a mindless slog on Anna pressing his authority: "You feel it's my province? Well, you're down right. It is my province. I'm glad someone is showing a bit of taste at last. Of course, it is my bloody province. I'm her husband" (IV, 62). Kate's response, however, is stunning as she dismisses his claims singularly: "If you don't like it go" (IV, 63). Thus, Deeley's dismissal is complete as the final blows are delivered by Kate. Though victory eludes Anna too, she still maintains her dignity in her detachment.

That Deeley finishes at the bottom in this gruelling battle for supremacy is clear as in the final moments he is shown to be "sobbing" (IV, 69). Since the other two characters are shown to be more composed and placid, they assert their authority. Moreover, Deeley is finally shown to be "sitting slumped" (IV, 70), a posture which suggests his defeat. Contrastingly, Anna is "lying on divan" (IV, 71) and Kate is "sitting on divan" (IV, 71), the posture of both the ladies suggests their calm, poised position that the battle renders them.

Obviously, both Kate and Anna have been projected as far more powerful persons than Deeley in the play. Their real strength is their absence of weakness, which Deeley, in turn, reflects in plenty. Like Edward of *A Slight Ache* he becomes angry and obviously cheap, both of which are the signs of weakness and never the symbols of power, strength and assurance. In this way, Deeley's maleness is overpowered by the feminity of Anna and Kate, who in togetherness, outplay him assuming the dominant position in *Old Times*.

This is not true only in *Old Times* but is a repetitive design of Pinter's plays. Almost as a rule, his female characters are much more powerful than this males. They are strong intellectually and are poised and composed. As most of the issues in contention are solved through a verbal tournament in his plays, the advantage clearly lies with Pinter's female characters as they are more in control of their verbal expression in comparison to their male counterparts. The females in Pinter's plays perform with precision at language while the males ramble aimlessly when they talk.

Moreover, Pinter's female characters are endowed with a vision which penetrates human behaviour. Thus, they easily see through the weakness of their male counterparts and outplay them. In fact, Pinter's female characters are shown to be capable of putting mind over matter. So, placing temperament over emotions, they outclass the males in contention with them with a better control, poise and placidity in their attitude, desire and expression. Thus, often in his plays we find the males alienated, subdued and exposed while the females assume the positions of superiority, dominance and control towards the end. In a suggestive manner thus Pinter provides an anti-thesis to the popular feminist question and indicates the meaninglessness of such talk.

REFERENCES

1. Victor, L. Cahn, *Gender and Power in the Plays of Harold Pinter* (London: The Macmillan Press Ltd., 1993), p. 6.
2. Alrene Sykes, *Harold Pinter* (St. Lucia: University of Queensland Press, 1970), 106.
3. Harold Pinter, "*A Slight Ache*," *Plays: One* (London: Methuen London Ltd., 1987), p. 173. All the subsequent references for *A Slight Ache* have been taken from the same edition of the play, hereafter cited in text, within parentheses, with Volume No. (I) and relevant page number(s).
4. Harold Pinter, "*The Homecoming*," *Plays: Three* (London: Methuen London Ltd., 1986), p. 25. All the subsequent references for *The Homecoming* have been taken from the same edition of the play hereafter cited in text, within parentheses, with the Volume No. (III) and relevant page number(s).
5. Bernard, F. Dukore, "What's in a Name?—An Approach to *The Homecoming*", *Theatre Journal*, 33 (May 1981), p. 177.
6. Dukore, Quoted by Guido Almansi and Simon Henderson in *Harold Pinter* (London: Methuen & Co. Ltd., 1983), p. 67.
7. Alan Hughes, "Myth and Memory in *Old Time*", *Modern Drama*, 17 (December 1974), p. 470.
8. Harold Pinter, "*Old Times*," *Plays: Four* (London: Eyre Methuen Ltd., 1986), p. 3. All the subsequent references from *Old Times* have been taken from the same edition of the play, hereafter cited in text, within parentheses, with the Volume No. (IV) and relevant page number(s).
9. Victor, L. Cahn, *Gender and Power in the Plays of Harold Pinter* (London: The Macmillan Press Ltd., 1993), p. 104.
10. *Ibid.*

❑❑❑

29

Nargis Dalal—The Woman Writer

MALLIKARJUN PATIL

Nargis Dalal is one of the greatest woman novelists in English in modern India. She has been the front-ranking woman novelist of her days. In this regard, she has excelled her contemporaries like Ruth Prawar Jhubvala and Anita Desai. By her deliberate purity of responsiveness and artistic dignity and sincerity, she has made her works vivid and enjoyable. Mrs. Dalal's works are in the line of English novelists. They are her exploration of human existence. Indeed, Nargis Dalal's intimacy of the world, and her vision of life is depicted in her novels and short stories with clarity and economy.

Nargis Dalal is a great Indian woman novelist. She is a versatile genius too. As a novelist, she has written *Minari* (1967), *The Sisters* (1973), *The Inner Door* (1975) and *A Birth Day Party* (1976). Besides, Dalal has also written *The Nude* (1977), a collection of short stories and *Never a Dull Moment*, a book of middles under the pseudonym *Aires*.

Minari: This is Nargis Dalal's maiden novel in the line of Sir Walter Scott and Alexander Dumas. The novel is full of historical and romantic elements like love, chivalry and idealism. It deals with the people of aristocratic background. The novelist depicts a variety of people of different races, religions and classes. Even the characters differ from each other in their tastes and temperaments.

Nargis Dalal presents the old way of life with clarity and precision. However, she depicts bizarre lovers and meritocratic geniuses, she does not fail to make them consistent and attractive. Her characters are from different socio-economic interests. Nonetheless, they persistently try to transcend the man-made barriers. They honestly strive towards harmonizing their endeavours. They liken their lives to the people who are in the higher strata of society. Since they are rational and educated, they work towards progressive enlightenment.

The characters of *Minari* are from different colourings. Some of them are intellectuals and many of them are aristocrates. A few of them are of varied nationalities too. Tejpore, the hero of the novel is a prince of a maharaja family of Minari, an advanced townlet in Rajasthan. Dowager Maharani is Tejpore's mother, a scholarly and affectionate lady. While Iqbal Sing is a waywarded genius rather untamed. He turns a *bandit*. Vikram Sing is a retired General, a DSO, MBE and MC. He is a militia man, known for his adventures and dismal vision of life. Anita, the daughter of Vikram Sing, Ranjan's docile husband, Bim and Riki, their children are the other interesting characters. Anita emerges as a lady of free-sexual desires in quest of sexual fulfilment. While Ranjan appears a lovable figure, for he represents niceties of life. Then we find a host of Europeans who reside in India either, for they like to remain in India or, for they are unable to return to their homelands. In this class Mr. Wilton, Mr. Evans, Mr. Philip, Mrs. Wheeler and others are exceptional. There are also Mrs. and Mr. Delfront, Americans who, in the words of Oscar Wilde; "Passed from barbarism to decadence without the customary interim of civilization".[1] Besides, Mrs. Rula Ranganathan, the unfortunate wife of Mr. Nicky, who died of drinking, is an unforgettable personality. She is a Eurasian, for she was born to an Indian father and Greek mother.

The novel is set in Minari, a fascinating advanced village in Rajasthan. The lovely descriptions of topography, nomenclature, old customs and beautiful landscapes add their own glamour to the theme of *Minari*. The village is very attractive and picturesque. Indeed, in Nargis Dalal's view:

> Minari is a small hill-station jutting out improbably from the plains of Rajasthan. Below it, the sandy wastes of the deserts stretch away into infinity, but

> here everything is cool and green and damp. Eucalyptus trees with their blue-green leaves and enamelled white trunks grow side by side with the date palms. The silver oaks were in flower, and everywhere the blaze of gold rippled against a monotone background of hills and shimmering and glowing for miles around.[2]

The village is amidst hills, vales and woodlands. Therein are the mansions of many aristocratic people. The artificial lake constructed by the then British officer adds its own charm to it. The hilly tarrian and the ridge ways of Minari exactly recall Thomas Hardy's depiction of nature in his first poem "Domicilium" and in his pastoral novel *The Return of the Native* (1878). Although it is unnecessary to bring a comparison between Dalal and Hardy, it is somehow inevitable. The description of Minari in Dalal's novel veraciously resembles Hardy's depiction of his grandfather's cottage in his poem "Domicilium":

> Red roses, lilacs, variegated box
> Are therein plenty, and such hardy flowers
> As flourish best untrained. Adjoining these
> Are herbs and esculents; and further still
> A field; then cottages with trees, and last
> The distant hills and sky.[3]

In such natural milieux of Minari, human inhabitation is varied and complex. Owing to the admixture of people of diverse culture, custom and the like, the village is filled in by the people of 'full-scale variation'. In the words of Dalal, they seem as the people of vary advanced lifestyles:

> Minari was like some beach in a far corner of the world where all sorts of people were washed up, for all sorts of reasons.[4]

The names of the mansions in Minari sound vary natural. The house names 'Misty Heights', 'Hill View' and 'Spring Fair' which are amidst Gold Monar trees, Oaks Bougainvillea certainly recall Wordsworth, Hardy and Frost's nature poems.

The 'denizens' of the beach-like village are free-thinking and scandalous people. They have their own clubs, viz. Cooking Club and Red Cross. However, like Hardy's Casterbridge,

Minari has no railways, it has many cars and two wheelers. Like the men and women of Jane Austin's social novels, the characters of *Minari*, 'know each other well', 'know each other's business, and exchange all the gossip'.

The gist of the novel in this background of natural surrounding is this: there are some important characters and human activities. Tejpore is the prince, a modern easy going man of a royal family. He is a bachelor, but a womaniser interested only in luxurious mode of life. Life's faiths and failings do not interest or bother him. A half-educated man, Mr. Tejpore has already toured the continent. After he returns from Europe he finds a variety of ladies married, unmarried and widowed, by chance or design, run after him. In this circumstance Rula Ranganathan, a Eurasian, who is till then the wife of Mr. Nicky, a foreigner becomes a widow. Her husband who was addicted to drinking dies and leaves her in a miserable position. However, Mrs. Rula Ranganathan is wise and beautiful. Her work as a journalist brings her an immense importance in the village. Similarly, her elegance, charm and beauty makes her a 'thing of beauty' always aspired by many aristocrats including Tejpore, Colonel Rejendra Singh and Kunjara. All desire to marry her. However, the prince's love for her becomes immense. As a result, he befriends her and their courtship continues. But Tejpore's love is unsteady, not integrated one. He has already many ladies in his clutch. He has Zora as his 'kept'. When he went abroad he enjoyed many ladies there too. Besides, Anita the daughter of Vikram Sing a retired General, and the wife of Ranjan, is strongly fallen in love with him. So in this atmosphere when all higher persons desired from her, at least, 'a word, a smile, or a kiss', Tejpore takes her to his mansion, to his bed and to his body. 'They dance, sing and sleep'. Rula's beauty, which is portrayed by Dalal as follows, bewitches him:

> ...a woman in her middle thirties with mangnolia skin, grey-green eyes that tilted a little of the corners, and jet black hair of an unusual feathers. There was, however, more to her than her beauty. She had the poise, the serenity, and the easy grace of an eighteenth century elegante.[5]

However, Tejpore loved her for sexual fulfilment and his love for her is less in proportion to her love to him. The reasons are very clear. Tejpore's sexuality with Zora, a mean woman, and his love and adoration for Anita, Ranjan's wife weakens his love for Rula, a lady of pure heart and docile temperament. Consequently, Rula changes her attitude towards him. The early death of Nicky, her husband, and Tejpore's indifference to her emotions and feelings make her rather atheistic and frustrated. In her saddest mood, she expresses thus:

> No. My father is a Brahmin, my mother a Greek. Both of them believe in God, but a God who does not seem too greatly concerned with what happens on earth. I can't accept this, so I prefer to believe nothing.[6]

On the other hand, Tej, as he is known in the ladies' circles, falls in love with Anita, the innocent and unhappy wife of Ranjan. Since she did not receive Tej's invitation to the royal party when he came from Europe, she eagerly desires his company most. The other and more important reason for Anota's love to Tej is her carnal desires are not fulfiled by her husband. However, Tej is unfaithful to her, to her, the unheard melodies seem to be sweeter than the heard ones. When she celebrates her birth day, Tej who is already fallen in love with her presents her many packs of lipsticks, and chocolates to her lovely son Bim and daughter Riki. Their companionship develops to such an extent that they meet each other as often as possible. Their sexual desire which was till then unfulfilled dances and stimulates them to day dreams. His romantic fascination, love and sexual desires can be put in the following verse:

> He wanted to swim
>   Across her waist
> He desired to drink
>   The cream of her sexy breast.

Subsequently, Anita goes to Tej, so does her chastity. They dance, love and linger on each other. Her breast becomes heaven to Tej, a just stricken man. Likewise, Anita who is extremely after him gets abundant ecstasy. But her sexual gratification through illicit love brings 'disgust' as well:

> Under his moving hands, his caressing fingures, all thought was blotted out by a sort of anaesthesia. His complete silence, the intenseness with which he caressed her began to frighten her. This was some-thing quite beyond her experience.[7]

Nevertheless, Anita gets an attachment with Tej and tries intensely to mingle with him sensuously, due to Tej's lack of steadiness, she fails to gratify herself. The problem lies in Tej's disloyalty to her. As she yearns for him, he does not, for her. So, their illicit sexual relationship withers. Dalal says, "And it was not his fault either. She had come to him openly, asking for it, and then to turn all girlish on him".[8] As a consequence, Anita, being guilty of adulteress tries to recover her character. Besides, Ranjan's doubt about her faithfulness leads her to tension. But in her quest for 'self-hood', she regrets for her misdeeds and stops her relationship with Tej. In the environment of her children, father and pure-hearted husband, she turns spiritual.

On the other hand, Tejpore, torn by his lust ruins himself, his social status and family image. Nor does he obey his affectionate royal mother Dowagarh Maharani. His only intention, like Hardy's Eustacia is to enjoy love, lust and life to their fullest extent. In the novelist's words:

> He brought to the art of making love a sophistication, a subtlety, a finesse, all transmuted by experience into perfection.[9]

However, after the earthly desires of his flesh fade, Tejpore, decided to take vengeance for the death of Iqbal Singh, his friend, a royal fellow, turned bandit, goes abroad to manufacture guns. So his life in India ends in skirmishes.

While among the minor characters of *Minari* Mr. Wilton, a foodie, Mr. Philip, Mr. Evans and the Delfronts add a fine colour to the plot-construction and characterization. Mr. Ferdie, a wicked gossip manger, Mr. Shastri, a jovial figure provide humour whenever the events turn monotonous. The novel *Minari* has plenty of wise sayings too—"Marriage should be first of all, a companionship—a friendship lit by passion"[10], "Zora liked to eat and she liked to make love"[11], "a word, a smile, or a kiss".[12] Real love has 'little to do with physical pleasure', "Women were not meant to live alone"[13], "Women attach a great deal of importance to small things"[14], etc. The statement "Most civilized races acknowledge that men are capable of unspeakable cruelties and injustice"[15], represents the crux of the theme of *Minari.* Although *Minari* is Nargis Dalal's first novel, it is in the view of Dr. P.G. Javalgi, "the master piece of Nargis Dalal that certainly assures her a permanent place in Indian English fiction"[16].

The Sisters: It is another exploratory novel of Nargis Dalal. It is written in the line of *Pride and Prejudice* of Jane Austin. The novel shows Dalal's depiction of conflicts and contradictions of family web. Dalal pictures the story of two sisters, their married family relations and their enmity, distrust and indifference to each other. It is a fine portraiture of a broken tense-stricken family relationship. In the novel, two sisters Rita and Nina are realistically depicted. They are twins. They are of equal age, physique and fortunes. But Rita is not beautiful like her sister Nina. Her dark complexion and sad childhood have made her unhappy. She is very much disgusted with her own life. Besides, she blames her sister for her own misfortunes. Nonetheless, Nina's dislike mainly stems from her embittered heart. Her whims and fancies too are unfulfiled owing to her ugly appearance. So this leads her to frustration. Hence, she states:

> How to explain; after all these years, the feeling of blackness and hatred that enveloped me? I wondered in that radiant garden, shuddering under the blows to my pride and my, Oh! So vulnerable heart. At that moment I knew was convinced, that Nina was more loved because she was beautiful. I walked aimlessly till I came to one of the small enclosed gardens, hidden by tall trees and grassy around a shallow pool. Here I sat down in the dampness and began to pick at the hated dress.[17]

She thinks that she is ugly and Nina is pretty. This darkens her life and makes her a star-crossed despaired woman. So she often looses her heart at life's oddities and failings.

On the other hand, Nina is tenderer and more beautiful. She is brought up with a reasonable care by her father, a Parshi and Sophie, her mother, an English woman. The reason for Nina's optimism and Rita's despair is that the former owing to her prettiness is looked after well. While Rita was under estimated and neglected by her parents. This partiality in bringing up the daughters hurts the tender feelings and sentiments of Rita. Besides, the society too adds its own mite in intensifying this imbalance between the sisters. Many people, unconsciously praise Nina. They speak thus:

> "My dear, she grows prettier every day."
>
> "She looks like a little fairy."
>
> "Did you ever see such hair. Sophie you must spend hours brushing it."
>
> "You'd better look out-it won't be long before you have all the young men on your doorsteps."[18]

The partiality in treatment meted out to Rita causes her unhappiness. Therefore, she expresses her anger:

I, of course, was invisible, did not exist at all, for them. Then there were the men, already fatuous and drooling about Nina. I particularly recall an elderly Englishman—Mr Holt... Her greeted Sophie and father and then would turn beaming to Nina.[19]

So the passage brings out a sense of the double standards of life that persists in the sister's house. Even the parents fail to bridge up the gap that grows fast between Rita and Nina. Rita writes that there are many contrasts between Nina and herself save their blood relation. This furthers her grim experience. She, for many times, does not tolerate those who directly or indirectly insult her. Moreover, with a view to forget her heartache, she begins to love solitude. Even her annoyance and wretchedness, oblige her to avoid the company of Nina, grandma and her parents. So Rita tries to alienate herself from 'others' just in order to be happy alone. Although, to many, loneliness is a malediction, to her it is a comfort and an opportunity to forget her heartbeats and achings. Whenever, Nina, already married to Bobby Mehta, a rich man comes home, she arranges her a private room in the upstair. Once it so happens:

> I took her to upstair to her room and left her to lie there and rest. "Don't come down for tea Nina I'll send it up to your room." I had become used to living alone. There are who can't bear to be alone even for an hour, but I have always enjoyed it. To be alone for long stretches of time is as necessary for me as food. Perhaps, it had been a mistake inviting Nina to stay with me. By her very presence she seemed to stir up waves of restlessness in the atmosphere, as though her innermost being searched without finding, for something on which to anchor itself.[20]

However, Rita is lucky in one sense. She inherits all the assets of her rich grandma which Nina does not get. Nor her father inherits his own mother's property. A happy encounter with Ramesh, a gentleman, leads her to love him. This fellow mostly allured by her wealth marries her and builds a fine mansion. But he does not live with Rita at Missourie, for he dislikes her. What makes him to alienate himself from Rita is that he finds Nina, who recently has become a widow. He gets a house in Delhi and is often lost himself in the company of Nina, Rita's sister. Nina an unsatisfied woman, comes to Ramesh naturally. When her husband who died in Belgrade left her no property, 'Ramesh's company', she thinks, becomes 'inevitable for her'. Besides, Bobby Mehta left her sexually not gratified too. As a result, she moves towards her sister's husband to such an extent that she asks her to divorce Rita and marry her. This is clear in her letter to Ramesh which unfortunately goes to Rita:

My dearest darling,

Your letter made me wildly happy. At last, After all these months, we will be together always I can't tell you how I have lived all this time, for only this moment, with only this hope. It does not matter at all to me whether R. divorces you or not, but if it affects your career then, of course, we must be properly married. You say you do not anticipate any trouble and that Rita has never been either possessive or emotional. But you don't know her as I do. She is capable of violence and viciousness. I can't see her letting you go without a struggle, even though you are now making enough money not to be dependent on her. But together we will cope with anything. You say you plan to tell her soon. I will be praying for us both.

Your very own
Nina[21]

When Rita, a woman just happy with Ramesh received this news, she finds the harsh reality too. Soon her husband asks her that,

> I want you to divorce me. I want to marry Nina....[22]

This brings another shock to Rita, already a bereaved woman. As a result, she tries to kill him, for he became unfaithful to her as well as Nina wanted to fish in the troubled water:

> I thought everything out very carefully. There must be no mistakes. I wished I could put my hand on him softly, while he slept, and extinguish his life gently, like a candle. Yes gently, since I had no desire to see him suffer.[23]

Indeed, he dies not by her conspiracy but by his own heart-failure, and the sisters move towards their own amicable settlements.

The Sisters presents a burning issue of our day. Man's indifference towards his or her own kith, kin and dear ones is delineated with clarity and vividness. The characteristic failures, limitations and contrasts of the sisters are lucidly portrayed. The cover paper of the novel puts the theme of the novel very impressively:

> How unlike can twins be? How much hatred can blood generate? Here is the story of Nina and Rita unidentical twins who, from small beginnings in childhood, go on to poison each other's lives to a ghastly climax.[24]

The Inner Door: It is Nargis Dalal's third novel. It is as interesting as her first novel *Minari.* The theme of it is 'the importance of *Yoga* in human action and meditation'. "Yoga", Dalal says, "is essential for man's all round development". In this regard, Gandhi said prayers are inevitable for the purification of mind and heart as physical exercises are so for the building of good health. But Dalal says, yoga is helpful for the mind and body alike. Yoga which is a Hindu system of meditation and self-control brings man the rarer and finer qualities like self-control, unity betwixt faith and practice and physical health. This system of meditation is practised in the breadth and length of India right from the Vedic times. Particularly, Himalaya is the best-known region for yogis and saints who practise it. Places like Rishikesh, Haridwar, Kashi and Prayag have several ashrams where yoga practice is on war-footing. Since yoga helps for Hindu *Vernashram dharma*, it has attained a special significance in India. Many temples too have become centres for yoga tired of their materialism have turned for this most useful and bewitching art and practice. The reason for this can fairly be that the practice of yoga is scientific and if it is properly put into practice, it definitely helps man for a progressive enlightenment of his mind and body. Therefore, many Europeans as well as Americans come to India to acquaint themselves with this unique art and science.

Like *Minari*, *The Inner Door* is set in an auspicious religious shrine town Rishikesh in North India. Like the huts and mansions of Minari, the cottages and palatial buildings of Rishikesh are lovely and gigantic. There are many natural lakes and the town is built by rishis on the river bank of Ganga. Besides, there are as many as forty ashrams built by sadhus and saints. As during the 19th century, British-ruled India, many British as well as other Europeans and Americans used to frequent the places either for site-seeing and pleasure or for wisdom. To many foreigners the first reason was a primary motif. However, they were more interested in yoga studies than the natives. So to them Rishikesh provides ample opportunities:

> Rishikesh, on the banks of the Ganges is one of those places that could only exist in India, invented to fulfil a distinct need a town dedicated to the salvation of men's soul.... Every person, it seemed, wore the orange robes of the holy man. It was not so much a town as a pattern of consciousness, emphasising the illusion of identification. Pilgrims, sought here an adjustment

> between reality and dreams, secure in the knowledge that no matter what they did, one dip in the holy water relieved them of all past sins.[25]

Attracted by the spiritual or materialistic or sensual allurements of yoga studies of Rishikesh, many people from abroad come here every year. Among them the Stuarts-Myra and Chris play an important role in the novel. Dalal says the Stuarts were exploring the town, looking for something else which they might buy up and sell to unsuspecting guests at a hundred per cent profit. To them the town looks like Hollywood with narrow roads, the eternal river Ganga and a high dazzle of light. Even Chris desires to make a film here where people come in throng for cleansing their sins. The mythology built about this city stimulates them to do something.

The theme of the novel is importance, study and spread of yoga—a way of life. The title of the novel *The Inner Door* which is taken from Gitanand's poem "Beyond Peace" on yoga, implies that yoga is an inner door for self-realization. However, for attaining mastery over yoga—a way of selfhood, the rishis advocate man simplicity, purity and celibacy. Since sex is the root-cause of many unavoidable ills and diseases, Swami Jagdish, Rahul, the hero's uncle says that sex must be controlled. He thinks unless one cannot sublimate one's sex, one cannot be able to attain divinity through yoga. In this significant atmosphere, the Stuarts financially assisted by Govindas and Clive Holmes set up Sukhanand Ashram on the seven rishi hills. Jed Allen, a spoilt boy of Italy becomes its secretary and Mr. Rahul, turned Sukhanand becomes the Swami of yoga in the ashram. Once Jed Allen asks Rahul about free sex and the latter advises him:

> But Jed, too much sex is not good for you. In fact, in yoga they teach that sex should be avoided if one wants to learn higher practice. They believe that the semen when properly controlled, can climb up the spine and turn into power, in the brain. The most powerful force in the body is this sex force and this can be controlled and turned into spiritual force, lifted from the lowest to the highest.[26]

So, according to the rishis, yoga gives man power to strengthen his mind and body. True it brings man patience and purification.

The Inner Door has many characters—Indian, foreign, theistic, atheistic, rich, poor good and bad. Rahul, the hero of the novel is the only child and son of a late engineer and Ishwar Devi, a dominating woman. Swami Jadgish, the brother of Ishwar Devi, a frustrated man in family life has retired to Rishikesh hills for leading a luxurious life with the foreign disciples of yoga studies. As a yoga master, he acquires much wealth, but his knowledge of yoga is negligible. Panditji is another important yogi who runs Ramkrishnashram. He is a yogi in the true sense of the word. He has earned much wealth and has built a five-star building for the sake of the foreigners. It is panditji who teaches Rahul, the essential yoga knowledge. As a result, Rahul, intelligent and virtuous, a B.A. graduate, learns all yoga knowledge assisted by the Stuarts. He becomes the yogi of Swami Sukhanandashram. At the end, we see Rahul become Sukhanand and excel even his guru panditji. In fact, he becomes a lovable figure, for he is very handsome and scholarly. Subsequently, all foreign ladies, even married ones including Francoise Myra and Goldie fall in love with him. So what Rula Ranganathan was to the rich and handsome male persons in *Minari*, Rahul is to the foreign belles in *The Inner Door.*

As already planned, the courses on yoga begin in the Sukhanandashram. The Guru Swami Sukhanand imparts yoga education to the foreigners. He is a master of *Hath Yoga* which helps for physical health and mental purification. The courses go well. Rahul's excellent teaching, handsome personality, innocence charm satisfy the disciples. As the events and years turn by, Chris Stuart and his wife Myra plan to start *Yoga for Sex*, another subject in the faculty. They do it when many Americans and Europeans urge them to learn some measures for healthy sexual inter-courses. The mischievous boy Jed Allen, the secretary of the ashram, tries to execute his design too. He who is jealous of Rahul's radiant personality built because of celibacy, tries to see him seduced. One day Allen asks Myra, the innocent woman to seduce the Swami who is unaware of sexuality, though it went illicitly in the ashram. However, Myra simply tries to awaken Rahul sexuality:

> Myra was the first to go in search of Rahul. Since he had been more or less on her mind, ever since she met him, her new assignment, was merely a projection as it were of her thoughts for him. The feeling that she would be doing him a favour as well, was irresistible.[27]

But Rahul frankly says her that he does not like to enjoy woman. Then, as Jed Allen proposed, Fran, a French woman, goes to Rahul to seduce him. But, like Myra, she tries to seduce him directly which he is afraid of. As a result, Fran's desire is thwarted. At the end, Goldie too tries her best but she succeeds. She is neither dark like Myra in complexion, nor older like Fran to Rahul. Besides, she is very lovely and pleasing. She also employs a better approach to tempt him. She, like him, begins to say that 'yoga is essential for spiritualization' and for that too much sex must not be enjoyed. Nevertheless, she does not forget to make him aware of love, sex and woman for satisfying the bodily desires, as a pre-course for self-realization. Her lively words, stimulating approach and behaviour stained in love, and his own changed taste about sex bring a temporal union between Rahul and Goldie. Dalal's description of Rahul's transformation or change in his attitude towards sex and woman is noteworthy:

> Take your clothes off, she said softly, helping him. He felt her wonderful smoothness, the skin so cool, so delicate and then she was lying under him, welcoming him into. her body and the stiffness, the tenseness drained out of him and left him limp and a little sad. She held him close, petting him, murmuring words that could hardly be distinguished till he was relaxed, drowsy, content.[28]

This drives home a remarkable point that sex is uncontrollable. Even it is said that control over sex is undesirable. The experience of Rahul Gurudev with Myra and Fran shows that had Rahul been aware of sex earlier, he could have also enjoyed Myra, the dark-complexioned young lady and Fran, the red-complexioned middle-aged woman. However, Rahul becomes a fallen man, he does not indulge in sexual activities further. This first sexual act of him with a foreign lady makes him sad and disappointed.

As a consequence, he looses his desire for lust and wealth. He seeks one more good guru and from him he learns the higher knowledge. Hence, he becomes a great master in his field. This brings immense respect and devotion for him. His mother too respects him. So do the other persons of Rishikesh. His spiritual power rapidly grows and spreads in all directions. His blessings become effective and the number of foreign as well as Indian disciples grows. Owing to his blessings, Myra's health is recovered, Carl Hanes, recovers his interest in novel-writing, and Duncan, the art designer gains faith in God. So the Guru Swami Sukhanand's influence becomes far-reaching and powerful. No doubt, people in large number come to the ashram for self-realization.

The Inner Door is a fine novel of Nargis Dalal. In fact, like *Minari* and *The Sisters*, it is very vivid and interesting. Its yoga knowledge is very informative and authentic. *The Inner Door* will surely enrich Mrs. Dalal's fame as a rare Indian Woman novelist. Indeed, it is a well-written classic.

Apart from these novels, Nargis Dalal has also written *The Nude*, a collection of short stories and a book of middles. In her short stories, Dalal deals with fate that works in human lives, military life, the then important aspects of society and woman's importance in the male-dominated society. As a distinguished woman writer, she thinks about feminism too. Her obsession with the present-day woman's problems, difficulties and aspirations makes her to write for woman's emancipation. What Ruth Prawar Jhubvala writes in her *Heat and Dust* (1975) and Anita Desai in her *Clear Light of Day* (1980) and *Where Shall We Go This Summer?* (1975) about woman, Nargis Dalal writes about feminism both in her novels and short stories. Even in her 'Middles', Dalal, dwells upon the theme of love, woman and military life. Her *Never A Dull Moment*, a collection of 'Middles', a genre of column writing displays her grand and varied interest in journalist. Dalal's career as a journalist, novelist and short story writer in lucidly seen in her works.

Nargis Dalal is the best-known woman writer in English in India. In this regard, she has already done a good deal of work.

Her views on the art of fiction and her vision of life is explicit in her novels, stories and middles. Like Raja Rao, Mulk Raj Anand, R.K. Narayan, Ruth Prawar Jhubvala and Anita Desai, Nargis Dalal is undoubtedly a noted name in Indian English fiction. Indeed, her fame as a first grade writer will be everlasting as long as the letters linger on.

REFERENCES

1. Oscar Wilde, qt. by Nargis Dalal, *Minari*, Bombay: Pearl Pub., 1967, p. 216.
2. Nargis Dalal, *ibid.*, p. 1.
3. Thomas Hardy, *The Complete Poems*, ed. by James Gibson, London Macmillan, 1976, p. 3.
4. Nargis Dalal, *Minari*, p. 8.
5. *Ibid.*, p. 13.
6. *Ibid.*, p. 79.
7. *Ibid.*, p. 98.
8. *Ibid.*, p. 99.
9. *Ibid.*, p. 20.
10. *Ibid.*, p. 25.
11. *Ibid.*, p. 52.
12. *Ibid.*, p. 71.
13. *Ibid.*, p. 112.
14. *Ibid.*, p. 134.
15. *Ibid.*, p. 203.
16. P.G. Javalagi's letter to the author, December 15, 1995.
17. Nargis Dalal, *The Sisters*, Delhi: Hind Pocket Books, 1973, p. 11.
18. *Ibid.*, p. 121.
19. *Ibid.*, pp. 121-22.
20. *Ibid.*, pp. 15-16.
21. *Ibid.*, p. 138.
22. *Ibid.*, p. 144.
23. *Ibid.*, p. 140.
24. *Ibid.*, Cover page.
25. Nargis Dalal, *The Inner Door*, Delhi: Orient Paperbacks, 1975, pp. 15-16.
26. *Ibid.*, p. 63.

27. *Ibid.,* p. 93.
28. *Ibid.,* p. 101.

A SELECT BIBLIOGRAPHY

Nargis Dalal's Works

Novels:

1. *Minari,* Bombay: Pearl Pub., 1967.
2. *The Sisters,* Delhi: Hind Pocket Books, 1973.
3. *The Inner Door,* Delhi: Orient Paperbacks, 1975.
4. *A Birthday Party*, Delhi: Hind Pocket Books, 1976.
5. *The Girls From Overseas*, Delhi: Hind Pocket Books, 1979.

Short Stories:

1. *The Nude*, Delhi: Orient Paperbacks, 1977.

Middles:

1. *Never a Dull Moment*, Delhi: Hind Pocket Books, 1976.

30

Concept of Woman in *Nectar in a Sieve*

VIBHA JAIN

Manisha Roy makes a thoughtful comment in her paper on "Women and New Consciousness", "Fortunately and unfortunately India's unique political history makes it irritable that we have learned much from the West. But we cannot do it for our advantage unless we also know what unconscious tendencies our own system created or still creates in the unconscious."[1]

The writer has drawn a thoughtful conclusion giving us a line of thought that if we take the initiative to assess and philosophise on the concept of Indian woman, it is desirable that we should look towards our own mythology, tradition and ancestral legacy. From the earliest times when during the Vedic period the scholarly women like Ghosha and Apala helped considerably in composing the Vedic rich as we find the creditable role of women in the development of Indian culture. Historical and Sociological upheavals have managed to trammel the image of the Indian woman to such as extent that there grew numerous female writers to uphold and protect the cause of Indian women.

Amongst the eminent personalities and writers who were fraught with the pathetic feelings towards the Indian woman, Kamala Markandaya comes foremost. In almost all of her novels beginning with 'Nectar in a Sieve' she seems to be undergoing strenuous efforts to upgrade the status of women in the Indian society. She is never satisfied with the stand of the Indian woman that "A woman's place is with her husband."[2] It is a general out look of an Indian woman about the Indian women due to which again Shanta Krishnaswamy writes about the virtues and merits of this Indian lady of Nectar in a Sieve 'faced with great odds like famine, death, infidelity and prostitution amidst a backdrop of bone-chilling poverty, she wages a constant battle."[3]

The first novel of Kamala Markandaya published as *Nectar in a Sieve* by Putnam and company, London in the year 1954 is centered round a poor lady Rukmani, who is the symbol of the deepest and crudest poverty of India. Emerging from the dreams of childhood when she sees her 'heaven' of husband, all her castles of cards are flown and she says: "I wanted to cry. This mud hut, nothing but mud and thatch was my home."[4]

There is no end to the grievances and misfortunes of this poor lady, who continues to suffer as a wife, as a mother and then as a grandmother. Poverty, inertia, famishment and disease torure her till the end of her life, when even her husband leaves her on his eternal journey. An Indian woman can hardly endure that her own daughter should go for prostitution to maintain the family-life. Kamala Markandaya has been crude and unflinching to the extent of Romantic Ferver in her narration of the unfortunate conditions of the Indian woman. Though at times she realises this fact, also, that is directly related to the human psychology.

Basically, mind and physic have got immense elastic powers, due to which, a woman, poverty-stricken so despairingly, can have an eye to smile. Rukmani of this novel also is the same kind of lady. The writer says: "While the sun shines on you and the fields are green and beautiful to the eye and your husband sees beauty in you, which no one has seen before and you have a good store of grain, laid away for hard times, a roof over you and a sweet stirring in your body, what more can a woman ask for?"[5]

While, on the one hand, the novelist has given vivid descriptions of the crude realities of a poor unfortunate woman, we realise at the same time that the lady Rukmani, downtrodden and miserable though she has been, does not accept the defeat. As Shanta Krishnaswamy comments about her "If Indian womanhood evolved towards this larger concept of love and caring then there need be no fear about its endurance."[6]

While the intention of Kamala Markandaya here has been to ventilate the grievous scars in the image of Indian woman, on the other hand, she was always embellished this image with the virtues of endurance, forbearance, compassion and self-sacrifice. So, this enterprising effort does not project an Indian woman as an image with a weak physic but an image of a far stronger moral concept. Sometimes these women remind us of the pious heroines of Thomas Hardy, but we know simultaneously that Hardy's heroines are guided by supernatural powers and they develop an epos-making mythology. In that comparison the women of Kamala Markandaya are restricted to the phases of Indian society. We find some close resemblance of these women in the women characters of Virginia Woolf. B. Sudipta is justified in writing in her article on "A Feminist Perspective of Women Characters" in the novels of Virginia Woolf and Kamala Markandaya, "The travails and tribulations which she encounters are labeled as her predestined faith or as the reprisals of her past Karmas, Rukmani was one such creature, born to shoulder the plough and reap the harvest if any."[7]

While Kamala Markandaya presented the degraded condition of the Indian woman, not only in *Nectar in a Sieve*, but in other novels also, she has tactfully upgraded her status in the moments of adversity and doom. This she has not under the overwhelming lap of emotions but through a tactful strategic plan. The long discourses on the women persecution, fraught with political zeal, have been of little significance, viewing the continuous injustice being done to the women society even today. The superfluous thinkers have become satisfied with certain idealistic comments like the one quoted here "Philosophers and Feminists" have concluded that submission is the only virtue, compulsorily nurtured in woman as her faculties have been numbed by restrictions."[8]

Kamala Markandaya in this way has devised a method to idolise the image of woman by showing her downtrodden to the extremity but in that condition retaining the degree of confidence and forbearance to the extent where commonly the male character fails. She has looked outside the limitations of nationality and has tried to look towards the Western world also for guidance, but it is needless to comment that she had to come back to the same concept of Indian woman as nurtured by the Indian sociologist. Gayle, Greene and Coppelia, Kahn have made a significant comment about the versatility of the woman concept. They write "Actual behaviour is likely to be more varied than is suggested by social myths or stereo-types and the relation of the Idealogy of woman to social reality remains difficult to measure."[9]

Literature presents the personality not through the political concept but through such deeper layers of aesthetics and psychology which have far greater impact upon man and its history. Though C.T. Indra considers the achievements of Kamala Markandaya on the basis of normal human thought so she writes "Kamala Markandaya has managed to give full play to a women's self-cast in a relatively unadventurous social milieu and that is a remarkable achievement".[10]

Through all the dimensions of woman, as a daughter, then as a wife, as a mother, Rukmani has defeated the traditional concept of a weak woman. Kamala Markandaya, the artist in fiction, has drawn forth a new vision and image of Indian woman, dormant behind the garb of poverty helplessness, inertia and famishment. It is to be concluded that the achievement of Kamala Markandaya is not limited to the field of fiction and philosophy only but she has come forward as an explorer, an inventor as well.

BIBLIOGRAPHY

Markandaya Kamala, *Nectar in a Sieve*, Putnam and Co. Limited (New York, 1954).

Roy Manisha, Women and New Consciousness, published in a *Journal of Women's Studies*, Vol. 1, Women's Study Research Centre, Calcutta, 1996.

Krishnaswamy Shanta, *The Women in Indian Fiction in English*, Asia Publishing House, New Delhi, 1984.

Sudipta, B., A Feminist Perspective of Women Characters, *Indian Women Novelist*, Vol. 2, Set 2, Prestige Books, New Delhi, 1996.

Kahan Coppelis, Gayle and Green Making a Difference, *Feminist Literary Criticism*, Mathuen Publisher, London, 1998.

Indra, C.T., The True Voice of Endurance, *Feminism and Recent Fiction in English*, edt. Sushila Singh, Prestige Books, New Delhi, 1991.

Iyengar, K.R., Srinivasa, *Indian Writing in English*, Sterling Publisher, Patna, 1990.

Khan, M.K. and A.G., Changing Faces of Women in *The Indian Writing in English*, Retalive Books, New Delhi, 1995.

Prasad Madhusudan, *Perspective on Kamala Markandaya*, Vimal Prakashan, Ghaziabad, 1984.

REFERENCES

1. Roy Manisha, "Women and New Consciousness", published in the *Journal of Women's Studies*, Vol. I, No. 1 (Calcutta, 1996), p. 124.
2. Kamala Markandaya, *Nectar in a Sieve* (New York, 1954), p. 108.
3. Shanta Krishnaswamy, *The Women in Indian Fiction in English*, New Delhi, 1984, p. 162.
4. Kamala Markandaya, *Nectar in a Sieve* (New York, 1954).
5. *Ibid.*, p. 7.
6. Shanta Krishnaswamy, *The Women in the Indian Fiction in English* (New Delhi, 1984), p. 162.
7. B. Sudipta, "A Feminist Perspective of Women Character", *Indian Women Novelist* (New Delhi, 1993), Vol. 2, Set 2, p. 84.
8. *Ibid.*, p. 85.
9. Gayle Green and Coppelia Kahn, "Making a Difference". *Feminist Literary Criticism* (London, 1985), p. 18.
10. C.T. Indra, "The true voice of endurance, A Study of Rukmani in Markandaya's *Nectar in a Sieve*" *Feminism and Recent fiction in English*, edt. Sushila Singh (New Delhi, 1991), p. 71.

31

The Novels of Tony Morrison—A Feminist Study

S.P. SWAIN and A. NAIK

Toni Morrison's novels revolve round the theme of isolation and identity. Tales of the dispossessed and disillusioned feminine black voice, they portray the lacerated self's struggle for freedom of speech and expression in an incarcerating milieu. Her accent is on the diversity of black sensibilities, horrors of slavery, modes of expression and independent thinking. Professor Anniah Gowda maintains: "Her feminist attitude is fierce but her language is poetic. It has a worldly and sometimes satiric purpose. She acts against the myths that dignify black women by taking away their initiative" (*The Literary Half-Yearly* 28).

Woman to Morrison is a creative force and not a burden of continuity. A disgruntled self, a woman is at war with the patriarchal societal forces which impede the growth of her feminine instincts. But in Toni Morrison's novels the black women invariably lived for children, for parents, bereft always of an autonomous self. Hence, the emergence of black female expression in drama, poetry and fiction in American literature. Most of the Afro-American women like Toni Morrison gave themselves up to the task of writing because they felt that their presence as a black woman and their perspective as a woman, in general, had been under-represented in American literature.

We propose to study the nature of the struggle of the black American voice of the Morrison protagonists who are frantically endeavouring in their state of isolation to establish their identity and emotional sensitivity in an impersonal and threatening social milieu.

Toni Morrison's novels stress the need for self-discovery and self-identity leading to self-actualisation. They emphasise the individual self's need to actualize his/her minor potentiality in order to enhance self-esteem. Morrison portrays the alienated individual's odyssey for attaining the integration of the self by assimilating or discarding the social values of the community they live in. In the United States, the contemporary feminist movement started with the white, middle class women's struggle to do away with the sexist oppression and to attain equal opportunity, with the white, middle-or-upper class men. For a variety of causes the black women failed to see this "as addressing their concerns" and felt alienated from the "mainstream of the white feminist movement" (Powell 1990: 2). The black American women were concerned as much about ethnic and racial discrimination as about sexism since to be "black and female" is to be in "double jeopardy" (Beal 1970: 90).

Racism figures as a dominant theme in the works of black authors, irrespective of sex. But the "double-edged persecution of the Afro-American woman finds full expression only in black feminist writings (Sengupta 88) where she is depicted as a stifled and anguished being. The black authors depict the Afro-American woman's pain of being black and that too a female. Further, these women are shown desperately searching for their genuine self. The allied themes of racism and gender discrimination echo through the heroines of Morrison. Insisting on the relationship of woman as self and as part of a community, she prefigured the major themes of black women's fiction in the 1970s: the black woman's potential as a full person and necessarily a major protagonist in the socio-cultural issues of the times. Morrison makes the silent speak, the inarticulate and the repressed, explode and articulate.

Her novel *The Bluest Eye* (1970) has the ingredients of a black voice railing against the myth of the black monolith and the racist supremacy. The story of a year in the life of Pecola Breedlove, a young black girl in Ohio, *The Bluest Eye* squeezes the great spectrum of black feminine voice into the pseudo mould of stereotype. It probes deeper into the black woman's psychic dilemmas, oppressions and trials symbolised by the tragic life of Pecola "driven literally insane by the pressures towards absolute physical beauty in a culture whose white standards of beauty...are impossible for her to meet, though no less alluring and demanding" (Hedin 49-50). The "unsettling emptiness" and the "enemy within" drives Pecola to the need of a man who could make her happy. The emotionally depraved life of Pecola's parents propels her to a state of schizophrenia. Her mother Pauline is troubled by the feelings to motherhood in her life: "...the daily needs of her children are like lighted matches to the fuse of her disappointment as a black woman denied beauty and romantic love" (Wade-Gayles 74), the very tenets of an ideal feminine life. Even the life of Pecola 's father Cholly is an instance of negligence, frustration and a quest for identity. Without parental affection and care, he feels himself alienated from his family. Pecola, thus, becomes the victim of her parents bitter discontent with life, a dissatisfaction that can be directly traced to the various forms of discrimination on which blacks have to endure in white America. Trapped in a world of taunts and threats, Pecola yearns for love and protection. But neither pauline nor Cholly can provide her any emotional or moral support since they themselves are without roots and are emotionally and spiritually depraved. Pecola's desire is for "blue eyes"—coveted by the black and "in wanting blue eyes, pecola wants, in fact to be white" (Weever 406). Like her mother pauline, she wants to identify herself with the white woman. Through pecola's character, Morrison traces the cautious and careful process of growing up from adolescent sensuality into womanly repression. "To get rid of the funkiness, the dreadful funkiness of passion, the funkiness of nature, the funkiness of the wide range of human emotions" (*The Bluest Eye* 68), is what the Morrison women crave for. Sensuality in Morrison is related to sexuality, which symbolically portrays the image of the liberated woman in Tom Morrison's novels. Alienated from her own body, the Morrison woman hopes that "she will remain dry between her legs—She hates the glucking sound they make when she is moist" (*The Bluest Eye* 69). The Morrison woman is defined by the dictates of her husband's desire. Morrison writes against the erosion and the repression of female sexuality as it is channeled by male desire and stifled by domestic hang-ups. Ruth in *Song of Solomon* (1977) has been defined by her father's overprotection and her husband's rejection. The connection of desire and hatred is a contradiction generated by the male domination of heterosexual relationships and black woman's fiction echoes this polarity not only as it moulds adult heterosexual relationships but also as it pertains to women's feelings towards their children and mothering.

Morrison's Sula has no strong sense of the self at the centre: "She had no centre, no speak with which to grow" (118). Her quest is to fill the void caused by her alienational experiences. Without any father figure to relate to, Sula is dependent upon her grandma Eva Peace and her mother Hannah, neither of whom seems to be able to show any affection or understanding for Sula. She grows up isolated from them unable to relate to either. But she has to grow into an autonomous self—to discover her "me-ness". Neither "white nor Male, and all that freedom was forbidden to her" (52) and hence, she sets about creating something else to be. In order to assert her freedom as a female self, she "sleeps with a white man". This way she also asserts her sense of equality with the white. Sula's life is a challenge to male-dominated heterosexual roles for women. She is an affront to the way men have traditionally defined women as either mother or whores. Sula's adult female sexuality grows under male domination which in her sensual and pre-sexual girlhood did not exist. She has sex with Nel's husband because she wants to reveal how heterosexual, nuclear family life stifles women's aspirations. Her challenge has been to suggest the possibility of creating a female equivalent to male bonding. But should women accept Sula's challenge?

In *Song of Solomon*, Ruth's house fails to bring about the fruition of the feminist principle. The house symbolises male domination in the form of Macon's ruthless authority and his son's egotism. In almost all Morrison novels, we find that women develop open relationship with men to assert their female freedom but this liberty often degenerates into licentiousness culminating in harlotry which to Morrison is a viable alternative to male domination. This relegates women to a dependent being.

Tar Baby (1981) is about "incest, the motherhood cast in dialogue between the sexes" (Gowda 31). It portrays the harrowing relationships between black and white cultures in the Caribbean and America. Jadine is almost self-ruined by the white societal values and ideas of prosperity. She is obstructed in her assays to asserts her female self in the teeth of the cankerous societal values of the white from which she finds difficult to release herself.

In *Song of Solomon* (1977), the three—woman household, a recurring pattern in Morrison novels finds its utopian realisation in Pilate's house, and its dystopian cancellation in the house Ruth shares with Macon Dead. Although both houses comprised women and were defined upon different economic models, Ruth's house fails to bring the feminist principle (i.e. the principle of fusion and togetherness) into being. On the other hand, it symbolises male domination in the form of Macon's ruthless authority and his son's egotism, sometimes degenerating to male chauvinism. Whereas Pilate's household is a striking contrast to Ruth's. Composed of three heterosexual women, it negates male domination. Women, here, have their relationships with men but men are disallowed to either live or define the space and economy of the household. Eva Peace's house in Sula is a "bricolage of stairways, rooms and porches, as befits its everchanging social mark-up" (Willi's 1985: 235). It is a contrast to the confining and cribbing atmosphere of the centripetal family, defined by a phallocentric social order, where the patriarchal domination enacted by the notion of male sexual and economic domination which relegates all women to the state of a binding vine.

Feminism in Morrison's novels is grounded upon "the structure of a Culture...which defines women, as worthless and invisible victims" (Ruthven 1984: 3). Her fictional characters struggle for their liberation from being manipulated by a corporate society reeling under the throes of capitalism and thereby save themselves from self-mutilation. They are in dynamic involvement with and at the same time are critically opposed to the system of society in which they live in order to assert their feminine self.

REFERENCES

Beal, Frances, "Double Jeopardy: To be Black and Female", *The Black Woman: An Anthology*, Ed. Toni Cade, New York: Signet, 1970.

Gowda, Anniah, "Feminine Black Voice", *Literary Half Yearly,* Vol. XXXV, No. 1, January 1994.

Hedin, Raymond, "The Structuring of Emotion in Black American Fiction", *Novel*, 16.1 (1982).

Morrison, Toni, *The Bluest Eye*, New York: Simon & Schuster, 1972.

——, *Song of Solomon*, New York: New American Library, 1978.

——, *Sula*, New York: Bantam, 1980.

(All citations from Toni Morrison's novels followed by page numbers in parentheses are from these editions of the text.)

Powell, Faye, "African-American Feminist issues: An Overview", *IJAS*, 20.1 (1990).

Ruthven, K.K., *Feminist Literary Studies: An Introduction*, Cambridge: Cambridge Univ. Press, 1984.

Sengupta, Ashis, "Afro-American Women's Fiction: Perspectives on Race and Gender", *New Quest,* 110, March-April, 1995.

Wade-Gayles, Gloria, *No Crystal Stair: Vision of Race and Sex in Black-Women's Fiction,* New York, Pilgrim, 1984.

Will's, Susan, "Black Women Writers: Taking a Critical perspective", in Gayle Greene and Coppelia Kahn (eds.) *Making a Difference: Feminist Literary Criticism*, London and New York: Routledge, 1985.

❑❑❑